MW00779685

THE GOLF
100

THE GOLF

100

A SPIRITED RANKING OF
THE GREATEST PLAYERS
OF ALL TIME

Michael Arkush

Doubleday | New York

Published by Doubleday, a division of Penguin Random House LLC, 1745 Broadway, New York, NY 10019.

DOUBLEDAY and the portrayal of an anchor with a dolphin are registered trademarks of Penguin Random House LLC.

Book design by Betty Lew
Composite title image of Golfers: (males) by frilled_dragon; (females) by Jan Stopka, both Adobe Stock
Golfball with tee by snyGGG / Adobe Stock

Library of Congress Cataloguing-in-Publication Data
Names: Arkush, Michael, author.
Title: The golf 100 : a spirited ranking of the greatest players of all time / Michael Arkush.
Other titles: Golf one hundred
Description: First edition. | New York: Doubleday, [2025] | Includes bibliographical references.
Identifiers: LCCN 2024024407 (print) | LCCN 2024024408 (ebook) | ISBN 9780385549691 (hardcover) | ISBN 9780385549721 (ebook)
Subjects: LCSH: Golfers—Rating of. | Golf—Records.
Classification: LCC GV964.A1 A75 2025 (print) | LCC GV964.A1 (ebook) | DDC 796.352/092/2—dc23/eng/20240605
LC record available at https://lccn.loc.gov/2024024407
LC ebook record available at https://lccn.loc.gov/2024024408

penguinrandomhouse.com | doubleday.com

PRINTED IN THE UNITED STATES OF AMERICA

1 3 5 7 9 10 8 6 4 2

The authorized representative in the EU for product safety and compliance is Penguin Random House Ireland, Morrison Chambers, 32 Nassau Street, Dublin D02 YH68, Ireland, https://eu-contact.penguin.ie.

To Pauletta,

my bride, my friend, my life

Contents

Author's Note

In March 2022, I introduced myself to Jim Furyk at the Hoag Classic, a Senior tour event in Newport Beach, California, sharing with him my idea to rank the top one hundred golfers, men and women, of all time. (Memo to PGA Tour commissioner Jay Monahan: Get rid of the name *PGA Tour Champions*. Not every member of the Tour, and I mean no disrespect, has been a champion.)

Furyk, the 2003 U.S. Open winner, didn't have much to say.

"Tough task," he told me.

Gee, thanks a lot, Jim.

About three hours later, as I was stuck in traffic on Interstate 405—one is always stuck in traffic on the 405—it dawned on me:

This is not a tough task. This is an impossible task.

I thought of the profound changes the game has undergone over the past 150 or so years with better balls and clubs, more manicured courses, and, most significantly, the players themselves.

Today's golfers employ extensive support groups, which include agents, managers, trainers, instructors, psychologists, hypnotists (I made the last one up . . . I think).

How then could I stack up the accomplishments of Old Tom Morris or Young Tom Morris, who won multiple British Opens in the 1860s and '70s against Tom Weiskopf, who starred in the 1960s and '70s? Or compare Johnny Farrell, the 1928 U.S. Open champion, to Johnny Miller, the 1973 Open champion?

Maybe I needed to give back my advance from the publisher and find another project.

Or find a psychologist myself. It wouldn't be difficult. You can't go two blocks in Southern California, where I live, without running into one.

Bobby Jones summed it up perfectly after Ben Hogan won the British Open in 1953:

"I think we must agree that all a man can do is beat the people who are around at the same time he is. He cannot win from those who came before any more than he can from those who may come afterward."

Thanks, Bob. You're as helpful as Furyk.

Even so, once I arrived home and glanced at the dozens of golf books and tattered magazines in my office, I stopped worrying about what Furyk or Jones thought. I was too curious—obsessed, my wife would say—to see which golfers would make the top one hundred and in what order, and, just as important, whom I would leave out.

So now that I had decided to proceed, the question was how.

From the start, it occurred to me that I needed a formula to measure the credentials of every potential candidate. To explain, for example, why I put Ernie Els ahead of Vijay Singh. Or, better yet, John Ball, a legendary English amateur, ahead of Rory McIlroy.

One aspect of a player's career would be valued more than any other: how he or she performed in the game's biggest events.

The majors.

That's how, for the longest time, we have determined who the best golfers were, not by where they finished on the money list or, in recent decades, how they fared in the FedExCup playoffs. (If God were to grant me one wish, it might just be to rid the world of the FedExCup.)

Rick Reilly, the former *Sports Illustrated* writer, put it best when Fred Couples broke through in the 1992 Masters: "If he never did [win a major] he would get thrown in the heap over there with Tom Kite [who would end his long drought two months later in the U.S. Open at Pebble Beach] and the rest of the very good players who got off the bus one stop short of greatness."

The majors feature the strongest fields and, more often than not, are staged on the most demanding courses.

When history is on the line.

Thus, I chose to award a player 2,000 points for each major victory; 500 for second place; 250 for third; 100 for fourth; and 50 for fifth—

a rather substantial gap, I know, between first and second, but that's how much emphasis I place, as Tiger Woods would say, on getting the "W."

Only, which tournaments should count as majors? And in which years?

That's not as easy to determine as you might assume. The four in the current rotation—the Masters, U.S. Open, British Open, and PGA Championship—obviously qualify, but what about the United States Amateur and British Amateur (now known as the Amateur Championship but I'm going to stick with its original name. Nor will I refer to the British Open as the Open Championship)? For decades, they were among the most prestigious events in golf, comprising two of the four majors Jones won in 1930 to attain the Grand Slam.

Except they don't possess the same luster today. Not even close.

Can you name the five most recent U.S. Amateur champions? Of course not. Don't feel bad. I can't, either, and I've been writing about the sport for more than thirty years. The question became: When should I stop counting the Amateurs as majors?

At first, I figured the cutoff would be the 1920s, when more top players began turning pro. Until I took into account the caliber of those who prevailed in both amateurs during the 1930s, '40s, and '50s, and factored in how much the events still meant to the game itself.

Besides, they were considered majors back then. So who was I to mess with tradition?

Ultimately, I chose 1961, which was when Jack Nicklaus captured his second U.S. Amateur at Pebble Beach. He was, after all, the last amateur with the potential to make it big as a pro to give serious consideration to maintaining that status. When he applied for membership in the PGA of America a few months after Pebble, it marked the end of an era.

At the same time, to discount the U.S. Amateur and British Amateur entirely over the last sixty-plus years didn't seem appropriate.

Consider the golfers who have won one or the other Amateur during that stretch: Lanny Wadkins, Craig Stadler, Jerry Pate, Mark O'Meara, Hal Sutton, Justin Leonard, Sergio Garcia, Phil Mickelson, and, of course, Tiger Woods. Therefore, I counted a victory in either Amateur, starting in 1962, as worth 1,000 points, half as many as in previous years, 250 for the losing finalist, and 125 for the other semifinalists.

Whoever fell in the quarterfinals, as was the case before '62, didn't earn any points.

As for the non-major tournaments, I awarded only the champion, and with 300 points. To close with a 65 with no pressure on to squeeze into the top five of, say, the John Deere Classic, isn't worthy of receiving points. Again, it's about the "W."

I also decided not to allocate official points for performances in the Ryder Cup or Presidents Cup. Think of all the golfers who, because they were born too early or in the wrong part of the world, didn't compete in those team events.

Still, I didn't ignore those performances, either.

I was similar to a juror who, despite a stern warning from the judge not to let evidence deemed inadmissible be a factor in the verdict, couldn't help its affecting his thinking in one way or another. That goes, too, for players who excelled in individual events outside the United States.

Case in point: Bernhard Langer's forty-two victories on the European Tour. Only Seve Ballesteros, with fifty, won more.

On the other hand, with all due respect to Langer's record forty-seven wins on the Senior tour, that is something I most definitely could ignore. Congrats to the players fifty and over who have been able to take a "second bite of the cherry," as the late Scottish golfer Brian Barnes referred to the tour in the late 1990s. Yet success as a senior has nothing to do with true greatness. True greatness was what they had hoped to attain in the first bite.

In any case, no matter how many points a golfer accumulated in majors, or non-majors, the total shouldn't solely determine if he or she belongs in the rankings, or where. A number of deserving players would be left out entirely or wind up in the wrong spot. Other variables needed to be factored in; most significantly, an individual's impact or contributions to the game.

A prime example is Francis Ouimet, whose shocking win as a twenty-year-old amateur in the 1913 U.S. Open at the Country Club of Brookline over English stars Harry Vardon and Ted Ray gave golf on this side of the Atlantic the boost it sorely needed. Bobby Jones is another. He was an enormous figure in the 1920s, and not just because

of what he achieved on the course. Jones was the epitome of class, setting a standard that will probably never be matched.

A quarter century later, Arnold Palmer arrived, right out of central
casting: handsome, talented, charismatic, and fearless. He won eight
majors—I'm including the 1954 Amateur—but also lost his share, no
loss more gut-wrenching than the seven-shot lead he squandered to
Billy Casper on the back nine of the 1966 U.S. Open at the Olympic
Club in San Francisco. No matter. Arnie's Army loved him just as much
for his failures, if not more.

Finally, toward the end of the twentieth century, when golf needed
another shot in the arm, along came Woods. Even those who couldn't
tell the difference between a three-iron and a nine-iron knew who
Tiger Woods was. As Roger Maltbie, a longtime NBC commentator,
put it: "Tiger Woods doesn't just move the needle. He *is* the needle."

I also gave additional weight to the elite players who would have put
up more impressive numbers but left the game prematurely—some
voluntarily, others the victims of fate.

They include: Byron Nelson, who quit the Tour at age thirty-four to
buy a ranch; Tony Lema, killed in a plane crash at thirty-two; Young
Tom Morris, who passed away—some say of a broken heart—at
twenty-four; Willie Anderson, a four-time U.S. Open champion in the
1900s, who died—I'll fill you in later—at thirty two; Lorena Ochoa,
who retired at twenty-eight to start a new life, and England's Joyce
Wethered, who rarely competed after turning twenty-four.

Only, how would I incorporate such subjective elements into my
final calculations?

Bonus points, that's how. Which I tacked on to roughly thirty players, male and female.

On the flip side, I took away points from those who, while piling up
victories in regular Tour events, didn't come through in a single major.
Like Harry "Lighthorse" Cooper, who won twenty-nine tournaments
in the 1920s and '30s but could do no better than four second-place
finishes in majors.

Perhaps my toughest task was how to integrate into the list the top
female golfers of all time, given that they competed in entirely different events—and against entirely different opponents.

Initially, I thought of compiling separate lists but women have been marginalized enough already. Ultimately, I elected not to compare women's totals (including the bonus points) to the men's—only to other women—and I relied on my expertise as a golf writer to determine where they belonged. I'll go to my grave wondering whether I put Joyce Wethered high enough. She was incredible.

Let me be clear: I'm under no illusion the list is perfect. Far from it.

Many will make a case for a player to be ranked higher or lower, and I might agree with them. Or for someone who isn't on the list at all, such as Scotland's Colin Montgomerie, who won the European Tour's Order of Merit eight times, the equivalent of the money title in America. I have nothing personally against Monty, who might be a fine bloke, for all I know.

Only, he never won a major.

Or any tournament on the PGA Tour. In 142 starts.

In conclusion, please keep the following in mind:

Just because someone is ranked number 40 doesn't mean that person would defeat number 80 in a head-to-head match. All it means is that the player at number 40 racked up more total points.

I hope you enjoy the trip down memory lane. See you on the other side.

THE GOLF
100

100
John McDermott

Leave him out, I kept telling myself.

Leave out the poor soul who spent much of his life in a psychiatric hospital. All you will do, Michael, is raise more questions than you can answer. Let him rest in peace. He had too little of it when he was alive.

I didn't listen. I couldn't.

John McDermott, in 1911, was the first American-born player— no, not Francis Ouimet, as many would assume—to win the U.S. Open and, at nineteen, the youngest ever (he still is). He took the title again a year later. McDermott needs to be given his due, and it wasn't his fault he lost his way . . . there but for the grace of God go us all.

Let's pick up the trail in the 1910 Open when McDermott, the son of a mailman, and who dropped out of high school to turn pro, lost by four strokes to a Scottish immigrant, Alex Smith, in a playoff at the Philadelphia Cricket Club. One would expect that McDermott, who regularly attended mass, would show respect to the better man that day.

Not exactly.

"Hard luck, kid," Smith said.

"I'll get you next year, you big tramp," McDermott replied.

Well, as Muhammad Ali used to say, it isn't bragging if you can back it up, and that's what McDermott did against Smith and everyone else in 1911.

First in the Open at the Chicago Golf Club, where, after starting out with an 81, he prevailed in a playoff (despite hitting his first two shots out of bounds) over Mike Brady and George Simpson, and then in three challenge matches against other top pros in Philly in which he put up $1,000 against their $100. (Phil Mickelson would have loved a piece of that action.) And once McDermott won the first three, according to longtime golf writer and editor Robert Sommers, "the competition dried up."

A year later, at the Country Club of Buffalo, when he became the first to win the Open while breaking par, he outdueled the 1909 runner-up, Tom McNamara, by two.

For McDermott, who endorsed clubs and balls and played in exhibitions, "the world," Sommers wrote, "was a lovely place."

In 1913, he won the Western Open, a huge tournament in those days (although it's not considered an official major), tied for fifth in the British Open at Royal Liverpool, the highest finish to date for an American, atoning for his failure to qualify the year before, and beat Harry Vardon by thirteen and Ted Ray by fourteen in the Shawnee Open shortly before the U.S. Open at Brookline.

If only McDermott hadn't opened his big mouth. And hadn't had the audacity to bring his U.S. Open trophy to the presentation ceremony.

"There's been a lot of loose talk about 'the great English champions' coming over here and competing in our Open," he said. "Mr. Vardon, I understand you won this baby [in 1900] once before. But let me tell you this; [McDermott was addressing both Ray and Vardon] you are not going to take our cup back!"

The Brits hadn't heard fighting words like that since ... I don't know, the War of 1812?

The other players couldn't believe what they had heard and apologized to Vardon and Ray. So did McDermott, but the damage had been done, the United States Golf Association warning it might not allow him to play at Brookline. McDermott, according to *The New York Times*, was "worried greatly over the affair and has almost broken down under the strain." In the end, the USGA backed off, though McDermott could fare no better than eighth. America anointed a new hero in Ouimet, with another, Walter Hagen, who tied for fourth, on the horizon.

McDermott, with one setback after another, starting with heavy losses in the stock market, would soon be a factor no more.

Some point to the summer of 1914 as the beginning of the end. Missing a ferry, he missed his tee time to qualify for the British Open at Prestwick Golf Club in Scotland. He was told he could still give it a go, but rules were rules and McDermott, to his credit, wasn't willing to be an exception.

On his way back to the States, the vessel he was on, the *Kaiser Wilhelm II,* a high-end liner, collided with a grain ship in the fog. It was badly damaged—McDermott was among those put in lifeboats—but reached land in England.

In August, he tied for ninth in the Open at Midlothian Country Club outside Chicago. Two months later, his "mind cracking," as one writer put it, McDermott collapsed at the pro shop in Atlantic City where he worked. In June 1916, he was sent by his family to the State Hospital for the Insane in Norristown, Pennsylvania, where, according to Philadelphia golf historian James Finegan, he didn't speak to the other patients, reportedly spending "endless hours scribbling unintelligibly in notebooks, claiming he was writing his mother's and father's names."

McDermott was gone but not forgotten. At least not by his peers.

In 1928, Hagen played with him on a short six-hole course on the hospital grounds. His swing, according to Hagen, was "as fluid as ever."

As the years rolled on, McDermott got opportunities to play.

"I'd pick him up at Norristown," said Bud Lewis, a club professional from Philly. "He'd have his golf shoes on. He'd come down ready-made, wearing a suit and tie.... He would shoot in the 80s. He had big grips, still the biggest I've ever seen."

Fast-forward to June 1971 and the U.S. Open at the Merion Golf Club outside Philadelphia, where an elderly, poorly dressed McDermott was ushered out of the clubhouse by an assistant pro who had no clue who he was. Just then, who happened to come by but Arnold Palmer?

Palmer, who knew exactly who he was, put his arms around McDermott and brought him back inside.

"They talked golfer to golfer, champion to champion," wrote historian John Coyne, "and Palmer then arranged for McDermott to stay at the tournament as his special guest with all clubhouse rights and privileges."

I hope you now understand why I can't leave John McDermott off the list.

"There isn't any question," Grantland Rice, the famous sportswriter, claimed in 1916, "but that McDermott would have been to American golf what Vardon is to British play if John J. had not been forced out through fate just at the moment when he was coming upon the uplands of his career."

99

Roberto De Vicenzo

Argentina's Roberto De Vicenzo, who had won dozens of tournaments around the globe, couldn't believe what just happened.

No one could.

Which led De Vicenzo, in the best broken English he could muster, to deliver a response almost as memorable as the incident itself.

"I play golf all over the world for thirty years," he told the press, "and now all I can think of is what a stupid I am to be wrong in this wonderful tournament."

What a stupid, indeed.

This wonderful tournament was the 1968 Masters. The Masters he lost. Not by a mistake he made with his clubs. By a mistake he made with his card.

In the final round, on the day he turned forty-five, he failed to notice that on the card kept by Tommy Aaron, his playing partner, the number jotted down for the par-4 17th hole was a 4 instead of the 3 he had recorded. But because De Vicenzo signed it, he was forced to accept the higher score and miss out on what would have been an eighteen-hole playoff with the now-declared champion, Bob Goalby.

Those, ladies and gentlemen, were the rules.

That doesn't mean everyone agreed with the rules.

"In an event like the Masters," suggested the esteemed writer Herbert Warren Wind, "with hundreds of spectators lining each hole (and millions more watching on television), no one is going to 'win with the pencil.' ... The score that the player makes on the course is the score that he should be credited with. ... If an error is discovered, the important thing is to see that it is corrected. No penalty should be imposed. Golf, like every other sport, is meant to be a test of athletic ability, and not of bookkeeping."

Wind made a good point, but the club had no choice. "There was enough body of evidence of players getting penalized before Roberto," said David Fay, the longtime executive director of the United States Golf Association, "and if Augusta National had waived the rule, the outcry would have been pretty dramatic."

In any case, it's impossible not to feel sorry for De Vicenzo.

Not just for throwing away an opportunity to win a major, which doesn't come along too often. Also, for one lapse in concentration being how he would be remembered forever. The first sentence of his 2017 obit in *The New York Times* mentioned how he committed "one of the game's most storied gaffes." Ouch.

If not for the gaffe, this is how Roberto De Vicenzo would have been remembered, and still should be:

As the winner of 231 tournaments—that's not a typo—highlighted by the 1967 British Open at Royal Liverpool.

"I saw very few golfers in my lifetime who were better than Roberto," Gary Player told me. "He was physically strong, was an aggressive player, and had a marvelous swing. If he had been born in America, there's no telling how many majors he would have won."

In the '67 Open, De Vicenzo beat Jack Nicklaus, who was at the height of his powers, by two to become, at forty-four, the oldest to take home the Claret Jug in the twentieth century, his 10-under 278 only two shy of the Open record. He arrived at Royal Liverpool so confident that he placed five hundred pounds on himself to win. At odds of 70-to-1.

The club that won it for him was the putter, often his most glaring weakness.

De Vicenzo tried a new one that week. He was always trying a new one. The putter, which he had found on a visit a few months earlier to America, featured a gray mallet head. He made one big putt after another.

The fans were pleased with the outcome. "The English were tired of Americans winning [four of the previous six Opens]," he suggested, "and in this case they wanted De Vicenzo to win. In the final moments, that helped me."

The British Open was very good to him. In his first two appearances, in 1948 and 1949, he came in third, and only once in fifteen starts through 1971 did he finish out of the top twenty. Not too bad for the fifth of eight children born to a house painter in Villa Ballester, a suburb of Buenos Aires, and who used to pick up lost balls in the pond from a course across the street.

When he was six, he became a caddie at a local club.

"Even though I liked other things in life," De Vicenzo said, "I could not tear myself away from golf."

He dropped out of school at fifteen, landing a job at the Ranelagh Golf Club, about forty miles away. By the early 1940s, De Vicenzo was winning tournaments all over the country—nine Argentine Opens before he was done.

The time came to see if he could take his act on the road.

The answer was yes.

In 1951, he won the Palm Beach Round Robin and the Inverness Invitational Four-Ball with Henry Ransom. Even so, he didn't feel comfortable in America. "The greens were faster, especially at Augusta and the U.S. Open, and would give me trouble," he pointed out. "Some years I did not go at all. It was a choice I made."

Prior to 1968, his best finish in the Masters had been a tie for tenth the year before. In '68, De Vicenzo trailed Player, the leader, by two when he teed off on Sunday.

Not for long.

He holed out for an eagle on 1 to tie him and birdied 2 and 3. At 17, he hit his approach to within three feet. He made the putt, and once Goalby eagled 15 the two were tied, and that's where they stood after Goalby putted out on 18 ... until, well, the mistake with the card.

De Vicenzo went to his grave believing Goalby should have apologized for how things turned out. "Of course, it was my fault for signing the incorrect scorecard," De Vicenzo said, "but the way the public reacted wasn't my fault. It was his [Goalby's] fault. ... All he had to do was say one thing before they presented him with the green jacket: 'Sorry, I prefer that we play off tomorrow.' That would have been sufficient. Then, everything is fixed."

Maybe so, but we shouldn't come down too hard on the late Goalby, an eleven-time winner who received hate mail over the incident. He didn't make the rules.

"The presentation ceremony wasn't what it could have been," he said a half century later. "I sat next to Roberto and did what I could to console him. There's video of me patting him on the leg. I felt no elation, nothing like you'd expect from winning the biggest tournament of your life."

98 Tony Lema

Champagne Tony Lema—I'll explain the story about the nickname later—had gotten his act together. At last. He won three tournaments in 1962, one in 1963, five in 1964, including the British Open at St. Andrews, two in 1965, and another in 1966.

At first, Lema wasn't sure about playing in the '64 Open. It was a long way to go for a first prize of only $4,200. Urged on by Arnold Palmer, who wasn't in the field, he arrived thirty-six hours before the tournament kicked off on Wednesday morning. He got in ten holes on Monday and eighteen on Tuesday, hardly the way to prepare for a major.

And for a course he had never seen.

Lema did have one factor in his favor, and it was huge. His caddie was Tip Anderson, a Scot, who carried Palmer's bag when he won the Open in 1961 and 1962. If anyone could navigate Lema around the subtleties of a links course, Anderson was the man.

"At the British Open, you really need a good caddie," Gary Player said. "When you're on an American course, you can see everything, but over there you can see nothing. That year, Tony had the best caddie."

The fans on the Old Course took a liking to Lema, and the sentiment was mutual.

"I feel like I am back visiting an old grandmother," he said. "She's crotchety and eccentric but also elegant, and anyone who doesn't fall in love with her has no imagination."

The golfing gods were on his side, as well. On Day One, he teed off when the conditions were at their most benign, posting a one-over 73. By contrast, Jack Nicklaus, the tournament favorite, was stuck with the worst end of the draw, the winds gusting up to sixty-five miles per hour. Known for taking his time, he took almost three minutes for a shot on number 11 when he had ended up short of a bunker.

"Every time I was ready," Nicklaus said, "sand from the bunker would swirl out and hit me in the eyes. My eyes were watering so badly I could hardly see." He did well to turn in a 76. On Day Two, Lema, also using a putter that Palmer had given him, shot a 68 to go up by two over England's Harry Weetman, and more importantly, by nine over Nicklaus.

On Friday, the third and final day—the Open wrapped up with thirty-six holes back then—Nicklaus made his move while Lema headed in the opposite direction, the lead suddenly down to one. The two spotted each other from different fairways, Lema on the 6th, Nicklaus on the 13th. If ever there was a moment for Lema to be intimidated, this was it.

"I felt lousy," he said. "I thought, 'here he goes again.' We grinned at each other after glancing at the scores. Mine was sickly. His was happy."

Lema, however, proceeded to record five 3s in a row, three of them for birdies, shooting another 68. Nicklaus matched the course record with a 66 but still trailed by seven going into the final round. He wasn't about to catch Lema. No one was.

Tony Lema was on top of the golfing world, and what a journey it had been to get there.

When he was three, his father, a factory worker, died of pneumonia. His mother, supporting four kids in an industrial section of Oakland, California, worked as a department store clerk, shoe salesperson, and drugstore cashier. Lema, as you might imagine, got into his share of trouble. One time, he and a friend siphoned gas from a patrol car.

Golf entered his life, and not a moment too soon.

"Those are years I would love to have the chance to do over," he wrote. "We would sit around and booze it up from time to time, then start talking big and pump ourselves full of a lot of false courage. Phew! Talk about close calls!"

He became a caddie at Lake Chabot, a municipal course, when he was twelve. Six years later, he won the Oakland City Amateur Championship, though trying to make a living in golf wasn't on his mind.

The Marines were.

"I was at loose ends," Lema wrote, "and couldn't think of anything better to do."

With the fighting in Korea coming to an end, he spent much of his tour on courses in Japan and, upon returning to the United States, became an assistant pro at the San Francisco Golf Club.

Now trying to make a living in golf was definitely on his mind.

In 1956, Lema finished fiftieth in the U.S. Open at Oak Hill Country Club near Rochester, New York. A year later, he won the Imperial Valley Open, an unofficial event in El Centro, California. There's a story that goes with that victory. There's a story that goes with everything in the life of Tony Lema. Figuring the leader, Paul Harney, had the tournament wrapped up, Lema headed to the clubhouse bar.

He figured wrong.

Still, he gathered himself together to defeat Harney on the second playoff hole.

After a fine season in 1958, he struggled in 1959 and 1960. In his memoir, Lema referred to that period as *Two Years in Purgatory*.

"I had reached the point," he wrote, "where I hated to look at a golf club or a golf ball or a golf course."

Enter television writer and producer Danny Arnold to the rescue.

Arnold, who would later create the hit comedy *Barney Miller*, became good friends with Lema after they were paired together for a pro-am in Palm Springs. "He convinced me," Lema wrote, "that . . . if I stayed calm and kept the ball in play, the breaks would come my way."

Speaking of breaks, Lema, known as a playboy, met Betty Cline, a flight attendant, on a trip from Dallas to San Francisco in 1961, and they were married two years later. "I feel I am a better person, a more complete person and even a better golfer," he wrote. "I'm now playing for someone besides myself."

So anyway, how did he get the nickname of Champagne Tony Lema? Another story. Of course.

In October 1962, when Lema, leading by two, was interviewed after the third round of the Orange County Open at Mesa Verde Country Club in Costa Mesa, California, he indicated he wasn't thrilled with the beers in the pressroom.

"If I win tomorrow," he promised the reporters, "it's champagne, not this stuff."

Lo and behold, Lema defeated Bob Rosburg, the 1959 PGA champion, for his first official tour victory, sinking an eleven-foot birdie putt on the third playoff hole.

Only, he forgot his promise.

Good thing Lester Nehamkin, a photographer for the *Los Angeles Times*, didn't, and as a result, the press was able to enjoy three bottles of champagne.

From then on, Lema ordered the bubbly for members of the fourth estate whenever he won.

Given everything he'd been through, success couldn't have tasted any sweeter.

"I wonder how I had the nerve to start out on the tour or stay with it as long as I did," he wrote. "Most of the players at least got in on the ground floor. I climbed in through a basement window."

In July 1966, on the way to a pro-am only hours after tying for thirty-fourth at the PGA Championship in Akron, Ohio, he and Betty, who was pregnant, were killed in a plane crash. The private charter, running out of fuel, went down, in the cruelest of ironies, in a water hazard near the 7th green of a course in Lansing, Illinois.

He was thirty-two.

No one can say what Lema, still in his prime, would have accomplished in the years ahead. The game is too fickle. One week, you're hitting every fairway and green. The next, you're grinding to make the cut. Yet, given how talented he was and where his priorities were, there would have been few limits.

"I don't think he really found himself until right before the accident," said Dave Stockton, a two-time PGA champion. "He would have won more majors. There is no question about it."

97

Macdonald Smith

He was the youngest of the five Smith brothers to immigrate from Scotland to America around the turn of the twentieth century, and considered the most talented. So in 1910, when Macdonald Smith lost in a three-way playoff in the U.S. Open to his brother Alex, it was hard to feel sorry for him.

Mac Smith was twenty years old. There would be plenty of opportunities to win a major.

Unfortunately, he didn't cash in on those opportunities—would I have started the chapter this way otherwise?—although he had an outstanding career: twenty-five victories, including three Western Opens (the first in 1912, the last in 1933), four Los Angeles Opens, and a Canadian Open.

Smith did everything but win a major championship.

Boy, did he come close. In twenty-nine tries, he posted seventeen top tens... twelve top fives.

"Dame Fate took a particular delight in mocking his genius," one writer suggested, "encouraging him with lesser prizes but always refusing his demand for stellar honors."

Let's start with the Open in 1910, the first major he played in, coming just two years after he arrived in the States. Smith turned in a 71 in the final round to tie Alex and, you may recall, eighteen-year-old John McDermott.

Too bad Mac Smith shot a 77 in the playoff to come up six short. There is no telling how his career might have unfolded if he had gotten the first major out of the way and at such a young age. No less a figure than Harry Vardon stated in 1913 that Smith, who would be in the hunt on the back nine of the Open at Brookline—he tied for fourth, three shots back—was the best golfer he had seen in America.

Before long everything changed. With the world. And with Smith personally.

Word is he lost a good deal of his hearing fighting for the Allies in France during World War I, or perhaps it happened after the war while working at a shipyard in San Francisco, where he hit the bottle.

"He was such a drunkard that his [future] wife picked him up out of the gutter, and I mean the gutter in the street," claimed Bill Mehlhorn, a top golfer in the '20s.

Smith, according to Mehlhorn, hit a thousand balls a day for a whole year to get his game back in shape.

The hard work paid off. In 1924, he won his first Tour events in twelve years, the California Open and the Northern California Open.

Yet he still came up short in the majors: third in the British Open at Royal Liverpool and fourth in the U.S. Open at Oakland Hills outside Detroit.

Leading to the heartbreak of all heartbreaks: the 1925 British Open at Prestwick.

All Smith, up by five heading into the final round, needed to take home the Claret Jug was a 78. "A 78 for a golfer like Mac Smith," Herbert Warren Wind wrote, "was as simple as stirring sugar."

So much for the simplicity of stirring sugar.

Smith shot an 82 to finish fourth.

His fans didn't do him any favors, either.

"They killed Old Mac with their ardor," Wind went on. "Whatever chance he might have had for coming home in 36 was smashed in the unruly rush of unmanageable thousands, strangling the pace he wanted to play at, forcing him to wait ten minutes and more before playing a shot until they had filed across the narrow foot bridges and pounded through the bunkers ahead and grudgingly opened an avenue to the greens."

Smith wasn't done teasing us just yet: two more seconds in 1930, in the U.S. Open at Interlachen Country Club outside Minneapolis and the British Open once more at Royal Liverpool.

Then one more heartbreak for the road: the 1931 Open at Carnoustie in Scotland.

Now forty-one, he went five over his last three holes to hand the Claret Jug to another Scot, Tommy Armour.

"At no other moment in all the time I've played and won in golf tournaments," Armour wrote, "was I so depressed as when I saw Mac Smith walk into the clubhouse at Carnoustie, again the patient victim of the unkind gods of golf."

Give Smith credit. He kept up his winning ways—five victories from 1932 through 1936, including two L.A. Opens—even if the gods, when it came to the majors, would remain unkind forever.

It could have been worse.

"Mac's comeback is something unique in sports," Armour wrote. "At one time he was through—through as completely and conclusively as an athlete can be. The jitters had him. There was hopelessness in his carriage and in his eyes. He pulled himself together.... He won something far more important than a dozen National Open Championships. He won Mac Smith."

Charles Price, the distinguished golf writer and historian, watched Smith hit balls one day on the range.

"Mac Smith was well past 50 then," Price wrote, "but the balletic sweep of that swing was still there. He had a certain flair just holding a golf club that I had seen before only in Hagen, Jones and Snead and that I had seen off a golf course only in the way Ted Williams handled a bat, Leopold Stokowski a baton and Franklin D. Roosevelt a cigarette holder.... Merely by addressing the ball, Mac Smith gave the impression that he could bring off a golf shot if he had to stand barefoot on a cake of ice."

Yet, believe it or not, Smith isn't in the World Golf Hall of Fame.

Granted, not winning a major is a factor against him, as it should be. That's why I have him this low on the list. On the other hand, what about those twenty-five victories, including the three Western Opens?

I reached out to someone familiar with the selection process, who assured me Smith's name has been brought up and that he will get in "eventually."

Eventually can't come soon enough.

96

Padraig Harrington

Padraig Harrington was pulling a Jean van de Velde. On the same course, amazingly enough, and in the same event.

For those not familiar with the story, van de Velde was the French fella who, with one lapse in judgment after another—you think Roberto De Vicenzo was a stupid?—threw away the 1999 British Open at Carnoustie after leading by three on the final hole. You can catch the entire meltdown on YouTube. Viewer discretion advised.

For Harrington, from Ireland, the first mistake he made on the 72nd hole of the 2007 British Open was, like van de Velde, with the tee shot.

Not the choice of club. The execution.

"I got to the top of my backswing, and I got a little doubt," said Harrington, who was leading Sergio Garcia by a stroke at the time.

Don't hit it left, he thought.

He didn't. He hit right.

Right into the Barry Burn, a water hazard, and if that weren't disturbing enough, Harrington found the hazard again with his next shot.

He was beside himself, certain he had lost the Open.

"That's probably the first time in my whole career," he said, "I would have been quite happy if the ground had opened and swallowed me up."

Even so, his caddie told him the tournament wasn't over.

"For 50 yards I wanted to kill him," Harrington said. "The next 50, I was listening to him. The last 50, I actually believed him."

His caddie was correct. It wasn't over.

From about fifty yards away, Harrington, given the circumstances, hit the shot of his life, the ball coming to a rest about five feet from the cup.

"I chipped it exactly as I would have done as a fourteen-year-old showing off to my mates," he said.

And once he knocked in the putt for a double and Garcia made a bogey on 18 roughly fifteen minutes later—his eight-footer for the win hit the lip—the two headed to a four-hole playoff, which Harrington won by a stroke.

Jean who?

The problem with the errant tee shot on 18 was that he was too complacent. "You're told by the psychologists that fear is a terrible emotion, but I think fear is a great motivator," he said. "I play great with fear. I play terrible with complacency."

That wasn't the case with the pitch shot. He was in no position to be complacent now.

The 2007 British Open was only the beginning.

Over the next thirteen months, he won his second Claret Jug and the PGA. He was on a roll no one saw coming.

Harrington learned a lot about himself in the 2006 U.S. Open at Winged Foot, where he recorded bogeys on 16, 17, and 18 to finish fifth, two behind the champion, Geoff Ogilvy. In the final round, "I couldn't have left more shots on the course," he claimed.

Dr. Bob Rotella, the renowned sports psychologist, waited for him afterward.

"Bob was there to talk me off the ledge," Harrington said.

There was no need.

"I came out with the biggest smile on my face," he explained. "I said to Bob, 'I know I can win a major.'" Prior to that, Harrington assumed that "for me to win, I'd have to get some help. I [now] knew it was within my control."

Nonetheless, in 2008, while defending his title at Royal Birkdale in England, he needed help and from a most unlikely source—Greg Norman, who led Harrington and K. J. Choi by two heading into the final round. Norman, fifty-three, hadn't won a tournament in eleven years.

Harrington couldn't have drawn it up any better.

"Greg Norman was the story," he said, "and I was really afraid of this idea of nostalgia. The fairy tale was very much in my mind at all times."

Norman closed with a 77, tying for third, while Harrington shot a 69, to prevail by four. As elated as he had been to pick up his first major, the second was more gratifying.

"I had come from the wrong side of the draw and swung the club the best," he said. "There was no doubt this was my tournament."

In the PGA three weeks later at Oakland Hills, Harrington trailed by six after rounds of 71 and 74.

"It's hard to hype yourself up to win a major, get excited, come down, and get yourself back up," he explained.

Enter Mother Nature to bail him out. Due to rain suspending play on Saturday, he got a much-needed break and was fresher for the twenty-seven holes he needed to navigate on Sunday. After putting the finishing touches on a third-round 66, he followed with another 66 to outduel Garcia and Ben Curtis by two. All of a sudden, Harrington, who was once 0-for-36 in majors, had won three of the last six.

So what if Tiger Woods missed the British Open and PGA in 2008 to recover from knee surgery? That should take nothing away from what Harrington accomplished.

"If you want to say I was the next-best player to Tiger, I'll take that," he said.

Harrington knows how cruel the golfing gods can be.

In the second round of the 1996 Benson & Hedges International

Open in Thame, England, only a week after he had collected his first European Tour victory in Madrid, he made a *Tin Cup*–like 13 on a par-5, finding the water four times.

"The only way I could tell what score I had on the hole," he recalled, "was to count how many balls I had and how many balls I started with."

The Times of London poked fun at him with a diagram that tracked where his shots went. His parents put it in a crystal picture frame, and while the paper has become a bit faded, Harrington gets a kick out of it every time he visits his mum.

"It reminds me of why I love the game," he said. "It tests your mental fortitude to be able to deal with the good and the bad."

Harrington, who had his first lesson at fifteen, thought so little of his prospects as a junior golfer that he took classes in accounting at Dublin Business School to have something to fall back on.

"I didn't ever expect to be a star in the game of golf," he said. "I didn't have the swing for it. Everybody said so."

95

Glenna Collett Vare

Her drive that day in the summer of 1917 went more than one hundred yards and down the middle of the fairway. The others in the group at Metacomet Golf Club in Rhode Island, which included her father, George, a former national bicycling champion, were blown away.

The fourteen-year-old who hit it couldn't have been more excited.

"My head was bursting," Glenna Collett Vare wrote, "with the soaring dreams that only the very young and ambitious live and know. As I came off the course after the first game, my destiny was settled. I would become a golfer. It was in retrospect as simple as that. No bypaths, no hesitations, no doubts. . . . I dreamed of some day becoming the champion! With such a goal in mind, I labored to find out the shortest route to the top."

She made it to the top, all right, and stayed there for years to come.

From 1922 through 1930, Collect Vare won the U.S. Women's Amateur five times, with a sixth—and final—title coming in 1935 when she defeated seventeen-year-old Patty Berg, a future LPGA Hall of Famer.

Collett Vare was known as the "female Bobby Jones" but the game didn't come easy to her in the beginning.

"My first round of eighteen holes was something of an ordeal," she wrote. "I don't remember a more unpleasant afternoon. Struggling along, missing more shots than I made, getting into all sorts of hazards, and finishing with the embarrassing score of 150, I was ready to give up the game."

Around the same time, a foursome that was playing in exhibition matches across the country for the Red Cross—the United States had entered World War I in the spring of 1917—showed up at the Wannamoisett Club outside Providence.

Providence, indeed.

The foursome included Jones, fifteen, already an important figure in amateur golf.

Watching such talented young players—she was very impressed by Alexa Stirling, the 1916 U.S. Women's Amateur champion—proved anything was possible.

Within two years, she broke 100. Though only five feet six and weighing about 130 pounds, she hit the ball a mile. When she was eighteen, one tee shot traveled as far as 307 yards—"the longest drive," according to Collett Vare, "ever made by a woman golfer."

A lot of the credit goes to her instructor, Alex Smith, Macdonald's older brother, who, you may recall, had won the U.S. Open in 1910—and in 1906, as well. Smith, the pro at Shennecossett Country Club in Groton, Connecticut, met with her twice a week.

"Alex gave me a happy philosophy as well as an improved way of handling the putter and mashie [a five-iron today]," she wrote.

In 1919, Collett Vare lost in the second round of her first U.S. Women's Amateur and came up short again in 1920 and 1921. Her breakthrough was in 1922 at the Greenbrier in West Virginia in a field that included Marion Hollins, the defending champion, and Edith Cummings, another top player. Collett Vare shot a 75, her lowest score ever, two days before the matches got under way.

She was very pleased, although wondered: Where did *that* round come from?

Her guess was it had something to do with dinner the night before: two lamb chops, creamed potatoes, and string beans. Which would now be her dinner every night.

She was also superstitious about her wardrobe—the same skirt, sweater, and hat.

It worked. Collett Vare beat Cummings in the semifinals and took down Margaret Gavin in the final. "Even when it was over, and I had won the championship, I couldn't believe it," she wrote. "My eyes, which had been for days riveted on the little white ball sailing and rolling over the fairways and greens of the lovely Greenbrier course, were raised for the first time."

Collett Vare failed to defend her title in 1923 and fell in the semis (her only loss in sixty matches that year) in 1924 to Mary K. Browne, the U.S. Women's Open champion in 1912, 1913, and 1914—in tennis, not golf. Browne was quite fortunate. On the first playoff hole, her ball caromed off her opponent's and dropped into the cup. Players didn't mark their ball back then unless within six inches of another ball.

She won her second Amateur in 1925, beating Alexa Stirling Fraser (she had married Wilbert G. Fraser), 9 and 8, and prevailed again in 1928, 1929, and 1930.

Glenna Collett Vare—the LPGA's annual award for lowest stroke average is named after her—beat everyone at one point or another.

Except Joyce Wethered.

The two squared off for the first time in the third round of the 1925 British Ladies Championship at Royal Troon in Scotland, Wethered winning the thirty-six-hole match, 4 and 3. "After fifteen holes of the best golf I ever played—I was just one stroke over par at this stage—I was out of the tournament, beaten by four holes," Collett Vare wrote. "She is as good as it is possible to be."

The second time they met, in the final of the same tournament at St. Andrews in 1929, was like a heavyweight title bout, Wethered, the ex-champion, coming out of retirement to play a course dear to her heart. Through eleven holes—this match was also set for thirty-six—Collett Vare, who had shot a 34 over the front nine, was 5 up.

"The finest sequence of holes I have ever seen a lady play," Wethered wrote, referring to the first nine.

The turning point came on number 12.

After Wethered three-putted, Collett Vare lined up about a three-footer to go 6 up. If she were to make it, the match might very well be over.

She missed.

Given new life, Wethered sliced the deficit to two after the first eighteen and by the midway point of the second eighteen was 4 up. Needing just 73 strokes during an eighteen-hole stretch, she prevailed 3 and 1.

Nonetheless, Collett Vare maintained fond memories of that day on the Old Course.

"The match was so exciting," she said nearly a half century later. "There were so many Scots watching the match and in those days the crowds followed the matches very, very closely. I was lucky to have a few friends, strong ones, who linked arms to keep the gallery from getting to me. Even still, I was very lucky to ever see a shot land. When I was winning, the silence was deafening. When she started to win, there was a noise like I never heard."

The two went head-to-head one last time in 1932 at the Wentworth Golf Club in England for the inaugural Curtis Cup Match, which pitted the best women amateurs from the U.S. against a squad from Great Britain and Ireland. Although the Americans took home the Cup, Wethered defeated Collett Vare in the singles, 6 and 4.

In 2022, I reached out to golf writer/author Jim Dodson, who wrote a magazine article about Collett Vare when she was in her eighties.

Dodson asked if he could caddie for her at an event in Rhode Island.

"Absolutely not," she told him. "No one should ever have to see my golf swing again."

Dodson showed up regardless and was blown away.

Just like the group on that summer day in 1917.

"She walloped the ball," Dodson said, "and it was so natural."

94

Bernhard Langer

In evaluating the career of Germany's Bernhard Langer, let's not focus on what happened that memorable Sunday at the 1991 Ryder Cup, known as the *War by the Shore* (to refer, if you'll permit me to vent for a second, to a sporting competition as a war is insensitive beyond belief) on the Ocean Course at Kiawah Island in South Carolina.

Let's focus on what happened the Sunday after.

On the first Sunday, Langer lined up a par putt from six feet away. Make it and Europe, as the defending champion, retains the Cup. Miss it and the United States wins the Cup for the first time since 1985.

Langer, all square with Hale Irwin on the final hole of the final singles match, took his time. Nothing unusual there. He always took his time.

At long last, he brought the putter back.

And missed.

He was devastated. Yet after the tears came perspective.

"What really helped," Langer told me, "was the reality that we were just playing a game of golf. It wasn't life-or-death. My self-esteem didn't rely on making or not making a putt. I got my self-esteem by being a child of God."

Which takes us to the Sunday after. In the German Masters at Stuttgart, Langer, the tournament host, knocked in a ten-footer on the 72nd hole to force a playoff with Australia's Rodger Davis.

The putt meant nothing—with all due respect, who cares about the German Masters?—and everything.

He won it on the first extra hole, proving he was as tough mentally as any golfer over the past half century not named Jack or Tiger. He needed to be tough. Born in Anhausen, a village near Munich, the odds of his becoming a championship golfer were stacked against him from the start. His father, Erwin, was a bricklayer who worked twelve-hour days.

"He built our house with his own hands, literally," Langer said.

In the mid-1960s, when he was nine years old, Langer became a caddie at Golfclub Augsburg, about five miles away. He didn't carry bags for the love of the game, mind you, but for the love of the Deutschmarks. Hanging around the course, his love for the game came soon enough.

In his early teens, Langer went with his parents to a job placement center. It didn't go well.

"I want to become a golf professional," he told the man they met with.

"What's that?" he responded.

At one point, the man left the room. When he returned a few minutes later, the news was the last thing Langer wanted to hear.

"We have no documents on the golf professional being a recognized job in Germany," he said. "I would highly recommend you learn something decent."

Langer feared the worst.

"I was thinking my dream was gone," he recalled.

He wasn't down for long, becoming an assistant pro at the Munich Country Club.

For much of the day, Langer, who rode to the course on his bicycle from a farmhouse about a mile away, operated the pro shop, set up tournaments, and fixed clubs. From five p.m. on, he practiced and played with teaching pros and the club's top amateurs. "The eighth and ninth holes," he said, "we'd play in total darkness."

He had heard of Jack Nicklaus—there was a swing sequence of him plastered on the wall in the caddy shack—but that was pretty much all he knew.

In 1976, Langer, eighteen, joined the European Tour. The early days were a constant struggle. Unable to afford a hotel, he spent more than a few nights sleeping in his car, which could get awfully cold. And when he was fortunate to find a room, "there were crawling creatures at times."

That was nothing compared to what came next: fifteen months of compulsory military service.

One morning, around seven thirty, the group leader explained to his troops the drill for the day: "If an enemy airplane flies at you and they are shooting machine-gun bullets, what do you do? You throw yourself on the ground as quick as you can because you're a smaller target on the ground than you are when you're standing up."

Langer followed orders . . . to a point. Lugging a thirty-pound backpack, he kept throwing himself on his side to keep from getting injured. The group leader wasn't pleased.

"I told you guys to throw yourselves straight on your stomach," he insisted.

Langer followed orders to a tee this time. And to his detriment.

"Every time you hit the ground, the backpack hit you from the top," he said.

The next morning, when his alarm went off at six, "I couldn't move any part of my body without it feeling like someone was stabbing me with a knife," he recalled. "I just lay in my bed, crying. Finally, someone got help."

Langer, who suffered stress fractures to a pair of vertebrae and had two bulging discs, spent six weeks in the hospital.

"I was thinking my golf career is finished," he said.

His body healed, thank goodness, although he has endured his share of back and neck problems ever since.

As the years went on, he faced another test, the dreaded yips. (The definition on the Mayo Clinic website: "Involuntary wrist spasms that occur most commonly when golfers are trying to putt.") Langer would, on occasion, reach sixteen or seventeen greens in regulation and still shoot a bunch of strokes over par. "The worst I remember," he said, "was once when I hit the ball twice. I hit it, but it only moved a few inches, and before it stopped I hit it again."

Nick Price, a three-time major winner, was often paired with Langer in those early days.

"I never thought he would make it," Price said. In one tournament, "he was four-putting or three-putting just about every hole. It was horrible to watch."

Yet he persevered. Given what he had overcome to get this far, it was not surprising.

By the spring of 1985, Langer had won eleven times in Europe. This brings us to a tournament they hold every April in Augusta, Georgia.

The focus that Sunday afternoon was on Curtis Strange, who had rebounded from an opening 80 to seize a three-shot lead on the back nine.

The winner that Sunday afternoon was Bernhard Langer, who birdied 12, 13, 15, and 17 to defeat Strange, Raymond Floyd, and Seve Ballesteros by two.

Langer earned his second green jacket in 1993. He was at even par for the final round until he eagled 13 to go up by three over Chip Beck. Which was still the margin when Beck chose not to go for the green on 15 from 236 yards away.

A lot of people have been critical of Beck for laying up. Langer isn't one of them.

"It was touch and go," he said in 2024. "We had persimmon heads and steel shafts and the ball wasn't going as far as it does now." Even if his ball had carried the pond, Langer said, there was no guarantee it would have stayed on the green.

Price, having seen the worst of him, couldn't be more impressed with the player Langer turned out to be.

"He won at Augusta National on what are probably the hardest greens in the world to putt on," Price pointed out. "His determination and resilience, I have never seen it matched in golf."

93

Ken Venturi

Ken Venturi is one of the most inspiring golfers of all time. Not just for what he accomplished: fourteen victories, including the 1964 U.S. Open. Also for what he overcame, on and off the course.

Before his game fell apart in the early 1960s, Venturi came close to winning the Masters in 1956 (an amateur, he blew a four-shot lead with a final-round 80), 1958—we'll get to that later—and 1960 (Arnold Palmer birdied the last two holes to beat him by one). He was supposed to be the next Ben Hogan. Instead, he was a has-Ben. At the ripe old age of thirty-one.

In 1962, a ten-time Tour winner, he earned just $6,951 to finish sixty-sixth on the money list.

In 1963, he made less than $4,000. When he showed up in Las Vegas for the Sahara Invitational, he was told he hadn't been invited. He assumed it was a mistake. He was Ken Venturi.

There was no mistake, though officials allowed him in after a few players pleaded his case.

"I was a washed-up loser," he wrote in his memoir, "closer to selling cars—my former line of work—than to winning them. My swing had vanished, along with my confidence."

He turned to alcohol.

One afternoon in September 1963, he walked into a bar on Geary Street in San Francisco.

"My car was already there from the night before, another night I couldn't remember," he wrote. "Another night I was too drunk to drive home."

Good thing the bartender was Dave Marcelli, who had played football for the University of San Francisco. When Marcelli told Venturi he was wasting his life, he did something he hadn't done for a long time. He listened.

He thanked Marcelli and, after one last Jack Daniel's, made a promise:

"I give you my word. I will not have another drink until I win again."

The next day, Venturi practiced at the California Golf Club, pretending his mentor, Byron Nelson, was cheering him on. Yet in early 1964, he didn't show any progress. He tied for thirty-ninth in San Francisco and missed the cut in Palm Springs.

Finally, in March, his game started to come around. He recorded two top 15 finishes in Florida and then in June, he tied for third in the Thunderbird Classic outside New York City, where he had practically begged to get an invite, and tied for sixth a week later at the Buick Open in Michigan.

The Open at Congressional Country Club in the D.C. area was next.

The story has been told hundreds of times, and it is worth telling hundreds more.

Going into the final round on Saturday afternoon—they played the last thirty-six on Saturdays back then—Venturi trailed Tommy Jacobs by two.

Only, Jacobs wasn't his toughest opponent. Mother Nature was. And she was a beast.

With the temperature around a hundred degrees, Venturi suffered from heat prostration. "You can't go out there [on the course]," a doctor told him in the locker room. "It could be fatal." Venturi didn't give a damn. "It's better than the way I've been living," he said.

So with cold towels around his neck and equipped with salt tablets, he walked slowly to the 1st tee.

Jacobs, meanwhile, began to falter. It didn't help he'd eaten beef Stroganoff between his two rounds. ("By the time we got to the clubhouse, they had run out of sandwiches," Jacobs said in 2000. "It was beef Stroganoff or nothing." After a few holes, "my arms became very heavy, and I had absolutely no drive.")

Venturi didn't have much left, either, but made the pars down the stretch one needs to make in a U.S. Open.

After putting out on 18, he dropped his club to the ground. His playing partner, Raymond Floyd, twenty-one, with tears in his eyes, picked the ball out of the hole. Venturi, who closed with a 70 to prevail by four over Jacobs, couldn't believe it.

"My God," he said, "I've won the Open."

It was no fluke.

Later that summer, he won the Insurance City Open near Hartford and the American Golf Classic in Akron. He was named the *Sports Illustrated* Sportsman of the Year for 1964.

In 1965, however, he was diagnosed with carpal tunnel syndrome, which became so debilitating that clubs would fall from his hands without his realizing it. Winning only once more—fittingly, in 1966 at Harding Park in San Francisco, where he played as a kid—Venturi, in his mid-thirties, was done for good this time. Between the ropes, that is.

He became an analyst for CBS, where he lasted for thirty-five years, quite an accomplishment for someone who stuttered growing up. One speech therapist warned his mother he was "an incurable stammerer" who would not be "able to speak right for the rest of his life."

No wonder many were taken aback when Venturi, in his 2004 memoir, *Getting Up & Down*, which I co-wrote, was critical of Arnold Palmer.

He claimed Palmer broke the rules on number 12 in the final round of the 1958 Masters, which he won by a stroke over Doug Ford and Fred Hawkins. According to Venturi, who was paired with him, Palmer needed to declare his intention to play a second ball before playing his first, which was embedded near the green, resulting in a double bogey. With his second ball, Palmer made a par, and that's the score that was counted by Augusta National.

It was as if Venturi had gone after the pope.

"So what we have here," one writer suggested, "is Palmer, promoter of the game, being taken to task by someone whose main objective can only be described as self-promotion."

Nothing could have been further from the truth.

Venturi's objective was to get something off his chest that had been bothering him for more than forty years. Can you blame him?

Even so, my responsibility as his collaborator was to protect him, and I wondered if I had failed to do that. At the very least, perhaps I could have persuaded him to tone down his remarks on Palmer.

When an excerpt of the book came out, I received an email that felt like a punch in the gut:

"Ken's reputation is now cemented as an angry old man."

Yet the more I thought about it, the more I felt at peace. I didn't see what happened on the 12th green in 1958, and if he wanted to call out Arnold Palmer, that was his right. Besides, his reputation is not cemented as an angry old man. Ken Venturi, who passed away in 2013, is remembered as a major champion and respected commentator.

And one of the finest ambassadors the game has ever known.

92
Tony Jacklin

In my chats with Tony Jacklin, one hole from his past came up more than any other—the 17th at Muirfield, a reachable par-5, on the east coast of Scotland, where they played the British Open in 1972. When he got to the green in the final round, Jacklin, twenty-eight, was in position to claim his third major in three years. Twenty minutes later, he was a wreck and would never be the same player again. All because of what happened at 17.

I didn't believe him for the longest time. I kept thinking to myself: *Come on, how can one lousy hole cause so much damage?*

Lord knows, it did.

He was tied with his playing partner, Lee Trevino, who had knocked his third into the thick rough, tossing his club in disgust, and his fourth over the green. Jacklin, meanwhile, was lying on the green in three about eighteen feet from the cup.

"I was so mad I was just going to hit it and then hit it," Trevino said. "I didn't care if I made an eight."

Only, he didn't make an 8. He made a 5.

For Jacklin, who had seen Trevino chip in a couple of times that week already, the shot on 17 was "the straw that broke the camel's back."

Even so, all was not lost.

He could still make his putt for a birdie or, at the very least, two-putt for a par that would keep him and Trevino even headed to 18. As the cliché goes, there was still plenty of golf to be played . . . if only Jacklin had realized it.

"My instinct was, *You're not going to beat me like this.*"

So, taking a bold run at his birdie attempt, he knocked it a few feet by and missed the comebacker. While only a shot behind, he might as well have been a hundred shots behind. That's how out of sorts he was. "I ran out of patience," Jacklin said. "I could have rolled the damn thing around the hole and tapped it in. My emotions got the better of me."

What offended him wasn't that Trevino won the golf tournament. It was *how* Trevino won the golf tournament, the chip-ins violating a sacred code about the game Jacklin had believed in for as long as he could remember. That, on any given week, the player who executes the best will prevail.

"I didn't think luck could play that big a role," he explained. "I had never seen anything like it."

In six British Opens from 1967 through 1972, Jacklin finished in the top five on five occasions. From 1973 on, he didn't post one top ten. Or a top ten in any major.

Trevino isn't the only one who made things difficult for Jacklin. Another was his agent, Mark McCormack, the IMG founder who represented Nicklaus, Palmer, and Player, golf's Big Three in the 1960s. Jacklin contends McCormack steered him in the wrong direction by claiming that, to capitalize on winning the British Open in 1969 and the U.S. Open a year later, he needed to be based in Europe instead of the States. Jacklin flew back and forth six times a year, burning himself out. "I was living on airplanes," he said.

Heading into the '69 Open at Royal Lytham & St. Annes in England, Jacklin, who had won in Jacksonville the year before, was very confident, and with good reason. With rounds of 68, 70, and 70, he was up by two through fifty-four holes and was still in the lead, when his mind began to wander as he walked down the 14th fairway.

"I wondered if an hour from then, I would be lifting the Claret Jug," he said. "I physically smacked my face to say, 'Don't you dare go there. Stay in the moment.'" Which he did, winning by two over Bob Charles to become the first Open champion from the UK since England's Max Faulkner in 1951.

Two months later, Jacklin took part in one of the most memorable matches of all time. The opponent was Jack Nicklaus in the Ryder Cup at Royal Birkdale.

The two, in the final battle of the entire competition, were all square on the 18th green. As were the teams themselves. A tie would allow the United States, as the defending champion, to retain the Cup, while a victory for Jacklin would hand it over to Great Britain and Ireland.

Nicklaus was four and a half feet from the cup, Jacklin about half that distance. Both would be putting for a par. Jacklin expected Nicklaus to knock his in. He was Jack Nicklaus. *T.J.,* he told himself, *you're going to have to make a putt.*

No, he wouldn't.

After Nicklaus canned his putt, he picked up Jacklin's coin in a gesture of sportsmanship that would be known as *The Concession.*

"I was surprised," Jacklin said.

He was also relieved.

Not that he was afraid he would miss it. He wasn't. Only one can never be too certain, especially given what was at stake.

Which brings us to the 1970 U.S. Open at Hazeltine National Golf

Club in Chaska, Minnesota. During a practice round, club pro Jim Yancey, whose brother, Tour veteran Bert, was one of Jacklin's closest friends, asked him:

"Have you ever tried looking at the hole while you putt?"

Nope, Jacklin said.

No harm in giving it a try.

No harm, indeed.

"We went to the putting green and stayed out there for an hour or so," he recalled. "I got this amazing sort of feel for distance."

In round one, he made a twenty-footer for birdie on the 1st hole and putted lights out the rest of the week. His attitude was also on target. While other players criticized the course—Dave Hill said it "lacked only 80 acres of corn and a few cows to be a good farm"—Jacklin focused on the task at hand.

Ahead by four going into the final round, he was anxious.

"I'm not an overly religious guy," he said, "but I took time to pray hard that morning. Not to win. I prayed for the strength to get through the day. If I blew it, I would be known forever as a guy who blew a four-shot lead."

After bogeys on 7 and 8, the lead was down to three. "I remember saying to myself, *Oh, God, please not now.*"

On number 9, his thirty-foot putt for birdie had too much speed, but the ball hit the back of the cup and, as Jacklin put it, "decided to go in." If it hadn't, he would have faced about a five-footer coming back. "At that moment, all the pressure just fell away," he said. "I thought, *This is mine now.*" Jacklin, who closed with a 70 to win by seven, now held the two Open titles at the same time, a claim few in this game have been able to make.

The first player from the British Isles to claim America's national championship since Ted Ray in 1920, Jacklin ascended to a whole new level of fame.

"Tony was a genuine hero to everyone in Britain at the time," said the late English pro Peter Oosterhuis. "He did something, two things, that no one else from Britian had done for so long. And he did both with a bit of dash and style."

Jacklin had his chances in the 1971 Open at Royal Birkdale but finished two behind Trevino.

A year later came Muirfield. And the dreaded 17th.

Fortunately, it wouldn't be the last we heard of Tony Jacklin. No, siree.

In the early 1980s, he took over as the captain of Team Europe in the Ryder Cup, insisting on first-class treatment for his boys, and they came through for him, as well. Under his helm, the Europeans went 2-1-1, winning the Cup in 1985 for the first time in twenty-eight years, and in 1987, for the first time on American soil. "The Ryder Cup," as one writer put it, "is the biggest event in golf outside the four major championships, a fact in large part due to the difference Jacklin made."

I sometimes wonder: What if Trevino had not chipped in on 17? Or what if Jacklin had made his short putt for par to keep the match even going to 18?

If, if, if.

91

Henry Cotton

The folks in the UK cheered for Bobby Jones and Walter Hagen and the other Americans who walked off with the Claret Jug every year from 1924 through 1933. Even so they looked forward to the day when they could again honor a champion who was one of their own, as had been the case in the British Open from its inception in 1860 until Frenchman Arnaud Massy broke the string in 1907.

They got their wish in Henry Cotton.

The talent was apparent from the beginning. At twelve, Cotton, who grew up in London, could beat his father, an avid player, and before long everyone else. He turned pro at seventeen and two years later became the professional at Langley Park Golf Club in the county of Kent.

Golf wasn't his sport growing up. Cricket was.

And if not for a dispute with the authorities, it might have remained that way. Cotton believed the prefects on his cricket team shouldn't be excused from carrying, like others, the equipment to matches on the road, and put his opinion on the school's noticeboard. Which didn't go over very well.

The punishment was to be hit with a stick, but when Cotton wouldn't submit to it, he was told he couldn't play anymore.

"What will you do now?" someone asked.

"In that case I will play golf," he said.

At Langley Park, when he wasn't on the job, Cotton was working on his game, often skipping lunch, and every night after dinner he hit balls for a few hours into a net in the garage.

He focused on building the strength in his arms, forearms, and fingers. One way was to swing his club at a car's tires on the ground.

It's a wonder he didn't break something. Or maybe he did.

Cotton, who took lessons from John Henry Taylor, a five-time champion, won the Open on three occasions, starting in 1934, and if not for World War II—there was no tournament from 1940 through 1945—he might have won one or two more. By the time the Open resumed on the Old Course in 1946, Cotton was thirty-nine.

He was the Champion Golfer of the Year in 1937 and 1948, as well, and registered top tens in 1952, 1956, 1957, and 1958.

The 1934 Open at Royal St. George's stands out. In how Cotton played—and what he did after he played.

During the first round of qualifying—players needed to fare well enough over thirty-six holes to secure a spot in the field—Cotton, according to Bernard Darwin, the premier golf writer of his era (an outstanding player himself, he was the grandson of the renowned naturalist Charles Darwin) "proceded to play such golf as had never been seen on the links...he made the game look almost laughably easy... every drive split the fairway and every approach ended within six or eight yards of the hole."

Add 'em all up and it came to a 66, a new course record.

Was he peaking too soon?

Apparently not.

On Day One of the tournament, Cotton turned in a 67, matching Hagen for the lowest score to date in a British Open. On Day Two, he shot a 65 to go up by nine. (To honor the accomplishment, the Dunlop company would name its new rubber-core ball, which Cotton used, the Dunlop 65.) He cooled off with a 72 in the third round, the first of two on the final day, but with the course soggy from a hailstorm, he increased his lead to ten.

No one could stop him.

Except perhaps Cotton himself.

It didn't help that his tee time was delayed fifteen minutes to allow officials to manage the crowd.

"I went and sat in an empty tent by the first tee, where my closer friends talked to my well-wishers, keeping them away from me," he said. "Those 15 minutes dragged by. I was waiting to see my life's ambition realized and I was powerless to get on with it.... This anxiety proved more than my delicate stomach could stand and I had a terrible stomach cramp. I could hardly stand up."

Little wonder why Cotton, who had finished in the top ten of the Open five times, was in such a state.

For nearly a decade, "he had been trying to win [the Open]," wrote Michael McDonnell in his book about golf's greatest moments, "and while nobody would argue that he was not the best golfer in Britain, and of late had even touched world-class, he could never deliver the documented proof of that fact with his name on the trophy."

When people congratulated him after the third round, Cotton "tried to shut his ears to them," McDonnell wrote, "lest the gods overheard and damned him for his presumption."

Fortunately, despite a closing 79, he wound up winning by five.

After the ceremony, Cotton went to the Guilford Hotel to find the man he spotted in each of the first three rounds standing alone atop a hill at the 6th hole but who didn't show up for the fourth round.

He was none other than Harry Vardon, sixty-four, who wasn't feeling well.

"Cotton gave him the trophy," according to McDonnell, "without speaking, and Vardon looked at it and began to weep. Perhaps it was the joy at meeting an old friend, for this trophy had been his [on six occasions] and nobody had bettered that record."

Henry Cotton drove around in a Rolls-Royce and occupied a suite in a five-star hotel. In 1939, he married Isabel-Maria Estanguet de Moss, the daughter of a wealthy businessman in Argentina. Everyone knew her as Toots.

"He liked his life the British way," Tony Jacklin said.

In the 1937 Open, Cotton rallied from three down after fifty-four holes at Carnoustie to win by two over Reg Whitcombe.

In 1948, he turned in a 66 in the second round at Muirfield and went on to prevail by five over Fred Daly. King George VI (the father of Queen Elizabeth II) was in the gallery, the first reigning monarch to attend an Open. Cotton hit every "tee shot with a resounding thwack," one observer noted, the ball heading like "an arrow straight down the middle of the fairway, always avoiding the many sand traps that Muirfield has to offer."

Too bad he played very little golf in the United States. Knowing him as well as he did, Jacklin wasn't surprised.

"He was never going to be one for traveling around motels," he said.

Besides, Cotton had nothing to prove.

"I don't think he had any weaknesses," Jacklin said. "He was as good as there was."

90

Se Ri Pak

Do you miss being out there? I asked Se Ri Pak.

No, not really, she said. She missed her friends, all right, but didn't miss playing in tournaments and everything that came with it.

She has a life now.

Pak, who retired in 2016 at age thirty-nine, was more than a golfer; she was a pioneer. Which led to numerous changes: the loss of privacy. The soaring expectations. A new land and language to learn.

That would have been a lot for anyone, let alone a twenty-year-old South Korean who still had plenty of growing up to do. The LPGA tour would soon be filled with players from her country. The Se Ri Kids, the press called them. They looked up to her and relied on her. And, inspired by her, they would soon live a life beyond their wildest dreams.

Becoming a professional golfer wasn't her dream. Not at first.

Pak was into track, once running the 100 meters in thirteen seconds.

She also ran the hurdles and threw the shot put. Not until her early teens did Pak begin to take the game seriously, urged on by her father, Joon Chul, a very good player himself. At five thirty every morning, she got out of bed to run up and down the stairs of their fifteen-story apartment building about a hundred miles from Seoul.

"I wanted to teach her that to win in golf," Chul said, "she first had to win the battle within herself. Once, I told her to run down the stairs backward, not realizing how difficult that was. I tried it myself and I could only go down five floors. But Se Ri endured my training without any complaints."

Some of the stories I read said he forced her to spend nights sleeping in a cemetery to make her tougher.

Not true, Pak said several times as I continued to press the matter. I will take her at her word.

Pak, who turned pro in 1996, signed a $10 million, ten-year sponsorship deal with Samsung, which paid a top swing instructor, David Leadbetter, a six-figure salary to work with her in Orlando. She put in a lot of twelve-hour days. If you're going to dream, her parents told her, dream big.

Leadbetter was impressed. "As a worker, she's in Nick Faldo's class," he said. "I have to make sure she doesn't work too hard."

In the fall of 1997, Pak tied for medalist honors at the LPGA Qualifying Tournament. She was on her way.

Life in America presented its challenges.

"First couple months," Pak said, "everything [was] lonely. I was not close to any players. I never used the locker room because they spoke English and I didn't know [how]. Only parking lot, to the course, back to the car, back to the hotel, back to the course in the morning. Just lonely, lonely, lonely."

Lonely or not, she had quite a rookie year.

In the 1998 LPGA Championship at DuPont Country Club in Wilmington, Delaware, Pak led wire to wire, hitting 55 of 72 greens to win by three over Donna Andrews and Lisa Hackney.

"All I can say is she beat the heck out of us," said Nancy Lopez.

Pak's next big test came two months later in the U.S. Women's Open at Blackwolf Run in Wisconsin.

She passed and then some.

In an eighteen-hole playoff against another twenty-year-old, Jenny Chausiriporn, an amateur from Duke who had made a miracle birdie putt from forty-five feet on the 72nd hole to force a tie—the look of disbelief on her face was priceless—Pak was down by four after five holes.

She didn't panic. "I had a lot of holes left," she said. "That was too early to decide [that the game was] going to be over."

Too early, indeed.

Pak, who still trailed by two at the turn—it would have been a lot worse had Chausiriporn not tripled number 6—birdied three of the next five to seize a one-stroke lead. The two arrived at the par-4 18th all even. Pak then hit a terrible drive, the ball coming to a rest by a water hazard.

Going for the green was out of the question, leaving her with two options:

Take a drop, which would result in a penalty stroke. Or try to whack it out of there to an area where she could get on the putting surface with her third.

Pak, with Chausiriporn waiting in the fairway, took a long time before hitting her second shot. Some may have felt it was too long, but if it had been up to me, they would still be playing. That's how compelling it was—two twenty-year-olds battling for the biggest title in women's golf.

Standing in the water, her shoes off, she found the right rough about 140 yards from the pin. Par was still a possibility. "As soon as I hit it," she said, "I think I closed my eyes. It's probably the best-ever contact in my career."

Pak didn't make par, as it turned out, missing about a twenty-footer, but in avoiding a double, she stayed alive when Chausiriporn also made a bogey. On the second playoff hole, Pak knocked in an eighteen-footer to become the youngest U.S. Women's Open champion ever...until Inbee Park won in 2008 at the age of nineteen.

"First time I [cried] in my life," Pak said.

In South Korea, young girls woke up in the middle of the night to watch on TV, and soon started to have dreams of their own.

"She was Michael Jackson, Michael Jordan, and Bruce Springsteen wrapped into one," said agent Jay Burton, who represented Pak for more than fifteen years. Burton never ceased to be amazed at the crowds that gathered to see her. "We'd be driving through tollgates like a presidential motorcade with four or five black armored vehicles," he said. "Guys would be jumping up and down going, *'Pak, Se Ri, Pak Se Ri.'*"

Among those watching the 1998 Open was Inbee Park.

"After Se Ri won, it was on TV every day and they made advertisements of her hitting it out of the water," recalled Park, who would go on to win seven majors. "I watched it a lot of times and I said to my parents, 'I can do that.'"

Se Ri Pak, who ended up with twenty-five tour victories, including five majors, came along at the perfect time. A financial crisis in Asia in the late '90s had put about 1.5 million Koreans out of work.

Her Open win, she believes, "gave a lot of Korean people a lot of hope."

Since 1998, eighteen women from South Korea have combined to win thirty-three major championships, while five players, including Park, have occupied the number one spot in the world rankings, the most of any country, including the United States.

"She transformed golf globally more than Tiger Woods did," according to Christina Kim, an LPGA member for more than twenty years. "There always would have been someone else, but would it have been to the same magnitude?"

89

Larry Nelson

By the time Larry Nelson turned twenty-one years old in September 1968, he had yet to play a round of golf.

"There were no golf courses where I grew up," explained Nelson, who lived in Acworth, Georgia, about forty-five minutes from Atlanta, "and nobody I knew personally played golf."

Until, while serving in basic infantry at Fort Hood in Texas, another recruit mentioned during a card game that he had played in junior college before he was drafted. Nelson filed the information away for another day. Where he was going, there would be no time to learn.

He was going to Nam.

When drafted in the fall of 1966, that's not where he expected to wind up. But with the war not going according to plan—how's that for an understatement?—President Lyndon Johnson called for additional troops while Nelson was at Fort Hood.

Nelson, who became a squad leader in the 198th Light Infantry (their mission amounted to Search and Destroy), spent ninety days in Vietnam.

Which must have seemed like an eternity.

"The bad thing was, the Viet Cong knew that's what we were doing out there," Nelson recalled. "We would come under fire pretty much every day. They'd set ambushes."

One night, everyone under his command was asleep except him and a few others when dozens of North Vietnamese soldiers marched by about ten yards away. He was terrified it "would be all over" if any men woke up and made the slightest noise.

"We saw the morning," Nelson told me, "so it was okay."

Once he got word that he would be heading home in ten days, Nelson couldn't have been more excited. Or more cautious.

"You hear the sad stories all the time about people dying in their last day or two of combat," he said. "I didn't want that to happen to me."

In the States, Nelson found it difficult to leave the war behind.

"One night, not thinking, I jumped out from behind a refrigerator to scare him," said his wife, Gayle. "I thought he was going to level me."

Nelson landed a job as an illustrator for Lockheed, drawing the inside of aircraft to help electricians route the wires, and took engineering classes three nights a week. His dream was to play in the big leagues—he was a star pitcher in high school—but he injured his shoulder while throwing the ball one day for a local team and that put an end to the dream.

Thinking back to the recruit from the card game, he began to spend time on the driving range. Nelson knew little about golf other than keeping his left arm extended, which he'd read in a magazine.

"Because of my baseball experience, I hit the ball really straight," he said.

Not long afterward, he purchased a junior membership at Pinetree Country Club in Kennesaw, Georgia, playing mostly by himself. "I'd play two balls and take the worst score of the two," he said. Nelson became friendly with the members as well as the head professional, Bert Seagraves. When the assistant pro left, Nelson got the job.

One day, Seagraves gave him a copy of Ben Hogan's *Five Lessons: The Modern Fundamentals of Golf.* Nelson read every word. A fast learner, he broke 70 within nine months. "I was a math major in college so working on one thing before going to the next was pretty easy to me," he explained. "I could do fundamental one, then two, then three."

After a couple of years at Pinetree, Nelson applied for the head pro job at another club but was turned down.

Tough break.

Make that tremendous break.

Several Pinetree members came up with an idea: *Why don't you go out and play professionally? We'll put up the money.*

To borrow a line from *The Godfather,* it was an offer Nelson couldn't refuse. He competed on the mini tours in Florida, and by the end of a year had won a handful of events. In 1973, he made it through the PGA Tour's Qualifying Tournament (Q-school) and never looked back. Among his ten victories: the PGA in 1981 and 1987, and the U.S. Open in 1983.

The Open was held at Oakmont Country Club outside Pittsburgh. There isn't a course in the galaxy tougher than Oakmont.

Midway through the second round, it dawned on Nelson, who made the cut by a few strokes, that the more he looked at the fairways before hitting his tee shot, the more trouble he saw and stress he felt. From then on, he picked a spot six to eight inches in front of the ball and looked at nothing else.

Out of sight. Out of mind.

He fired a 65 in the third round to climb within a stroke of the co-leaders, Tom Watson and Seve Ballesteros. On Sunday, Watson, the defending champion, went low on the front nine, but once he stumbled a bit, Nelson took advantage with one well-executed shot after another. A storm halted play for the day, setting up a Monday finish with the two tied for the lead.

On number 16, his first hole, Nelson faced a downhill birdie putt from about sixty feet.

He was hoping to get it close.

He did better than close.

"The last ten feet, when it went over the last hump, I knew I had made it," said Nelson, who edged Watson by one.

Winning the Open was the high point of his career. As for the low point, it has to do with the Ryder Cup and it wasn't his fault.

Here's what happened:

Nelson figured he would be the captain of the U.S. squad for the 1995 matches at Oak Hill. He would have just turned forty-eight, around the typical age for captains. Until—and keep in mind this is his version—he spoke to Lanny Wadkins, the PGA champion in 1977.

"Let me do it in '95," Wadkins supposedly told Nelson. "You can do it in '97 because of your record against Seve."

That sounded like a pretty good idea to Nelson, who had gone 4-0 against Seve in the 1979 Ryder Cup, which the U.S. won rather handily. In 1997, Seve would be Europe's captain at Real Club Valderrama in his native Spain.

Lo and behold, the PGA of America, which picks the U.S. captains, had another idea in mind.

"I was in Japan playing when my manager called," Nelson said. "He said, 'You're not going to like this, but they named Tom Kite as Ryder Cup captain.'"

No, he did not like this. Not one bit.

Nearly thirty years later, the snub still bothers him, as it should.

The PGA, he claims, never reached out afterward to explain.

"I won the PGA twice," Nelson said. "I was a PGA member for three years before I went on the PGA Tour."

Of the five Americans (the others: Jack Nicklaus, Raymond Floyd, Dave Stockton, and Lee Trevino) who won the PGA Championship at least twice between 1958, when it switched to stroke play, and 1999, Nelson is the only one who didn't become a captain.

So, why was he passed over?

I don't have a clue, nor does Nelson, but perhaps the powers that be didn't feel he had enough charisma.

"The guys who got most of the press, if they weren't winning majors, it was because of the controversy they caused," Nelson pointed out. The perception at the time was that "golf was dull, and so we were all put in a certain class and I happened to be the quietest of that dull class."

If that, indeed, was the reason, it makes no sense. I think highly of Tom Kite, but let's face it: Kite isn't known for his charisma, either.

Besides, Larry Nelson was a proven leader of men.

"I figured if I could get ten people through Vietnam," he said, "I could have probably gotten twelve people through the Ryder Cup."

88

Fred Couples

There are two ways to look at Fred Couples, a fifteen-time winner on Tour.

One way is to be in awe of how far he could hit the ball and how laid-back he always seemed.

The epitome of cool, 007 in spikes.

"A few women," Couples said long ago, "would come right up to me and say, 'I would love to take you out to dinner.' I have had some letters, too, and some photographs."

Another way is to see promise unfulfilled.

If not for an incredibly fortunate break in the final round of the 1992 Masters, he might have been left without a major on his résumé. On the short but dangerous par-3 12th hole, instead of vanishing in Rae's Creek as every other ball that landed in a similar spot had done, his came to a rest in the steep embankment below the green. (More on that later.)

Couples was something to behold. John Cook, an eleven-time winner, ran into him for the first time in the 1979 NCAA Championships at Bermuda Run Country Club in Winston-Salem, North Carolina. Couples was playing for the University of Houston.

"They had a straight drive contest and a long drive contest," Cook recalled. "He won both of them, hitting three balls on the line and over three hundred yards. We're looking at each other, going, 'Who is this kid?' A couple of years later, he's on Tour."

Jim Nantz, his teammate in Houston, will never forget what took place when they were paired together in a Southwest Conference tournament. After Couples sent his drive OB on a 410-yard sharp dogleg par-4, "he reteed a ball on a pencil," Nantz said, "hit it soaring over the pine trees, and what seemed like twenty or thirty seconds later, the ball landed on the green. And he made the putt for a par."

Couples often took the road less traveled.

While on vacation during the summer before what was to be his senior year of college, he stopped at El Dorado Park in Long Beach, California, the site of the upcoming Queen Mary Open.

He asked if he could play.

No problem, they told him, as long as you turn pro.

So the next day, borrowing a couple hundred bucks, he signed his name on the dotted line, and, presto, he was an amateur no more.

Finishing in a tie for sixth, he left town with an extra three grand in his pocket.

Not everyone was thrilled, however, his dad hanging up when Couples called home to share the news. "It was very much a shock for us," his mother, Violet, said years later. "As far as we knew he was going back to school. We were a little upset because it wasn't a decision he talked over with us. But it turned out to be the right decision."

You can say that again.

In his first three years on Tour, however, Couples won only one tournament, the Kemper Open in the DC area. And, after capturing the Players Championship in 1984 by a shot over Lee Trevino, he picked up just one more victory the rest of the decade, the 1987 Byron Nelson Classic. His fans loved him anyway. His appeal never depended on his scores.

"He exudes a genuine, almost childlike, innocence that endears him to people," Nantz suggested. "There is simply no bad side to him."

If there was a knock on Couples, who once admitted golf was about his "fifth priority," it was that he came across as *too* easygoing. Which some interpreted to mean he didn't care whether he won or lost. "It's a hundred percent incorrect," his longtime caddie Joe LaCava told me. "I spent enough time with him after rounds to know that if he didn't get as much out of the round as he wanted or thought he should, he was extremely disappointed and it ate at him, and I think it still eats at him. He cares quite a bit."

I agree with LaCava, and I will give you an example: The 1989 Ryder Cup at the Belfry in England.

Couples lost to Ireland's Christy O'Connor Jr. one up in the singles, Europe retaining the cup with a 14-14 tie. If Couples had managed even a half point… well, do the math.

"I'm not afraid to say I cried," he admitted years later.

Couples brought up the loss during our conversation in March 2024. "I felt like I had let down everybody," he said.

In a 1991 interview, Tom Weiskopf, a former British Open champion, said this about Couples:

"Great talent. No goals in life. Not one."

"Why would a guy put someone else down like that?" Couples wondered. "I have goals. My goal since I was eight years old was to win the Masters."

He accomplished that goal, all right, though not without the aforementioned gift from the golfing gods on number 12. Who knew they could be that generous?

Couples arrived at the tee with a three-stroke lead over his friend Raymond Floyd. Still, it was far from over.

"This is the shot that will make or break it right here," said CBS analyst Ken Venturi.

The smart play at 12 was to aim for the middle of the green, away from the traditional pin placement on the right. So much for the smart play.

"I didn't want to [shoot for the flag]," Couples said, "but there's this thing in my brain that just shoved the ball over there."

The ball hit the bank about eight feet from the green and rolled down the steep slope, coming to a stop about a foot above the water.

No one could recall that ever happening before on 12.

"Unbelievable," Couples said. "Luckily it didn't hit way up on the bank, otherwise it would have picked up speed coming down and would have gone in."

As he walked toward the green, LaCava was still anxious.

"It was the longest three or four minutes of my life," he said. "I thought the ball could fall back into the water."

Couples hit a lovely pitch and hung on to win by two. Still only thirty-two and the first American to be number one in the world since the ranking system was adopted in 1986, there seemed no limit on what he could accomplish.

That all changed in March 1994.

After hitting an eight-iron on the range at the Doral Open outside Miami, he felt like a hand grenade had gone off in his back. "If I move in any direction," Couples told his coach, Paul Marchand, "I'll scream." The troubles with his back—a spinal disk had herniated—would restrict for the rest of his career how often he could play and practice.

"When my back is [hurting]," he said in 2008, "I just get really edgy. Every move you make it's like a toothache. By the end of the day, I'm physically spent.... I want to play better but I can't try any harder. Pushing it a little, like hitting 15 more balls, that's the biggest thing I can't do."

Couples won only six times after the 1992 Masters. What would his record be if he had stayed healthy?

"Hard to put a number on it," LaCava said, "but I can say confidently he would have won more tournaments. He would have contended more, which would have led to another win, maybe two wins, in the major category."

I agree with LaCava, but regardless, how Couples carried himself is what we will remember most.

"It's the image that we all wish we could be," Nantz told me, "to be cool and unburdened by pressure. We would all like life to feel that easy."

87

Jackie Burke Jr.

When he teed off in the final round of the 1956 Masters, Jackie Burke Jr. didn't have a prayer. He was eight strokes behind Ken Venturi, the twenty-four-year-old amateur from San Francisco who was tearing the place up.

Burke, however, held one advantage over Venturi and practically everyone else in the field. A low-ball hitter who grew up in Texas and had been the head pro at Galveston Country Club, he knew how to cope with the winds that were blowing about forty miles per hour that Sunday in Augusta.

Because of those winds, a record twenty-nine players shot 80 or worse, including his good friend Jimmy Demaret, a three-time Masters champion who turned in an 81. The average score was 78.3. As the day wore on, the casualties piled up, which included Venturi, who three-putted six times on his way to an 80. Which meant that Jackie Burke Jr., the son of a club pro who had finished second in the 1920 U.S. Open, might actually pull off the impossible.

A pivotal moment took place on the par-4, 17th hole. Burke's choice of club showed how windy it was. Normally, for his approach, he would have gone with a two-iron or a wood, but he went with an eight-iron instead, the ball coming to a rest about twenty-five from the cup. (Earlier on number 4, a 225-yard par-3, he hit driver and still came up sixty yards short.)

The wind was blowing so hard there was sand from the bunker scattered across the 17th green.

No problem. Burke was used to playing on sandy greens, as well.

He settled into his routine and released the blade. "I just touched that putt," he recalled, "and I immediately thought, 'Oh, no, I didn't get it halfway there.' Then the wind grabbed that thing and kept blowing it down the hill, until it plunked dead in the middle of the hole. It was a miracle, the best break of my career.... A golf ball weighs 1.62 ounces. Can [heavy winds] affect that ball as it rolls? You tell me."

Burke was fortunate to be paired that day with Mike Souchak, who, with no hopes of winning himself, acted as his cheerleader. After the putt fell in on 17, "[Souchak] ran to pick the ball out of the cup," Burke said, "and then clapped me so hard on the back I had to walk around on the 18th tee to recover."

"C'mon, man!" Souchak urged Burke. "They're still making bogeys out here. Let's go!"

On 18, after finding the fairway with his drive, his goal on the approach was to avoid going left, which could very easily result in a bogey, perhaps a double. He avoided the left, all right, but the ball ended up in a greenside bunker on the right. From there, he blasted out to about four feet from the hole.

"This is how I see it, Pappy," Burke said to his caddie. "What do you think?"

Willie "Pappy" Stokes, who had caddied for former champions Ben Hogan, Claude Harmon, and Henry Picard, agreed with the read.

"Just go on and cruise her on in there," he said.

Burke did just that, and before long his wardrobe included a new green jacket.

"It still makes me almost ill," he said in 2002, "to think about that putt with the outcome riding on it."

Burke, who turned in a one-under 71, and Sam Snead, who also shot a 71, were the only two golfers to break par on Sunday. His comeback was the largest in the final round of a major until Paul Lawrie rallied from ten behind to defeat Jean van de Velde in the 1999 British Open at Carnoustie.

"Pappy's gone," Burke wrote years later, "but when I get to the big clubhouse in the sky, I'm going to thank him again for handling me just right."

Three months later, Burke picked up his twelfth Tour victory—he would wind up with 16—and a second major, the PGA at Blue Hill Country Club outside Boston.

In the semifinals, he made one clutch putt after another, rallying from five down to defeat Ed Furgol on the 37th hole. "One of the prettiest putters I have ever seen," Ben Crenshaw said. "He looked like he was born with a putter in his hand. People went to him all the time for advice."

In the final against Ted Kroll, Burke fell behind again, this time three down through nineteen holes. But he rallied once more, eliminating Kroll 3 and 2.

Burke was blessed from day one.

His father, Jack Burke Sr., who had been one of the first club pros in the Lone Star State, worked at River Oaks Country Club in Houston, where he taught stars such as Henry Picard, Craig Wood, and Babe Didrikson Zaharias. "A lot of pros came to visit him," said his grandson, Mike. "My dad absorbed a lot of that knowledge. He used to sit on the practice tee with him while he gave lessons."

Every so often, he got a chance to play with Babe.

"C'mon, little Jack, let's go," she would say.

"When I got to where I could hit it past Babe," Burke explained, "I thought, 'Man, I'm on my way.' I was about fourteen then."

He attended Rice University, spent four years in the Marines, and then worked at a series of clubs back east.

In 1950, Burke, twenty-seven, tried the Tour full-time.

"I had always played the whole winter circuit," he said. "So now I just kept right on going."

In January 2024, Burke, who was a mentor to many golfers—like father, like son—passed away at the age of one hundred. Until almost the very end, he showed up at work every day at the Champions Golf Club in Houston (the host of the 1967 Ryder Cup and 1969 U.S. Open), which he and Demaret founded in the late 1950s.

He never hesitated to let others know what was on his mind.

"I hadn't seen the guy for two or three years," recalled Jack Nicklaus, who had been practicing on the putting green during a U.S. Open long ago. "He walks up, yelling, 'Nicklaus... what do you mean putting with your left hand like that? Get your right hand on the putter facing the line and roll it!' And I've only won ten majors by then and he's giving me this. But that's Jack Burke."

86

Sergio Garcia

First of all, the shot itself was too good to be true.

From 189 yards away, the ball inches from the base of a tree, Sergio Garcia, with his eyes closed at impact, hit his approach onto the putting surface.

And yet, the shot isn't what I remember most about that summer afternoon at Medinah Country Club outside Chicago, and I got to believe I'm not alone.

What I remember most is Garcia sprinting down the 16th fairway with a scissor-kick leap in the air to see where the ball would wind up.

Tiger Woods won the tournament, the 1999 PGA Championship, but Garcia, nineteen, who came up one stroke short, reminded us what it's like to be young and fearless and have more fun than any person has a right to have. (Yes, Tiger was just twenty-three, but he always seemed much older, didn't he?)

Other summers, however, came and went, and Garcia couldn't stay young forever.

He achieved a great deal of success—eleven Tour victories, including the 2017 Masters, sixteen wins in Europe, as well as his heroics in the Ryder Cup. Still, there will always be a feeling that Garcia should have achieved more.

Perhaps I, and others, expected too much, but if you watched the shot at Medinah in real time and the sprint that followed, you can't help but feel let down.

That's not to suggest Garcia should have won a half dozen or more majors. Not in the Woods Era. Two or three more would have been plenty.

Even Woods had an inkling of what he might be up against in the years to come.

"I see in him a lot of similar qualities to myself," he said in 1999. "I love that emotion he has about what he does. And he is a great competitor—you can see it in his eyes."

The promise of stardom had been there from the outset. "We met for the first time in 1990," said European Tour pro Gonzalo Fernández-Castaño. "It was a Spanish 10-and-under, only nine holes. I remember he showed up playing golf in a bathing suit, and I think he beat the field by nine shots. He was already playing a different game."

At fifteen, Garcia became the youngest to win the European Amateur. The same year, he took part in an exhibition with Seve Ballesteros, José María-Olazábal, and Miguel Ángel Jiménez.

"It was very obvious that he already hit the ball better than the other three," according to José Manuel Lara, who would later play on the European Tour. "They knew it, and so did Sergio."

In 1998, he captured the British Amateur at Muirfield, defeating Craig Williams 7 and 6, and lost in the semis of the U.S. Amateur after eliminating Matt Kuchar, the defending champ, in the quarters.

He went through some rough stretches, as well, such as the 89 he shot on Day One of the 1999 British Open at Carnoustie, his first major as a professional.

Afterward, he cried in his mother's arms.

"I was suffering," said Garcia, who would follow with an 83 to miss the cut by a mile. "I couldn't do anything. I felt I couldn't swing the club. Today everything came out the wrong way."

Too bad Carnoustie wasn't done with him yet.

In the 2007 British Open, his ten-foot par putt to win it on the 72nd hole lipped out, and he went on, as you may recall, to lose in a playoff to Padraig Harrington.

I generally don't like to play the What If game—there would be no end to it, although I do it often anyway—but if the putt had gone in, I wonder if Garcia, still only in his late twenties, would have become the player we thought he would be. And, in losing, he showed the side of him that we have seen too often. The whiny side.

"I'm playing against a lot of guys out there, more than the field," claimed Garcia, who had allowed a three-shot lead on Sunday to slip away.

The losses in majors got into his head. After shooting a 75, which included thirty-five putts, in the third round of the 2012 Masters, Garcia said something rarely, if ever, expressed by any athlete of his caliber:

"I'm not good enough. I don't have the thing I need to have. In thirteen years, I've come to the conclusion that I need to play for second or third place."

He certainly wasn't good enough on the greens, no putt too short to miss—a shame, really, because his ball striking was among the finest of his time.

As the years wore on, Garcia seemed destined to join those who jumped off the bus one stop short of greatness. Then, in the spring of 2017, at age thirty-seven, when we least expected it, he picked up a green jacket.

After leading by three early in the final round, he fell two behind England's Justin Rose with seven holes to go. The Garcia of the past might have lost hope.

Not this Garcia.

Not even after he nicked a tree with his drive on 13, the ball ending up beneath a bush, unplayable.

"If that's what's supposed to happen, let it happen," he told himself.

"Let's try to make a great five here and see if we can put on a helluva finish to have a chance."

He got the five, all right, making an eight-footer, then birdied 14 and eagled 15, thanks to a 330-yard drive down the middle of the fairway and eight-iron from 192 yards to within fourteen feet.

The Rose lead was gone.

Garcia put Rose away on the first playoff hole, ending his 0-for-73 drought in major championships.

"It's been a long, long wait," he said, "but it's that much sweeter because of that wait. People believed in me, sometimes more than I did, and that mattered a great deal."

Was this the beginning of a new Garcia?

"If Sergio's actually learned how to put things behind him and just play, and it wasn't just a one-week thing," Dr. Bob Rotella suggested, "he's going to win a lot of tournaments."

It was a one-week thing.

Garcia, who jumped to the Saudi-backed LIV tour in 2022, has become such a nonfactor that it sometimes feels as if the 2017 Masters was a mirage. He has registered only one PGA Tour victory since then, the 2020 Sanderson Farms Championship, and in his last twenty-five majors, he hasn't recorded a single top ten, missing the cut fifteen times.

I yearn for that summer day at Medinah.

The shot. The sprint.

The promise of tomorrow.

85

Lorena Ochoa

Lorena Ochoa was gone from the LPGA tour before we knew it. Before we could fully appreciate what she had brought to women's golf. To golf, period.

By how she played and how she conducted herself.

Ochoa, the Player of the Year in 2006, 2007, 2008, and 2009, retired in the spring of 2010 at the age of twenty-eight.

In February 2003, I spent a day with Lorena at her home in Guadalajara, Mexico. I was struck by how mature she was for twenty-one (although my ego took a massive hit when she toyed with me on the clay courts, 6–3, 6–1), and how she had so many dreams for the future. Not only for herself, but for her country, too.

"I would love to help establish a public golf course and a public range so that people can go hit balls," she said. "I want to see golf on advertisements, in magazines, on national TV. I would like to do things the right way so that little kids can follow me."

Mission accomplished.

Ochoa, now in her early forties, runs a foundation for low-income children to receive a quality education. As of 2024, more than seven thousand had been awarded scholarships to La Barranca, a school for ages six to fifteen in Guadalajara. She plays in exhibitions all over Mexico, raising money for the foundation.

Her dreams for herself were also big. When she was five, she bugged her two older brothers, Javier and Alejandro, to take her with them to the golf course. No, they kept saying. Until they said yes.

By the time she was eight, Ochoa, one of just a few girls to tee it up at Guadalajara Country Club, was the top-ranked junior in Mexico.

In 1990, she won the first of five straight Junior World Championships in San Diego. "We really didn't know much about my level of play," Ochoa said in her 2017 induction speech at the World Golf Hall of Fame. "Mexican girls didn't play golf. So after the opening ceremony, I saw the previous year's winner and I said to myself, 'I can beat these girls.'"

Ochoa worked with Rafael Alarcón, a club member who played on the PGA Tour in the 1980s and '90s. Watching him hit balls on the range day after day, she was inspired by his talent and dedication.

"I want to be the number one player in the world," she told him when she was twelve. "Can you help me?"

"Do you know what you are saying?" he asked.

She knew exactly what she was saying.

"Did you tell your parents?"

"No."

"Did you tell your brothers?"

"No."

Alarcón agreed to help but told her he couldn't do it alone: "You get your family together and tell them. They need to make a lot of sacrifices."

The family was all in. As always.

It hadn't been easy for Ochoa at first. The boys she played with, who were a couple of years older, routinely hit their drives thirty or forty yards past her. No problem. She worked on her short game.

"I knew I could make par from everywhere," Ochoa said, "and, all of a sudden, I started beating them."

And anyone else who stood in her way.

In three years at the University of Arizona, she won twelve tournaments (in just twenty starts) including a record seven in a row. With nothing left to prove, Ochoa turned pro, winning the money title on the Futures Tour, the LPGA's developmental tour.

In 2003, she was the LPGA's Rookie of the Year with eight top tens. Even so, her new life was more difficult than she anticipated.

"I returned home crying and complaining," Ochoa said. "I said I didn't want to play anymore. I felt a lot of pressure. The funny thing is that after three days without playing, I got up, put on my golf clothes and [went] to the golf course."

The first victory came in May 2004 at the Franklin American Mortgage Championship in Tennessee, the second a few months later in Pennsylvania, and the third the following June in New York.

In 2006, she won six times and posted twenty top tens in twenty-five starts. The following spring, her dream came true: Lorena Ochoa was the number one player in the world—and would remain number one for 158 straight weeks, a record until it was broken by South Korea's Jin Young Ko in 2023.

"It has taken a bit of time," Ochoa said, "but I have got there."

A few months later, she went wire to wire to pick up her first major, the Women's British Open at St. Andrews.

Ochoa captured eight events in 2007 and seven (four in a row) in 2008, including a second—and last—major, the Dinah Shore in Rancho Mirage, California. (FYI: I don't give a damn if it was, officially, the Kraft Nabisco Championship. To me, the tournament, which no longer exists, I'm sorry to say, will always be *The Dinah Shore* or, better yet, *The Dinah*.)

Ochoa was at her best that week in the desert. And not just inside the ropes.

As about eighty members of the maintenance crew were having breakfast, she stopped by to express her appreciation, even scrambling some eggs. I can't think of any other professional golfer, male or female, who would have done that. During the week of a major, no less.

"They are good people and work hard to help their families," she said. "I want them to know I support them and that I play for them."

In December 2009, Ochoa married Andrés Conesa, the CEO of Aeromexico. The end of one chapter was coming—and beginning of another.

"In her last year, you could see that some of the joy was starting to wane," Christina Kim said.

When she retired, Ochoa was following her heart. A heart the size of North America.

That didn't mean it was easy.

"I was brave enough to listen to that inside voice," she told me. "I'm thankful to God to give me the strength to make the decision."

Her abrupt departure was also difficult for those left behind.

"Borderline devastating," was how Kim put it. "Lorena was such a dominating force, and she never walked around like she was better than anyone else."

As she travels these days across Mexico, Ochoa, a mother of five—three from her husband's previous marriage—is reminded of how much the game has grown since she took it up in the mid-1980s. "Every time I visit a course," she said, "the president of the club tells me, 'Lorena, look at what you have done. There is no room for the members. They can't practice or go out to the course because it is full of kids.' It's a good problem to have."

84

Chick Evans

Year after year, Charles E. "Chick" Evans Jr. kept knocking on the door. Only fate wasn't ready to let him in.

In three straight U.S. Amateurs (1909, 1910, 1911), he was eliminated in the semifinals, falling to Chandler Egan, William C. Fownes Jr. and Fred Herreshoff, respectively.

At last, in the 1912 Amateur at Chicago Golf Club, he made it to the final.

This was fitting for Evans, who had led nearby Evanston Academy to the Western Interscholastic Golf Association championship in 1908. After moving from Indianapolis when he was two, he grew up on Chicago's North Side and became a caddie at Edgewater Golf Club.

Now, with practically the whole city cheering him on, Evans, twenty-two, needed to win just one more match against Jerry Travers, the U.S. Amateur champion in 1907 and 1908, and the title would be his.

Alas, it wasn't meant to be, and the wait for that first major championship would continue.

Evans, one up after the morning round of eighteen, was outplayed in the afternoon, succumbing to Travers, 7 and 6.

To suggest he was disappointed would be an understatement.

"After the usual exchange of congratulations, I went back to the clubhouse and took the silver medal that I had won and threw it as hard as I could up against the wall," Evans wrote years later. "Trains began to bear the people away and dinner time came on, but I did not care for food that night. I got up from the bed on which I had thrown myself and walked in the darkness ... my world had gone wrong somehow."

Fortunately, he found a way out of his misery.

"I walked far into the night," Evans went on. "I do not know exactly what village I came to, but through the woods came the sound of music and it was soon evident that a Saturday night dance was in progress. It did not take me long to join the dancers."

Evans fell in the semis again in 1913 to John G. Anderson at the Garden City Golf Club in New York, but returning to the Chicago area a year later, he made quite a run in the U.S. Open at Midlothian Country Club. After converting a twenty-five-footer on 17, he arrived at the 72nd hole, a 277-yard par-4, needing an eagle to tie Walter Hagen, who was finished for the day.

He crushed his drive, the ball ending up on the edge of the green, about fifty feet from the pin.

Evans, with Hagen in the gallery, hit a beautiful pitch. It didn't miss by much.

Still, he was a bridesmaid once more.

And this, ladies and gentlemen, could easily have been how we'd remember Chick Evans... if we were to remember him at all.

It's not.

The 1916 Open at Minikahda Country Club in Minneapolis came first in late June.

Evans turned in rounds of 70 and 69 to lead at the halfway mark by three over England's Wilfrid Reid. No one had ever broken 140 in the first two rounds of a U.S. Open. On the second and final day—the tournament wasn't extended to three days until 1926—Evans faltered in the hot morning weather, but was still up by three heading into the afternoon.

On the 4th hole, he made a 7, but on the tee at number 5, he took stock of the situation.

Forget it and keep going, he told himself.

Thanks, in part, to an aggressive approach over a creek on the 535-yard 13th hole, Evans prevailed by two with a score of 286, a record that would stand for twenty years.

"I never played a better shot in my life," he wrote. "I listened for the gallery at the green and when the encouraging sounds came echoing thrillingly from the little wood near by, I was overjoyed."

Next up was the U.S. Amateur at Merion, where Evans was one of the favorites.

"Control of the long iron is one of the key essentials to success," Grantland Rice wrote, "and control of the long iron is one of the strongest features of Chick's play."

Evans was better than ever. After a close opening match, he demolished his next two opponents, W. P. Smith and John G. Anderson, and defeated D. Clarke Corkran in the semis 3 and 2.

This left just one man to beat: Robert Gardner, the defending champion.

Evans was up to the task, the match coming to a conclusion on the 33rd hole. Someone in the gallery said it all: "The double crown for Evans."

How ironic, indeed, that the man who seemed like he might never win the big one had become the first to win the U.S. Open and U.S. Amateur in the same year. Only Bobby Jones, with the Grand Slam in 1930, has ever matched him.

"Winning two championships in one season," Evans wrote, "realized my fondest hopes and exceeded my greatest expectations. It is true that I had dreamed of capturing one or the other for a good many years, but I had never really counted on both and certainly not in 1916."

Even so, Evans was in no mood to celebrate. Not with a war raging across Europe.

"Golfers who had spent much time in Britain and France had their hearts wrung by the loss of friends," he wrote.

In 1919, with the hostilities over, the U.S. Amateur resumed after a two-year absence. A year later, Evans beat Francis Ouimet 7 and 6 in the final at the Engineers County Club in Roslyn Harbor, New York, for his third major title. He competed in the Amateur more than fifty times, his last appearance in 1962, when he was in his early seventies.

Few have contributed more to the game than Chick Evans, and not just as a player. In 1930, he established a scholarship fund for caddies that has sent thousands of youngsters to college. His experience as a caddie in the 1890s set the tone for the rest of his life.

The first day was one he would never forget.

"It was nearly dark, when, on the ninth green, Miss Jones removed the bag from my shoulders and handed me thirty-five cents!" Evans wrote. "I hastened home with all my riches and my family had to stand a great deal of detailed information about golf, that night, and for many other nights since that time."

83

Jim Ferrier

The list of major champions from Down Under include familiar names: Greg Norman, Karrie Webb, Peter Thomson, Jan Stephenson, David Graham, Adam Scott, Jason Day, Ian Baker-Finch, and Cameron Smith.

As well as a name that isn't familiar:

Jim Ferrier, the first of all the Aussies to win one.

Known as "The Undertaker" for burying opponents, Ferrier, who collected eighteen Tour victories, was an American citizen by the time he captured the 1947 PGA Championship at Plum Hollow Country Club in Southfield, Michigan, having served in the United States Army from March 1944 to November 1945.

He and Norma, his wife, arrived in the States in early 1940 for what was supposed to be a six-month visit. Six months that, for him, turned into forty-six years.

The move to America made a lot of sense. Ferrier, who walked with a slight limp due to a soccer injury in his youth, had done all he could back home, winning the Australian Open as an amateur in 1938 and 1939, and the Australian Amateur four times.

"If you wanted to play golf, the tour [in the U.S.] was it," he said.

He wrote about the game, as well, his articles appearing in *The Sydney Morning Herald*, *The Daily Telegraph*, and *The Australian Women's Weekly*.

"I didn't write all that well," Ferrier admitted, "but good enough to get by, and after the boys in the office worked on it, well, you know…"

The columns he wrote in the States helped pay for the trip, he and Norma making stops in Florida and Georgia, including at Augusta, where he finished twenty-sixth.

His entry form, however, to participate in the 1940 U.S. Amateur was rejected because he had benefited financially from the game, which isn't permitted for amateurs, through his work as a writer.

He made his case to the president of the USGA but got nowhere. So in the spring of 1941, Ferrier turned pro.

Around six months later, Japan attacked Pearl Harbor.

"I was drafted," Ferrier said, and "in those days, they could draft non-citizens, and if you didn't want to serve you could never become a citizen."

That settled that.

"It was our new home, the United States," he explained. "We liked it, everything was fun, and joining the army to become a citizen was a cinch."

He was assigned to the artillery, but when the higher-ups discovered what he did for a living, he was placed in special services and gave golf lessons. While stationed in California in 1944, Ferrier picked up his first Tour victory in the Oakland Open, earning $1,500 in war bonds. Once the war ended, he was off and running.

Upon his arrival at the PGA in 1947, his game from tee to green was in good shape. His putting, not so much.

No sweat. Norma knew exactly what to do.

Norma, a three handicap at one point, told her husband to practice his putting and not hit any irons or woods. "She was like a video," Ferrier said. "She could look at me and could tell when my pace was quicker or the movements were different, and that was all I needed."

They spent a day and a half on the putting green.

Mission accomplished. Ferrier required just fifty-four putts in the final to take care of Chick Harbert, 2 and 1.

"The only time my putter hit a second putt," he said, "was on the last green, the thirty-fifth hole. It was a foot from the hole and Chick said I'd better knock it in, because it was for the victory. The rest of the day I had been putting so close he was just giving me the second ones."

Heading into the match, Ferrier didn't take any chances.

Believing that his opponent, who was raised in Michigan, had been aided in his semifinal triumph over Clayton Heafner—"a couple of balls that were out of bounds were found a foot inside the fence," Ferrier said—he came up with an idea.

"There were a couple of cops at the course drinking Cokes, and I said to them, 'Would you guys like to make fifty bucks apiece today? . . . I want one of you on the left side of the fairway, one of you on the right on every hole. When my ball comes to rest, I just want one of you standing close to it, maybe four feet away. I don't want anybody to touch it. I don't care what they do to his ball, but I don't want mine stepped on, kicked in a bunker or under a tree.' To me that was the best $100 I've ever spent."

Three years later, in the final round of the Masters, Ferrier assumed a five-stroke lead on the front nine and was still three clear of Jimmy Demaret, who was done for the day, with only six holes to go.

A green jacket was going to be a nice addition to his closet.

Or not.

As one writer put it, "the ceiling fell on Ferrier's huge frame in one of the most tragic finishes ever." He bogeyed 13, 14, 16, 17, and 18 to lose by two, which was the first of a string of missed opportunities for the Aussies at Augusta National. Not until 2013, when Adam Scott defeated Angel Cabrera in a sudden-death playoff, did someone from Down Under come out on top.

"Now I know what they say about golf is true," Ferrier said after shooting a five-over 41 on the back nine. "It isn't over until you finish."

At forty-five, he made one final stab at a major, finishing second by a stroke in the 1960 PGA at Firestone Country Club in Akron, Ohio.

Looking back at his career, he realized how fortunate he had been.

"I came along in the Hagen-Sarazen-Jones era, played with Snead and Hogan, and ran into the Palmers and Nicklauses," he said. "A great span."

Whether his name is familiar or not.

82

Juli Inkster

I'll tell you what I liked most about Juli Inkster. How emotional she got on the golf course.

In victory and defeat.

Unlike with Fred Couples, no one believed for a second she didn't care.

She acted as if every shot was a matter of life or death. I wish more players were like that.

Let's start with a defeat. The most crushing of her career.

With two holes to go in the final round of the 1992 U.S. Women's Open at Oakmont, the championship she craved more than any other, Inkster led Patty Sheehan, her playing partner and former San Jose State teammate, by two.

Mother Nature then intervened. The nerve of her.

After the delay, Sheehan canned a twelve-footer on 17 to narrow the deficit to one. At 18, she received, like Couples, the break of a lifetime.

Because her tee shot, which ended up in the rough, was sitting in casual water, Sheehan was permitted to drop in the fairway, that being the nearest point of relief. This irked Inkster to no end.

"It was a big gray area," Inkster told me in 2024. "Did she really have water over her shoes? It was stupid on my part that I didn't go over there and make sure it was a correct ruling or even get a second opinion."

Why didn't you? I asked.

"I don't like controversy," she explained. "I didn't want to make a big deal. But I should have."

(Inkster said the USGA official who made the ruling later "told me that if she had to do it over, she wouldn't have granted relief.")

Anyway, Sheehan capitalized, hitting her approach to within eighteen feet and making the putt to force an eighteen-hole playoff the next day, which she won by two.

Losing the 1992 Open, Inkster said, felt like "a punch in the gut."

Here's another example that showed how much she cared:

In January 1983, during the second round of the LPGA Qualifying School at the Bent Tree Golf Club in Sarasota, Florida, Inkster lost a contact lens on the eighth hole. Her husband, rushing to the hotel to pick up another, received a speeding ticket. She didn't get her card.

Other players might have brushed it off as a bad week. It happens. Besides, another Q-school would come before too long.

Not Inkster. She didn't pick up a club for three months.

"I was pissed and embarrassed," she said. "I needed time to get my head together."

During her second attempt in Texas, she finished as the co-medalist, and once on tour, notched victory number one at the Safeco Classic (by a stroke over the great Kathy Whitworth) in just her fifth start.

In 1984, her first full season, Inkster won two majors: The Dinah Shore and the du Maurier Classic in Canada.

*

She was fifteen when she took up the game. Growing up with two ultracompetitive older brothers and a father who spent three years in the Cincinnati Reds farm system, golf was a chance to excel in a sport of her own. Her home course was Pasatiempo Golf Club in Santa Cruz, California (she lived in a house adjacent to the 14th fairway), which was designed by one of the best, Alister MacKenzie.

At Pasatiempo, she met Brian Inkster, the club's assistant pro, who, in 1980, added a new role to his portfolio: husband. Brian and Juli, twenty, went on their honeymoon shortly before the U.S. Women's Amateur at Prairie Dunes in Kansas, which she was planning to skip.

"We played once on our honeymoon," she explained, "and I shot like 90. I said, 'I'm not going to the U.S. Amateur.'"

Brian wouldn't hear of it. "Yeah, you are," he told her. "Your mom and dad would kill me if you don't go."

Lo and behold, she won the tournament, defeating Patti Rizzo in the final, 2 up. She took the title again in 1981, using clubs borrowed from Sheehan, and in 1982, became the first to win the Amateur three years in a row since Virginia Van Wie in 1934. Inkster nearly didn't make it out of the first round, canning a fifteen-footer for par on the 18th hole to force a playoff against Caroline Gowan.

As accomplished as she was—thirteen wins and three majors before giving birth to her first child, Hayley, in 1990—she was more successful after: eighteen wins and four majors, thanks in part to her instructor, Mike McGetrick. In late 1994 or early 1995, Inkster, who had gone winless since the summer of '92, visited McGetrick in Colorado.

"I was always a good worker," Inkster said, "but I needed a game plan."

McGetrick was the right man for her swing. And her psyche.

"Can I get my game back?" she asked.

"A hundred percent!" McGetrick said.

That's all she needed to hear. "He was so positive," she recalled. "I could call him any time and he'd get right back to me."

Even so, for Inkster, trying to balance the three jobs in her life was never easy.

"I was not doing very good at doing the golf thing," she said, and "I didn't think I was doing any good at the Mommy thing. And I always [stunk] at the wife thing. I felt like I wasn't doing anything great."

Others would beg to disagree.

"She was a mom first, every step of the way," said Greg Johnston, her caddie for seventeen victories. "And when it came time to do the golf stuff, she put everything into it."

In 1998, she helped lead the United States to a victory over Europe in the Solheim Cup at Muirfield Village in Ohio. Hayley, eight, and sister Cori, four, were there to root for Mom and her teammates.

"I get it," Hayley told her mother on the bus to the airport the next day.

"You get what?" Inkster replied.

"I get why you do this. This was so much fun. You need to keep playing golf."

A year later, Inkster, thirty-eight, won her first U.S. Open at Old Waverly Golf Club in West Point, Mississippi, by five over Sherri Tuner. Three weeks after that, she captured the LPGA Championship for her fifth major. Those victories meant a lot but her defining moment, whether she cares to admit it or not, came in the final round of the 2002 U.S. Open at Prairie Dunes when she outdueled Annika Sorenstam, the best player in the world.

On the 15th hole, Inkster lined up an eighteen-footer for par to stay one ahead.

One thought raced through her mind: *I got to make it.*

She made it, all right, followed with a birdie on 16 and wound up prevailing by two.

"The fact I won that Open is amazing," Inkster said, "'cause I hit the ball [terribly]. But that really summed up my whole career. It's all in your heart and your stomach. I always loved being in that moment."

81

Jim Furyk

When he came out on tour in 1994, the first thing people noticed about Jim Furyk was his swing.

No one had seen anything like it.

He moved the club straight up and away from his body on the backswing, before returning it to a more conventional position on the inside as he initiated the downswing.

"Like an octopus falling out of a tree," television analyst David Feherty joked.

Furyk didn't mind one bit.

"If you can't laugh at yourself, you can't have much fun," he said.

Besides, before he had won a single tournament, the swing helped him stand out from the pack.

"When I played well, I'd go to the press room and we'd literally spend the whole time talking about my golf swing and very little about the round and how I played," recalled Furyk, who used to catch fans in the gallery swinging an umbrella to mimic him.

Amusing or not, the swing had its share of skeptics. Gary Koch was working the Tucson Open for ESPN when he spotted Furyk in action for the first time. "With this swing," Koch, wondered, "is it going to last? Is it going to work?"

The answer: an emphatic yes.

For two decades, Furyk, who won seventeen tournaments, including the 2003 U.S. Open at Olympia Fields outside Chicago, was one of the best players in the game. His knack for hitting fairways and greens was made for the Open. Come to think of it, Furyk could have won three or four of them. The wrong shot at the wrong time killed him.

So, how did he come up with that swing of his in the first place? And why on earth did he stick with it?

"My swing solely developed because it was a natural move to me," Furyk explained.

He said his father, Mike, a club pro in Pennsylvania before becoming a sales rep for an equipment company, knew him well enough that attempting to break his swing down and rebuild it from the ground up wouldn't work.

"My dad always believed that what was natural was repetitive," Furyk told me, "and if you had to manufacture a swing, it probably wouldn't hold up under pressure. It would be hard to repeat."

When a college coach said he couldn't wait to "get Jim down to our school to change that swing," Mike Furyk, the only instructor his son has ever had, didn't hesitate.

"Coach," he said, "he will never go to your school."

Furyk wound up attending the University of Arizona, where he was an honorable mention All-American his freshman and sophomore years. As a junior, however, he played so poorly that he wasn't invited to join his teammates at the NCAA championship.

Still, the week wasn't a total loss. Furyk made it through Monday qualifying at the PGA Tour's Buick Classic in Rye, New York. With rounds of 71 and 78, he missed the cut by six strokes.

"I had myself in pretty good position," he said, until leaking "some oil in the second round. But it was a great learning experience for me."

In 1993, Furyk, who had regained his form as a senior to help lead the Wildcats to the NCAA title, earned his card at Q-school in Palm Springs. The hard work was only beginning. He'd now have to take on the likes of Davis Love III, Fred Couples, and Greg Norman.

"That was a rude awakening," he said.

He was a fast learner. Furyk once asked Tom Kite why he walked around every green and jotted down notes in his yardage book. Kite said he was tracking the direction of the grain in different sections of the putting surface.

The takeaway: no detail is too small.

Paul Azinger, the 1993 PGA champion, said every time he played a practice round with Furyk, he felt outprepared.

"That is the one quote that has given me the most satisfaction in my career," Furyk said. "If guys thought I was beating them on Tuesday, that is pretty damn good."

In 1995, Furyk picked up victory number one in the Las Vegas Invitational with a five-day total of 29-under 331. For somebody known as a grinder, he could go awfully low. He's the only player with two rounds in the 50s: a 12-under 59 at the BMW Championship in 2013 and a 12-under 58, the lowest score ever, at the Travelers Championship in 2016.

He's proud of the 58, but "just as cool to me," Furyk said, "is the fact I've [broken 60]—twice."

In the 2003 Open, Furyk cruised to a three-shot triumph over Stephen Leaney.

One of toughest parts of that Sunday was holding his emotions together to wish a Happy Father's Day to the man who taught him so much.

"I kept avoiding it," Furyk said, "and finally we had a nice moment on my way to the range in the afternoon. He gave me a hug and we went to work."

As for those aforementioned missed opportunities…

In the 2006 Open at Winged Foot, he stood in the rough on the 72nd hole two strokes behind the leader, Phil Mickelson. A par, as it turned out, would've put Furyk in a playoff the next day with Geoff Ogilvy, the eventual champion. He hit his approach into the greenside bunker and didn't get up and down.

In the 2007 Open at Oakmont, he was tied for the lead when he arrived on the tee at number 17, a 306-yard risk/reward par-4—for him, unfortunately, more risk than reward. He drove it too far left, into some of the worst rough on the course, and then made a mess of things around the green, leading to a bogey five.

"I'm a little surprised my ball went as far as it did," said Furyk," who tied for second, a stroke behind Angel Cabrera.

Finally, there's the 2012 Open at the Olympic Club.

On 16, a par-5, Furyk, who was tied for the lead, hit, given the urgency of the situation, the worst shot of his life. The ball ended up near the cypress trees, just 150 yards from the tee. As NBC's Johnny Miller pointed out, the duck hook was a carbon copy of Arnold Palmer's drive on the same hole in the 1966 Open, and like Palmer, Furyk made a bogey he couldn't afford.

"What pissed me off most at Olympic was that it was a mental mistake, not a physical mistake," Furyk said. "I took an aggressive club and made a tentative swing. I should have hit a hybrid or iron off the tee and made an aggressive swing." He, like everyone else, had been caught off guard by the USGA's moving the tee forward by ninety-nine yards.

I asked Furyk last year if, while daydreaming, he ever thinks about the Opens he came so close to winning.

"You can't," he told me. "It happened. You got to put it behind you."

Call me a skeptic—and it won't be the last time—but I don't believe him. He's got to think about those losses. Anyone would.

In any case, Furyk is grateful for what he did achieve.

"No one would have ever imagined I would have won seventeen times on Tour, a major, and played in nine Ryder Cups," he said.

Not with that swing.

80

Karrie Webb

During the late 1990s, Karrie Webb was better than Annika Sorenstam, and that's saying something.

Even Sorenstam's caddie, Terry McNamara, wondered: *How the hell are we going to beat Karrie Webb?*

"She could do everything," McNamara said.

No wonder the press wanted to know more about the five-foot-six woman from Ayr, a farming town of about 8,500 in the northeast part of Australia.

Too much, in her opinion.

Webb, who had joined the LPGA tour in 1996 at age twenty-one, said she believes she "subconsciously backed off the pedal a little bit, because I wasn't really enjoying everything that came with it." She saw how the media went after her countryman, Greg Norman, and didn't want that to happen to her.

"I had a couple of camera crews show up [unannounced] on my front doorstep," she said. "I built a fence so they couldn't get in."

Webb, after a short period of time, gave everything she had. And the sport was better off because of it.

"You work hard to be the best you can be," she explained, "and if the best you can be is the best player in the world, you can't hold yourself back."

She wishes, however, she had handled the spotlight better. "You don't really know what that is about before it happens to you," she said.

Webb, fifty, also wishes she had savored more of her success.

She didn't realize she had the most top tens in a row [sixteen in 1998 and 1999] until another player closed in on the record some years later. [That doesn't account, according to the LPGA, for tournaments prior to 1980.]

"That tells you how much I wasn't appreciating how good my golf was," Webb told me.

A lot of that good golf was because of Kelvin Haller, the greens-keeper at Ayr Golf Club.

"Kel's parents ran a news agency next to my grandparents' toy and gift shop," she said. "He got Mom and Dad into playing golf. I can remember when I was a little girl, wanting to caddie for him. He was the best player in the club. I asked Mom, 'Is Kelvin a pro?'"

When Webb was eight, Haller worked with her on rhythm and timing. She practiced before and after school and played every weekend. "He'd get me to hit nine-irons," she said, "just nine-irons. 'Repeating it is the key,' he'd say. 'If you can't repeat it with a nine-iron, you can't with anything else.' I'd be there all day hitting that nine-iron. Picking up the balls and hitting them again. The other kids would be hitting drivers."

Haller saw no fear in her. "When it came to the little tournaments, going off by herself, she loved it," he recalled. "She always knew there was a big journey ahead."

In 1991, Webb, sixteen, won a junior tournament sponsored by Norman's foundation, which led to a week she'd never forget. Staying at Norman's home in Hobe Sound, Florida, she and a young male player saw the sacrifices it would take to make the life she wanted come true.

"It gave my dreams more of a visual," Webb said. "I wanted to play in the States."

Norman was quite impressed.

"If I was up at dawn, they were up at dawn," he said. "If I lifted weights, they lifted weights. If I hit four hundred balls, they hit four hundred balls. Karrie was right there the whole way, whereas the boy couldn't keep up. She had the right attitude. It was obvious that she had the game and the mental toughness to succeed."

Webb also learned there are things more important than chasing a little white ball. At thirty-six, Haller suffered a stroke that would leave him as a paraplegic for the rest of his life.

As the years wore on, he coached Webb by reviewing videos of her swing sent from all corners of the globe. "Even before they arrive," Haller said, "I kind of know what to look for" because Webb's caddie "emails me the distances and the locations of every shot, which side of the fairway, exactly where in the rough ... I'll study the numbers and be thinking, 'I wonder if she's blocking it a little.'"

Inspired by his example, she became more determined than ever.

"I knew my success was fueling his positivity and outlook on life," she said.

After turning pro in 1994, Webb took her talents to Europe, where she exceeded expectations, including her own. She won the 1995 Women's British Open at the Woburn Golf Club in England by six over Sorenstam and Jill McGill, one of her eight top-ten finishes on the Ladies European Tour. The Open wasn't a major at the time, but it was a major breakthrough. Overcome with emotion on the final hole, Webb backed off the tee on two or three occasions.

"I knew she was good," Haller said, "but I didn't really have any idea. None of us did. It's a small town. When Karrie played in that first British Open and—bang!—she won it, I guess we all started to catch on."

Her plan had been to return to Europe for the 1996 season. The Open changed those plans.

Off she went to the States, securing her card at the LPGA Qualifying Tournament.

Webb finished second, first, and second in her first three tournaments, and with four victories was named Rookie of the Year. She also won the money title, the first woman to surpass $1 million in a single season.

In 2001, Webb captured the McDonald's LPGA Championship to become, at twenty-six, the youngest woman to attain the career Grand Slam.

Her final major came at the Dinah Shore in 2006, when she defeated Lorena Ochoa in a playoff.

"She was a shotmaker," said Hall of Famer Beth Daniel. "Karrie didn't market herself. She let her clubs do the talking."

79

Doug Ford

In the five years between Ben Hogan's final major title in 1953 and Arnold Palmer's first *professional* major title in 1958, the Tour lacked a true superstar.

There were, however, some outstanding players. Jackie Burke Jr., as profiled earlier, was one; Doug Ford another.

His birth name was Douglass Fortunato. His father, a club pro in the Northeast, changed it to find work in a golf shop. Back then, Italians typically didn't advance beyond greenskeepers, caddie masters, and cooks.

Ford, who won nineteen tournaments, including the 1955 PGA and 1957 Masters, grew up belonging to a gang in Manhattan.

Some members of the gang became FBI agents. Others joined the Mob.

"In that neighborhood, to survive you had to have guts," he said. "You had to be street smart; you really had to learn how to read people and size up situations."

He cleaned tables at a pool hall, which allowed him to play for free. Pool served as the ideal preparation for another game in which he'd have to knock a ball into a small hole. "It gives you such a natural feel for angles," Ford said. "You tend to aim the putter very squarely, and of course you have nice touch. It's funny, you hear [golfers] talk all the time about how good greens are 'just like a pool table.' But none of them play pool."

Baseball was another sport he loved. Ford, a third baseman, said he was offered a contract by the New York Yankees. He gave it serious consideration.

Until his father set him straight.

"How long will you last playing baseball?" he asked Ford.

"Maybe ten years," his son responded.

"Why don't you stay with the golf? You'll last forever."

Ford didn't turn pro until 1949, when he was twenty-six.

Before then, he did quite well in gambling games. "I was stationed in Florida during the war," he said, "and when it was over, all the hustlers were around Miami Springs."

He picked up his first Tour victory at the Jacksonville Open in 1952 and won five more times over the next two years, leading to the 1955 PGA, a rigorous test in those days: two rounds of medal qualifying to make the top sixty-four, followed by two eighteen-hole matches and, potentially, four thirty-six-hole matches.

No problem for Ford, who advanced to the final against Cary Middlecoff, the reigning Masters champion, at Meadowbrook Country Club outside Detroit.

The two couldn't have had less in common.

Ford was one of the fastest players in the game—"the joke," one of his peers said, was that he would "play through his own group"—while Middlecoff, as his opponent would put it more than a half century later, was "as slow a player as ever walked this Earth." In his thirty-six-hole semifinal, Ford took five hours and ten minutes to defeat Shelley Mayfield, 4 and 3, while Middlecoff needed almost seven hours to eliminate Tommy Bolt by the same score.

In the final, with the temperatures in the nineties, Ford had a decision to make: Would he allow the pace of play to get under his skin or stay calm?

The latter, thanks to his wife, Marilyn.

Marilyn suggested that their ten-year-old son, Doug Jr., carry a stool, so often, when Middlecoff got ready to hit a shot, Ford took a seat.

"She didn't want him pacing and pacing," Doug Ford Jr. told me.

On the 14th hole, Middlecoff was on the green in three while Ford was in there closer lying two.

Time for the stool.

"Doc [a former dentist] lit a cigarette," Ford said, "and he didn't putt until the whole cigarette was gone. The gallery really got on him, but you couldn't rush Doc. I didn't care. I just sat in that chair."

After Middlecoff made his putt, Ford knocked his in to go 3 up and finished him off on 15.

Two years later, he took down Sam Snead in the Masters, the moment of truth occurring at number 15. Ford, leading by a stroke, was about 230 yards from the flag. The safe play was to lay up, especially after what happened the day before. From roughly the same area, he had knocked his three-wood approach into the water, resulting in a bogey.

His caddie, George "Fireball" Franklin, was in favor of laying up. Fireball had his reasons.

"Use your four-iron," he told Ford. "Gonna cost me $100 if you go in the water."

Ford didn't care about some damn bet. He had a Masters to win. And if he was going down, he would go down his way, and it wouldn't be by playing it safe. The two were arguing so vehemently, Ford said, that the gallery started laughing.

"Give me the three-wood," he told Fireball. "They only remember you around here if you win."

The gamble paid off. Ford two-putted for a birdie to extend the lead to two and holed out from the bunker on 18 to win by three. In the 1958 Masters, he missed birdie attempts on 17 and 18 to come up one short, putting the green jacket on a new winner, Arnold Palmer, which launched a new era.

Ford was never again a factor in the Masters, his best finish a tie for eleventh in 1963, but in 2002, he made headlines of a different sort at Augusta National.

Along with former champions Gay Brewer and Billy Casper, Ford received a letter from the club *suggesting* he stop using the lifetime exemption given to every winner. He hadn't made the cut since 1971 and had withdrawn ten times, including the last four years.

Boy, did the club get that one wrong. Even Palmer weighed in.

When asked why he had decided the 2002 Masters would be his last, Palmer, who would change his mind, quipped: "I don't want to get a letter."

Ford, who appeared in forty-nine Masters—only Gary Player (fifty-two) and Palmer (fifty) played in more—later claimed the letter was no big deal.

"I was finished anyway," he said. "Hell, that course was a tough walk even in my prime."

And what a prime it was.

78

Walter Travis

Walter Travis, aka the "Old Man," was thirty-four when he began playing golf in 1896.

He made up for his late start, winning three U.S. Amateurs and a British Amateur, and eventually became a highly respected architect, author, and magazine editor.

And if not for him, Bobby Jones might never have been … Bobby Jones. (Be patient, I'll get there.)

Travis, from Maldon, Australia, had preferred tennis and cycling. The only reason he took up golf was because a few friends at Niantic Club in Flushing, Long Island—he'd moved to New York in the late 1880s—were interested in building a course, and he wanted to show his support.

He didn't take lessons. He learned by reading everything he could get his hands on and practicing whenever he could.

Within two years, he made it to the semifinals of the U.S. Amateur.

His first Amateur title came in 1900 at the Garden City Golf Club, his second a year later at the Country Club of Atlantic City in New Jersey. In 1902, he tied for second in the U.S. Open, also at Garden City, the closest an amateur had come to winning since the event got under way in 1895.

If Walter Travis had stopped after capturing his third Amateur at Nassau Country Club in 1903, his place in golf history would have been secure.

He didn't.

The following year, he took on his toughest challenge yet, the British Amateur at Royal St. George's in Sandwich, England.

"If the weather is calm, I think you will win the thing," wrote his friend, Devereux Emmet, who would wind up making it to the quarterfinals. "They don't begin to know how good you are over here, and that will be greatly to your advantage."

Nonetheless, the odds were not in his favor. Travis was a short hitter, and Royal St. George's was a long course, and he had looked awful during practice rounds in St. Andrews and North Berwick, also in Scotland, before heading to Sandwich. So awful he bought a new set of clubs.

History wasn't on his side, either. No one from outside the United Kingdom had won the British Amateur.

Travis did a smart thing before the tournament began.

Instead of playing a practice round and running the risk of becoming prejudiced against the course, he walked the grounds with just his putting cleek. Every so often, he hit a few shots. For the first time in two weeks, Travis wrote years later, "I could feel the ball," and when he regained his normal "touch and timing," he was "at once transported into the golfer's seventh heaven of delight."

Too bad the caddie assigned to him was, according to Travis, anything but normal.

"A natural-born idiot," he called him, "and cross-eyed at that, too nervous to think of performing the customary duty of teeing a ball and rarely knew where it went." He tried to get rid of the caddie, but to no avail.

Travis felt that club officials treated him poorly from the outset.

He couldn't get a room, Herbert Warren Wind wrote, "in the buildings usually reserved for guests of the Royal St. George's," instead staying at the Bell Hotel with the other Americans, or a locker in the clubhouse which forced him to dress in the hallway and keep his clubs in the shop.

And after winning his first-round match in a downpour, he wasn't given time to put on dry clothes before his next match.

Yet, drenched or not, Travis won the match, one up. The Old Man wouldn't be denied.

Not with the confidence he had on the greens thanks to a putter made by Mr. A. W. Knight of Schenectady, New York.

"It seemed to suit me in every way," he wrote, "and I decided to stand or fall by it."

Travis cruised to a 5 and 4 victory over four-time major champion Harold Hilton in the fifth round and defeated the long-hitting Edward Blackwell 4 and 3 in the final.

The Old Man had made history. A foreigner wouldn't capture the British Amateur again until 1926.

"If anyone had prophesied that one of [the Americans] was likely to give trouble or get into the final heats," wrote Horace Hutchinson, an English golfer who won the tournament twice in the 1880s, "he would have been looked on as a lunatic."

The Brits weren't overjoyed with the outcome, especially one Brit in particular: Lord Northbourne, the captain of the Royal St. George's Club, who, I think it's fair to say, had a gift for hyperbole. "Never, never since the days of Caesar has the British nation been subject to such humiliation," he said at the ceremony afterward.

After speaking for more than an hour, Lord Northbourne grudgingly handed the trophy to Travis, but not before landing one last jab:

"Here's hoping such a disaster never happens again."

In 1908, Travis founded a magazine, *The American Golfer*, which he later handed over to Grantland Rice. He also designed about fifty courses across the United States and Canada.

And was influential as a teacher, which leads us to Bobby Jones.

In 1916, Jones, fourteen, competing in the event for the first time, made it to the quarterfinals of the U.S. Amateur at Merion before falling to Robert Gardner on the 15th hole. That week, Rice asked Travis how Jones might become a better player.

"He can never improve his shots, if that's what you mean," Travis said. "But he will learn a great deal more about playing them. And his putting method is faulty."

One thing led to another, and arrangements were made for Travis to give Jones a putting lesson the morning before the final match between Gardner and Chick Evans. Except Jones missed an early train and arrived twenty minutes late. By then, Travis was gone.

Eight years passed before Jones got another chance.

Travis was at Augusta Country Club when Jones, now in his early twenties, showed up for an exhibition. He suggested Jones keep his feet closer together, adjust his grip to a reverse overlap, and take the club back in a longer sweeping stroke.

"I was privileged to be present when Mr. Travis gave Bobby, in the guise of a lecture," wrote O. B. Keeler, the *Atlanta Journal* reporter who was Jones's Boswell, "a lesson which so changed his putting in a single season that from one of the worst performers among the champions, he became one of the finest and most consistent putters the game has seen."

77
JoAnne Carner

Big Mama, as JoAnne Carner would be known—for the length of her tee shots and, later on, the size of her waistline—has always been a big believer in...

JoAnne Carner.

Check out what she, as an amateur, told the press in early 1969 after winning the LPGA tour's Burdine's Invitational in Miami, the richest event of the season:

"Most of the pros don't show me much," suggested Carner, a five-time U.S. Women's Amateur champion from 1957 through 1968. "Some of [them] think they are the greatest thing walking. But give me the top 10 amateurs and we would beat the top 10 professionals."

Fighting words, if there ever were any. A couple of years ago, I asked Carner, who was eighty-three at the time, if she harbored any regrets over being so brash.

None whatsoever.

"It was what I truly believed," she said.

God bless her.

No wonder some of her peers didn't welcome her with open arms when she joined the tour in 1970.

Carner wasn't fazed one bit. About a decade earlier, when she was competing in the Western Open in Seattle, a golfer who will remain nameless tried to mess with her head. "She used intimidation to her advantage," Carner recalled, "telling players where to stand when she was hitting and so forth."

The golfer was messing with the wrong woman. Carner, who tied for second that week, dished it right back.

"I'm a nice person, but I'm also one of the most stubborn people on this earth," she said. "I ran that woman all over the place, telling her she was away, don't move when I'm swinging, and rolling my eyes at her puny tee shots. I sensed that if I caved in to her that it would hurt my game. And that just wasn't going to happen."

In each of her first five tournaments as a pro, however, she recorded at least one round in the 80s.

"I had to eat some crow," she said.

She didn't eat crow for long. Carner was the LPGA's Rookie of the Year, winning the Wendell West Open in a playoff over Marilynn Smith, and finished eleventh on the money list. In 1971, she picked up two more victories, including the U.S. Women's Open at the Kahwa Club in Erie, Pennsylvania, going wire to wire to defeat Kathy Whitworth by seven strokes.

Growing up in Kirkland, Washington, Carner played golf on a nine-hole public course near her home. Since her older brother worked there, she was allowed to hit once everyone else had teed off. Darkness would not be far behind. "You could follow the ball with the moonlight on the back of the ball," she said. "You learn to know where the clubface was. It was probably the best training ever. Like swinging blindfolded."

So why did she wait until she was thirty to turn pro?

Because she and her husband, Don, whom she married in 1963 and was about twenty years older, were content with the life they had.

Don had done very well for himself, running an electronics company and jewelry business before he and his wife built the Firefly Golf Course, a par-60 facility in Seekonk, Massachusetts, a few miles from Providence. Their day began around six a.m. and ended around ten p.m. She didn't have a spare moment during the busy season, signing players in and helping out in the snack bar.

In the fall, with fewer visitors, Carner found a unique way to work on her game.

Standing about twelve feet inside a clubhouse that had glass windows, "I would hit five-irons out through the door onto one of the greens," she said, never causing any damage.

The time came, eventually, to try a different life.

"It was my husband's idea," explained Carner, who had participated in only a handful of amateur events each year. "He thought I was running out of enthusiasm and competition and the next step was to play against the best in the world."

So they turned the course over to a manager and got themselves a thirty-one-foot trailer to travel from one tour stop to another.

But in 1972, her third season, the wheels came off, and I'm not referring to the trailer.

She didn't win a single tournament, and none in the following year either. Carner had never been through a slump before.

"I was shooting 80 or right around there," she said. "It was awful."

Of all people, it was Billy Martin who came to her aid.

Yes, *that* Billy Martin, the fiery major league baseball manager who later, with the New York Yankees, would have constant run-ins with the owner, George Steinbrenner, the slugger Reggie Jackson—they almost got into a fight in the dugout—and Lord knows how many others. What can I say? The man had a gift.

Martin possessed a soft side, too, according to Carner. (I would love to hear Reggie's reaction to that.)

While they were enjoying dinner with mutual friends, Martin, who had never met Carner, told her she was spending too much time on the driving range—an hour, maybe longer—before she teed off. She analyzed every swing and took the same mindset to the course. *Just hit about ten balls to get loose,* he said, *and go out and play.* That was difficult for her. She assumed being a professional meant you practiced more than ever.

After a while, it dawned on her that Martin was right.

"If you analyze every swing, by the time you get to [holes] 12, 13, or 14," Carner said, "you're convinced you're not hitting it very good. That's when everything falls apart."

The advice from Martin, along with swing tips from Gardner Dickinson, a PGA Tour veteran, put Big Mama back on track. For good.

Carner won six tournaments in 1974, three in 1975, and four in 1976, including a second U.S. Open (in a playoff over Sandra Palmer), ending up with forty-three victories, remarkable for someone who turned professional at such a late date. She was the LPGA's Player of the Year on three occasions and won the Vare Trophy five times.

Just think of the numbers she might have put up if she had joined the tour in her early twenties.

As for her nickname, which was given to her by Palmer, Carner claims it didn't bother her one bit.

The same can't be said of her husband.

"He once picked up a caddie and slammed him against the hood of the car for calling me that," she recalled.

The Carners were quite a couple until Don's passing in 1999. Whenever he felt she was pressing too hard, he made sure they took a week off.

"Usually, it involved fishing somewhere," she said.

Good thing he convinced her to turn pro when she did.

It's impossible to imagine women's golf without her.

76

Davis Love III

Davis Love III had a career most tour pros would have taken in a heartbeat: twenty-one victories, including a major (the 1997 PGA at Winged Foot) and two Players Championships (1992, 2003). In the '03 Players, he closed with an eight-under 64 in cold, windy conditions.

"That 64 is one of the best rounds ever," said Jay Haas, who finished second. "A 64 here in the summer with no wind and the greens rolling at seven on the stimpeter would be impressive."

On the other hand, Love, similar to Fred Couples and Sergio Garcia—and there will be others to come—didn't have the career we expected him to have.

Not with the talent he possessed.

In 1986, his rookie season, he led the tour in driving distance at 285.7 yards. "Love is scary long," Paul Azinger said, "and he's scary straight for being so long."

Length wasn't the only thing he had going for him.

"He's got the psychological makeup to be a superstar," suggested Bob Toski, a former tour player and highly respected teacher.

Love was born on the Monday after the 1964 Masters.

His father, a teaching professional, was in the field, sharing the first-round lead with, among others, Arnold Palmer and Gary Player, before fading over the weekend to finish in a tie for thirty-fourth.

Growing up in a house on the grounds of Atlanta Country Club, DL3 was in love with golf from the start.

"From our backyard Dad could hit pitching wedges to the second green and drivers to the third green," he wrote. "The ball just seemed like it was going miles, and I remember the terrific whistling sound it made as it left the clubface and went off, soaring."

In 1974, Love accompanied his dad to Tanglewood Park in North Carolina for the PGA Championship that Lee Trevino won by a shot over Jack Nicklaus. "All the stars of the game were there," he wrote. "Newspapermen wanted to talk to these men, kids wanted their autographs, and my father would chat with them like they were a guy down the street thinking of buying a used car. I thought to myself, 'Man, this is the life.'"

Davis Love Jr. was fine with his son wanting that life. On one condition.

"If you are going to do it," he told him, "do it right. If not, just play for fun. I don't want you to be anywhere in between."

Love did exactly what his father said.

"I remember serious swing instruction way before I had a driver's license or knew it was fun to chase girls," he said. "I was working on my swing plane, doing drills."

The time was well spent. He led his school to the state championship in his senior year of high school. On a 600-yard par-5, he reached the green in two.

With back-to-back one-irons!

Love, an all-American his first three years at the University of North Carolina, won the ACC Championship in 1984, as well as the North & South Amateur. He skipped his senior year to turn pro, and when he made it through Q-school, the life he wanted would now be his.

In those early days, as his father had advised, he did everything Tom Kite did.

"When he practiced long putting, I practiced long putting," Love wrote. "When he practiced pitch shots over bunkers, I did the same.... I learned how to learn a golf course from Tom."

In 1987, Love registered his first Tour victory at Harbour Town in South Carolina by one over Steve Jones. And although he missed twelve cuts and posted only three top tens in twenty-nine starts the following year, the future looked bright.

Until that horrible day in November 1988.

Heading from St. Simons Island, Georgia, to Jacksonville, Florida, the single-engine plane carrying, among others, Davis Love Jr. and his son's best friend, Jimmy Hodges, crashed while approaching the airport through the fog. None of the passengers survived.

Weeks later, hitting balls on the practice tee they'd spent so much time at together, Love said he "never felt so alone in all my life."

He would be blessed in the years ahead to work with such outstanding instructors as Butch Harmon and Jack Lumpkin.

Except they weren't his dad.

Would it have made a difference in the trajectory of Davis Love III's career if the plane hadn't crashed? Would he have developed into the multiple major winner he seemed destined to become?

"Davis and his father shared the game through his instruction," his mother, Penta Love, pointed out. "It gave him this wonderful foundation that probably doesn't really require all that much more coaching. But without his dad he might not have pursued it as diligently as he would have."

Gary McCord, a former Tour player and TV commentator, offers another explanation for why Love won only one major.

"I don't really know if he had that killer in him," McCord told me. "He was one of those guys who was always really nice, and those guys become good players, but the next step is you have to have a lot of nasty in you to win the majors. You had to have that edge."

McCord might be on to something.

"I wanted to win," Love admitted, "but maybe not as bad as some. I always looked at someone like Nick Price, who among all the dominant players was always the nicest guy out there, as who I wanted to be like."

Love singled out a couple of his peers who "put their family first, friends second, golf game after that. Golf was their job. And that's the way I always looked at it."

Of the majors that got away, the 1996 U.S. Open at Oakland Hills has to top the list.

In the final round, Love, who came up one short, hit his tee shot on number 17, a 200-yard par-3, to a bad spot and could not get up and down. On 18, he three-putted from twenty feet for another bogey, missing the second putt from three feet. "I guess I'll be explaining those putts for a long time," he said.

Thank God for Winged Foot.

In the 1997 PGA, he turned in three 66s to win by five over Justin Leonard. As one writer put it, Love "finally played the kind of golf that people had been expecting of him for about 10 years."

That Love had been expecting from himself, as well.

"So many times I felt like I should have won and didn't," he said.

Many will never forget the rainbow that appeared in the sky as Love walked down the 18th fairway.

"He knew his dad was with him," his mother said. "When it was over and he hugged me, I said, 'Dad knows.' And he said, 'Yes, I'm sure he does.'"

75

Jock Hutchison

A little over one hundred years ago, both the United States and Scotland claimed Jack Falls "Jock" Hutchison as one of their own.

Hutchison, who became a two-time major champion with his win in the 1921 British Open on the Old Course, had lived in the U.S. since 1904. *The Glasgow Herald,* on the other hand, pointed out that Hutchison was a Scot, born and bred (in St. Andrews) who had "come over disguised as an American."

Herbert Warren Wind later wrote he had "the map of Scotland written all over his face."

Well, whether his allegiances laid with Uncle Sam or the Union Jack or both, he was a heck of a player—if, and I mean no disrespect, a bit peculiar. Whenever he found himself in the heat of battle, according to Wind, Hutchison was "dourness itself and as nervous as a mosquito. He walked around restlessly between shots. He sweated lavishly and took to waving his arms in the air to dry them. He literally twiddled his thumbs."

Yet, Wind wrote, "Jock could play one plus-perfect hole after another, each shot, like mountain views in Switzerland, seemingly more breathtaking than the one that went before."

Hutchison got to know a course as well as he could before a tournament began. Nothing wrong with that, right?

No, but in his case, there were times he might have overprepared.

He looked unbeatable leading up to the 1919 U.S. Open at Brae Burn in West Newton, Massachusetts, and the 1920 Open at Inverness in Toledo, Ohio. In 1919, however, he could do no better than a tie for third, five behind Mike Brady and Walter Hagen, who won in a playoff, and in 1920, he lost by a stroke to Ted Ray.

As Wind put it, Hutchison "had spent his brilliance during the qualifying rounds and was relatively played out when the championship proper began."

In 1921, as meticulous as ever, Hutchison, whose dad was a caddie on the Old Course, arrived in St. Andrews four months before the tournament. He played every day, even thirty-six holes on occasion. His "supporters," Wind suggested, "were afraid that he might go stale before the championship got underway."

It finally came time to find out.

Hutchison seized the lead by a stroke with a one-under 72 that included an ace on the 135-yard 8th hole and, believe it or not, nearly another on 9 . . . a hole measuring 278 yards! His tee shot rolled onto the green, hit the cup, and lipped out. His playing partner, Bobby Jones, said Hutchison "was set like a piece of flint to win."

Round two was another matter. Although he turned in a respectable 75 to maintain his one-stroke advantage, he looked, Wind wrote, "over-golfed."

In round three, he shot a 79 to trail by four, but then went out in 36 and came home in 34 to qualify for a thirty-six-hole playoff against amateur Roger Wethered, whose sister, Joyce, would soon be the greatest female golfer of her time.

The playoff was no contest, Hutchison prevailing by nine.

"The most remarkable day of golf that any of us can remember," according to *The Glasgow Herald*.

During the ceremony afterward, he pretended to take a sip from the Claret Jug.

"He is that slender, bowlegged, blond-haired Scotch comedian of the links," was how *The New York Times* once referred to him.

He came close to repeating in 1922.

With one round to go at Royal St. George's, he led by a stroke, but closed with a 76 to finish fourth, opening the door for Hagen to become the first American-born player to win the British Open.

Hutchison's other major title had come in the 1920 PGA at Flossmoor Country Club outside Chicago.

He arrived in wonderful form, having won the Western Open at nearby Olympia Fields by a shot over Jim Barnes and two others, and tying for second at Inverness. Hutchison wasn't initially in the field at the PGA but got in when other qualifiers failed to show up.

He remained in wonderful form.

On his way to the final, he coasted past his first four opponents: 5 and 3, 5 and 3, 6 and 5, and 4 and 3.

Would he ever meet his match?

Yup, his name was James Douglas Edgar, and he gave Hutchison one hell of a match.

Four down after twenty-eight holes, Edgar sliced the margin to one with three to go.

Which was when Hutchison pulled off what *The Times* called "one of the greatest shots ever played in an American tournament." His drive on the 34th hole, a par-4, had come to rest at the foot of a bunker, meaning there was a real possibility the club head on his next shot would hit the bunker instead of the ball.

The club head missed the bunker by maybe a quarter of an inch.

Incredibly enough, the ball ended up on the putting surface about 200 yards away, which rattled Edgar who followed with a mediocre approach. (I wonder if Hutchison sprinted down the fairway like Sergio Garcia.)

Hutchison, who wasn't the favorite among many bettors—he was seen as a perennial bridesmaid—won the hole, and the match one up.

"When the line formed on the right to pay off bets," *The Times* wrote, "it included most of the wiseacres, for there were more long faces at Flossmoor this afternoon than at an undertakers' State convention. Surprise? It was a complete upset."

One final note about Jock Hutchison:

In 1963, he and Fred McLeod, another Scottish immigrant, became the first two honorary starters at the Masters. Hutchison had won the 1937 PGA Seniors' Championship at Augusta National.

"Leading off the Masters," he said, "is the greatest honor we can ever have. I'd rather do this than win a tournament."

No matter which flag he saluted.

74

Tom Weiskopf

From the late 1960s through early 1980s, Tom Weiskopf won sixteen tournaments, including the 1973 British Open, but with the swing he possessed—described by *Los Angeles Times* columnist Jim Murray as "made in Heaven, part velvet, park silk, like a royal robe, so sweet you could pour it over ice cream"—he could have won twice as many.

So, why didn't he?

For starters, Weiskopf put too much pressure on himself to live up to his expectations and those of others who compared him to another Ohio State star, Jack Nicklaus.

"It's strictly a no-win position for Weiskopf," one sports psychologist said. "How can anyone be compared to Nicklaus? It's been an unfair burden to Tom for a long time. Heaven knows how much it's hurt him."

He also drank. Like a fish. It wasn't until 2000 that it dawned on him how much damage the bottle had caused to his game and his family. One night, while watching one of his buddies at a bar in Arizona try to talk "the barmaid who was a C- into an A," Weiskopf had an epiphany:

I need to change my life.

He never took another drink.

Then there was that temper of his. The nicknames he was given, *The Towering Inferno* and *Terrible Tom,* followed him his whole career. He became so angry—at himself, his playing partner, the golfing gods, who the hell knows?—that, on several occasions, he stormed off the course in the middle of a round.

"The shame here is not so much that Tom, by his continued failure to grow up is wasting a talent as great as any on tour," *Golf Digest* wrote in November 1976. "That's his business. The shame is that by his actions, he robs the ticket-buying public of a chance to see him display that talent. The fan who paid handsomely to sit on the 17th green at Westchester is waiting to see Tom Weiskopf [he had walked off earlier in the round] come through, and he doesn't care if Weiskopf is shooting 85 or 65."

No wonder I was anxious when I reached out to Weiskopf in the spring of 2022. I had no idea how he would react.

Well, much to my surprise, and relief, Weiskopf, seventy-nine, couldn't have been more gracious and candid.

Perhaps it had something to do with the fact that he was battling pancreatic cancer at the time. That dealing with one's mortality makes a person see everything in a whole new light.

"I wish I wouldn't have done what I did," he told me, referring to those occasions when he quit. "I disappointed a lot of people."

There was, however, one occasion that he did not regret. It happened, as cited by *Golf Digest*, in the second round of the 1976 Westchester Classic in Harrison, New York. His close friend, Bert Yancey, was losing it. On the 12th tee, "we tried to calm him down," Weiskopf said, "but he began picking on me and Rod [Curl, the other member of the group], to the gallery." Weiskopf tried to seek help and was fined $3,500 for withdrawing without a medical reason.

"I could have given a phony reason and been okay," he said, "but I couldn't do that and live with myself."

Nor did he feel any remorse about deciding to skip the 1977 Ryder Cup.

Weiskopf, who finished sixth on the points list, said he sent the PGA of America a letter well ahead of time to indicate he'd have another commitment that week. The PGA, he said, told him it never received the letter.

Nonsense, according to Weiskopf.

"I still have the receipt by registered mail that someone signed for," he told me.

The other commitment was a sheep hunt, his opportunity to secure the final leg in a sport which had its own Grand Slam. Weiskopf had collected the first three legs earlier in the 1970s.

Hunting was a passion, if not a necessity.

"It was how I treated myself to get away from golf," said Weiskopf, who earned his precious Slam.

As for his main occupation, the highlight was, without a doubt, the summer of 1973.

"I wasn't afraid of anything or anybody," he recalled. "I'd look up at the scoreboard, and think: 'Is that all they could do today was 66?'

It was the first and only year I felt like Jack Nicklaus did his whole career, or Tiger."

Weiskopf's father had died of cancer in March. Losing him drove Weiskopf to be the player everyone thought he would be.

The player he thought he would be.

He won five of his next eight tournaments, including the British Open at Royal Troon, where he was in the lead after each of the first three rounds. When anyone made a run at him that year, he had a chat with his father.

"They're getting closer," Weiskopf told him. "But watch this. We'll slam the door right in their face."

Slam it he did. With Johnny Miller, the reigning U.S. Open champion, trailing by only two, Weiskopf hit a beautiful one-iron on 17, a 220-yard par-3. He two-putted for a par, extending the lead to three thanks to a Miller bogey.

The Claret Jug would soon be his.

Walking down the final fairway, his emotions took over.

"I don't know if my feet ever hit the ground," Weiskopf recalled. "It felt like I actually was running, but I wasn't."

He thought of the people who had helped him along the way, and you can put Jack Nicklaus on the list.

"You're hitting it solid," Nicklaus told him on the driving range before the last round.

"I am," Weiskopf said.

"Then just go out there and play the golf course and you'll be fine."

Too bad that attitude didn't work as well at Augusta National, where Weiskopf finished second on four occasions, a record for a non-winner, most memorably in 1975. After a birdie on 15, Weiskopf was up by one over Nicklaus, who came up forty feet short on 16, a par-3. Lo and behold, he knocked it in, raising his putter in the air to celebrate.

Weiskopf, who was on the 16th tee, had seen this movie before.

"I was thinking," he said, " 'Nicklaus, you SOB, I knew you'd do that to me.' "

He promptly bogeyed the hole to fall a shot behind.

Weiskopf hit approaches to within about fifteen feet on 17 and eight feet on 18 but missed both birdie putts.

Gone was another chance at a green jacket. And a lot more.

"I think the '75 Masters was a turning point for me," Weiskopf said. "I don't think I ever really recovered. It was like Arnold when Casper beat him at Olympic. He was never the same. After that Masters I was pretty much confused and lost."

In our last interview, Weiskopf said that nearly a half century later he still thought about the putt he missed on 18. He said he hit it too firmly to compensate for the one he didn't hit hard enough on 17.

Over the next decade or so, Weiskopf won five tournaments, his last the 1982 Western Open.

"I knew then and there that I was through," he said.

As a player perhaps, but not with the game itself. Always intrigued by how courses were laid out, he turned to golf architecture for a second career and became one of the most respected in the field. With his partner, Jay Morrish, he designed more than seventy courses around the world, including Loch Lomond in Scotland and Troon North in Arizona.

"He created another legacy with his golf course design," said former Tour pro and fellow Ohio State alum Ed Sneed. "As time goes on, people will recognize him as much for that [as his play]."

As for that other Ohio State alum...

"First let me say that he [Nicklaus] couldn't drive the ball better than I could, nor could he hit his long, middle or short irons as well," Weiskopf said, "but he had three things I didn't have, and they made a huge difference. I didn't have Jack's concentration...I couldn't form a game plan and stick to it the way he could...and he had tremendous patience."

In the 1986 Masters, when the forty-six-year-old Nicklaus, in the midst of his historic charge, arrived at the 16th hole trailing by only two, Jim Nantz asked Weiskopf, now an analyst for CBS, to speculate on what might be going through the Golden Bear's mind as he got ready to hit his tee shot.

"If I knew the way he thought," Weiskopf said, "I would have won this tournament."

73

Curtis Strange

In June 1989 at Oak Hill, Curtis Strange won the U.S. Open for the second year in a row, a feat accomplished to that point by only Willie Anderson, John McDermott, Bobby Jones, Ralph Guldahl, and Ben Hogan.

"Move over, Ben," Strange told the press.

At age thirty-four, surely there would be more victories to add to his total of seventeen, including perhaps another major or two.

That's not what happened.

From that day forward, Strange went 0-for-258 through his last appearance on Tour in 2004. It was hard to believe then and still hard to believe now.

First, let's go back to the beginning. Strange owes a great deal to his father, Tom, a club pro at Bow Creek Golf and Country Club in Virginia who played in six U.S. Opens, his best finish a tie for forty-eighth at Baltusrol in 1967.

During the summer, Tom Strange often took his son with him to work at seven in the morning and didn't get home until seven or eight at night. One day, when he was thirteen, Curtis came into the office in tears because he couldn't figure out what was wrong with his swing. His father dropped everything, and the two went to the range. Problem solved.

A year or so later, his father was gone. Lung cancer. He was thirty-nine.

"He was a big part of me for quite a while," Strange said.

(Having lost my father when I was twelve, I wanted him to go a lot deeper. I don't know, maybe he couldn't. Or wouldn't.)

In the spring of 1974, Strange, a freshman at Wake Forest, eagled the final hole, a par-5, to claim the individual title in the NCAA Championship at Carlton Oaks Country Club outside San Diego.

When he called home afterward, "my mother started crying," he said. "I knew this was different."

Three years later, after failing by a shot in his first attempt, he made it through Q-school.

A big step but only that, a step.

He still had to qualify every Monday for that week's tournament. If he secured a spot and made the cut, he could play the following week. If not, he went back to Monday qualifying. There had to be an easier way to make a living.

Yet Strange wouldn't trade those days for anything. They made him tougher.

His first Tour victory was in 1979 at the Pensacola Open in Florida. He won two more times in 1980, including in Houston when he defeated Lee Trevino in a playoff.

Which brings us to the 1985 Masters.

After shooting an eight-over 80 on Thursday, his chances of making the cut were slim, so he phoned the airline to book an earlier reservation. Naturally, he fired a 65 on Friday. Not only did he make the cut, he was only five back, and following a 68 on Saturday, he trailed Raymond Floyd, the leader, by one.

With six holes to go on Sunday, Strange, ahead by three strokes, was on the verge of making history: no one in modern times had won a major after starting off with a round in the 80s.

He would also have a chance to pay tribute to the man who had made it possible.

"If I ever were to win something big," Strange said, "I told myself for the longest time, I would thank my dad in public."

But going for the green in two on 13 and 15, he found the water both times, resulting in two bogeys, and lost by two strokes to Bernhard Langer.

So much for that chance to thank his dad.

"God, that would have been a hell of an experience," Strange said. "But it wasn't meant to be. You have to expect those times as well as the good times."

He will never forget the kind words he received from Jack Nicklaus.

"Keep your head up," Nicklaus told him. "You'll be fine."

Better than fine.

Strange won the Canadian Open a few months later over Nicklaus and Greg Norman and was the leading money winner in 1985 and 1987.

In 1988, as well, when he became the first player to surpass $1 million in earnings over a single season.

Nineteen-eigthy-eight was quite a year. With two holes to go in the U.S. Open at The Country Club of Brookline, he led Nick Faldo by one. Strange promptly three-putted number 17 from fifteen feet away, and after finding the rough with his drive on 18, sent the approach into a greenside bunker.

Under normal circumstances, it was a straightforward bunker shot.

This wasn't a normal circumstance.

And if Strange failed to get up and down, it would be fair to wonder:

Does he have what it takes to win the big one?

Absolutely.

The ball ended up about a foot from the cup, and in the eighteen-hole playoff the following day, he shot a 71 to defeat Faldo by four.

After walking off the 18th green, Strange was interviewed by ABC's Bob Rosburg who brought up Curtis's father. I don't remember a single shot from the playoff but I remember him tearing up a bit. I wish I knew what I was thinking, maybe of my father.

After defending his title at Oak Hill in 1989—he rallied on Sunday from three behind with a closing 70—the question was:

Could he win three Opens in a row?

He gave himself a chance. Heading into the final round at Medinah, he was only two back but fired a three-over 75 to finish in a tie for twenty-first.

Strange lost more than a golf tournament that week.

"I knew after Medinah something was missing," he told me, sounding like Tom Weiskopf after the 1975 Masters and Tony Jacklin after the 1972 British Open.

Strange figured it had something to do with his driving or putting, which he could probably fix. It didn't. What he lost was the edge that made him as intense as anyone on Tour.

"Where I noticed it was when I missed a cut or didn't play well, it didn't hurt nearly as bad," he said.

In the 1990s, the Virginia Sports Hall of Fame informed Strange they were planning to induct him.

"I have a tough time thinking I'm going to go in before my dad," he told them. "He won five State Opens and was a leading ambassador for the game."

"All our golfers are internationally known," they responded.

Strange didn't give in.

In 1998, Tom Strange was inducted, and six years later, Curtis followed him.

Father and son together again.

72

Mark O'Meara

Prior to the afternoon of Sunday, April 12, 1998, Mark O'Meara was considered a good player.

Strike that: a very good player.

Among his fourteen victories were the Canadian Open in 1995, the Mercedes Championships in 1996 (the season opener for the previous year's winners), and five times from 1985 through 1997, the pro-am at Pebble Beach. He also won the 1979 U.S. Amateur at Canterbury Golf Club outside Cleveland, beating his friend and defending champion John Cook, 8 and 7.

Very good, however, is a long way from great, and with time running out—O'Meara was forty-one—it didn't seem likely he'd ever reach the next level. Especially with the young guns—Tiger Woods, Phil Mickelson, David Duval, Ernie Els, etc.—taking over the sport, as young guns are wont to do. All that was left for O'Meara was to pick up as many paychecks as he could until he turned fifty when, thanks to the Senior tour, the mulligan of all mulligans, he would suddenly be young again.

On that April day in 1998, O'Meara, tied with Duval and Fred Couples, lined up a twenty-foot birdie putt on the 72nd hole to win the Masters.

He circled the cup to check the break and speed from every angle. He might never have a putt this big again.

A putt for his legacy.

Finally, after two practice strokes, O'Meara brought the putter back, the spectators (sorry, not patrons, as Augusta National and CBS, its broadcast partner, refer to them. This is a golf tournament, not *The Marriage of Figaro*) rising to their feet.

The ball was tracking... tracking...

*

In 1996, a new kid moved into the neighborhood. His name was Tiger Woods.

O'Meara became a big brother to Woods, who had recently turned pro. They practiced and played together at Isleworth outside Orlando, the old man winning his share. Woods couldn't have come along at a better time. To suggest O'Meara was burned out would be going too far. Still, the end would arrive sooner than later and he knew it.

Cook, a former Isleworth resident, summed it up:

"Tiger Woods comes and all of a sudden, that little downside on the top of that mountain kind of plateaued out a bit. You could see a renewed interest [in O'Meara] to compete and at a high level. If we didn't improve and have the same enthusiasm that Tiger did, he wouldn't have let us be part of what he was trying to accomplish."

O'Meara doesn't speak to Woods very often these days.

"But he knows I'm there for him whenever he needs me," he said. "I love the kid."

*

O'Meara was at peace. He knew, at the very least, he had hit a good putt, and that's all he could ask for. Whether it went in, well, that was for the golfing gods to decide.

As the ball edged closer to the cup, another thought crept into his head:

This might go in!

Then, ever so slightly, it began breaking to the left—"my last thought," he said, "when it was about three inches from the hole was, *Please don't lip out.*"

It didn't.

Mark O'Meara was the 1998 Masters champion.

"My feeling was shock and disbelief at what the hell just happened," he said.

O'Meara didn't arrive at Magnolia Lane that week with a lot of confidence, a 2, he estimated, on a scale of 1 to 10: "I wasn't hitting it good, and I wasn't putting good."

Other than that...

He opened with a two-over 74, five behind Couples, the leader.

"I yipped a putt on Thursday on the 10th green from ten feet," O'Meara said. "I thought, *How the hell can you ever win a tournament playing like this?*"

Soon, however, the putts began to drop. He finished the week with one hundred five putts, twelve less than Woods the year before, and didn't have a single three-putt.

Three months later, on the other side of the Atlantic, he lined up another putt.

From about fourteen feet, it was for a birdie on the 71st hole at Royal Birkdale, a Claret Jug up for grabs. Glancing at the leaderboard, O'Meara noticed he was tied with Woods, who was done for the day. Most players would have been intimidated to see that name up there.

Not O'Meara.

"I said to myself, 'You know what? I make these all the time at home when I'm playing against him,'" he said. "'He is going to be so ticked off when I make this putt.'"

He made it, all right, and went on to defeat Brian Watts in a four-hole playoff.

Prior to the 1998 Masters, O'Meara was 0-for-58 in majors, missing the cut close to one third of the time. One writer suggested that O'Meara could be branded as the *King of the B's* after he won two lesser events in 1997.

When O'Meara spotted the writer in the pressroom after winning the green jacket, he couldn't resist:

"I don't know if I'm still in that B category, buddy."

No, he was not, and after he had added the second major at Birkdale, Mark O'Meara was now better than very good. Dare, I say, great.

Few would have thought that was possible if they had seen him on the range at Pinehurst on a cold, snowy morning in late 1982. O'Meara, who had fallen to 118th on the money list after being the Rookie of the Year in '81, was working with Hank Haney, his instructor.

Haney was trying to get his swing to be more rounded, but O'Meara hit one poor shot after another. He became so fed up that he tossed his wedge thirty yards in the air. After hitting several nine-irons, with similar results, he threw that club, as well. Then the eight. The seven. The...

Before long, O'Meara had emptied his entire bag.

"Well," Haney said, "I guess we have one more thing we can swing."

The umbrella. And that, too, was heaved in frustration.

O'Meara promptly picked up the clubs, put them into his bag, and started over. People say Tiger Woods practiced a lot, and he did. So did O'Meara. "Listen, I was around Tiger for ten or eleven years," he said. "I promise there is no way Tiger Woods would have hit more golfs balls than I hit. No way."

The hard work paid off.

He played a little better in 1983, and in 1984 he picked up his first Tour victory at the Greater Milwaukee Open by five over Tom Watson.

"When I putted out on 18," O'Meara recalled, "he shook my hand and said, 'Congratulations, I hope, and I believe this could be one of many.' I just beat the best player in the world, I'm thinking. No matter what happens, at least I won one of these things."

He notched two more victories in 1985 and finished with sixteen overall.

I asked O'Meara why he never won on Tour after Birkdale.

"Good question," he said. "I wish I could answer that."

It soon occurred to me how fitting it was that the British Open was his last victory. He's on the short list year after year of Best Player to Never Win a Major, and just when you think his window is closing, he picks up two in three months.

You can't top that.

71

Harry Cooper

Harry "Lighthorse" Cooper should have been higher on this list. A lot higher.

After all, only Paul Runyan, with twenty-seven, collected more

Tour victories in the 1930s than Cooper's twenty-four, and only nineteen players have more than his total of twenty-eight.

So, why this far back?

Because of the victories he didn't collect. The ones that people remember. The ones that spell greatness.

The majors.

Cooper had no excuse, try as he often did to come up with one. Whenever he was in position to break the drought, which may have led to winning others, he played more like Winnie Cooper. (Kevin Arnold's girlfriend on the 1980s–90s TV show *Wonder Years.*)

Three missed opportunities stand out, starting with the 1927 U.S. Open at Oakmont.

Cooper, born in England and raised in Texas—his father was a club pro who had served as an apprentice under Old Tom Morris at St. Andrews—hit his approach on the 71st hole to within eight feet. If he were to knock it in, the tournament, in all likelihood, would be his. If he two-putted, that still might be good enough.

He three-putted, missing the comebacker from four feet.

"If I knew what was going on," Cooper said decades later, "I couldn't have lost it. . . . I thought I needed [the birdie]."

Even so, Cooper was informed after finishing on 18 to get ready for the trophy ceremony. No one was going to catch him.

Except Tommy Armour.

Cooper watched from the balcony of the clubhouse as Armour lined up a fifteen-footer for the tie.

"I had my fingers crossed," he recalled. "I was mumbling, 'Miss it. Miss it. Miss it.' But he made it." (That reminds me of a Senior tour event in 1999 when I sat next to Jim Thorpe in the pressroom as Tom Jenkins had about a fifteen-foot putt to win in regulation. "Miss it for Thorpie," Thorpe said. Jenkins did, indeed, miss but prevailed in a playoff.)

Cooper would now have to regroup for an eighteen-hole playoff the following day.

No problem.

Tied after nine holes, he looked like he might gain a few strokes on Armour at number 10.

Until a fan got in the way.

"[Armour] hit a one-iron that was going like a bat out of hell over the green, but a spectator kicks it back," claimed Cooper, who lost by three. "That would have made a difference."

Fast-forward to 1936 and two more heartbreakers.

The first was in the Masters, known then as the Augusta National Invitation Tournament. Due to rain on Thursday and Sunday, the final two rounds were played on Monday. Cooper shot a 71 in the morning to seize a three-stroke lead over Horton Smith but followed with a 76 in the afternoon.

Teeing off long before Smith—the leader in those days didn't automatically play in the final group—Cooper was forced to cope with the rain.

"Then the sun came out," he said. "Horton Smith had good weather for the back nine."

The nerve of him.

Still, Smith needed a two-putt on the 72nd hole to win the tournament.

Easier said than done.

Which was when, according to Cooper, Smith received some unfair assistance.

"The pin was cut on the upper right," Cooper recalled. "Horton and Lawson Little were both down on the lower left. Horton had a sixty-five-footer, Lawson a forty-five-footer. Horton was clearly away, but Lawson putted first. He gave Horton the line and the speed, then Horton two-putted.... Lawson came up to me later and apologized, but Horton never said a word to me about it all the time I was with him later."

The second heartbreaker was in the U.S. Open a few months later at Baltusrol.

Cooper was up by two with eighteen holes to go.

"Harry, all you've got to do to win is to be standing up when you finish," Johnny Bulla, a fellow pro, told him fairly late in the final round. "You can't lose. It makes no difference what you do from here in."

Bulla was badly mistaken. What Cooper did down the stretch would make a massive difference.

It started with a three-putt bogey on 14, and then on 15, a par-3, instead of waiting for the gallery to clear—there were no ropes or marshals—Cooper hit a tee shot that bounced off a spectator and into the bunker, which led to another bogey. (What was the deal, anyway, with him and spectators?)

"Whether Bulla saying what he did to me had anything to do with [the poor play] or not, I don't know," he said years later.

Finally, you won't believe what happened on 18.

On second thought, since it involves Harry Cooper, maybe you will.

He was a fast player; hence the nickname Lighthorse, given to him by Damon Runyon, the writer, during the 1926 L.A. Open at Los Angeles Country Club when Cooper, the eventual winner, and George Von Elm got through the final round in just two and a half hours.

You can understand then how frustrating it must have been for Cooper to wait almost ten minutes on the 18th green at Baltusrol for his playing partner, a fella by the name of Leslie Madison—sounds like a character from *The Great Gatsby*, doesn't it?—who, the story goes, was trying to find a wallet someone had stolen from him.

"Apparently, it affected me," said Cooper whose approach ended up about thirty-five feet away "and I three-putted the damn green."

Even so, someone still had to play well enough to beat Cooper, and that turned out to be Tony Manero, a thirty-one-year-old club pro from Greensboro, North Carolina, who closed with a course-record 67 to win by two.

Poor Harry. Robbed again.

"What really hangs over me about my career," said Cooper, "is that I never won a major title, despite all my success otherwise. And it was simply a matter of luck. First, you've got to be good, but then you've got to be lucky." Luck definitely plays a role—don't get Tony Jacklin started—but you still have to be at your best, mentally as well as physically, when it matters most.

"Coopy was a great shotmaker, one of the three best fairway-wood players ever with Bobby Jones and Byron Nelson," Paul Runyan said. He was also "the most pessimistic, negative thinker I've ever known. He made things too hard for himself. It kept him from being a superstar."

Jim Ferrier played with Cooper when a team of pros from the United States toured Australia in the mid-1930s.

"He'd hit two beautiful shots and be twelve feet from the hole," Ferrier pointed out, "but it seemed like even before he hit the putt, he'd be saying how the s.o.b. hit a spike mark and that cost him a birdie. All this while the ball's still running!"

70

Hubert Green

During the final round of the 1977 U.S. Open at Southern Hills in Tulsa, Oklahoma, Hubert Green was four holes away from changing his life. Then, out of nowhere, more than a dozen men in blue showed up.

With reason to believe someone might try to *end* his life.

The FBI office in Oklahoma City had received a call from an unidentified woman who claimed three male friends were planning to murder Green on the 15th hole.

"I know they're serious," the woman said. "They showed me their guns."

Frank "Sandy" Tatum, the head of the United States Golf Association's competition committee, Harry Easterly, the president of the USGA, and Lieutenant Charles Jones, who was in charge of security, filled Green in after he putted out on 14. They presented him with three options: he could quit, ask for a suspension of play, or keep going. Meanwhile, the TV cameras scanned the gallery for any suspicious characters.

"You can have all the time you need to decide," Tatum told Green.

"I don't need any time," he said. "Let's go."

Green, leading by a stroke over Lou Graham, the 1975 winner, hooked his drive on 15 toward the trees. He was fortunate, the ball hitting a tree trunk and coming to a rest in the rough above the fairway bunker. From there he reached the putting surface with an eight-iron and got out of there alive.

In more ways than one.

"I was on the green in two but a long way from the hole," Green said years later, "and when I stood over the putt, I suddenly got the sensation I was going to be shot at any second. As soon as I hit the putt, I knew I'd left it short. I also knew I hadn't heard a gunshot. I said out loud, 'Chicken!' And I wasn't talking about leaving the putt short."

On number 16, a par-5, Green hit a superb pitch to set up a birdie that gave him some breathing room, and he wound up winning by a stroke.

The victory, his fourth in fifteen months, proved something. To Green perhaps more than anyone else.

"The majors are where you stand up to be counted in this game and when my turn came I was always sitting down," he said about his performances prior to Southern Hills. He too often hit what he described as a "typical stupid Hubert Green major championship shot."

His success also affirmed that in golf, it doesn't matter how. Only how many.

Jim Murray, the LA columnist, likened his swing to a "drunk trying to find a keyhole in the dark." With a wide-open stance on his chips and putts—he bent over so far he could probably smell the dirt—Green choked down to the shaft, gazed at the ball, the target, the ball again, the target again... to where you felt your life was passing you by.

"There were some shots I swear he did this ten or twelve times," Gary Koch said. "To watch him, you would have never thought he would have that type of career."

A career—nineteen victories including two majors—that earned him a spot in the World Golf Hall of Fame.

Green, whose family belonged to the Birmingham Country Club in Alabama, was five when he took up the game, playing with sawed-off clubs.

"I'm holding the U.S. Open at my place tomorrow," he told his friends.

His place was named Green Acres. He sank tin cans to make holes in the backyard and used plastic golf balls. The total purse was $1, the winner walking off with thirty-five cents.

He once lost by three-putting the final green.

Good thing he didn't do that at Southern Hills. He might have shot himself.

Failing to earn his card at Q-school in 1969, Green, who had played at Florida State, took a job as an assistant pro at Merion. "I learned what

I didn't want to do for a living, and that's be a club pro," he said. "It's one of the toughest, most underpaid jobs in the world. I worked long hard hours and made $80.45 a week after taxes."

In 1970, on his second attempt, he earned his card and never looked back.

Green, the Rookie of the Year in 1971, notched his first victory in Houston when he defeated veteran Don January in a playoff. He struggled in 1972 (only three top tens in thirty-two starts) but rebounded the following year to win two tournaments, and four in 1974.

Too bad the press didn't pay much attention.

"I don't know what I did wrong," he said. "I keep readin' about all those young lions and they're all the same guys I played junior golf with. Maybe it's because I have one gray hair."

No doubt he added a few more after the 1978 Masters.

Green, trailing Gary Player by a stroke, hit his approach on the 72nd hole to within three feet. Lining up his putt, he looked, as usual, at the ball, the hole, the ball, the ... It's a wonder his head didn't come off.

Just then, he heard the voice of CBS radio announcer Jim Kelly doing the play-by-play.

Green backed off and smiled.

And lined it up again. And missed.

To his credit, he didn't throw Kelly under the bus. (If it were me, I would have called for a convoy.)

"I've known Jim a long time, and he's a friend of mine," Green said. "I know he feels bad, but I should still have made the putt. He was doing his job and I was doing mine." (Can you imagine if that happened to Sergio Garcia? He'd still be complaining.)

Shortly afterward, with darkness approaching, Green took a half dozen balls out of his bag and returned to the scene of the crime, attempting one three-footer after another. They all went in except for one.

"Want to go get Gary and start the sudden death, Hubert?" some smart aleck asked.

"Naw," he said. "Gary's the guy who played good enough to win it. I'm the guy who played just good enough to blow it."

At least he didn't blow it at Cherry Hills Country Club outside Denver in 1985.

Ahead by three with one round to go in the PGA, Green made a couple of early bogeys but parred the last seven holes to prevail by two. "He gave a chipping display the likes of which I'd never seen before," said Nick Price, who was in the final group with Green and Lee Trevino. "I can't begin to find enough words to describe how well he played around the greens."

69

Willie Park Sr.

I have all the respect in the world for Old Tom Morris and his son, Young Tom, who won a combined eight British Opens from 1861 through 1872.

Who knows where the game would be today without them?

I feel the same about Willie Park Sr., who doesn't get anywhere near the same attention, and that's a shame.

In 1854, Park Sr., whose son, Willie Park Jr., would become a two-time Open champion himself, boarded a train from his home in Musselburgh to St. Andrews, about seventy miles away, in hopes of taking on Allan Robertson, regarded as the finest golfer of his day. Park, only twenty, issued his challenge through other players and placed an ad in the local paper.

"When he played a match," a Scottish amateur later suggested, "it was never merely for people's amusement, never a matter of indifference whether he won or lost but a serious, stern reality.... With him it was always death or glory."

One day, after failing to elicit a response from Robertson, he showed up at his cottage.

Robertson still wouldn't budge. Park would have to prove himself against someone else. Which turned out to be George Morris, the older brother of Old Tom, who was out of town.

George lost the first eight holes in a row. No one could blame him for what he said to Park:

"For the love of God, man, give us a half!"

Robertson, who was following the match, was quite impressed.

"Willie frightens us with his long driving," he said.

Little wonder that Robertson didn't take on Park next. The task went instead to Old Tom, who had a chance to get revenge for the Morris family.

He didn't come close.

A week later, the two faced off again, Old Tom losing in another rout. Park, according to one observer, "was now the rising, or rather the risen, sun."

Willie Park Sr. versus Old Tom Morris would grow into quite a rivalry over the years, each winning their share, with one hundred pounds or more often on the line.

"Those battles spurred the growth of professional golf," author Kevin Cook suggested. "Newspapers dispatched reporters to the latest 'great match' between the two. Bettors shouted odds while vendors hawked lemonade and ginger beer to spectators. Before long there were dozens of challenge matches pitting local heroes against the best golfers from other towns, with civic honor at stake."

As for the match he desired most, Park never got the chance. In 1859, Robertson came down with a case of jaundice and died. He was forty-four years old.

Which left the issue unresolved: Who was the best golfer in the land?

Well, there was one way to find out.

At noon on October 17, 1860, three weeks before Abraham Lincoln was elected the sixteenth president of the United States, eight men, all professionals, teed off at Prestwick, a links course with only twelve holes. The competition was set for thirty-six holes, each golfer to go around three times, and even with a break at the Red Lion Inn between rounds two and three, they finished in less than five hours. That is how the British Open, the oldest major championship in golf, got its start.

Old Tom was the man to beat. Not only was he a magnificent player, but he had designed Prestwick.

So much for local knowledge.

Park shot a 55 in the first round to seize a three-stroke lead over Old Tom, and maintained the same margin heading to the final twelve holes. Old Tom hung in there like the fighter he was, but it wouldn't be his day, Park canning a thirty-footer on the last hole to prevail by two.

As the first Open champion, he was entitled to the Challenge Belt, which was awarded to each winner before it was replaced by the Claret Jug in 1872. The belt was Park's to borrow, not keep, and that was only if he left a security deposit until bringing it back a year later.

Willie Park Sr., it's fair to say, was a rather odd fellow.

Word has it he once played a match while swinging one-handed and hopping on one leg.

There was also the time, according to a Scottish golf writer, that "a gentleman promised Park an expensive watch if he could drive a ball off the watch without scratching the face. Park did just that, but the man died two days later and had the watch in his pocket when he was buried."

Anyway, the belt was safely returned, allowing Park to pick up his security deposit.

He almost took the belt home with him again in 1861.

Up by three in the final round, the typically aggressive Park attempted to get over the dune in two on number 2, known as the Alps Hole, which would require two pokes of nearly four hundred yards, but the ball ended up in the hazard and he wound up losing by four to Old Tom. No matter. Park won the Open in 1863, 1866, and 1875. From 1860 through 1867, he came in first or second every year except 1864, when he finished fourth.

He and his son weren't the only ones in the family to make a name for themselves in the Open. His brother Mungo took the title in 1874, while another brother, Davie, recorded five top six finishes, including a runner-up in 1866.

In 1886, Willie Park Sr., fifty-three, competed in his last Open, tying for thirty-sixth. He spent his final years running a golf shop in Musselburgh: making clubs, selling balls, and, as always, ready for the next challenge.

So history hasn't treated him as warmly as it has treated Old Tom and Young Tom. Willie Park Sr. was a very important figure in the game, nonetheless.

Not long after his triumph in the 1860 British Open, "Park posed," Cook wrote, "for his official photograph... wearing a satin bow tie and a houndstooth suit, one jaunty thumb under his lapel: Willie the Conqueror."

68

Jerry Travers

Jerry Who?

Exactly.

Jerry Travers was once the best amateur in the United States, and it wasn't close. His problem was that he came too early. Before Francis Ouimet and Bobby Jones. Before people in America cared about golf.

Travers, like Jones, left the game when he was on top.

He went to Wall Street, taking a seat on the New York Cotton Exchange, not even bothering to defend the U.S. Open title he won in 1915.

Travers enjoyed success in his new life. Until...

Wait, we're getting way ahead of ourselves.

When Travers was about ten, he designed a three-hole course on the front lawn of his father's country estate on Long Island. "Hour after hour," he wrote, "I would make the circuit of my little course, and day after day I would work hard to lower my record for the three holes."

A few years later, he took his talents to a real course, where he made friends with three brothers by the last name of Mahon and saw how golf was meant to be played.

His streak of good fortune was just beginning.

In 1902, when his father joined Nassau Country Club in nearby Glen Cove, he became a junior member. One day, the club's Scottish-born professional came up to Travers, fifteen, after he lost to another boy his age.

"Do you want to become a real golfer, kid?" the pro asked, "or are you just going to dub around at the game?"

Travers chose the former, and, as a result, the pro taught him what he knew, which was quite a bit. The pro was Alex Smith, who, you might recall, came to the aid of another ambitious young player, Glenna Collett.

Smith got Travers to reduce the length of his backswing and place his right hand under the shaft instead of over it. Before long, he was hitting the ball farther than ever.

If not for Smith, he wrote, "I doubt if I ever would have won a national title."

In 1904, on his home course, Travers, seventeen, took on none other than the Old Man himself, Walter Travis, in the final of the Nassau Invitation Tournament. Travis had won the British Amateur a few months earlier.

Smith gave Travers some words of encouragement.

"Don't pay any attention to the 'Old Man.' You know how you can play this course—day after day you turn in cards between 75 and 80—so just go ahead and play your game."

Play his game, he did.

Two down with five to go, he took the 14th and 17th holes to even the match. Heading into the playoff, he figured he had nothing to lose.

"Even if fortune went against me on the extra holes," Travers wrote, "the tie at 18 would be glory enough."

Fortune didn't go against him. He put Travis away with a ten-footer on the third playoff hole.

Travers won his first U.S. Amateur in 1907, over Archibald Graham 6 and 5, at the Euclid Club in Cleveland, and successfully defended his title in 1908, beating Max H. Behr 8 and 7, in Garden City.

He didn't play in the Amateur in 1909 or 1910, Travers learning, according to Herbert Warren Wind, "that during his two lean years a young man" can't be a "professional playboy and an amateur golf champion."

In the final of the 1912 U.S. Amateur, Travers beat Chick Evans 7 and 6—that's when Evans threw his silver medal against the wall and went for a walk in the dark—and took care of John G. Anderson 5 and 4 in the final a year later.

The 1913 Amateur was significant for another reason.

After dispatching Francis Ouimet 3 and 2 in the second round, Travers told him in the locker room what he could improve on. The chat, author Mark Frost wrote, "made Francis believe he truly belonged."

The U.S. Open at Brookline was only two weeks away.

Travers's winning the 1915 Open has to be considered a surprise. He wasn't cut out to win an Open. Not with his tendency to spray the ball off the tee. Good thing he was a superb putter, which bailed him out on more than a few occasions.

Leading by a shot heading into the final round, he turned in a 39 on the front nine, sailed one OB at 10, topped a drive at 11, and airmailed an approach over the green at 12. Yet he pulled himself together with a birdie at 15 and pars on the last three holes to join Ouimet as the only amateurs to win the Open.

Not long afterward, he left the game again.

Travers, according to his son, David, hoped to provide a better life for his family, and as one financier supposedly told him, "Jerry, anybody can make money on the cotton exchange."

The move to Wall Street paid off until the crash. In 1931, he sold his seat on the exchange.

He had no choice but to turn pro, which was the last thing he wanted to do.

"My father had the reverse mores of today," David Travers pointed out in 2009. "A good golfer never played for money."

It did not go well.

The rest of the '30s were a constant struggle. In the early '40s, he became an inspector for Pratt & Whitney, an aircraft company in East Hartford, Connecticut.

He didn't play much golf, but when he did, the magic was still there.

"The minute he stroked a putt," said Fred Calder, recalling a round with Travers in the late '40s, "I knew he was a great putter.... I could see that he must have been a hell of a competitor."

67

Joyce Wethered

The train: that is where we must begin.

The train that passed by just before Joyce Wethered struck her four-foot putt on the 17th green at Sheringham Golf Club, which, if it were to go in, would give her the 1920 English Ladies' Championship.

"What train?" Wethered, eighteen, said afterward.

The story has been told for years and years, including in her *New York Times* obituary in 1996.

Too bad it might not be true.

"The point of it," she wrote in her memoir, "seems to depend on whether I heard the train or not—whether, indeed, I was so oblivious of my surroundings that my oblivion became a glorious instance of concentration—and that is a question which for me is still wrapt in mystery."

Where, I'm afraid, it will remain forever.

What isn't a mystery was her talent.

Wethered made the putt to cap an astounding comeback—she had been six down with sixteen holes to go—to prevail 2 and 1 over the favorite and defending champion, Cecil Leitch, and went on to become the top female golfer in the world. Bobby Jones, her partner years later in a match on the Old Course, wrote: "She did not even half-miss one shot, and when we finished, I could not help saying that I had never played with anyone, man or woman, amateur or professional, who made me feel so utterly outclassed."

No one thought she had a prayer to win the English Ladies' Championship in 1920, including Wethered herself, competing in her first national event.

"When I went down to Sheringham in June," she wrote, "it was really more as a companion to a great friend of mine—Miss Molly Griffiths, who had already made a name for herself in the previous year—than with any ambitious ideas of my own.... I began this championship with the hope that I might at least produce one good day's golf before being knocked out."

Try a whole week. And not just good golf. Great golf.

From then on, the expectations grew and she wasn't the only Wethered who could play. Her older brother, Roger, was one of the leading amateurs in the United Kingdom, losing, you may recall, to Jock Hutchison in a playoff in the 1921 British Open at St. Andrews.

Wethered, who took her one and only formal lesson when she was twelve, won the English Ladies' Championship five consecutive times in the 1920s and the British Ladies' Championship on three occasions. She also captured the Worplesdon Mixed Foursomes, another prestigious event, eight times.

With seven different partners.

Unfortunately, the pressure took a toll. In 1925, she retired at the age of twenty-three.

"I felt that I had had a sufficient experience to make me wish never to be other than a carefree spectator in the future," she wrote. "I can enter into the emotions of the game and enjoy them just as I like without having to preserve a state of elaborate calmness as a player over incidents which are in reality causing me acute excitement and probably no little apprehension and alarm."

Retirement suited Wethered just fine. "I simply wanted to do other things," she explained. "I had played golf very hard for five or six years." She returned, remember, when she found out the 1929 British Ladies' Championship was to be held on the Old Course.

"The appeal of St. Andrews," Wethered wrote, "proved too irresistible."

The British press suggested she came out of retirement to keep an American from taking the title away from where it belonged.

Nothing, according to Wethered, could have been further from the truth.

"I must really protest against this rather pretentious statement," she wrote. "The fact that Glenna Collett and I actually met in the final lent some color to the rumor, but I feel I should never be justified in entering for the sole purpose of hoping to prevent some other particular player from winning. A championship in my opinion is an event originally instituted solely for private enterprise and for the best player to win, and it seems to me a pity that it need necessarily be converted into an international match on a larger scale."

The thirty-six-hole match against Collett Vare was something to behold. Not just because Wethered rallied from five down after eleven holes.

Because of where she did it, at the Home of Golf, and whom she beat.

After being gone for four years.

"The greatest ambition of my life had been realized after all—the winning of a championship at St. Andrews," Wethered wrote.

Even so, she had no desire to resume her old life. "It was only when the prize-giving and the speeches were over," she wrote, "that I began to feel really free once more."

Free or not, she wasn't done with the game just yet.

In 1930, when she and Jones were paired together against her brother and Dale Bourne, another top amateur, Wethered turned in a three-over 75 on the Old Course.

From the back tees!

No wonder Jones was blown away. And he wasn't the only legend to rave about her.

She "had a better swing than any woman I've ever seen," according to Gene Sarazen, "a swing you could almost compare with Vardon's, that's how good it was. Her swing went with the person. She had class and grace. She had the hands of a pianist. She was so good she could have played with the men."

Or as Willie Wilson, another professional, put it, "she could hit a ball 240 yards on the fly while standing barefoot on a cake of ice."

She played with Jones again, in 1935 at the East Lake Golf Club in Atlanta, shooting a 74 to his 71. Wethered, who had turned pro by then—the crash in 1929 led her to taking a job as a golf advisor for a London department store—participated in more than fifty exhibition matches across the United States and Canada, establishing several dozen course records.

Too bad Wethered, who lived to the age of ninety-six—in her later years, she was known as Lady Heathcoat-Amory, the widow of a British baronet—and Glenna Collett Vare never played each other on American soil.

"Wethered and Vare have to be judged on what they did as amateurs," Sarazen said many years later. "But they were still the best women golfers I've ever seen. As good as some of the players on the LPGA tour have been, I think Wethered and Vare were better."

66 Johnny Farrell

In 1921, Johnny Farrell, twenty, captured his first Tour event, the Garden City Open on Long Island, and won six more times over the next five years. It wasn't enough. "I tuned myself up to fighting pitch and I scored a few victories, but did nothing to boast about," Farrell said. "I hadn't learned what it is that gives a winning edge."

In the winter of 1927, Farrell was laid up back east for two months while his friends played in tournaments down south.

All he could do was think. Which was just what he needed.

"I thought of something that had happened more than once," he explained. "Coming up one fairway toward the finish of a tournament, I would hear the gallery applauding some player in the adjoining fairway with whom I was having a struggle. Naturally, I would say to myself, 'Well, he's making a birdie while I'm missing one.' The result was that I'd get to pressing and soon lose out. There was the secret, I concluded. I hadn't been playing my own game but some other fellow's. Ever since I've been playing my own game."

Case in point: the 1927 Metropolitan Open at Wykagyl Country Club in New Rochelle, New York. Coming from three back with three holes to go, Farrell made a twelve-footer on number 18 to defeat Bobby Cruickshank for one of his seven victories that year, which included five in a row.

Or was it more?

Grantland Rice and O. B. Keeler claimed Farrell won eight straight. Byron Nelson seemed to agree.

"I broke his record then, for sure," Nelson, who won eleven straight in 1945, told a reporter. "But you've got to remember back then that the tour would make all sorts of changes with dates and things like that. I won 66 tournaments, but I'm only credited with 52." (A Tour representative said one of Farrell's victories in 1927 wasn't official. For his career, he's credited with twenty-two.)

Either way, it was quite a year.

In 1928, he arrived at Olympia Fields for another crack at the U.S. Open. He had tied for fifth in 1923 and for third in 1925 and 1926.

In the first round, he was paired with Bobby Jones. After Jones putted out, his fans hurried to the next tee, as the fans of Arnold Palmer and Tiger Woods would decades later. This can be unnerving for the player left behind with a putt of his own.

He said something about it before the second round to Jones, who being the class act he was, apologized. Still, Farrell, who had opened with a 77, could manage no better than a 74, and after a 71 in round three still trailed Jones by five.

Game, set, and ...

Wait, this just in from the newsroom: Bobby Jones is human. Film at 11.

During a six-hole stretch, starting with number 6, Jones went seven over on his way to a 77, opening the door for Farrell, who closed with a 72. A playoff was set the next day for thirty-six holes.

Jones, with seven majors, was the clear favorite.

"Nobody could beat Bobby Jones back then," said Farrell's son Billy.

Maybe not, but he sure didn't look unbeatable over the first eighteen. Farrell, finishing with four straight birdies, assumed a three-shot advantage heading to the second eighteen. Still, he couldn't afford to let up for a second.

Not against Jones.

Lo and behold, the lead was gone after two holes.

When they arrived at 18, Farrell was up by one. With Jones in there tight, Farrell needed to make an eight-footer to avoid another thirty-six holes, and who's to say he would get a chance like this ever again?

Let's have Keeler (with help from Grantland Rice, who penned *The Bobby Jones Story*) take it from there:

"Just as he started his backswing, a movie camera began to whir, a sound beside which, to a tense golfer, the buzz of a rattlesnake is bland innocence itself. Johnny checked the stroke, stepped back from the ball, and smiled. Then despite all the strain, he struck the ball as smoothly and crisply as the beat of a Curtiss engine. It rolled along a curving line, beautifully predestined on the—"

Sorry to interrupt, guys, I love your prose, but the suspense is killing me:

The ball disappeared!

Johnny Farrell was the 1928 U.S. Open champion. Gene Sarazen and a few others carried Farrell, known as *Handsome Johnny*, off the green on their shoulders.

Now back to Keeler and Rice to put a bow on it, and gentlemen, please keep it brief this time:

"I had seen Lou Tellegen [a stage and film actor] in his blazing younger days when he was leading man for Sarah Bernhardt, and was rated the handsomest man in the world, but I think he was never handsomer than Johnny was on this memorable occasion."

One of the best dressers on Tour—for the first eighteen holes of the playoff, he wore a gray-checkered sweater, blue socks, and white plus-four trousers—Farrell hung around Babe Ruth and boxer Jack Dempsey and dated Fay Wray, the blonde King Kong carried to the top of the Empire State Building.

"I went to a dinner with Babe one night," Farrell recalled, "and people were all around us, shaking hands. But later Babe told me, 'Kid, in 10 years nobody will know who you are.'"

Farrell was friends with celebrities but not in awe.

"Grandpa," Bobby Farrell once asked, "how come you didn't get Babe Ruth's autograph?"

Grandpa didn't miss a beat: "He didn't ask me for mine."

For months after the 1928 Open, thanks to clothing endorsements and exhibitions, Johnny Farrell earned close to $100,000, an ungodly sum back then. He also appeared in vaudeville and in a few golf movies.

Except the Bambino was right.

"At the [1929] Open at Winged Foot, I shot 46 on the front nine in the first round," Farrell said, "and I thought of what Babe had told me. Nobody was clamoring to meet me then. I didn't even have to wait ten years. I had burned myself out in 1928 playing all those exhibitions."

Farrell, who retired in his early thirties, was the head pro at Baltusrol for close to forty years.

He taught the Duke of Windsor, Bing Crosby, Bob Hope, Douglas Fairbanks, as well as presidents Eisenhower, Kennedy, Nixon, and Ford.

"You never knew who was going to call and ask my dad for a lesson," said Peggy McGuire, his daughter.

In June 2024, Farrell was inducted into the World Golf Hall of Fame at Pinehurst.

"Definitely long overdue," his grandson told me. "It validates where he should be."

I couldn't agree more.

65
Nancy Lopez

The sixteen-year-old girl waited outside the locker room. She was excited beyond belief. She was about to get her hero's autograph.

Then it happened.

When the player—she has kept his identity secret for more than a half century—was approached by another fan during the 1973 L.A. Open at Riviera Country Club, he barked:

"I don't have time for this. I have to go."

The girl couldn't believe it. From that moment on, he would be her hero no more.

"If I ever turn professional," she promised herself, "I will never do that to someone."

Nancy Lopez lived up to her promise and then some, signing autograph after autograph, year after year, no matter how long it took. "I didn't want people to feel the disappointment I felt," she explained. "We are role models whether you like it or not."

Lopez was the Arnold Palmer of the LPGA tour. No female golfer has been more popular.

That's not the only promise she lived up to.

Lopez won forty-eight tournaments, including nine—five in a row—as a rookie in 1978.

She didn't see it coming. "My goal that first year was to win one tournament," Lopez told me. "I wanted to finish, if I could, in the top twenty every time I played." Almost. In twenty-five appearances she didn't finish worse than twenty-fifth.

Some members of the media wondered if there might be a sophomore slump in 1979.

She won eight times. Some slump.

Her success was only part of her appeal. People connected with Lopez for the same reason they connected with Palmer. Because she connected with them.

"If you were in the gallery and Nancy walked by, she would look at you and smile," Beth Daniel said. "She made you feel like she was happy you were out there."

Daniel, who joined the tour the year after Lopez, experienced Nancymania for the first time at a tournament in Tucson. "I'm going to the range," Daniel recalled, "and this mass of humanity is leaving the course. I said to someone, 'Is there a delay?' " 'No,' " she was told. " 'Nancy just finished her round.' "

Lopez learned the game from her Mexican-born father, Domingo, who owned an auto-body shop in Roswell, New Mexico. "My first memory was walking with my mom and dad on the course," she said. "My dad would shut down the shop early and play almost every afternoon."

One day, when she was eight, he let her hit a few.

"He told me, 'Every time you swing, make connection,' " she recalled. "He had a really strong Spanish accent, so instead of saying 'make contact,' he said, 'make connection.' That was my goal. I kept on hacking and running up to the ball and hitting it again."

Hitting the ball wasn't the only fun she had.

"I would put on my dad's golf shoes, with spikes, and the sound of the shoes on the pavement stuck with me," Lopez said. "I'd want to go back and make that sound again."

Her first victory came at the Pee-Wee Junior Tournament in Alamogordo, New Mexico.

By 110 strokes.

She shot close to a 70 in each of her three rounds. Over nine holes, not eighteen.

"We were terrible," Lopez said. "On one par-5, I made a 15. I told my dad I could make a 10 instead of a 15. That was my goal the next day." (I asked her last year if she accomplished that goal, but she couldn't remember.)

Her scores improved and it didn't take long. When she was twelve, she beat future LPGA tour member Mary Bryan, who was in her early twenties, 10 and 8 to win the New Mexico State Amateur. Lopez was so talented she played on the boys' team at Goddard High, helping the school win two state championships.

She didn't hide her emotions when she hit it big, and that, too, made her so appealing. So human.

She still doesn't hide them.

When I asked about her mother, Marina, who passed away in September 1977 from heart failure when Lopez was only twenty, she teared up. "My mom was a perfectionist," she said. "Everything I did, she told me I had to do it right or not do it."

Along with the victories came the photo shoots, the requests for interviews, the corporate outings that went from $500 a day to $25,000...Nancymania.

Lopez grew up in a hurry. She had no choice. Otherwise, it would have been too much for her. Though there were times in her rookie season "the pressure was so great," Lopez said, "I just wanted to scream."

She didn't try to make sense of it all. She was too busy living it.

"The press liked me, which helped," Lopez explained. "They always wrote positive things about what I did that week. They're the ones who brought the crowds out to see what I was all about on the golf course."

Some players were jealous of Lopez—there was, according to *Sports Illustrated*, cheering in the locker room when she lost a playoff in 1979 to JoAnne Carner at the Women's Kemper Open in California—although most recognized a good thing when they saw it.

"She's a real asset to the tour," Kathy Whitworth said. "I've seldom seen anyone out here handle herself with such grace."

Lopez played well throughout the 1980s, notching twenty-five of her forty-eight victories, including two of her three majors: The LPGA Championship in 1985 and 1989. Still, like Sam Snead and Phil Mickelson, she never won the U.S. Open. She finished second in 1975 (as an amateur), 1977, 1989, and 1997.

In the '77 Open at Hazeltine, Lopez, making her pro debut, was on top with five holes to go but was having trouble with the zipper in her shorts.

"That was really the U.S. Open I should have won," she said. "I was in a panic mode much of the day. My whole focus became my zipper; I couldn't bend down to read a putt for a fear my pants would break."

Her last real opportunity came at Pumpkin Ridge Golf Club near Portland in 1997. At forty, "I was in the best shape I had ever been in," recalled Lopez, who had dropped about thirty pounds. "My golf game was great and I didn't think she [England's Alison Nicholas] could beat me."

Nicholas was up by two in the final round when they reached the fairway at number 5. Lopez, going first, hit a wedge to tap-in range.

It looked like the lead might soon be one.

Make that three.

From fifty-six yards away, Nicholas holed out for an eagle. "It was a kick in the face," Lopez said. "I was pretty numb."

She hung in there, however, and on 18, trailing by one, sent her approach to within fifteen feet of the flag.

Lopez thought her putt for the tie was going in . . . until it broke sharply to the right. Breaking her heart.

Again.

She was the first to post four rounds in the 60s in a U.S. Women's Open, and it wasn't enough.

Lopez cried a lot that day and in the days to come.

At sixty-eight, she's still not over it.

"Every U.S. Open," Lopez said, "I just couldn't beat the one person who was better than me that week."

64
Payne Stewart

In February 1996, I met Payne Stewart for the first time. I wasn't impressed.

Stewart, the guy on Tour who wore knickers, was on the putting green at Torrey Pines preparing for that week's event. I waited for him to finish before asking if I could interview him for a few minutes. He agreed but was dismissive from the start. I don't believe I used a word of what he said.

About eighteen months later, I approached him again, this time for a book I was writing about golfers and the fathers who inspired them.

I braced myself for another unpleasant exchange.

How wrong I was.

In the months ahead, Stewart gave me whatever time I needed on the phone or in person to talk about his father, a traveling furniture salesman who taught him about golf and about life. (Bill Stewart, who had played in the 1955 U.S. Open—he missed the cut—passed away from cancer in 1985.)

This was a different Payne Stewart, it occurred to me, and I wasn't the only one to notice. "He was becoming a better version of the guy that we knew for all those years," said his friend and fellow Tour pro Peter Jacobsen.

On October 25, 1999, Stewart, forty-two, and five others were killed in a private jet headed from Orlando to Dallas. The aircraft lost cabin pressure and ran out of fuel after about four hours, crashing into a swamp near Mina, South Dakota.

In 2000, I wrote a book, *I Remember Payne Stewart*, filled with observations from family members and friends who knew him well. I received a bunch of calls after the book was released.

One call stood out—from his widow, Tracey, who said I'd done justice to his legacy. No compliment for any book or article I've written has meant more to me.

In 2022, I asked Tracey, whom I hadn't spoken to since, about the last years of her husband's life. About the peace he found that had been lacking no matter how many tournaments he won or awards he received. She talked about the day in April 1999 when their ten-year-old son, Aaron, arrived home from First Academy, a Christian school in Orlando, carrying bracelets with the initials W.W.J.D.

"What does that mean?" Payne Stewart asked.

"What would Jesus do?" Aaron said.

"That really struck a chord with him," Tracey told me. "He thought that made a lot of sense."

Aaron asked if his father would be willing to wear a bracelet, as well. He was, and it was on his wrist two months later when he won the U.S. Open at Pinehurst No. 2, his third major title and eleventh win overall.

"I've got to give thanks to the Lord for giving me the ability to believe in myself," he said. "Without the peace I have in my heart, I wouldn't be sitting here in front of you right now."

Stewart came through over and over down the stretch on a Sunday that, because he would leave us only four months later, will always have a special place in our hearts:

On 16, a thirty-footer for par that would keep him tied with his playing partner, Phil Mickelson.

On 17, a par-3, a four-footer to go up by one.

And then the thrilling climax on 18.

Sending his drive into the rough on the right, he had no alternative—"it was the worst lie he'd had all week," said his caddie, Mike Hicks—but to knock it onto the fairway about eighty yards short of the green.

An eighteen-hole playoff on Monday was a strong possibility.

But after Mickelson missed his birdie attempt from twenty-five feet, Stewart converted a fifteen-footer, the longest putt ever to win a U.S. Open, and celebrated with a memorable fist pump, his right leg in the air. He then cupped Mickelson's face in his hands, telling him there is nothing like being a father. Lefty's wife, Amy, was home in Arizona. Their first child would be born the next day.

"For him to think about Phil at that stage was pretty amazing," Tracey said.

He had come a long way since 1989.

That year, in the final round of the PGA at Kemper Lakes Golf Club in Illinois, Stewart birdied four of the last five holes for a 67 and would soon trail the leader, Mike Reid, by just one.

If only he'd kept his mouth shut.

"I said a prayer in the [scoring] tent," Stewart told the press. " 'How about some good stuff for Payne Stewart one time?' He obliged by letting me win [by a stroke]."

Two months later, after blowing the season-ending tournament at Hilton Head by three-putting the final hole of regulation and the second playoff hole versus Tom Kite, Stewart turned toward the Atlantic and yelled an obscenity.

"I didn't handle myself as a professional after that golf tournament was over," he said.

Ya think?

When I asked Tracey about the final day in Pinehurst, I wondered if my questions might stir too many memories.

Of the man she loved. And lost.

"I told him, 'I'm so proud of you.' " Tracey said. "He said to me, 'I did it, lovey. I did it.' He said, 'I kept my head down all day long.' "

The day before, while watching on TV, Tracey had noticed that her husband was moving his head on his putts. When she told him about it after the round, he went to the putting green to fix the problem and didn't leave the course until it was dark.

Payne Stewart wasn't always a winner. As a matter of fact, he came in second so often—on thirteen occasions from 1984 through 1989—the caddies called him Avis.

Ouch.

A prime example was the 1985 Byron Nelson Classic in Texas. Leading by three on the 72nd hole, Stewart made a double bogey and doubled the first playoff hole, as well, losing to Bob Eastwood.

The 1986 U.S. Open at Shinnecock Hills on Long Island was another.

Up by one with six to play, he made four bogeys coming home while Raymond Floyd, who he was paired with, went two under during the same stretch to win by two.

"I got to watching those eyes," Stewart said, referring to Floyd, "and forgot what I was supposed to be doing."

Stewart was able to rid himself of the Avis label . . . eventually—though he did wind up with twenty-five seconds and nineteen thirds to go along with the eleven wins—and a lot of the credit goes to Dr. Richard Coop, a professor of educational psychology at the University of North Carolina.

"I never wanted to admit I needed some help," said Stewart, who suffered from Attention Deficit Disorder (ADD). "I was having a hard time producing my best golf when I wanted it. It was inside me, but I couldn't get to it. Coop has helped me tap my best."

ESPN's Jimmy Roberts, who interviewed Stewart that evening at Pinehurst, reflected on the brief chat the two had before the camera rolled.

"Payne was worn out and it might have been his first chance to take a deep breath," Roberts recalled. "He talked about how he felt bad about the type of person he had been. He could be a little prickly, as you know. But he had kind of seen the light."

63

Tom Kite

In June 1992, when he arrived at Pebble Beach for the U.S. Open, Tom Kite was forty-two years old. Time was beginning to run out.

Over the previous two decades, Kite had checked every box:

Rookie of the Year, check.

Leading money winner, check. (Twice.)

Players Championship, check.

Vardon Trophy (for the lowest scoring average), check. (Also twice.)

Okay, not every box.

Kite had yet to come through on the game's biggest stage, and if he didn't win one soon, it would follow him to the grave, as it followed Macdonald Smith, Harry Cooper, and Doug Sanders.

He had his opportunities. One after another.

In 1984, he led by a stroke with one round to go in the Masters and was still in the hunt when he came to the dangerous 12th hole. He was out of the hunt when he left the dangerous 12th hole. Thanks to Rae's Creek and a triple bogey.

In 1986, again in the final round at Augusta National, he lined up a ten-foot birdie putt on the 72nd hole that, if he had knocked it in, would have eventually put him in a sudden-death playoff with Jack Nicklaus. "I made that putt," Kite said. "It just didn't go in."

In 1989, he was ahead by three in the final round of the U.S. Open at Oak Hill. Until he hit his drive into the water on number 5.

Another triple bogey. Another blown opportunity.

Even so, Kite told me the absence of a major title wasn't "eating at" him in June 1992. He'd had a blessed life before Pebble Beach and would have one after no matter how he finished.

"I was not going to be defined by what I did on the golf course," he insisted. "At least, in my mind, I was not going to be defined that way."

Fine, let's take him at his word. Who are any of us, really, to question what is inside the soul of another human being? On the other hand, his triumph that week did, indeed, forever alter how his career would be judged. Pebble Beach saved Tom Kite, it's as simple as that. He won nineteen times. Of the forty-five golfers with nineteen or more tour victories, only the aforementioned Cooper, Smith, and Sanders, along with Bill Mehlhorn, failed to win a major. Now there's a foursome you wouldn't want to join.

"All of a sudden people started looking at the whole picture," Kite acknowledged in 1993. "I was the leading money winner of all time *and* the U.S. Open champion. Until you can put a major championship with it, there's always the buts. Yeah, he did this, but. Yeah, he could do that, but. Now there's none of those."

In addition to beating the field, Kite, who had trailed by one after fifty-four holes, beat the elements, closing with an even-par 72 in winds blowing at roughly forty miles per hour. The average score in the final round was 77.3, the third highest in an Open since World War II, eight players in the last seven groups unable to break 80.

The shot of the week came in the final round on number 7, the breathtaking 107-yard par three that borders the Pacific Ocean, my favorite hole in the world, by far. (I asked my wife, Pauletta, to spread my ashes there—I had planned to phone Jack Nicklaus and Mark O'Meara to suggest an exact spot—but she refused. Any volunteers?) Players chose six- and seven-irons on Sunday, and, as one writer put it, "if a player didn't aim for Honolulu, his ball would settle near the eighth tee, in wiry, ankle-deep grass, or worse, down the cliff."

Kite pulled out a six.

"You've got the elevated tee, so there's almost no way to keep the ball down," he said.

The wind blew his ball hard to the left. Good thing it ended up in an area where the fans had been walking. His lie could have been a lot worse.

The goal was to get up and down.

He chipped it in!

The shot brought back memories of the chip Tom Watson holed on number 17 in the 1982 Open. Only Kite didn't jog onto the green and point to his caddie as Watson did.

Too many holes to go. Too many chances to blow it. Again.

"I don't know why it took me so long," said Kite, who hung on to prevail by two over Jeff Sluman. "I think my game is right for the Open.

Oak Hill was my Open to win or lose and I lost it. This one was mine to win or lose and I won it."

No one in the game was more consistent than Tom Kite. In 1981, he finished in the top ten in twenty-one of twenty-six starts. Nor did anyone spend more time on his craft. He lived on the range, although he never saw himself as a workaholic. "I have a problem with that term," Kite said. "I don't know who said this and I have repeated it a couple of times... *The man who finds a job that he truly loves never works another day the rest of his life.*"

In 1980, he became the first player on Tour to carry a third (sixty-degree) wedge to add to his pitching and sand wedges. (Which he'd use for his chip-in on number 7 at Pebble.)

Before long it seemed everyone carried a third wedge.

Kite got the idea from short-game expert Dave Pelz, who claimed that the additional loft would help him have more control over his full wedge shots. "That's when I really became a good player," he said. "I found out the data Dave was giving me was accurate. I wasn't as good inside 70 yards as I should be." (Kite won his first money title the following year.)

He also worked with Dr. Bob Rotella before sports psychologists were in vogue.

"Some others who blew him off," Kite once said, "are no longer playing." Rotella taught him that "playing great was not just about working hard. He made me appreciate that taking time off was very positive. You're not worn out by the time Saturday afternoon comes around or Sunday. You're ready to go."

Give him credit, as well, for what he overcame.

Kite, like Tom Weiskopf, was unfairly compared to another star from the same college; in his case, Ben Crenshaw. They both attended the University of Texas and were taught from an early age by Harvey Penick at Austin Country Club.

Crenshaw "has a classic, rhythmic swing, hits the ball with crunch, and chips and putts with dexterity," one writer suggested in the early 1970s, while "Kite, by contrast, is a bit on the pudgy side.... He wears glasses and a cap that shields his pinkish complexion and kinky curly hair from the sun. In addition, Kite bears the unfortunate burden of appearing disgruntled much of the time."

Nonetheless, he claims there was no rivalry between him and Crenshaw, and I believe him.

"Sooner or later, you realize," he said long ago, "that something is going on—that what people want is a feud—and you aren't the two who are causing it. By the time you're thirty, you take it in stride and understand that it's part of the circus."

Crenshaw wrote Kite a letter after he won the Open. Kite won't divulge its contents except to say it's a "letter I treasure very much." He returned the favor after Crenshaw's triumph in the 1995 Masters.

Yet I can't help wondering:

How could being linked with Crenshaw not have affected him in some negative way? As it affected Weiskopf.

"The thing I found so frustrating," Kite once said, "is that so many people assume there is a white hat and a black hat. I wonder, can't there be two white hats?"

62

Denny Shute

Herman Densmore "Denny" Shute, one of the top players in the 1930s, didn't relish the spotlight.

Shute, considered the "Calvin Coolidge of professional golf"—the thirtieth president of the United States (1923–1929) was also a man of few words—sometimes had his wife, Hettie, pick up his checks and trophies. "He was just so low-key and so quiet, Denny would have been easy to overlook," according to Larry Shute, his half brother. "He wasn't a Walter Hagen. He was modest... a professional gentleman."

Maybe so, but Shute, the son of a golf professional from England who moved to the United States in 1902, did have one thing in common with the Haig:

In the PGA Championship, when it was mano a mano, he could beat your brains out.

Shute won the PGA in 1936 and 1937. No one would go back-to-back again until Tiger Woods in 1999 and 2000. Overall, he won thirty-five of the fifty-one matches he played in the tournament.

He was a shot maker, a writer gushed, with a swing "as sweet as a Viennese Waltz."

As Larry Shute put it: "He played golf like he was taught by our dad—knock it down the middle, knock it on the green and something good will happen."

In the 1936 PGA at Pinehurst No. 2, Shute, who had rallied from two down with four to go to eliminate Bill Mehlhorn in the semifinals, outdueled Jimmy Thomson in the final, 3 and 2.

Thomson, "the mightiest hitter of a ball the world has ever seen," according to a *New York Times* reporter, outdrove Shute by huge margins.

"Jimmy hit it so far I wouldn't look at his shot from the tee," recalled Shute, who made up for the discrepancy with his wonderful approaches. "Every time Thomson walked down to his drive, I'd have one on the green, pretty close [to the cup]."

Nonetheless, he was only one up with eight holes to go.

He extended the lead to two by knocking in a thirty-footer on number 11, and on the 34th hole nailed a three-wood to about five feet from the pin. The match was over.

In the 1937 PGA at the Pittsburgh Field Club, Shute was two down to Jug McSpaden with only three holes remaining.

McSpaden promptly bogeyed 16, made a mess of things on 17, and missed a four-footer on 18—his concentration broken by the sound of a movie camera, he initially backed away from the ball—that would have given him the title. Shute put him away on the first extra hole.

"I will always remember these two hard-nosed competitors putting on as thrilling a battle as can be imagined," Hagen said.

Shute had collected his first major in the 1933 British Open at St. Andrews less than two weeks after three-putting from thirty feet—he missed the comebacker from four feet—on the final hole of the final match to hand the Ryder Cup to Great Britain.

Imagine if that were to happen today. He wouldn't be able to show his face for weeks.

Shute trailed by three heading into the last round at St. Andrews, and among those in the hunt were Hagen and Gene Sarazen, sixteen majors between them.

Both failed, however, to get anything going while Shute turned in his fourth straight even-par 73 to make it into a playoff with Craig Wood. Shute then prevailed by five to become the second U.S.-born player to win on the Old Course. The other was Bobby Jones.

Shute notched just one victory after 1937, the 1939 Glen Falls Open, although in the 1939 and 1941 U.S. Open, he was in it till the end.

In 1939, pars on the last two holes at the Spring Mill course in Philadelphia would have given him the nod over Byron Nelson, who had finished. But he bogeyed number 17 when his second shot ended up behind a tree and came up short in a playoff the following day.

In 1941, Shute, the first-round leader with a 69, finished second at Colonial in Texas, three back of Wood.

Shute, it may interest you to know, collected stamps. After he passed away in 1974 at age sixty-nine, his stamps were valued at more than $200,000—reportedly "one of the finest United States collections ever put up for sale."

He approached his hobby with caution. Which was no surprise.

"He never did take a chance in acquiring major rarities, preferring to buy twenty stamps rather than one," according to one writer.

In 2008, Shute was inducted into the World Golf Hall of Fame.

"I saw him play a lot of golf," Nelson said. "He was a lot better than people realize."

61

Ralph Guldahl

In the late 1930s, no one was better than Ralph Guldahl, and no, I'm not forgetting about Sam Snead and Byron Nelson. Guldahl won thirteen tournaments from 1936 through 1940, including three majors (as many as Snead and Nelson combined) and three Western Opens.

And he was still in his late twenties. The best was yet to come.

Or not.

Guldahl didn't win once after 1940. He went, as one observer noted, from *Who's Who* to *Who's He?*

Players go through slumps all the time but more often than not come out on the other side, sooner or later.

Why didn't he?

*

The son of Norwegian immigrants, Guldahl, like Nelson and Ben Hogan, grew up in the Dallas–Fort Worth area, and he, too, started out as a caddie. In 1929, he claimed the Dallas City Championship and led Woodrow Wilson High to the state title with rounds of 65 and 71.

A year later, skipping his high school graduation, he tied for eleventh in the Texas Open and turned pro on the spot.

He won the 1931 Santa Monica Open and 1932 Arizona Open, but it was during the 1933 U.S. Open at North Shore Country Club in Glenview, Illinois, that people started to take a closer look. Trailing by nine in the final round, he didn't have a prayer... until the leader, Johnny Goodman, an amateur, started to choke with a double bogey on number 6 and bogeys on 7, 8, and 9.

Guldahl took advantage, making one par after another down the stretch.

On 18, he was tied with Goodman, who was done for the day. However, after an excellent drive, Guldahl knocked his approach into a greenside bunker and was unable to get up and down, missing a four-footer.

"A look of keen disappointment came over Guldahl's bronzed face," *The New York Times* reported, "as he watched the white ball slide by the side of the hole, carrying with it his chance for the title."

Guldahl won one event in 1934 and finished second in two others, but after struggling in his few appearances the following year—he tied for fortieth in the Open at Oakmont, closing with back-to-back rounds of 82—he decided enough was enough.

He got a job selling cars in Dallas. America was still in a depression, and he had a wife and kid to support.

Unfortunately, he didn't fare well in that line of work, either, selling only one car. To himself.

Now what?

California, here we come.

He figured the warm, drier climate would do wonders for his son, who was experiencing some health issues. Guldahl worked as an assistant carpenter for one of the studios in Hollywood and during his off-hours gave lessons and played a few rounds on a nine-hole course in Palm Springs with two actors—no one you've ever heard of—who, as the story goes, handed him $100 to give the game another shot.

Sometimes that's all you need. Someone to believe in you. More than you believe in yourself.

Guldhal came in sixth at the 1936 True Temper Open in Detroit and tied for eighth in the U.S. Open at Baltusrol. Two weeks later, he closed with a 64 to capture the Western Open. He won twice more that year, posting the lowest scoring average on Tour, 71.63 strokes per round. Olin Dutra, a two-time major champion, was also a big help, urging Guldahl, who almost won the Masters in 1937—he double-bogeyed 12 and 17 to finish second, two behind Nelson—to change his grip from palm to finger control.

In June of '37, he was in command down the stretch of the Open at Oakland Hills.

"Just don't drop dead," Harry Cooper said, echoing what Johnny Bulla told him at the Open the year before. "That's the only way you can miss."

That, Guldahl could manage.

Approaching the green on 18, he combed his thick, curly hair. I'm not making that up. He did that quite often during tournaments.

"The tension of the 72-hole Open grind was over," explained Guldahl, who won by two. "The only reason I ran the comb through my hair was because I wanted to present a little better picture after all those rough holes."

His performance at Oakland Hills was only the beginning.

In 1938, he finished second again at Augusta, three-putting 16 and 18 to lose by two to Henry Picard, but two months later he became the fourth player to win back-to-back Opens, rallying from four behind at Cherry Hills to prevail by six over Dick Metz. There was little time to soak it all in, Guldahl boarding a train for St. Louis, where he claimed his third straight Western Open.

"Within a space of five days," one writer suggested, "he has accomplished a feat hitherto unmatched by any golfer in the history of the country's two ranking medal-play shows."

He wasn't done yet.

In 1939, Guldahl made up for his two missed opportunities in the Masters, edging Snead by a stroke. He won three more tournaments that year and another two in 1940.

Ralph Guldahl, the golfer-turned-carpenter-turned-golfer, was on top of the world.

Until, all of a sudden, he wasn't.

No one can say for certain why his game abandoned him. Only that it did.

Snead tried to turn him around. To no avail.

"I fixed his hands around the club," he recalled. "[Guldahl] tried my new grip a few times and said, 'It doesn't feel right.' I said, 'Well, I wouldn't think it would. That grip is the one you used when you were winning everything in sight. Now you've gotten away from it and you're doing something new—and that something new is wrong.'"

Of the various theories put forward, one gained the most credibility.

"When he sat down to write that book of instruction," his wife, Laverne, insisted, referring to *Groove Your Golf,* "that's when he lost his game."

Guldahl, according to this theory, began to think too much about swing mechanics and the position of his hands and feet, often checking himself in the mirror. It didn't help that the photos taken for the book showed him playing the ball more off his right foot than was actually the case.

"The angle was all wrong," Ralph Guldahl Jr. said. "Dad got it in his head that he needed to move the ball way up in his stance. He got a more upright swing, with less shoulder turn, and soon he was slapping at the ball, not making solid contact."

His father didn't blame the the book when speaking to the press. He said the problem was he'd lost his desire after many years on the road and wanted to spend more time with his family.

In private, well...

"Absolutely he thought the book destroyed him," said Doug Howe, the ex–general manager at Braemar Country Club in Tarzana, California, where Guldahl was the head pro in his final years. "I remember one specific lunch we had. He said, 'And then I wrote that dang book.'"

60

Henry Picard

In 1930, Henry Picard, the head pro at the Country Club of Charleston, was playing golf in Savannah, Georgia. In the group behind was none other than Bobby Jones, who hit into Picard's group with his second shot on a par-5. Jones felt awful, apologizing repeatedly over the next few holes.

Picard, in his early twenties, sensed an opportunity.

"Mr. Jones, what time do you start tomorrow?" he said. "I want to see you play, because I didn't think anyone could hit a ball as far as you did [back there]."

They met the next day.

"I started studying his swing," Picard recalled, "and the more I looked at it, I could see it was big and long. So I made up my mind that I would have a long swing, too."

He also learned a great deal from golf instructor Alex Morrison.

In 1935, Picard was giving an exhibition at a club in New York when he was introduced to Morrison, who made a small suggestion after watching him hit a few dozen balls.

"That I hold my head longer after impact—hold it steadier," Picard said.

It made a big difference.

He won the Metropolitan Open the same week and remained a believer in Morrison's theories of the golf swing till his dying day.

"I had already won on the tour before I met Morrison," he pointed out, "but I knew my plane wasn't right. He told me where it belonged. He made it, finished it."

Speaking of knowing how to finish, that's what Picard, who won twenty-six times on Tour, did in the final round at Augusta National in 1938. Leading by a stroke after fifty-four holes, he turned in a four-under 32 on the front nine to keep everyone at bay, prevailing by two over Harry Cooper and Ralph Guldahl.

Picard was pleased to come through, don't get him wrong, but winning the Masters wasn't the life-changing experience it would be for others in the years to come.

"I guess when they started the coat thing [in 1949, with Sam Snead the first winner] all of a sudden it got bigger than anyone could have imagined," he said. "When I won, I think they had to take up a collection from the members to pay me [$1,500]."

Morrison once offered Picard a $70,000 contract for ten years. Thanks but no thanks. "Everything I won he would get," he explained. "I told him that what he did is good, there's no system in the world that compares with it, but I don't want to put a burden on myself."

What Picard, meanwhile, did for Ben Hogan can't be stressed enough.

And the way it came about almost makes one believe the golfing Gods had something to do with it.

In late 1937, Hogan and his wife, Valerie, were having lunch at the Blackstone Hotel in Fort Worth when Picard walked in. "I was going across the country with Jack Grout [a fellow touring pro and future instructor]," Picard recalled. "Why we stopped in a hotel in Fort Worth I don't know, because I went across the country many times and never stopped in hotels during the day to eat or anything else."

Spotting the Hogans, he stopped by to say hello. This wasn't the confident Hogan we would come to know. This was a Hogan on the ropes.

"I've got to quit," he told Picard. "If I go back on the tour, we don't have the money for her to go with me."

Picard was glad to help.

"I'm not the richest man in the world," he said, "but go ahead and play. If you run out of money, I'll take care of it."

Hogan never took him up on his offer—he played well enough on the West Coast to keep going—"but knowing that help was there if I needed it helped me forget about my troubles," he wrote.

In the early 1940s, Picard was there for him again.

While he had shown some promise, Hogan wasn't close to where he wanted to be. "You told me I was going to be a great player," he said.

"But I hook too much." Picard assured Hogan he could get rid of the hook in five minutes, and that's what he did.

"I just told him to move his left hand to the left; weaken his grip, as we say," he recalled. "That's all there was to it. I said if he could hook it then, I'd eat the golf ball. He said later, 'I can't hook,' and I said, 'That settles it.'"

No wonder Hogan dedicated *Power Golf,* his first instruction book, to Picard.

Picard was there for Sam Snead, as well, helping him land a deal with the Dunlop Company and giving him a driver that made all the difference in the world.

The one he'd been using, Snead said, "was so whippy I had a heullva time controlling my tee shots. But this club was something else. The harder I swung, the straighter it went. That club gave me more control than I'd ever had in my life.... That act of generosity by Henry Picard could never be repaid because that wood was the single greatest discovery I ever made in golf and put me on the road to happy times."

Last, and certainly not least, was Picard's impact, indirectly that is, on a promising youngster in Columbus, Ohio.

His name was Jack Nicklaus.

Grout, who was Nicklaus's longtime teacher, passed on to him the ideas he picked up when working as Picard's assistant for three years at Hershey Country Club in Pennsylvania. "The more people get to thinking about how to swing, they all come up to the same genius," Picard said, referring to Alex Morrison.

*

In the 1939 PGA at Pomonok Country Club in Queens, New York, Picard's opponent in the thirty-six hole final was Byron Nelson, the reigning U.S. Open champion.

Lord Byron was one up heading to the last hole, a short par-4, when Picard hit his approach to about a foot from the pin and, better yet, directly in Nelson's line. Since the Tour was playing stymies back then—golfers weren't allowed to mark their position on the green—that meant Nelson, who was a couple of feet farther away, had to go over or around Picard's ball to get his three.

No chance. The match was all square.

Picard then won it by knocking in a twenty-footer on the first playoff hole.

When he left the tour in the early '40s, he was in his mid-thirties. There would have been time, even after the war, to add a few more victories.

Just no desire.

"I never regretted not playing more," said Picard who passed away at ninety in 1997. "I thought there were other things in life besides golf."

59
Jordan Spieth

I would have thought by now that Jordan Spieth, given what he achieved his first few years on Tour, would be a lot higher in these rankings, maybe even in the top thirty. After all, he won the Masters in 2015 with a record-tying, 18-under 270 at the age of twenty-one. And while he still might get much closer to the top by the time he's finished—give the man a break, he is only thirty-one—his decline proves once more how fleeting success can be in a sport that promises nothing and often delivers a lot less. And *decline,* I'm sorry to say, is the only way to describe it—of his thirteen victories, just two have come since the summer of 2017.

Spieth, to his credit, doesn't deceive himself.

"I think I've put an entire career of ups and downs into ten years," he told me in June 2023. "I accomplished a lot my first five years and not as much in the last five."

I wonder: Did he accomplish *too* much those first five years?

"Once you reach your end goal of something, maybe there is a little bit of a letdown," he acknowledged.

We first took notice in the spring of '10 when Spieth, sixteen, tied for sixteenth at the Byron Nelson tournament. The second multiple winner of the U.S. Junior Amateur—Tiger was the other—Spieth led the University of Texas Longhorns to the 2012 NCAA title in his freshman season and was the number one amateur in the world. All well and good, but the same year, he failed to advance past the second stage of Tour qualifying.

"I didn't make a putt outside of a foot and a half today or the first round, and made maybe three the whole week," he said. "It's extremely disappointing right now."

No matter. In 2013, Spieth, who had earned temporary member status on Tour, captured the John Deere Classic in a five-hole playoff over Zack Johnson and David Hearn to become, at nineteen, the youngest winner since Ralph Guldahl in 1931. (Guldahl, you recall, also lost his way after winning three majors in his twenties. Did I miss something? Did Spieth write an instruction book?)

In 2014, he was up by two at Augusta National through seven holes on Sunday but bogeyed 8 and 9 while Bubba Watson, his playing partner, and the eventual champion, birdied 8 and 9. Spieth didn't make a birdie the rest of the round, tying for second.

He made up for it in 2015.

First, the performance in the Masters. As Woods had said about him: "I think he can be great."

Two months later, Spieth won the U.S. Open at Chambers Bay in Washington.

Granted, he was fortunate—Dustin Johnson three-putted the 72nd hole from twelve feet—but he was also gritty. After a double bogey on number 17 (he had been leading by two), he nailed a three-wood to get home on the par-5 18th, securing the birdie he needed to keep his hopes alive.

Next up was the British Open on the Old Course, where he came within a shot of getting into a playoff with Zach Johnson, Louis Oosthuizen, and Marc Leishman, and then the PGA at Whistling Straits in Wisconsin, in which he finished second by three to Jason Day. With all the attention this century on Tiger Woods and Phil Mickelson, and rightfully so, it's easy to forget that it was Spieth who came the closest to winning the Grand Slam. (Woods won the first two majors in 2002, but finished in a tie for twenty-eighth at the British Open in Muirfield.)

Taking us—drum roll, please—to the final round of the 2016 Masters and the 12th hole.

I have watched what Spieth did at 12 at least a half dozen times,

and I still can't believe it. Up by one—the lead had been five before
he bogeyed 10 and 11 and England's Danny Willett birdied 13 and
14—Spieth hit his tee shot into Rae's Creek. Yet there was no reason
to panic. Get out of there with a 5, and he'd be only a shot back with
13 and 15 still ahead.

Spieth didn't get out of there with a 5.

He got out of there with a 7, sending his third into the creek, as well.

"It was a really tough thirty minutes for me that hopefully I never
experience again," said Spieth, who tied for second, three behind
Willett.

Well, at least he was able to put it behind him.

Spieth won at Colonial a month later and three times in 2017, including the Open at Royal Birkdale, where he did a wonderful imperson-
ation of the erratic, yet heroic, Seve Ballesteros on number 13.

His drive on the par-4 was to the right of Rush Limbaugh, the ball
buried in thick grass on a hill. Suddenly, alarmingly, it was looking
like the 2016 Masters all over again: Was Spieth, who had started the
day three ahead of Matt Kuchar, about to throw away another major?

After declaring an unplayable, he was allowed to take relief on the
driving range since it was considered part of the course and, facing a
blind shot to the green from an estimated 230 yards away, hit a three-
iron short of a pot bunker and got up and down for an all-universe
bogey. If you listened closely enough, you might have heard the dearly
departed Seve applauding from above.

Down by just one—it could have easily been two or more—Spieth
birdied 14, canned a fifty-footer for eagle on 15 and a thirty-footer for
birdie on 16. Heading into 18, he was 2 up. Spieth reached in regulation
while Kuchar found the greenside bunker. As the philosopher Porky
Pig would have put it: *"Th-th-th-that's all, folks!"*

Spieth, twenty-three, became just the second—Nicklaus was the
other—to win three different majors before the age of twenty-four.

The career Grand Slam—all he needed now was the PGA—seemed
to be a good bet.

Not anymore.

Since Royal Birkdale, he is 0-for-28 in majors, with only seven top
tens.

Spieth has had his moments—he closed with a 64 to make a run at the 2018 Masters—but has hit far too many errant shots. And while he has made his share of bombs, he has missed more short ones in recent years than he missed before.

"I lost the DNA of my golf swing and putting stroke to an extent," Spieth admitted, "so, mechanically, I made the game significantly harder."

In the third round of the 2019 PGA at Bethpage Black on Long Island, he was paired in the final group with Brooks Koepka. When he arrived on the 1st tee, it dawned on him:

I have no clue how I'm here right now.

One low point, and there's a lot to choose from, was when Spieth missed the cut at Torrey Pines in 2021 after shooting a 75 on Friday. "I had fear on how much longer I would be able to play the game professionally, to be fair," he said. "If it were like a two-week thing, where I said this was the low, I'd ask you not to feel sorry for me, but that was an all-encompassing three years of really feeling low and that was the low of the low."

A week later, he turned in a 61 during the third round in Phoenix to share the lead with Xander Schauffele but faltered the next day with a 72 to finish in a tie for fourth, two behind Koepka, the winner.

Which sums up the Jordan Spieth that we have seen over the last half decade or so.

No one knows what he will do from round to round. Shot to shot. I assume that includes him.

I hope Fitzgerald was wrong. I hope Spieth will have a second act.

His first act was something else.

58

Nick Price

The Nick Price era didn't last long.

To even call it an era is a stretch. Vardon, Jones, Hogan, Nicklaus, Woods, they had eras.

Price had a run. Yet what a run it was.

There were setbacks along the way, of course, the 1982 British Open at Royal Troon being one of them.

Price birdied 10, 11, and 12 in the final round to go up by three. The engraver who carves the champion's names on the Claret Jug would be at work before too long: *N...I...C...*

Then came number 15, a par-4.

Price, whose lead had been trimmed to two after a bogey at 13, hooked his drive into the rough. Catching a good lie, it appeared he might get away with it. He flushed his four-iron but the ball came out low and hit a ridge, ending up in a pot bunker in front of the green.

"The last place you want to hit it," said Price, who walked away with a double.

He was now tied with Tom Watson, the British Open champion in 1975, 1977, and 1980, who was done for the day. "I didn't fancy my chances having an eighteen-hole playoff with Tom Watson," Price said.

We'll never know.

Price bogeyed 17 and failed to birdie 18, losing by one. Driving to London the next day, he had a meeting of the minds. With himself.

This is going to have a long-term effect on me if I don't handle it correctly. How many people at the age of twenty-five have a chance to win a major championship?

"I couldn't wait to get back to the golf course the next week," he said.

Setback number two: the 1988 British Open at Royal Lytham & St. Annes.

Price was more confident and mature than he had been in 1982. Except he was in a duel down the stretch with Seve Ballesteros. First Watson and now Seve. The golfing gods weren't doing him any favors.

Seve, in pursuit of his fifth major, was in top form, closing with a 65 to prevail by two. "This was a tough one," recalled Price, who fired a 69. "I felt like I had played from tee to green as well as I could."

Once again, he knew how to handle defeat. Seeing Seve perform like a magician around the greens, Price concluded his own short game had been getting short thrift. The extra time he put in paid off, and in August 1992, the Nice Price era—sorry, run—got under way. He captured two PGAs and a British Open, ascending to number one in the world.

Price, who grew up in Rhodesia, now Zimbabwe, was supposed to serve for twelve months in the war between the white government and the black nationalists. After eight weeks of basic training, his tour was upped to eighteen months.

"That was depression like I have never known," Price said.

He was fortunate to make it through those eighteen months. A few of his friends did not.

The casualties included Graham Fanner, who was from the same block and went to kindergarten with Price. A half century later, he still thinks about Graham from time to time. "I wonder where he would be living and what he would have done," he said. "He was a brilliant guy and wanted to be a doctor."

Price had a few close calls himself. He was in the first or second truck of a convoy when the three trucks at the end were attacked. The enemy is supposed to hit the first three trucks to stop the others, not the last three.

"They were inexperienced," he explained.

In 1977, after his tour ended, Price went back to golf.

Nothing came easy there, either.

While competing in the 1978 British Airways Open on the Channel Islands, the pressure was definitely on. "If I didn't make money in that tournament," he said, "I was going home."

He didn't make a fortune—nine hundred pounds, if he's not mistaken—but it was enough to keep him on the road. Later that year, he came in second in the Dutch Open.

"That was a huge week for me," Price said.

Yet his game still wasn't close to where it needed to be. So he reached out to David Leadbetter, the teacher who had done wonders for Denis Watson, another young pro from Zimbabwe. Price had played junior golf with Leadbetter back in the day.

The two got together in the spring of 1982.

"First time I saw my swing broken down, I wanted to throw up," he said.

In 1983, he went wire to wire to defeat Jack Nicklaus by four in the World Series of Golf at Firestone and three years later, shot a record 63 in the third round of the Masters. (Price closed with a 71 to finish fifth.)

In 1991, he won the Byron Nelson tournament. On a scale of 1 to

10, his play from tee to green was maybe a 6. His short game was close to a 10.

"I won in a totally foreign way to any other way that I had won before," Price said.

A few months later, he skipped the PGA at Crooked Stick Golf Club in Indiana to be home for the birth of his first child, Gregory, opening up a spot for an alternate by the name of John Daly. As Price watched Daly turn into golf's new folk hero, he became concerned. His regular caddie, Jeff "Squeaky" Medlen, was carrying the bag.

"I didn't want him to jump ship," Price explained.

The phone rang a couple of hours after Daly won the tournament.

"Don't worry, Nick," Squeaky told him. "I'm staying with you. I had a great week with Daly but you and I have a great thing going."

It was about to become even greater.

In the 1992 PGA at Bellerive Country Club outside St. Louis, Price, who recorded pars on the first eleven holes, knocked in a thirty-footer for a birdie on 16 and a fifteen-footer to save par on 17, and wound up winning by three.

"All the planets were aligned for me that week and I knew it," he said.

They were aligned, as well, in the 1994 British Open at Turnberry in Scotland.

With two holes to go, Price trailed Sweden's Jesper Parnevik by two.

In all likelihood, he needed to birdie 17, a reachable par-5, to have a chance. His second shot from over 200 yards ended up about fifty feet from the pin. The putt for eagle started on a wonderful line but hit a spike mark a couple of feet from the hole.

A spike mark? Are you kidding me?

Just then, it slipped into the hole, tying him for the lead.

Or so he assumed.

As Price walked off the green, he saw that Parnevik had bogeyed 18. Wrongly believing he needed a birdie to win, Parnevik had gone for the flag instead of the middle of the green and paid—excuse the pun—the price when his ball ended up in the rough and he was unable to escape with a par.

"I walked as slow as I possibly could to the next tee to get my heart rate down," Price recalled.

He was so pumped up that he nailed a three-iron on 18 about 265 yards. He normally hit the club about two hundred. The fairways were fast, and the hole was playing downhill. Even so. He then knocked his approach to about thirty feet from the flag.

Two putts later, the Claret Jug was his. At last.

"I had climbed the mountain," he said.

One month later, Price, who would end up with eighteen Tour victories, went wire to wire in the PGA at Southern Hills to beat Corey Pavin by six.

His era was at its peak.

I mean, run.

57

Betsy Rawls

Betsy Rawls, who graduated Phi Beta Kappa from the University of Texas, would have been a physicist.

If it hadn't been for that other calling.

She was seventeen when her dad took her to the course for the first time.

"I immediately got hooked," said Rawls, who grew up in Burnet, a small town in Texas, "but I knew nothing about golf. The only name I knew was [future Hall of Famer] Betty Jameson because she lived right down the road in San Antonio, and I used to see news about Betty in the paper. I didn't know what to expect. I just started playing and loved it."

So in 1951, when the Wilson Sporting Goods Company asked her to join its staff to give clinics and play in exhibitions around the country, Rawls didn't require much convincing.

"I considered the offer carefully and decided that golf would be more interesting than physics," she said.

Her timing couldn't have been better.

The LPGA tour was just getting off the ground. The money wasn't great—the average purse, according to Rawls, was "$3,000, perhaps $4,000"—and wouldn't be great for a long time. Thank goodness for the folks at Wilson, who gave her a salary of about $3,000 and took care of any expenses.

As an amateur, Rawls, who took lessons from Harvey Penick, had captured the the Austin City Championship, the Texas Women's Amateur, and other important events. Once she turned pro, she won fifty-five times, including four U.S. Opens (her first as a rookie in 1951 by five over Louise Suggs) a record she shares with Mickey Wright, and eight majors overall. (In the 1957 Open, Rawls was awarded the title after Jackie Pung was disqualified for signing an incorrect scorecard.)

"I studied a lot," she said, "and that helped my concentration. Maybe it helps to have a very controlled, logical sort of mind to play golf."

It also helped to possess a superb short game.

In the 1960s, Rawls was paired one day with Donna Caponi. The other players told Caponi, an eventual four-time major winner, that Rawls could get up and down from anywhere. "She hit it all over the place and shot 68," Caponi said. "I hit every fairway and every green and shot 72. I was in the locker room with a bunch of the girls afterwards and said, 'You guys are right.'"

In 1952, when she won the tour event in Houston, Humphrey Bogart handed her the trophy.

"He took me in his arms, bent me back and gave me a big kiss," Rawls said. Bogart and Ingrid Bergman would always have Paris— sorry, I couldn't resist; *Casablanca* is my favorite film—but Bogart and Rawls would always have Houston.

In 1959, she became the first female golfer with ten victories in a season, in just twenty-six appearances, and earned nearly $27,000, thanks to a discovery she made after getting off to a disappointing start.

"I realized that many of my high scores were due to my giving up during a bad round," she said. "A couple of putts would jump out of the hole, and I'd get mad and start feeling sorry for myself. I'd figure it wasn't worth the effort to try to come back with a fairly good score." From then on, however, she said, "I would concentrate on every shot and try to play each one as best I could."

She won the Lake Worth Open by a stroke over Suggs and posted three victories, three seconds, and a fourth in her next seven tournaments. Not until 1966 did she go an entire season without a win. Her last triumph came at the GAC Classic in 1972.

In the summer of 2022, I reached out to Rawls, who was ninety-four at the time. (Janet Davis, a close friend for nearly forty years, emailed Rawls's responses to me.)

What were your first impressions of Harvey Penick?

"I liked him immediately," Rawls answered. "He was soft-spoken and very gentlemanly."

Penick sent Rawls a three-word telegram prior to her eighteen-hole playoff victory over Pung in the 1953 U.S. Women's Open at the Country Club of Rochester:

Take dead aim.

Rawls did just that, firing a 71 to defeat Pung by six.

Penick charged $3 for the first lesson but not a dime for any lessons after that. "The way I look at it," he wrote, "I was the one who got the bargain. To have a chance to teach a pupil with the brains and talent and charm of Betsy Rawls is a joy. I feel I have learned more from her than she has from me."

What were the most important lessons he taught you?

"The fundamentals of the golf swing starting with the grip," Rawls said, "and the proper stance and set up to the ball. He was not a psychologist. He stuck mainly to golf and trusted me to know the rest."

What did you think when you attended a clinic Byron Nelson gave in Fort Worth?

"It opened my eyes," she replied, "to how far a person could hit the golf ball and keep it under control."

In 1951, Rawls, along with Babe Didrikson Zaharias, Patty Berg, and others stunned the members of the British Walker Cup team at the Wentworth Club in England in a friendly—perhaps not so friendly—exhibition, winning all six singles matches after losing in the morning four-balls.

From the same tees!

"They stormed off the course," she said, "and didn't take their loss gracefully."

Rawls, who retired in 1975 and became the LPGA's tournament director, wasn't resentful when the purses grew to amounts she and her peers in the 1950s and '60s could never have ever imagined. "That's not why I played, for the money," Rawls said. "If it was a lot of money I was after, I probably would have done something else."

56

Lanny Wadkins

The numbers are impressive: twenty-one Tour victories, including the 1977 PGA at Pebble Beach, the 1979 Players Championship, the 1982 and 1983 Tournament of Champions, and two L.A. Opens. As well as the 1970 U.S. Amateur.

The numbers, however, do not tell the whole story. They never do.

They do not tell us about the man himself. Lanny Wadkins was afraid of no one, and I mean no one.

Take when he and Mark O'Meara battled Seve Ballesteros and Manuel Piñero in a four-ball match during the 1985 Ryder Cup at the Belfry in England. On the 1st hole, Wadkins had a birdie putt of about twenty feet. Since Seve's coin was in his line about ten feet ahead, he asked him to move it to the left.

No problem.

The ball hit the coin, veered to the right, and fell into the cup.

Big problem.

"You had me move that coin so you could make the putt," Seve charged.

"Yeah, I'm that fucking good," Wadkins fired back. "Don't forget it."

O'Meara, participating in his first Ryder Cup, couldn't believe it. "You just told Seve to basically fuck off," he said, as Wadkins remembers it.

"Yeah, I did."

He and O'Meara won the match, 3 and 2.

The toughness can be traced to his upbringing in Richmond, Virginia. Wadkins and his younger brother, Bobby, a future Tour pro, as well, competed against each other in every sport imaginable, neither conceding an inch.

That went for their old man, too.

"We had a Ping-Pong table in the basement, and there's no way in hell he was going to let me or Bobby beat him," Wadkins said. "He was going to kick our ass."

Wadkins planned to turn pro after a few months at Wake Forest.

Until his father set him straight.

"Get your ass back out there," he said.

Good thing he did.

In his sophomore year, Wadkins, the recipient of an Arnold Palmer scholarship—the King went to Wake in the late '40s and early '50s—finished first or second over and over. In the 1970 U.S. Amateur at Waverly Country Club in Portland, he edged Tom Kite by one. The amateur was a stroke-play event in those days.

The same year, Wadkins came in second in the Tour event at Hilton Head. Paired with Palmer in the final round, he had a chance to win until he made a double on 11. The following June, he tied for 13th in the U.S. Open at Merion.

With nothing else to prove, he skipped his senior year and turned pro.

His father didn't try to stop him this time.

In his rookie season, Wadkins beat Palmer by a shot at the Sahara Invitational in Las Vegas for his first Tour victory. The King brought out the best in him.

"He wasn't happy," Wadkins recalled. "I cost him a win and I was still supposed to be in school."

He won twice more in 1973 but wasn't the same player in 1974.

"It was a horrendous experience," said Wadkins, who lost more than thirty yards off the tee. "I'd never played badly in my life until then. I didn't know golf was so hard. I went from long and straight to short and crooked." One morning, at a tournament in Orlando, he woke up in so much pain he couldn't move. Over an hour went by before he could get out of bed.

The trouble was with his gallbladder. It would have to come out. So would his appendix.

Wadkins came back too soon, and that made the situation worse. He didn't win for four years, falling from fifth on the money list in 1973 to eighty-eighth in 1975.

He finally regained his old form in 1977:

Second in Los Angeles. Fourth in Miami. Second in Houston. Fourth in Atlanta. Sixth in Charlotte.

Setting the stage for the PGA at Pebble.

Wadkins took part in his usual money games early in the week: he and Arnold Palmer against Ed Sneed and Tom Weiskopf. "Everyone who played the money games back in the day," Wadkins pointed out, "we all seemed to play pretty damn well in tournaments."

Still, it looked like he'd come up short. Gene Littler, forty-seven, who had made quite a comeback of his own—he had a tumor removed from his left arm in 1972—was up by five with nine holes to go. He promptly bogeyed 10, 12, 13, 14, and 15.

When Littler was in command, Wadkins was rooting for him.

"My goal at that point," he explained, "was to finish in the top eight because that would get me in the Masters the next year."

Once Littler began to stumble, the goal changed.

"Littler was a nice man," Wadkins said, "but when it's me and you, nice goes out the window."

After a clutch birdie on 18, when he hit a wedge from ninety-two yards to within tap-in range, he was tied with Littler and one stroke ahead of Jack Nicklaus.

Nicklaus, as Wadkins recalled, lined up a birdie putt on 18 between fifteen and twenty feet.

"I didn't want Jack to make his putt," he said. "That would mean I would have to play Jack eighteen holes the next day at Pebble Beach and I didn't see that going really well. Jack had already won two majors [the 1961 U.S. Amateur and 1972 U.S. Open] there." (Wadkins was mistaken. A playoff in the PGA was sudden death, not eighteen holes.)

Nicklaus missed.

Still, there would be a playoff. With Littler.

Wadkins hooked his approach on the first extra hole—number 1 at Pebble—into the rough, which left him, eventually, with a downhill, double-breaking putt from about fifteen feet to stay alive.

It went in.

Littler was amazed.

"He could go out there again," he said, "and drop 30 or 40 balls and never make one."

They matched birdies on number 2 before Wadkins put Littler away with a four-footer on the 3rd.

The comeback was complete, and I'm not referring to Wadkins beating Littler. I'm referring to Wadkins again being the player he was before. "I don't think anybody gave me anything," he said. "I was on my own, figuring it out myself."

The same mentality also held him back, however. Wadkins took a few lessons with short-game expert Phil Rodgers, which led to three victories in 1982, but didn't stick with it. "I should have been working with Phil two times a year putting," he confessed. "Another set of eyes would have been invaluable. No question the biggest mistake I ever made."

He wasn't a poor putter. You don't win twenty-one tournaments unless you make your share. He just wasn't consistent enough.

"I had nine top threes in majors," he told me. "I could have put a couple of more over the line and I fault putting."

Maybe so, but the game today could use more players like Lanny Wadkins.

Who play fast. And go right at the flag.

"I probably cost myself some events by being too aggressive," he said, "but at the same time, I had a blast doing it. When I pulled it off, there was nothing better."

55

Peter Thomson

Each of the five Claret Jugs that Peter Thomson walked away with in the 1950s and '60s meant a lot to him.

Perhaps most of all the one he picked up at Royal Birkdale in 1965.

"I look upon my five wins like my children," said Thomson, an Australian native, who prevailed by two over Brian Huggett and Christy O'Connor Sr. "I love them all equally. But 1965 was slightly different. The championship was getting more worldly."

It sure was and that was because of Arnold Palmer, the game's biggest star, who came to play in the United Kingdom for the first time in 1960 and won the British Open in 1961 and 1962. Others soon followed.

Even so, I don't care who was in the field before Palmer and more top players arrived.

To win five Opens—only Harry Vardon, remember, with six, has more—while coping with the usual uncertainties (bad weather, bad bounces, etc.) in links golf proved what an exceptional player Thomson was.

For his time. For any time.

He started out at age twelve when his grandfather handed him some used clubs.

Within three years, he was the club champion at Royal Park, a nine-hole course across the road from his home in West Brunswick.

"I found out I got a great thrill out of winning," he said of his triumph at Royal Park. "The taste of it is without a doubt what kept me going all my life."

In 1950, Thomson, who was now a pro, headed to America, where the best players were.

He wasn't one of them.

Thomson shot an 80 at Cypress Point in the first round of the Crosby tournament, finishing in a tie for thirty-second, and tied for twenty-sixth two weeks later in Phoenix. "I realized the standard I had to attain to survive," he said, "and I was well aware I was not at that standard."

He kept plugging away, and in the summer of 1951 played in his first British Open at Royal Portrush Golf Club in Northern Ireland.

Thomson was taking a big gamble.

"When I first left Australia," he said, "I invested all my savings. I had a bit of help from a sporting manufacturer, but there was no question about it. I had to win enough money myself or I couldn't afford the fare to come home."

The gamble was worth every penny. Thomson tied for sixth, eight behind the winner, Max Faulkner. He had the fare to come home, and the talent to take off.

In the 1952 Open at Royal Lytham & St. Annes, Thomson came in second by a shot to South Africa's Bobby Locke, who'd wind up with four Claret Jugs of his own. The two played more than two hundred exhibition matches against each other over the years, Locke having his way—he won eleven of the first fourteen—until Thomson made some adjustments.

"I had known that golf was a psychological game," he said, "but up until then I had no idea just how much the mind came into play. I was trying to out-drive, out-approach, and out-putt him, while he just stood back and watched me defeat myself. At that stage I took up a new attitude and relaxed and tried nothing except to keep out of the trees and stick to par. I struck oil. . . . When I refused to take risks, Locke instinctively did so himself, and that was when I began to beat him."

In 1953, Thomson fared much better in the States, tying for fourth in the Pan American Open and tying for twelfth in the Western Open. In the Open at Carnoustie, he tied for second, four behind Ben Hogan. The next year at Birkdale, using Cecil Timms, Hogan's caddie in '53, Thomson won by one over Locke and two others.

The shot that saved him came on number 16 during the final round. His ball on a steep slope in the bunker about twenty-five yards from the flag, Thomson hit it to within a few inches.

"Had I made a mess of that one," he admitted, "I'd have been a goner."

He walked off with the Claret Jug again in 1955 at St. Andrews and in 1956 at Royal Liverpool to become the first to win three Opens in a row since Bob Ferguson in 1882.

One can make the argument it should have been four in a row.

In 1957, Locke, who beat Thomson by three on the Old Course, forgot to move his ball marker back to its original position on the 72nd hole—it had been in his playing partner's line—but the Royal and Ancient Golf Club of St. Andrews, the ruling body, which didn't learn about the error till sometime later, decided that "with his three-shot lead and no advantage having been gained, the equity and spirit of the game dictated that [Locke] should not be disqualified."

However, an article in *The Guardian*, a British newspaper, pointed out a half century later that Locke should have been disqualified for signing an incorrect scorecard.

In any case, Peter Thomson didn't just win golf tournaments. He covered them, too.

"After winning a tour event it would be common to see him accept the trophy," wrote Jerry Tarde of *Golf Digest*, "then go into the press tent and roll a piece of paper into a typewriter carriage and proceed to rap out a report on the final round as the golf correspondent to far-flung newspapers." Thomson enjoyed the writing process. "As a young man," he said, "it was something to fall back on if the golf didn't work out."

The knock on Thomson, and it's a fair one, was his failure to perform better on U.S. soil. He compiled his share of top tens but just one victory, the Texas International Open in 1956. Sorry, winning nine times on the Senior tour in 1985 doesn't count.

Bruce Devlin, a fellow Aussie and an eight-time winner on Tour, believes Thomson should have played more in America.

"He was the straightest player I ever saw," Devlin said. "I can't imagine that if he had spent the time over here that he did in Asia and Europe that he wouldn't have won more tournaments in the States."

Thomson had his reasons. On his first couple of visits, he felt there were "a lot of really, poor, second-class layouts," and that "everything cost about twice what it cost in Australia." By the early 1960s, he was busy helping launch a new tour in Asia. He also got heavily involved in the design business, building more than one hundred and eighty courses in thirty countries.

"[Thomson] was the greatest links player of the modern era," Tom Watson said, "and quite possibly the greatest links player in the history of the game."

54

Hale Irwin

No one was more competitive than Hale Irwin.

Not Tiger Woods. Not Jack Nicklaus. Not Ben Hogan.

Not even Pete Rose.

Strike that, maybe Pete Rose. Who else would knock over the catcher at home plate . . . in an All-Star Game? (In 1970, Rose crashed into Ray Fosse, who injured his shoulder and would never be the same player again.)

I'll give you two examples:

Number 1

In the early 1970s, Irwin was paired with Jim Colbert in the first round of the Jackie Gleason event in Florida. (God, I miss when tournaments were affiliated with celebrities, not corporations, and players didn't cover every inch of their clothing with one sponsor or another.)

On one hole, Colbert, with a bunch of trees between him and the putting surface, figured he didn't have a prayer of getting on in regulation. Somehow he pulled it off, the ball hitting the top of a hill and rolling down to less than a foot from the pin.

"You could give me a thousand balls," he told me, "and I couldn't do that again."

Even so, the shot itself was not what blew him away. It was Irwin's reaction.

"He had a long iron he was going to hit and just slammed the face into the fairway, the shaft bouncing up and down, up and down," Colbert recalled. "He's got his hands on his hips, staring at the highway. He was so pissed."

Number 2

Irwin, Mark O'Meara, and Seve Ballesteros were paired together for the first two rounds of the 1980 U.S. Open at Baltusrol. On Day Two, as Irwin and O'Meara prepared to tee off, there was no Seve. He thought his starting time was an hour later.

"Mark, did you see Seve on the range?" Irwin asked.

"No," O'Meara responded.

"Let me tell you how this works," Irwin explained. "When they call our names, I hit, and you hit and we're off. And when we get down there, we hit our second shots as fast as we can."

"Why is that?" O'Meara wondered.

"As soon as we tee off and [Ballesteros] doesn't show up, that's a two-shot penalty on him. As soon as we hit our second shots, he's DQ'ed [disqualified], and that's one less guy I've got to worry about."

Some may have been put off by his intensity—he didn't talk much on the course—but that's who he was.

"Am I going to go out and suddenly start changing how I play?" he once said. "Am I going to start lavishing all this friendly warmth upon everybody? No."

Here's a quote I love from Irwin that says it all:

"I feel alive when I'm competing."

I brought the issue up when we spoke last year. A few months shy of his seventy-ninth birthday, he sounded like the same Irwin I covered in the 1990s.

"It was never [about] somebody else," he said. "It was always me playing against me."

*

When he was four, he tagged along with his father on a nine-hole sand-greens course in Baxter Springs, Kansas, close to the borders of Missouri and Oklahoma. "Dad would cut down clubs for me and I'd find balls," he recalled. "Or he'd give me a ball or two. Man, those would last me forever."

Playing by himself, he learned to work things out on his own and that would be the case his whole career.

Dr. Deborah Graham, a psychologist who was counseling Tour pros, went to see him.

Not to give pointers. To get pointers to give to others.

"At this level, it's not about hitting the golf ball," Irwin said. "Everyone can do that. It's about the conversation between your mind and your heart. What can you do? What can't you do? And how do you accept those challenges?"

Irwin knew he'd never hit the ball like Jack Nicklaus but perhaps he "could prepare like Jack." Which was the same mindset he had as a defensive back for the University of Colorado, twice named to the All–Big Eight team. "I wasn't the fastest player on the field," he said, "and I certainly wasn't the biggest. But no one would try harder."

Or be more intense.

"He loved to dart up and crack a ball-carrier head-on at the line of scrimmage," recalled his teammate, ex–Miami Dolphins defensive back Dick Anderson. "He could have made it in the pros." Perhaps, but his heart wasn't in football. It was in golf, and winning the 1967 NCAA championship "was the catalyst to make that final step" toward being a professional.

The decision paid off, Irwin notching his first two victories at Harbour Town, one of the toughest tracks on Tour, in 1971 and 1973.

The toughest courses brought out the best in him.

Take the 1974 U.S. Open at Winged Foot Golf Club, about thirty miles from New York City. This was no ordinary Open. This was *The Massacre at Winged Foot* (the title of Dick Schaap's book about the tournament).

Blame Johnny Miller, who closed with an eight-under 63 the year before to win the Open at Oakmont. The USGA, many believe, made the fairways more narrow and the rough deeper to ensure no one shot a 63 this time. On Day One, there were forty-four rounds in the 80s and not one in the 60s. Irwin prevailed by two with a near-record-high total of seven-over 287.

The tournament wasn't over until he nailed a two-iron to within twenty feet of the pin on 18.

"I'd never won a major championship or even seriously contended in one," Irwin said. "When you hit a shot like that to seal the deal, you feel pretty darn good about it, and the feeling lasts."

Speaking of shots to remember, nothing in his career tops the putt he made in the 1990 Open at Medinah.

And what he did after he made it.

Irwin, forty-five, hadn't won in five years, and because he didn't qualify, he needed a special exemption from the USGA. "That was important to me," he recalled. "My first thought: 'I want to make their pick look good. I want to play well.'"

He played well the first three rounds but was still five back after nine holes on Sunday.

"I was focused on getting into the top fifteen to be exempt for next year," he said.

A birdie at 11. Another at 12 ... 13 ... 14.

He was now focused on this year.

On 18, he hit an approach that left him forty-five feet from the hole. Bingo.

After making the putt, Irwin, not known for showing emotion, jogged around the edge of the gallery, high-fiving fans and blowing kisses.

Who is this guy? And what has he done with the real Hale Irwin?

"People thought that was a little out of character for me," Irwin acknowledged. "The fact is, when I'm excited or on the go, my instinct is to run. I grew up running everywhere I went—to the golf course, to baseball, basketball and football practice; to the library and school. Everywhere."

The following day, he knocked in a ten-footer on the 19th playoff hole to beat Mike Donald and become the oldest Open winner in history.

"On putts like that, you have to eliminate the do or die," Irwin said. "It can't be that momentous. Even though it is. But you have to convince yourself it's not."

The only negative thing I can say about the man—you knew I'd find something—is that he didn't win any majors besides his three Opens. (The other Open was at Inverness in 1979, when he prevailed by two over Gary Player and Jerry Pate.)

He had an excellent chance in the 1983 British Open at Royal Birkdale but finished a stroke behind Tom Watson. Irwin had only himself to blame. In the third round, after missing a putt on 14, he whiffed on the next one when trying to backhand it from three inches away.

I'm not kidding. Whiffed.

"I've tapped in that way hundreds of times," he said. "I think the putter hit the ground and sort of bounced over the ball. I really don't know what happened."

In 1960, Irwin, fifteen, went to a practice round of the U.S. Open at Cherry Hills, the first golf tournament he attended in person.

He was blown away when he saw Ben Hogan drop a bag of new balls onto the driving range.

The only balls Irwin had ever used were the ones he found in the lakes or weeds, and they were usually stained and cut.

"It showed me that there was another world out there," he said.

53

Julius Boros

In the spring of 1948, Julius Boros played in the North and South Open at Pinehurst. The North and South was a big deal in those days, the field including Sam Snead, who was still in his prime.

Boros was not in his prime.

He was not a golfer, period. He was an accountant for a trucking company in Connecticut.

Boros, who had led his high school team to the state championship, made a fine accounting of himself, tying Snead for second place.

It wasn't the first time he had proven himself against top players. In

1947, he had won the Shoreline Open, a twenty-seven-hole event in Stratford, Connecticut, defeating, among others, future Hall of Famers Gene Sarazen and Tommy Armour.

After his success in North Carolina, Boros went back to his day job. His parents, Lance and Elizabeth, had immigrated to America from Hungary around 1910. Having steady work meant everything.

Even so, in December 1949, a few months after he had made it to the quarterfinals of the U.S. Amateur, Boros, twenty-nine, realized the time had come to give the Tour a try.

His mother wasn't crazy about the idea.

"You'll starve," she warned him. "Stick with your accounting."

Good thing he didn't.

Boros, known as "Big Jay" or "The Moose"—he stood six feet tall and weighed 210 pounds—was a top contender for well over a decade, finishing with eighteen victories. Prior to Phil Mickelson's triumph in the 2021 PGA, Boros, at forty-eight, was the oldest to win a professional major: the 1968 PGA at Pecan Valley Golf Club in San Antonio.

In late 1949, he married Ann "Buttons" Cosgrove. They met the week he tied Snead for second at the North and South. In 1951, Buttons, an accomplished golfer herself—she won the Massachusetts State Championship the year before—gave birth to a son, Jay Nicholas.

The future couldn't have been brighter.

Two days later, Buttons died from a cerebral hemorrhage. She was twenty-three.

Word is Boros was so overwhelmed with grief that he thought about putting his clubs away for good; he returned to the Tour after four months.

In 1952, he was in the field at Northwood Country Club in Dallas, though all eyes were on Ben Hogan, who was attempting to become the first to win three U.S. Opens in a row since Willie Anderson in 1905. Hogan shot back-to-back 69s and was up by two at the halfway mark.

Who was going to stop him? A former accountant from Connecticut?

Yep, that's exactly who.

Boros, who had finished ninth in the Open at Merion in 1950 and tied for fourth at Oakland Hills in 1951, went 68-71 in near one-hundred-degree temperatures to prevail by four, his first victory as a pro. Hogan finished third, five back.

"This was for Buttons and the boy," said Boros, who was the leading money winner in 1952, earning about $37,000.

I am happy to tell you he found love again. In 1955, he married Armen Boyle, a flight attendant. The couple had six children. Their youngest son, Guy, won the Greater Vancouver Open in 1996.

As for the 1968 PGA and the other major Julius Boros won, the 1963 U.S. Open in Brookline, they had something in common.

In both cases, he took down a legend.

Make that a king.

In the 1963 Open, he fired a one-under 70—one of only six rounds below par the whole week—to outduel the King, Arnold Palmer (76), and Jacky Cupit (73) in an eighteen-hole playoff. Boros should have been out of contention after turning in a 76 in Saturday's morning round, but with gusts of nearly forty-five knots and unforgiving rough, no one ran away with it.

"It was the most difficult wind I have ever played in," Palmer said.

In the afternoon, thanks to birdies on 16 and 17 and a critical six-footer to save par on 18, Boros rebounded with a 72 to put him in the playoff.

For Boros to beat Palmer, who was at the height of his powers, was as good as it gets. He said he was "pretty nervous during that playoff, although I may not always show it. But I'm human like everyone else. I guess it's just that my personality makeup is a little different than other people's."

You can say that again.

Good shot or bad shot, his demeanor didn't change. He came across, as one writer put it, "as if his main problem was just staying awake until the end of the afternoon." He took a while to get to his ball, walking well behind the other members of his group, but once he got there, he didn't take a practice swing. He just let it rip. "By the time you get to your ball," Boros said, "if you don't know what to do with it, try another sport."

In the final round of the 1968 PGA, about ten guys had a chance, including Palmer, who needed the title to join Hogan, Gary Player, and Gene Sarazen as the only players to achieve the career Grand Slam. On 18, Palmer, trailing Boros by a stroke, hit his approach from 230 yards to within eight feet.

Arnie's Army was ecstatic.

Until he missed the putt.

It wasn't over yet. After his second shot ended up thirty yards from the green on 18, Boros had to get up and down to avoid a playoff with Palmer. No problem. He hit a low pitch to about three feet from the hole and knocked it in.

Dan Jenkins of *Sports Illustrated* put it best:

"A middle-aged man struck a marvelous blow for tired, portly, beer-drinking, slow-moving fathers of seven."

52

Lawson Little Jr.

Lawson Little Jr. has been overlooked long enough.

He won both the British Amateur and U.S. Amateur in back-to-back years (1934, 1935)—the Little Slam, they called it—which no one else has ever done.

Not even Bobby Jones.

Little was victorious in thirty-two straight matches—thirty-six if you count, and there's no reason not to, his win as a professional at the San Francisco Open, a match play event in 1937.

Tiger Who?

Little, who went to Stanford—he was a teammate of Charlie Seaver, the father of Tom, the future Hall of Fame pitcher—captured the Northern California Amateur in 1928. In his first U.S Amateur in 1929, held at Pebble Beach, he knocked off Johnny Goodman, who had defeated Jones in a morning match, to make it all the way to the quarters.

In 1933, Little fell in the semifinals of the Amateur to George Dunlap Jr. 4 and 3 but earned a spot in the the Walker Cup the following year at St. Andrews, where he teamed with Goodman in the foursomes to defeat the formidable English duo of Roger Wethered and Cyril Tolley, 8 and 6. He beat Tolley in the singles, as well, 6 and 5.

The British Amateur at Prestwick was next.

Little was at the top of his game, winning all except one of his first seven matches rather handily.

In the thirty-six-hole final, which Bernard Darwin described as "one of the most terrific exhibitions in all golfing history," Little demolished Scotland's James Wallace, 14 and 13. (The last Wallace to be so thoroughly conquered in these parts, also a Scot, was Sir William Wallace of *Braveheart* fame, portrayed by Mel Gibson, who was hanged, drawn, quartered, and beheaded for treason in 1305. If you ask me, James Wallace got off pretty easy.)

A few months later, in the U.S. Amateur at Brookline, Little took care of David Goldman in the final, 8 and 7. Little didn't have a weakness. He was long off the tee—his nickname was "Cannonball"—accurate in his approaches, and more than efficient around the greens.

As well as an expert in course management.

"It's all mental," he explained. "The man who doesn't plan out every shot to the very top of his capacity for thought can't attain championship form. I say this without any reservations whatsoever. It is impossible to outplay an opponent you can't outthink."

When Little successfully defended his title in 1935 at the Country Club in Cleveland, defeating Walter Emery 4 and 2, Jones said it was the best he'd ever seen anyone play in an amateur competition. Little, who had put away Dr. William Tweddell, a former champion, in the final of the British Amateur one up, joined Jones as the only golfers to receive the Sullivan Award as the top amateur athlete in America.

Little, who carried as many as twenty-six clubs—some claim it was because of him that the USGA reduced the maximum to fourteen—turned pro a year later and didn't waste any time, winning the Canadian Open by eight strokes. He picked up two more victories in 1937 and finished his career with eight, including the 1940 U.S. Open at Canterbury.

In the Open, Little was in a duel with Gene Sarazen, who went two under on the back nine to force an eighteen-hole playoff the next day. After Little seized a four-shot lead, Sarazen cut the deficit to one with six holes remaining.

Little didn't blink, sealing the deal with birdies on 15 and 16.

Too bad the rest of the decade didn't proceed as smoothly.

First came the war, Little serving as a lieutenant colonel in the navy. Then a heart attack.

I wonder what his record would have been if he hadn't gone on three six-month exhibition tours across the country on behalf of the Spalding Company in the late 1930s with fellow pros Harry Cooper, Horton Smith and Jimmy Thomson. They played eighteen-hole matches and gave clinics.

Throw in the Tour events he played during that time he logged an estimated three hundred thousand miles and walked another four thousand.

And I thought Gary Player did a ton of traveling.

"It was quite a grind," Cooper said. "We spent as many as thirty straight nights on sleeper cars."

In 1948, Little beat Bobby Locke by three in St. Petersburg, Florida, for his final Tour victory, but will be remembered for what he did as an amateur.

"Lawson Little had everything a great match-player needed: golf, guts, stamina, a contempt for the breaks, an unquestioning belief in his ability to beat any other amateur golfer," wrote Herbert Warren Wind. "He was always the aggressor, tirelessly stalking his opponent, measuring him, hitting him where it hurt the most, and finally putting him away."

51
James Braid

The first Big Three wasn't Arnold Palmer, Jack Nicklaus, and Gary Player.

Nor, it may surprise you, was it Ben Hogan, Sam Snead, and Byron Nelson.

The first Big Three, referred to as *The Great Triumvirate*—they won sixteen of twenty-one British Opens from 1894 through 1914—was comprised of Harry Vardon, John Henry Taylor, and James Braid. The oldest of the three Brits by a few months was Braid, with five Claret

Jugs from 1901 through 1910. The five Opens he didn't win during that stretch, he came in second three times and fifth twice.

Braid, who stood six feet two and weighed 195 pounds, hit the ball a long way, was precise with his irons and a very good putter. "I have yet to meet the player," Taylor said, "who could hole the 10-yard putts with greater regularity than Braid."

That hadn't always been the case.

"His short putts at St. Andrews in the 1900 Open were enough to make the angels weep," suggested English golf writer Harry Everard. Enough for Braid, as well, who switched from a wooden-headed putter to an aluminum-headed one.

Which was when the putts began to drop.

Born in Earlsferry, Scotland, he had to overcome a father who saw no future in hitting a little white ball, chasing it, and hitting it again. His mother was no fan, either. Yet Braid wasn't deterred. When he was nine years old, he got a chance to watch his hero, Jamie Anderson, a three-time Open champion, play a match in a nearby town.

Anderson, aware of the boy's excitement, asked him to take a swing. Then a few more.

"He patted me on the shoulder," Braid recalled, "and told me to go in for as much golf as I could, and practise as thoroughly as possible, and that if I did that, I should be Open Champion myself one day."

By the time he was fifteen, he was a scratch player. After living for a while in St. Andrews and Edinburgh, he got a job as a club maker at the Army and Navy Store in London, working on his game as often as he could.

In 1896, he became the pro at Romford Golf Club, replacing the course designer, George McIntosh. His career as an architect—a fan of doglegs, he designed the Kings Course at Gleneagles in England— was off and running.

So was his playing career.

In 1897, he finished second in the Open at Royal Liverpool, losing by one to Harold Hilton. At 18, after coming within a foot of the hole on his approach, he missed a twenty-footer for the tie. Braid tied for fifth in 1899 and came in third in 1900 before breaking through at Muirfield in 1901.

The week didn't start out very well. Braid hit his tee shot out of bounds on number 1 and almost went OB again on 2 on his way to a 43 on the front nine. He rebounded, however, with a 36 on the back for a solid 79.

Harry Vardon, meanwhile, going for his fourth title, opened with a 77 to lead by one over Willie Park Jr. and two over Braid, Taylor, and James Kinnell. A 76 lifted Braid into a tie with Vardon at the halfway mark. No one else was within six.

In the end, Braid won by three, though it was a rather unusual finish.

The shaft of his club broke on his approach to the green, the head sailing toward the clubhouse. *Fore!* The ball still traveled more than two hundred yards, and Braid was able to secure a 4—and his place in history.

In 1908, he posted a record score of 291 at Prestwick that wouldn't be matched until Bobby Jones in 1926. Braid found a little trouble in round three—he made an 8 on number 3 and let another shot slip away on the 4th—but regained his form to prevail by eight. "When he had holed out," *The Guardian* reported, "there was a frantic outburst of joy by the enthusiastic Scots, who carried him shoulder high to the clubhouse."

Braid, according to Bernard Darwin, possessed "essentially a full swing, and in his earlier days, a most dashing one, with a very loose knee at the finish of the shot when he really went out for it."

And was sharp between the ears, as well.

"He plays all the time with his head, thinking out every shot, not only as he stands over the ball but while he is walking towards it," wrote Andra Kirkaldy, the St. Andrews pro who was a three-time runner-up in the Open.

Baird, forty, claimed his final Claret Jug in 1910 on the Old Course by four strokes over Scotland's Sandy Herd. He tied for fifth in the 1911 Open at Royal St. George's, two behind Vardon, and came in third in 1912.

"There could not be a cooler or better-tempered golfer than James Braid," Kirkaldy wrote. "...He is never beaten till he cannot win."

50

Paul Runyan

Paul Runyan, aka "Little Poison," was a 10–1 underdog when he took on Sam Snead in the final match of the 1938 PGA at Shawnee Country Club in Northeastern Pennsylvania.

Snead could hit the ball to Philadelphia. Runyan couldn't hit it out of his own shadow.

"On the drives, Runyan would be so far behind I'd lose sight of him at times," wrote Snead, who outdrove his opponent by fifty yards, maybe more.

Once they got near the green, however, it was a different story.

Through the first eighteen holes of the thirty-six-hole match, Little Poison was 5 up. Snead didn't put one in his column until the 24th hole, and that was the only hole he won. Runyan, who took four of the seven par-5s and recorded only one bogey the whole day, humiliated Snead, 8 and 7.

"I'd have a hole won, as everybody could see," Snead wrote, "and then he'd sink a shot from behind a bush or chip dead to the cup from a gully or make a pitching-iron recovery from a bunker that I'd have bet 50-1 against. . . . Runyan had me so bothered that after a while I couldn't have sunk a putt in a bathtub."

Which, by the way, was where Runyan went each morning that week before his first match and again each afternoon before his second. He lay in a tub filled with cold water for about ten minutes to bring his body temperature down and then took a nap.

"I was smarter than they were, all of them," he said. "There wasn't one of them who knew how to take care of himself in 100-degree sweltering heat. . . . I was getting stronger as the week went on, and they were all wilting."

Runyan was smart, all right. Prior to arriving in Pennsylvania, "I went to Bill Brown's health farm up on the Hudson River and stayed there for a week," he said. "I worked like hell, learning to perspire, learning what to do and what not to do. By the time the tournament came, I was ready."

Due to his slight physique—five feet seven and 125 pounds—Runyan figured out early in his career that his short game would have to be exemplary for him to have a prayer against the bombers. "Hard work, Sam, hard work," he told Snead. "Midgets like me can't cut the buck off the tee, so we have to compensate."

Runyan overcame one obstacle after another.

Starting at home.

Like James Braid's old man, Runyan's father, a dairy farmer in Arkansas, didn't think much of golf. So when his son, in his early teens, refused to stop caddying at the Hot Springs Golf and Country Club, he whipped him, and more than once—on "my fanny," Runyan recalled.

Yet he held his ground.

"I looked him in the eye and said, 'Dad, you can whip me if you want, but it won't do you any good, because I'm going over to the golf course and I'm going to become a golf professional,'" he said.

The whippings came to an end, mercifully, though his father held his ground as well.

"I still regret the fact that he would never come to watch me play," Runyan said. "He never saw me play one hole."

While working at Concordia Country Club, a nine-hole course in Little Rock, Runyan, on an average day, hit about six hundred balls.

After Concordia, he took a job at the Forest Hill Field Club in New Jersey and then moved on to the Metropolis Country Club in White Plains, New York. He had been there for a year when the members raised $3,500 for Runyan to play the winter Tour in late 1931 and early '32. The deal was he would split the profits with them.

The members didn't stick to the deal. They let him keep every penny and even gave him a $1,500 bonus.

Runyan collected nine victories in 1933, and six more in 1934—he'd end up with twenty-eight—including his first major, the PGA Championship at Park Country Club outside Buffalo, outdueling Craig Wood in a match that went 38 holes.

Wood, like Snead would four years later, outdrove Runyan all day, but he, too, was undone by Little Poison's short game.

The match-play format suited Runyan to a tee.

"I've taken some pleasure out of being the little guy who has beaten the big fellows," he said. "At match play, don't think that isn't an advantage, because a big guy would rather lose to a big guy. And I had a cocky attitude that boded well for me, especially if they had a tendency to get ruffled."

Once his days on Tour were over, Runyan gave lessons and wrote two instruction books.

"I can think of no one better qualified to write an authoritative book on golf instruction than Paul," Bobby Jones wrote in one of the forewords.

You won't get an argument from Frank Beard, the Tour's leading money winner in 1969.

In May 1975, Beard, who was going through a horrendous slump, spent three days with Runyan in Colorado. "He short-circuited my fears," said Beard, who tied for third a month later in the U.S. Open at Medinah. "Most of my life, I had lived in performance anxiety. I now had something positive to do instead of negative."

I met Runyan in the late '80s when he was giving lessons at Arroyo Seco, a par-3 course in South Pasadena, California. Working on an article for *The Pasadena Star-News*—the topic escapes me—I approached him on the range. After we spoke, he asked if I could give him a ride to the hospital a few miles away to visit his wife. I wish I could remember what we talked about. And that I'd known enough at the time to ask about his match with Snead.

He handed me a Callaway Great Big Bertha five-wood. As a gesture of appreciation, I assume.

After dropping Runyan off, I never spoke to him again.

A couple of years ago, I gave the club to a friend who was having trouble hitting fairway woods.

I'm certain Mr. Runyan would approve.

49

Craig Wood

Dear Greg:

Hi. The next time you think about the majors you threw away—you don't mind if I call you Shark from here on, do you? Good, I didn't think so—I suggest you look up what happened to Craig Wood, a hell of a player in the 1930s and '40s.

Let's start with the 1933 British Open at St. Andrews.

Wood, like you, came right out of central casting: blond hair, handsome, could hit the ball a country mile. "The Blond Bomber," they called him. Anyway, he couldn't have played much better in his four rounds on the Old Course, making it to a thirty-six-hole playoff against Denny Shute.

So, Shark, what did Wood do on the very first hole of that playoff?

He found the Swilcan Burn in front of the green, that's what, which led to a double bogey. He doubled the second hole, as well, losing by five.

Wood got his revenge by beating Shute 2 and 1 in the semifinals of the 1934 PGA, which set up the match against Paul Runyan that wasn't settled through the first thirty-six. On the 37th hole, Wood nailed his second shot on the par-5 to about eight feet from the pin.

Runyan, meanwhile, hooked his second, which was headed toward the rough when it caromed off the tire of a truck and onto the fairway.

Talk about the golfing gods being on your side.

Shark, I know, you can't relate.

From there, Runyan hit a wedge to within a few feet and stayed alive when Wood missed his eagle putt, and then won it on the next hole.

For Wood, another blown opportunity in a major.

That, you can relate to.

Like yourself, he won his share of tournaments—twelve through the 1934 season.

Just not any majors.

In 1935, Wood, who had finished second to Horton Smith the year before, birdied four of the final six holes on Sunday at Augusta National for a one-over 73. Understanding the course as well as you do, you can appreciate what a wonderful round of golf that was given the circumstances.

Everyone figured it was over. Wood's name was even written on the winner's check.

It was not over, of course, as Gene Sarazen—I'm sure you know this part already—hit "the shot heard 'round the world" from 235 yards away on number 15, the ball dropping into the cup for a double eagle that tied him with Wood, whom he beat by five in a playoff the next day.

Get this, Shark, the golfing gods weren't done with Craig Wood just yet. What did they have against him, anyway?

At the 1939 U.S. Open in Philadelphia, he found himself in an eighteen-hole playoff with Shute and Byron Nelson. On the final hole, Wood, up by one, sent his second shot on the par-5 into the gallery, beaming a man by the name of Bob Mossman, the owner of a nearby driving range and a distant relative, I kid you not, of Alf Landon, the Republican governor from Kansas who got shellacked by FDR in the 1936 election. Mossman, I should add, wound up spending six days in the hospital with a concussion.

Anyway, Wood hit his approach to within four feet and, after Nelson canned an eight-footer for a birdie, lined up the putt to win his first major. At last.

I don't have to tell you what happened.

Wood and Nelson, who each finished with a 68, battled for another eighteen holes the next day, Shute having been eliminated with a 76. On the 4th hole, a par-4, Nelson pulled out his one-iron. He was 210 yards from the cup.

It went in.

Of course, it went in. His opponent was Craig Wood.

Nelson, in the end, prevailed by three. Wood, who gave Mossman $200 of the $800 he earned to make up for the days lost at the driving range, made history, becoming the first golfer to lose all four majors in playoffs.

No one would have blamed him—he was known as "No. 2 Wood" for his close calls—for giving up right then and there.

He didn't.

Wood, the son of a timber company foreman who, reportedly, stood six feet eight and weighed 275 pounds—

Craig said he got his hand-eye coordination from swinging an ax—won the Masters and U.S. Open in 1941. The only others to win both in the same year: Ben Hogan, Arnold Palmer, Jack Nicklaus, Tiger Woods, and Jordan Spieth.

The golfing gods owed him. Big time.

He opened with a 66 at Augusta National to go up by five over four players, including Hogan and Nelson, and was still three clear of the field with a round to go. Nelson caught him on Sunday but fell three short. The win was well received. "If there was a popularity contest within the PGA Tour," golf writer Charles Price suggested, "[Wood] would win by so many votes the tally would look like a zip code."

Two months later, in the Open at Colonial Country Club in Fort Worth, Wood who was dealing with back issues—he wore a leather corset—made a double bogey on the 1st hole and a bogey on the 2nd.

He was ready to drop out.

Thank goodness Tommy Armour, his playing partner, convinced him to keep going. Wood managed a 73 to stay within four, followed with a 71 to seize a share of the lead, and closed with two 70s to win by three over Shute.

Craig Wood was on top of the golfing world.

Eight months later, the real world intervened. The Japanese attacked Pearl Harbor. Fate, a familiar foe, was messing with him one final time.

The Masters went on as scheduled in the spring of 1942—Wood tied for twenty-third—but the sport soon came to a halt. By the time the fighting ended overseas, he was forty-three years old. "If World War II hadn't interrupted his reign," your former instructor, Butch Harmon wrote, "Craig Wood might have been the Arnold Palmer of his era."

At least he came through—in Augusta, especially—before it was too late.

Got to go, Shark. I hope I was able to help.

Sincerely,
Michael Arkush

Ben Crenshaw

In the summer of 1973, after his junior year at the University of Texas, Ben Crenshaw turned pro.

The time had come to see if he would, as some predicted, be the next Jack Nicklaus. Consider how much Crenshaw, known as Gentle Ben (he wasn't always so gentle, which I'll get to later) had accomplished before the age of twenty-two:

- First freshman to win the NCAA individual title.
- Low amateur in the 1970 U.S. Open (tied with John Mahaffey) and the 1972 and 1973 Masters.
- A third straight NCAA title and ten other victories as a junior.

"I forget whether it was Jackie Burke or Jimmy Demaret who said, after playing with Ben, that every day Ben stayed in school it was costing him $100,000 a year," Tom Kite said.

In October '73, Crenshaw entered Q-school: a grueling eight-round test at the Perdido Bay Country Club in Pensacola, Florida, and the Dunes Golf Club in Myrtle Beach, South Carolina.

Pass and you play with the best golfers in the world—for a year, at least.

Fail and you play who knows where... Timbuktu?

Crenshaw passed.

He did more than pass. He finished first by twelve strokes.

One month later, in his first Tour start after securing his card, he captured the San Antonio Open with weekend rounds of 66 and 67 and came in second in his next event, the World Open Golf Championship in Pinehurst.

In February 1974, *Sports Illustrated* put him on the cover.

The headline: *Make Way for the Kid.*

Dan Jenkins, the fellow Texan who wrote the article, had spent a lot of time around Ben Hogan. He knew greatness when he saw it.

"Crenshaw . . . appears to be starting out with even more golfing ability than Palmer had . . . anyone familiar with his amateur record should have known that Crenshaw would not waste much time establishing himself as a professional star."

Needless to say, he did not become the next Nicklaus, ending his career with only two majors—the 1984 and 1995 Masters—among his nineteen victories overall.

He let one opportunity after another slip away:

The 1975 U.S. Open at Medinah

Tied for the lead on the 71st hole, a par-3, he hit a two-iron into the water and made a double bogey, finishing one shot out of the playoff between John Mahaffey and Lou Graham, the eventual winner.

"I just missed it," Crenshaw said. "I hit it in the toe."

The 1979 British Open at Royal Lytham & St. Annes

Trailing Seve Ballesteros by a stroke, he flubbed another two-iron, again on the second-to-last hole, leading to another double.

"I should have gotten rid of that club," he quipped.

The 1979 PGA at Oakland Hills

After a double bogey on the 72nd hole, David Graham canned putts of twenty and ten feet on the first two playoff holes before putting Crenshaw away on the third.

"I thought I had it on the first two holes," he said afterward, "but he kept making the putts. I'm sick of finishing second, and I know I've got a lot of work to do on my game."

I can't help wondering: Were the expectations unfair to begin with? Like the ones thrust upon a young Tom Weiskopf?

After all, there has been only one Jack Nicklaus, and there will probably never be another.

Which is why I prefer to focus on what Gentle Ben did accomplish— the highlight, without question, the 1995 Masters.

Crenshaw, forty-three, had missed three cuts in his last four starts and hadn't broken 70 in two months.

So he turned, as he did on so many occasions, to his longtime instructor, Harvey Penick.

Crenshaw was six or seven years old when the two first met at Austin Country Club. "He cut down an old mashie for me and he put my hands on the club," he said in '95, "and that's the grip I have to this day. Then he gave me a blade putter and he said, 'You chip this ball up on the green, then putt it in the hole and you're playing golf.'"

He was hooked. For good.

Crenshaw loved putting and it showed. If he's not the best putter ever, he's definitely in the conversation.

Give credit to Penick, who wrapped up each practice session on the putting green. "I don't care if you putt for a Coca-Cola or whatever," he would say. "I want you to make a game out of it."

One day, Crenshaw recalled, "I took about eight balls and had a ten-foot putt. I putted those putts over and over for a long time."

Penick, who was a father figure to Crenshaw and many others at the club—"the kindest individual I ever met," he told me—came out of his shop and onto the green.

"You look pretty good," he told him, "but I want you to putt to different holes. You'll never have this putt again for the rest of your life."

The two got together on Sunday, March 26. Too ill to get out of bed, Penick, ninety, told Crenshaw to go into the closet and find the hickory-shafted Gene Sarazen putter. After watching him take two practice strokes and then hit the ball, Penick knew what the problem was: the head of the putter was passing Crenshaw's hands.

"All you need to do is trust," Penick said.

"I love you, Harvey," Crenshaw said as he was leaving.

"I love you, too."

A week later, Harvey Penick was dead.

A week after that, Ben Crenshaw won the Masters.

He birdied 16 and 17 in the final round to break out of a tie with Davis Love III. Thanks to his caddie, Carl Jackson, who had told him early in the week to stand closer to the ball and move it back in his stance, Crenshaw hit it better than he had in ages.

After tapping in on 18, Crenshaw lost it. All the emotion he had kept bottled up had to come out. In front of millions, if necessary.

"Are you all right, buddy?" Jackson asked.

"No, I'm not," Crenshaw said.

The whole day he focused on getting from point A to point B.

"I did not think about Harvey until after I hit my tee ball on 18," he said. "At the bottom of the hill, I started thinking: *I can't believe this is happening this week.*"

Crenshaw didn't win another tournament.

To me, that's the way it should have been, as it was with Mark O'Meara. He could never have topped the 1995 Masters. And I have a hunch that Crenshaw, who is very familiar with the history of the game, would agree.

Working with his partner, Bill Coore, he has made his mark, as well, as one of the game's best course designers and was the captain of the Ryder Cup squad in 1999 that staged the miraculous comeback on Sunday in Brookline from four points down.

So, how did he get the nickname Gentle Ben? And why was it a misnomer?

The nickname was given to him when he was in high school by Dick Collins, a sportswriter for the *Austin American-Statesman*. Collins was being sarcastic, having seen Crenshaw lose control when things didn't go his way.

"There was a TV series about a kid and a bear," Collins said. "It was the bear that was Gentle Ben, but the name seemed appropriate at the time."

In 1980, after three-putting the 16th hole at Colonial, Crenshaw kicked an oil drum while walking off the green.

"I ended up having surgery on it," he said. "I do not push off the right toe anywhere near what I used to be able to do. It still bothers me."

In 1987, after another three-putt, on the 6th hole of his singles match versus Ireland's Eamonn Darcy in the Ryder Cup at Muirfield Village in Ohio, he slammed his putter to the ground, breaking the shaft. Putting with a sand wedge and one-iron the rest of the way, he fell to Darcy one up, the United States losing for the first time on its own soil.

Whenever Crenshaw ran into Ben Wright, the CBS commentator couldn't resist:

"You're not Gentle Ben. You are Violent Ben."

47

Johnny Miller

Any in-depth analysis of Johnny Miller and his place in history must start with the afternoon of June 17, 1973.

The day before, Miller shot a 76 in the third round at Oakmont, ruining any realistic hopes of winning the U.S. Open.

If any course demanded precise approaches to the green, it was Oakmont, but Miller had left his yardage book at the hotel. Without the book—he said there were "no yardage markers or sprinklers with anything on them"—Miller was flying blind.

"I just went over the top emotionally," he recalled. "I was five over after six. I could have shot 80 something."

Enter his wife, Linda, to the rescue.

Having to navigate through heavy traffic to retrieve the book, she got back in time to give it to her husband after he walked off the 9th green. Better late than never. Nonetheless, he trailed by six heading into the final round, chasing, among others, Arnold Palmer, Jack Nicklaus, Lee Trevino, Gary Player, Tom Weiskopf, and Julius Boros.

He told Linda to pack so they could catch a flight as soon as possible after the round to the next tournament in Ohio.

"I knew I had no chance," Miller said.

Yet while warming up on the range, he heard a voice:

Open your stance way up.

He listened to that voice, and as a result, was able to shorten his backswing and free up his follow-through.

A three-iron to five feet on 1. Birdie. A nine-iron to a foot on 2. Birdie. A five-iron to twenty-five feet on 3. Birdie. A sand wedge to six inches on 4. Birdie.

Telling himself he now did have a chance to win, "the hair in the back of my neck stood up."

After a bogey on 8, his only one the whole day, he birdied 9 for a four-under 32 and made four more birdies coming home for an eight-under 63—a lip-out at 18 kept him from a 62—the lowest round to that point in a major championship. One contender after another soon fell by the wayside, giving Miller, who missed just two fairways, reached every green in regulation, and hit ten approaches within twenty feet, a victory we're still talking about more than a half century later.

If you think the rain the day before made Oakmont more vulnerable, think again. The average score for the final round was 73.8, only four of sixty-five players shooting under par.

"The greatest eighteen holes of golf ever played," according to Billy Casper.

Miller was thrilled for the person who had made it all possible.

"I just wanted to win it for my dad," he said. "That's the one he wanted me to win the most."

Larry Miller, a Morse code specialist during World War II, worked the night shift as a supervisor for RCA Communications in the Bay Area. For two and a half years, he had his son hit ball after ball by a mirror in the garage, copying the swings of Hogan, Snead, and Nelson—he had bought their instruction books filled with pictures—before taking him to the course.

"The amount of time my father devoted to me was incredible," Miller said. "He was a very creative person, would write poetry and songs, and was really into how to make your psyche work with the game."

Miller said he knew when he was eight he would be a champion one day.

It didn't take long.

At seventeen, he won the 1964 U.S. Junior Amateur in Eugene, Oregon, and four years later the California State Amateur at Pebble Beach. He tied for eighth in the 1966 U.S. Open at the Olympic Club, where he'd been given a junior membership, the first for someone whose father didn't already belong.

He was paired the first two rounds with Lee Trevino, the third with Jack Nicklaus.

"Can't say it was a thrill finishing eighth," said Miller, who had signed up to be a caddie before he made it through qualifying, "but the more I thought about it, 'Hey, that's pretty cool, actually.' A confidence thing that I could play against these pros."

Could he ever.

In the 1971 Masters, Miller, who had joined the Tour two years before, tied Nicklaus for second, two behind Charles Coody. His first victory came later that year at the Southern Open Invitational in Georgia, his second at Harbour Town in 1972. Oakmont was his third.

In the fall of 1973, he teamed up with Nicklaus to win the World Cup in Marbella, Spain. "I got to compare my game with his," said Miller, who seized the individual honors by three over Player and four over Nicklaus "and all of a sudden, it was like, 'Hey, this guy is not invincible; you can beat this guy.'"

Miller could beat every guy.

"They say the common denominator of the super-athlete in his prime is a feeling of weightlessness," he said. "I've had that feeling. There's a power out there. You defy gravity."

He won eight times in 1974, including the first three tournaments, and four more in 1975: by fourteen in Phoenix and nine, thanks to a closing 61, in Tucson.

Over the four rounds in Tucson, he hit the hole or flagstick ten times. Miller said he could calibrate his swing for the ball to go exactly 147 yards, not 149.

"He played with a very weak left-hand grip, somewhat reminiscent of Hogan," Lanny Wadkins said. "The harder he hit it, the straighter he hit it. His natural ball flight was dead straight, so no matter where the flag was, he just aimed at it, and that's where it went. For a period of time, Johnny Miller was the best player I ever saw."

A period that was over before we knew it.

Although he won the 1976 British Open at Royal Birkdale (by six strokes over Nicklaus and Seve Ballesteros) he wasn't driven for the long haul like the Golden Bear. Then again, who was?

"I was just content," said Miller, "and when you are content, you're basically done. It was like, 'Well, that's done. I climbed that mountain. Check out the view and enjoy it. Be a good dad and go fishing.' I had lost that passionate love for the game."

The work he did on his ranch in Napa was also a factor.

"I went from 165 to 185 but kept a thirty-one-inch waist," Miller said. "But when I picked up the clubs again, they felt like toothpicks, and I'd also lost some flexibility."

He didn't ride off into the sunset—seven of his twenty-five victories came in the 1980s and '90s, including a shocking one at Pebble Beach in 1994 at age forty-six, when he was already the lead analyst for NBC (no one has ever been better)—but the magic, for the most part, was gone.

"My putting short-circuited everything," said Miller, another victim of the dreaded yips. "If I'd had good putting, even with no practice, and not being that dedicated, I probably would have won fifty tournaments."

Maybe so, but it would have been difficult to top the final day at Oakmont.

Others may shoot 62 or lower in an Open, as Rickie Fowler and Xander Schauffele did in the first round at Los Angeles Country Club in 2023, but unless they win the tournament—neither came within four shots—the rounds won't compare to Miller's 63.

"The secret of a 63," Miller said, "is the fact that I shot it on Sunday.... That's what makes the round what it is. It wouldn't have done any good if I finished second."

46
Old Tom Morris

He wasn't Old Tom Morris at first. Just plain Tom.

The old part was added later to distinguish him from his son, Young Tom.

Old Tom was born in 1821 in St. Andrews. That's also where he met his maker in 1908.

At fourteen, he started out as an apprentice to Allan Robertson. You remember Robertson, the one who didn't accept the challenge from Willie Park Sr. and later died of jaundice. Working in Robertson's cottage, Old Tom helped make close to fifty feathery balls a week, welcoming "any chance," as author Kevin Cook put it, "to leave the sweaty kitchen for the great green links."

He got to where he didn't need any strokes in his matches against Robertson. In 1843, Old Tom, by then a journeyman, beat his boss for the first time, a day he would never forget.

So was another day five years later.

There was a new ball on the scene, the gutta-percha, and Old Tom, out of feathery balls, used one given to him by a club member he was having a match with. Old Tom had sworn to Robertson he would never play with a gutta-percha—it might put an end to their business—but he couldn't quit in the middle of a match, could he?

Robertson didn't see it that way. Old Tom was discharged.

"Allan in such a temper cried out to me to never to show face again," he said.

It was the best thing that could have happened to him.

Old Tom was hired as the Keeper of the Green at Prestwick, which would end up hosting the first major ever, the 1860 British Open.

Prestwick needed a lot of work. "What Tom found," Cook wrote, "was fifty-odd acres of dunes, brush and ragged grasses with knee-high flagsticks scattered here and there. Some Prestwick golfers played randomly, aiming for any flag they could spot from wherever they found a ball."

Old Tom did everything at Prestwick: He gave lessons. He was in charge of the caddies. He figured out the handicaps. He played with the members.

And, lest we forget, he built the place.

Old Tom had never designed a course before, unless you count helping Robertson with a few holes at Carnoustie. What he lacked in experience he made up for in passion and ingenuity with new ideas of how to maintain the greens and hazards.

"By the end of his first year," Cook wrote, "club men were congratulating [Colonel James Ogilvie] Fairlie for recruiting this greenskeeper. Some went so far as to shake Tom's hand."

After losing to Willie Park Sr. in the 1860 British Open and beating him by four a year later, Old Tom won by thirteen in 1862, which remains the largest margin of victory in Open history.

Park came up with a way to get even:

Two rounds apiece at Musselburgh, Prestwick, North Berwick, and St. Andrews.

So much for getting even.

Over the eight rounds, Old Tom prevailed by seventeen strokes, which *The Scotsman* described as "unparalleled in the annals of golfing."

Old Tom won the Open again in 1864 and 1867—the latter, at age forty-six, and he is still the oldest champion ever.

By 1864, Old Tom was back at St. Andrews—a coup for the Old Course and a gamble for Old Tom. The job as head professional paid fifty pounds a year, plus twenty for expenses, but came with no security. If things went wrong, as they did with the last person who held the position, he could be on the street in no time.

Things did not go wrong. Old Tom remained at the home of golf for the rest of his life.

As for his own game, he continued to play well from tee to green. If only he didn't miss all those short putts.

Young Tom didn't let Old Tom off the hook.

"The hole'll not come to you, Da," he told him. "My father," he said, would be a "brave putter if the hole were always a yard nearer to 'im."

Old Tom expected to pass the baton to his son, who won the Open in 1868, 1869, 1870, and 1872.

"I could cope with 'em all, on the course," he said. "All but Tommy. He was the best the old game ever saw."

He didn't expect to bury his son. (Young Tom—I'll tell you the whole story when we get to his chapter—died on Christmas Day in 1875.)

In 1885, Old Tom, on the day he turned sixty-four, fired an 81 at St. Andrews, only four shy of the course record set by Young Tom in 1869.

"No' that ill for an old horse!" he said.

No' that ill, indeed.

In May 1908, the old horse had an accident at St. Andrews.

"What he used to do was come in, have a cup of tea," said author Roger McStravick. "He got up to go to the bathroom and he took the wrong door at the top of some really steep wooden steps. He took one step into the darkness and with nothing to grab on to, fell down the stairs and cracked his skull on the flagstones or wall at the bottom."

The loss of Old Tom Morris was felt throughout the land.

"Tom's was the biggest funeral I ever saw in St. Andrews," wrote Andra Kirkaldy, the Scottish pro. "Shopkeepers shut their shops and every house had drawn blinds. The coffin was followed by Professors of the University, members of the Royal & Ancient and of other golf clubs from far and near.

"Flags flew at half-mast. The greens were deserted. Not a golf ball was struck on the links that day, except in the very early morning."

45

Horton Smith

In 1929, Horton Smith reached a height in his profession no one saw coming.

Least of all Smith himself.

What he pulled off "would be remarkable," one writer suggested, "if it had been accomplished by some established star. As the achievement of a comparative unknown, the record is astounding." Smith, who turned twenty-one in May of that year, won eight tournaments, including three in a row, and finished second on six other occasions.

"He was the Tiger Woods of his generation," said Rick Grayson, a teaching professional who wrote a book about Smith. "He won more tournaments at an early age than anybody who had ever played the game."

Smith, who ended up with thirty victories overall, got his start as a caddie at Springfield Country Club in Missouri. No one was more meticulous.

"There is none of the hit-or-miss about his shot-making that characterizes the play of many young golfers who come by a good swing naturally without giving much thought to how or why," a writer explained.

In 1927, Smith tied for forty-fourth in the U.S. Open at Oakmont. A year later, he claimed the Oklahoma City Open for his first Tour victory and made it to the semifinals of the PGA at Baltimore Country Club, falling to Al Espinosa, 6 and 5.

"The boy is good," O. B. Keeler wrote. "...I really don't see why he ever misses a shot, except that he is human. But if ever there were a perfect mechanical golfer, Horton Smith is it."

And, boy, could he putt.

"To mention anyone else in the same breath is a travesty," Paul Runyan said. "He planted himself parallel to the intended line and was sound technically. But what made him a great putter was his attitude. He had a dogged determination to do it the same way, week after week and year after year."

Smith, who learned how to putt on flat, sandy greens, was victorious twice at Augusta National, including in 1934, the first year the tournament was held.

Going into the final two holes, he was in a tight duel with Craig Wood. Smith knocked in about a fifteen-footer on 17, the 8th hole today—the nines were reversed in 1935—to assume a one-shot lead. "Fortunately my third shot on the 17th was a short pitch," he recalled. "...I quite confidently stroked the ball in for the birdie I so badly needed."

On his last hole, now number 9, Smith hit his approach to about thirty-five feet above the hole and then left his first putt about three and a half feet short. "I studied the [second] putt," he said, "and at the moment I had one of those positive thoughts: Since the green was slippery and the break was fast, all I could do was hit the ball firmly and squarely.... So I stepped up and knocked the ball right in, to win."

In the 1936 Masters, Smith trailed Harry Cooper by three after three rounds. Cooper, you might recall, dealing with rain and heavy winds—many thought the round, the second of the day, should have been canceled—could fare no better than a 76.

Smith, teeing off much later, couldn't have been more fortunate.

When he got to the back nine, the winds had settled down. He chipped in from fifty feet for a birdie at 14 and made another birdie at 15. At 17, after rolling his first putt about fifteen feet past the cup, he knocked in the comebacker to maintain a one-shot advantage. A par at 18 gave him his second major title.

The *Joplin Ghost*, as Smith was known—he played for a short time out of a club in Joplin, Missouri, and was difficult to catch once he took the lead—was the last player, in the 1930 Savannah Open, to defeat Bobby Jones before he launched his quest for the Grand Slam.

Jones took the lead with a 67 in round one, but Smith turned in a course-record 66 in round two and wound up winning by a shot.

"The press decided," Mark Frost wrote, "that at long last a young pro had arrived who could give the Emperor Jones a fight for his crown."

The press could have used a mulligan.

Two weeks later, Jones, with baseball immortal Ty Cobb in the gallery, beat Smith by thirteen—he was ahead by eighteen with three holes to go—in the Southeastern Open in Augusta, his largest margin of victory ever.

"That's where I played my finest golf of 1930," Jones said.

Smith didn't win another major and notched only two victories after turning thirty, both in 1941.

The war—he served in the U.S. Army from 1942 to 1945 in mostly administrative posts—wasn't the only reason.

"As assiduously as he worked on it," Herbert Warren Wind wrote, "his swing was not the simplified and correct thing it had been in 1929. He had to battle a tall man's tendency to overswing and even when he periodically cut down the length of his arc, it did not always follow that he corrected a certain looseness in his swing."

Maybe so, but when Horton Smith was at his best, his swing "was sheer genius," Grantland Rice wrote, "as sound and as smooth a swing as Vardon, Braid, Taylor, Jones or anyone else ever had."

44

Dustin Johnson

On the short drive from the course to the house they rented for the week, no one said a word.

Not Dustin Johnson.

Not his fiancée, Paulina.

Not her father, Wayne Gretzky, aka the Great One, or mother, Janet.

No one.

Who could blame them?

They'd been hoping for the coronation of another Great One. Except Johnson showed he wasn't ready—sorry, Mr. DeMille—for his close-up just yet, three-putting from twelve feet on the 72nd hole of the 2015 U.S. Open at Chambers Bay to lose by a shot to Jordan Spieth.

"I had all the chances in the world," Johnson said.

You can say that again.

In addition to the debacle on 18, Johnson missed five other putts inside ten feet... on the back nine! "I didn't think I was hitting bad putts," he said. "I thought I was hitting them pretty good and they just weren't going in."

At least he didn't pull a Tom Kite and tell us he *made* those putts.

This wasn't the first major that had gotten away from him:

The 2010 U.S. Open at Pebble Beach.

The 2010 PGA at Whistling Straits.

The 2011 British Open at Royal St. George's.

Johnson was in the final group on Sunday each time, and each time someone else walked away with the trophy.

Anyway, on the ride from Chambers Bay to the rental house, Johnson felt the need to break the silence.

"Guys," he told them, "it's just a golf tournament."

Just a golf tournament? Was he out of his freakin' mind? Did he not know this was the United States Open and not the John Deere Classic?

He was serious. He wasn't going to treat what happened as life-or-death, nor should anyone else on his team.

"I was fine," Johnson told me. "We went from there, had some cocktails, flew over to Coeur d'Alene [in Idaho], and had a great week.... There's nothing you can do but move on."

Wow. Can you imagine Curtis Strange saying he had a "great week" after three-putting the final hole from twelve feet to throw away a chance to win the U.S. Open?

Or Lanny Wadkins? Or Ben Crenshaw?

All three, in their seventies now, would still be having nightmares.

That's what makes Dustin Johnson, for better or worse, who he is, and perhaps why his drought in the majors ended a year later.

Nothing fazed him in the final round of the 2016 Open at Oakmont.

Not even when the USGA told him on the tee at 12 that they were looking at an incident from the 5th hole. While Johnson was lining up a short putt for par, his ball moved. Which, if he were at fault, would result in a one-stroke penalty.

Ahead by two over Ireland's Shane Lowry at the time, Johnson remained calm.

"I never once thought I was going to get a penalty," he said. "I went right back to what I was doing."

Making one par after another, except for a miscue on 14, no small accomplishment in a U.S. Open.

At Oakmont, especially.

Johnson wouldn't have wanted it any other way.

The more challenging golf courses are "better for me," he said. "It helps me stay in the game. Every shot you hit, you have to think through it."

On 18, ahead by three—depending on the USGA, maybe two—he hit a six-iron to within five feet. Ballgame.

It was "a relief to finally get one," said Johnson—incidentally, he did receive a penalty—who prevailed by three over Lowry and two others. "At some point, you do start questioning a little bit: 'Am I ever going to win one?' I knew if I kept giving myself a chance, eventually I [would.]"

And once he nailed down his first—warning: here comes a cliché—many thought the floodgates would open.

The floodgates did not open.

While Johnson, who grew up near Columbia, South Carolina, about an hour away from Augusta, captured the Covid-delayed Masters in 2020 by five with a record 20-under 268, he hasn't come close to winning a major since. In sixteen starts, he's missed the cut six times and has only three top tens.

And now that he's in his forties, he will, in all likelihood, top out at two.

Every so often, when I watch Johnson rip one down the middle of the fairway or execute a gorgeous pitch—his wedge game improved significantly over the years—I think back to the 82 he fired in the final round of the 2010 Open at Pebble after starting the day with a three-shot lead. The only player to shoot a higher score on that Sunday was Jason Preeo, a high school golf coach in Highlands Ranch, Colorado, who turned in an 84.

I also think of the two-stroke penalty Johnson was assessed on the 72nd hole at Whistling Straits—he grounded his club in an area he didn't realize was a bunker—which kept him out of a playoff between Martin Kaymer and Bubba Watson.

"I still don't think I was in a bunker," Johnson said, "but it is what it is."

And, of course, the three-putt at Chambers Bay.

Johnson, with twenty-four victories, has spent 135 weeks at number one, behind only Tiger Woods (683) and Greg Norman (331), and is just the fourth player to win at least one tournament in each of his first thirteen seasons, the streak ending in 2021. The others: Arnold Palmer, Jack Nicklaus, and Woods.

I asked Johnson, who signed with LIV Golf in 2022, if he could envision himself at age sixty-four—having just turned sixty-four, I was doing some soul-searching of my own—being disappointed he didn't win more majors.

"When I'm sixty-four, hopefully, I'm sitting on my boat fishing," he laughed, "with a cold beer."

I asked him, as well, if he now looked at his younger days in a different light. I won't go into all the details—he was, reportedly, suspended in 2014 for failing a drug test, which the Tour denied—but, as he admitted back then, he was facing "personal challenges."

He wasn't defensive in the least.

"All of it made me into who I am today and you can't change the past," Johnson said. "All you can do is learn from it and get better."

43

Brooks Koepka

When Brooks Koepka, a four-time major winner from 2017 through 2019, wasn't himself in the 2022 majors (two missed cuts and two fifty-fifth place finishes), I began to wonder:

Have we seen his best days?

As I later learned, I wasn't the only with questions about his future.

"This is the worst I've ever struggled in my whole life," Koepka, who was dealing with knee and hip injuries, confessed on *Full Swing*, the Netflix doc. "I have to figure out how to get out of this thing before it gets too late. . . . Golf's so crazy. When you have it, you feel you're never gonna lose it, and when you don't have it, you feel like you're never gonna get it."

So, what happens? In 2023, a healthy Koepka comes close to winning the Masters—he led by two after fifty-four holes before shooting a 75 to tie for second, four behind Jon Rahm—and wins the PGA a month later at Oak Hill for his fifth major, tying him with Byron Nelson, Seve Ballesteros, Peter Thomson, James Braid, and John Henry Taylor.

Such resilience was nothing new for Brooks Koepka.

In 2012, after failing to advance past the second stage of Q-school, he took off for the Challenge Tour, Europe's developmental tour, which included visits to such popular golf destinations—please note the sarcasm—as Kenya and Kazakhstan.

Most ambitious young pros might have had a negative attitude toward the Challenge Tour. Not Koepka.

"I was excited and had no hesitation," he said. "Any chance to play against good players."

He won once in 2012 and three times in 2013—all by a total of twenty-three strokes—to secure his card on the European Tour.

People took notice, including Steve Williams, Tiger's former caddie, who watched him during a practice round before the 2014 British Open at Royal Liverpool.

"Once in a great while," Williams said, "a player comes along who hits a golf ball the way it was meant to be hit. Powerful, piercing, the perfect trajectory. Of the young players out there, one I've seen has that special ball flight: Brooks Koepka.... I haven't seen a ball flight like that since Tiger, and before that, Johnny Miller."

Koepka collected his first PGA Tour victory at Phoenix in 2015, and his first major two years later, the U.S. Open at Erin Hills in Wisconsin, where he averaged 322.1 yards off the tee and reached more than 85 percent of the fairways and greens in regulation. Only once did Koepka, who matched Rory McIlroy for the lowest score in relation to par in Open history, hit more than a seven-iron into a par-4.

"It hasn't sunk in, obviously," he told the press, "and probably won't for a few days. But that's probably one of the coolest things I've ever experienced."

He won the Open again a year later at Shinnecock Hills, the first player since Curtis Strange in 1988 and 1989 to go back-to-back.

The 2018 Open was similar to most of the Opens before.

Where par is a thing of beauty.

In the final round, he needed every one of them to outduel England's Tommy Fleetwood, who closed with a record-tying, seven-under 63, by a stroke.

Koepka, the great-nephew of former Pittsburgh Pirates shortstop Dick Groat (the 1960 National League MVP), had hoped to play in the big leagues himself one day. When he was ten years old, though, he fractured his nose and sinus cavity in a car accident. With baseball out for the summer, he took part in a junior golf program at a public course in West Palm Beach, Florida.

Fast-forward to Florida State, where he was the ACC Player of the Year as a sophomore and as a senior.

"Brooks had so much self-belief," his coach, Trey Jones, said, that he would grow "frustrated because his game wasn't as good as his vision of it. It's an old story with a lot of players who end up great. Once he learned some patience and to not force things, all that talent started to flow."

Looking back, the Challenge Tour might have been the best thing that ever happened to him.

"He's slept in his car," his longtime caddie, Ricky Elliott, said after Koepka captured the 2017 Open. "He's slept in a B&B with four of us [in one room] and struggled along the way, and that's helped him appreciate where he is."

With a good chance to win a few more majors before he's done. He won't turn thirty-five until May 2025.

"Double digits, that's what I'm trying to get to," Koepka said a couple of years ago. "I don't think it's out of the question for me."

Granted, he might not be the easiest person to root for—was it really necessary to rip his former LIV teammate, Matthew Wolff, in public? ("A lot of talent, Koepka said, "but I mean the talent's wasted")—but he can be intimidating, there's no doubt about that.

"He looks like he wants to punch you in the mouth," Steve Stricker, his ex–Ryder Cup captain, said. "You get a guy who is built like a linebacker and pounds the crap out of the ball, and then looks over like he wants to brawl, yeah that has an effect."

The slump in 2022 was another learning experience.

"Sometimes you have to hit the bottom to figure out where you're at," Koepka said.

On Sunday in the 2023 PGA, Koepka, who was ahead by one through fifty-four holes, extended the lead to three on the front nine.

Viktor Hovland applied pressure later in the round but Koepka didn't flinch, prevailing by two.

In 2024, he did not finish in the top twenty-five in a single major. And, of his sixteen rounds, only four were under par.

No matter. I have learned my lesson. I will never doubt him again.

42

Tommy Armour

The Third Battle of Ypres in the summer and fall of 1917, also known as the Battle of Passchendaele—about a half million were killed or wounded—was among the bloodiest in World War I, the war that was supposed to end all wars, the Germans facing an Allied force in Belgium that included soldiers from the British Empire.

One of those soldiers was Tommy Armour from Edinburgh, Scotland, who was eighteen when he enlisted, and from all indications, as brave as they come.

Word is that he captured a German tank on his own, strangling the commander when he refused to surrender. A fast machine gunner and member of the Tank Corps, he rose from private to major and met King George V, the grandfather of Queen Elizabeth II.

Not long afterward, Armour met his fate.

He was the victim of a mustard gas attack that initially cost him his sight in both eyes. Armour was in the hospital for months.

A decade later, he won the U.S. Open.

Armour, who would live the rest of his life with eight pieces of shrapnel in his shoulder, was fortunate. He regained the sight in his right eye, allowing him to have a future that wouldn't have to depend on the kindness of others.

In 1919, Armour, who had shown some promise as a golfer before the war, lost to England's Carl Bretherton in the final of the Irish Amateur Open at Royal Portrush but made quite an impression. "Mr. Armour fought a great fight," *The Glasgow Herald* reported, "and having fought so well he should have won, for he is assuredly the better golfer.... He is a young man with shots in his bag which are the envy and the despair of many, and he will assuredly come again."

A year later, he won the French Amateur in Versailles.

The next stop: the United States of America.

Armour, known as the Silver Scot—his hair was prematurely gray—turned pro in 1924. In 1927, he won five times, including, remember, the U.S. Open at Oakmont, when he birdied the 72nd hole to tie Harry Cooper and beat him in a playoff the following day.

"Whenever the Silver Scot played himself into a contending position," Herbert Warren Wind wrote, "he always seemed to have that extra something that was the difference between barely losing and barely winning.... His hands were hot, but his head was cool—one of the accidental rewards that only too rarely catch up with a war hero."

Three years later, in the PGA at Fresh Meadow Country Club in Queens, New York, Armour, who hit his irons as well as anyone, was again at his best when he needed to be. After dropping five of the first six holes to Johnny Farrell in the quarterfinals, he stormed back to prevail 2 and 1.

A one-up victory over Charles Lacey in the semis set the stage for a duel with Gene Sarazen.

What a duel it was, neither ever more than 2 up.

The match all square on 18, both faced par putts of under fifteen feet.

Advantage: Sarazen.

Putting was never one of Armour's strong points. Earlier in the match, he had missed a couple of very makeable ones.

He didn't miss this one.

And when Sarazen failed to make his putt, Tommy Armour was a major champion once more.

In 1931, Armour rallied from five back on the final day to win the British Open at Carnoustie. The leader, José Jurado of Argentina, found the Barry Burn on 17, resulting in a double bogey, and bogeyed 18 to finish one back.

"I am a Scotsman," Armour said afterward, "but I should like it to be known that I learned my golf in the United States."

The yips, I'm sorry to tell you—hadn't the man been through enough already?—claimed him as another victim. It was Armour, as a matter of fact, who came up with the term, writing of "that ghastly time when, with the first movement of the putter, the golfer blacks out, loses sight of the ball and hasn't the remotest idea of what to do with the putter or, occasionally, that he is holding a putter at all."

Armour, who finished with twenty-five victories, gave lessons to, among others, Babe Didrikson Zaharias and Lawson Little Jr. A familiar sight was the Silver Scot at the Boca Raton Club in Florida, where he taught for decades, "dispensing wisdom to pupils with a gin and tonic always in reach before going out in the afternoon to play matches for money."

41

John Henry Taylor

Willie Park Jr., who won two British Opens in the late 1880s, said "a man who can putt is a match for anyone."

England's John Henry Taylor put a different spin on the subject. In more ways than one.

"A man who can approach," he said, "does not need to putt."

He ought to know.

Taylor was such an accurate ball striker that at Royal St. George's in 1894, when he claimed the first of his five Claret Jugs, he had the directional posts on blind holes taken down because he feared his ball might strike one of them and ricochet into a bunker.

He was, as author Stephen Proctor noted, the "master of the mashie pitch to the green, which he played with enough backspin to stop it close to the flag."

Taylor, a former caddie and greenskeeper at Royal North Devon, also known as Westward Ho!, was the first of the Great Triumvirate to win the Open, and once he did, his life would never be the same. Between 1894 and 1914, he took part in hundreds of exhibitions throughout England and Scotland, adding about two hundred and fifty pounds to his yearly income.

In 1891, Andra Kirkaldy lost to Taylor, 3 and 2. When he returned to the Old Course, he heard it from the caddies:

Why did you let a young man like Taylor beat you?

"You will see more of Taylor," Kirkaldy replied, "and then you'll know why he beat me.... He's going to be the greatest golfer of the day, mark my words."

The victory at Royal St. George's was more than a personal one. Taylor—his friends called him J.H.—became the first professional golfer from England to win the British Open. The other pros were Scots. "Hitherto, when we wanted professionals, we had always been importing them from the North," Horace Hutchinson, the English amateur, pointed out. "It did not occur to the English caddie that he might become a professional, that there were possibilities, and money, in it.... It is not easy to overrate what that success of Taylor's meant for the professional golf of England."

Taylor won the Open again in 1895 by four at St. Andrews, closing with a 78, a heck of a round back then. Especially with the weather, as usual, refusing to cooperate.

Some were skeptical that Taylor's mashie approaches would be as effective on the Old Course's undulating greens.

They were wrong.

"It was a splendid exhibition of golf," *The Times* in London reported, "the good points of which were heartily applauded by the crowd, who notwithstanding wind and rain, followed the champion over the course."

Splendid, indeed, though for members of the Scottish press there was nothing to applaud.

For an English player to be triumphant at the home of golf, Mark Frost wrote decades later, was as if "the infidels had sacked Jerusalem."

The situation would only get worse for the Scots and their precious pride.

In 1896, Harry Vardon, another Englishman, defeated Taylor in a thirty-six-hole playoff at Muirfield for his first Open title. Taylor, meanwhile, won the championship in 1900, again at St. Andrews; in 1909 at Royal Cinque Ports Golf Club in Deal, England, and in 1913 at Royal Liverpool. Each victory was by four shots or more, two by eight.

In 1900, Taylor embarked on a trip to the United States. He wasn't a big fan.

"J.H. found less to admire in America than Harry [Vardon] did,"

Frost wrote. "Constant travel aggravated his delicate stomach and the presence of so many strangers increased his anxiety."

Taylor, who had bought an interest in a club-manufacturing factory in Pittsburgh, came in second in the U.S. Open at Chicago Golf Club, two behind Vardon.

In the 1909 British Open, Taylor was on target from the beginning. "Without, I trust, being an egotistical fool," Taylor said, "I may attribute my win at Deal to the pleasing recollection that for two days [they played thirty-six holes a day] I appeared to be inspired in my shots up to the hole." His approaches were so precise, they rendered "putting a simple proposition."

The triumph in the 1913 Open had to have been his most satisfying.

"Ever since my caddie days at Westward Ho!," he wrote, "I had looked upon [Royal Liverpool] as a second home . . . the thought that perhaps forever I should be thwarted from winning there not only disturbed my equanimity, but also injured my pride."

And to think how close he came to not playing in the tournament at all.

On the final hole of the two qualifying rounds, he needed to knock in a six-footer to make the field.

"I remember saying to myself: *'Well, Taylor my lad, there's only one place for this and that's the bottom of the hole.'* "

The bottom of the hole it was.

"The word relief," he said, "is not sufficiently intense in its meaning to describe how I felt when I saw the ball disappear, dropping with a sickening wobble on the right-hand side."

For Taylor, who won by eight, the 77 he shot in the third round in the worst conditions you can imagine—to call it a hurricane would not be that far off the mark—was a round to remember.

"How he did stick his chin out and pull his cap down over his nose and bang that ball right through the gale!" Bernard Darwin wrote. "It was the greatest of all golfing victories of man over nature."

In the 1925 Open at Prestwick, Taylor tied for sixth at age fifty-four. The following year, at Royal Lytham & St. Annes, he turned in another round to remember.

Jones, the champion in '26, called Taylor, who tied for eleventh, "the hero of St. Annes." In the third round, Jones wrote, he "shot a 71 in a hard wind... in his gallant effort to stave off the rush of the American invaders. It was better than I could do in any round....My hat is off to John Henry!"

40

Leo Diegel

Too bad the mental game coaches that players work with these days weren't around in the 1920s and '30s.

Leo Diegel sure could have used one. Who knows? An encouraging word here or there from one of them and he might have been a star.

Not that Diegel, who had himself psychoanalyzed at one point, didn't enjoy his share of success.

From 1920 through 1934, he won twenty-eight tournaments, including the PGA Championship in 1928 and 1929 and four Canadian Opens. Only Walter Hagen and Gene Sarazen won more often during that span.

No less an authority than Bernard Darwin wrote that Diegel was "in a way the greatest golfing genius I have ever seen." Willie MacFarlane, a top player back then, believed a course record would be broken whenever Diegel, as one writer put it, was "given a week's time."

The problem wasn't with his swing. The problem was with his psyche.

On occasion, for example, after hitting his drive, he climbed onto the tee box to get a better look at what he would be facing for his second shot. "He's a bundle of nerves," one writer explained, "keen, rarin' to go, and once off, going at break-neck speed either to win or to crash. He has always been that way."

Diegel tried walking slower between shots, which helped in every tournament except the U.S. Open.

Winning the Open wasn't meant to be.

His first opportunity came in 1920 at Inverness. All he needed was a 38 on the final nine holes and the trophy would have been his.

His troubles began on 14. Half-topping his drive was alarming enough, but as Diegel got ready to hit his approach, a friend told him the leader, Ted Ray, had bogeyed 17.

Diegel was anxious enough as it was.

"I don't care what Ray took," said Diegel who, according to one account, slammed his club to the ground. "I'm playing my own game."

A game that was deserting him. At the worst possible time.

A double at 14. A bogey at 15. Another bogey at 16. Diegel finished with a 40 to lose by one.

In the 1925 Open at Worcester Country Club in Massachusetts, the table was set again, but he went nine over his last six holes.

That included an 8 on the 18th hole to finish five behind Bobby Jones and MacFarlane, the eventual champion.

He wasn't meant to win the British Open, either.

Diegel, who had come in third in 1929 and tied for second in 1930, blew it big time on the Old Course in 1933. He took three from the edge of the green on 15, three-putted from forty feet on 17, the treacherous Road Hole, and three-putted again, whiffing on a tap in (maybe that's where Hale Irwin got the idea) on 18 when two putts would have put him in a playoff with Craig Wood and Denny Shute.

Thank God for the PGA.

In 1928, Diegel took on Hagen in the quarterfinals at the Baltimore Country Club. That was like taking on General Motors. Hagen, the four-time defending champ, had won twenty-two matches in a row, including victories over Diegel in 1925 and 1926.

Not this time, Sir Walter.

Diegel, a superb iron player—he "could put his second shots closer to the pins than any golfer in his day and he played in an age of giants," Herbert Warren Wind wrote—prevailed 2 and 1 and crushed Sarazen, 9 and 8, in the semis. Next was Al Espinosa, whom he defeated 6 and 5 in the final.

Diegel wasn't done slaying giants just yet.

In the 1929 PGA at Hillcrest Country Club in Los Angeles, his victims again included Hagen and Sarazen, along with Johnny Farrell, the 1928 U.S. Open winner, whom he beat in the final, 6 and 4.

Diegel and Hagen were good friends. In 1930, they appeared in *Match Play*, a twenty-minute comedy directed by Mack Sennett, a legend in silent pictures. As for his day job, Diegel constantly tinkered with his technique.

"In all my years of golf," Sarazen said, "I have never seen anyone whose devotion to the game could match Leo's. It was his religion. Between courses at the table, Leo used to get up and practice swings. Every night, he went to bed dreaming theory, and every morning he awakened with some hot idea that was going to revolutionize the game."

One idea was to spread his legs wide and point his elbows out parallel to his chest when he putted, his chin resting on top of the shaft. "If it didn't look so terrible," he insisted—like a "washerwoman at work over her tub" according to Darwin—"all the boys would use it. It's the most scientific method in the world. I've had any number of them try it out and tell me that."

The new method, which became known as "Diegeling," worked wonders.

When he captured the Shawnee and Canadian Opens in 1924, Diegel claimed he didn't miss a putt under four feet.

In 1951, cancer took him away at age fifty-two.

At a cemetery in Detroit, after the other mourners had taken off, Hagen placed a six-pack of beer on the casket, which contained Diegel's precious putter.

"May you and your putter rust in peace," he said.

39

Gene Littler

Some believed Gene Littler would one day belong in the same class as Ben Hogan, Sam Snead, and Byron Nelson. As Herbert Warren Wind put it, he possessed the "soundest natural golf swing since the days of the young Snead."

In 1953, Littler outdueled Dale Morey one up to win the U.S. Amateur in Oklahoma City.

Four months later, he captured the San Diego Open, the first Tour victory by an amateur in six years.

In the 1954 U.S. Open, Littler, now a professional, missed an eight-footer on the 72nd hole that would have put him in a playoff with Ed Furgol, and in 1955, he won four times, including the Los Angeles Open by two over Ted Kroll.

And he was still only twenty-five years old.

Well, I hate to break it to you—I know, here I go again—but Gene Littler did not become another Hogan, Snead, or Nelson.

Not even close.

He won only one professional major, the 1961 U.S. Open at Oakland Hills, in eighty attempts. On the other hand—see, I'm trying to reform—he had a hell of a career, with twenty-nine wins, the same as Lee Trevino, and more than Gary Player, Raymond Floyd, Ben Crenshaw, Johnny Miller, and Greg Norman. From 1954 to 1979, he only once finished outside the top sixty on the money list. As I wrote about Davis Love III, most guys would have taken that in a heartbeat.

Why, then, has Littler failed to receive more credit for what he was able to accomplish?

It's simple. His crime was that he didn't have charisma. Which, God bless him, he made no apologies for.

"I'm not a showboat or an actor and I don't want to be one," Littler stated. "I'm a golf professional. And I always thought golf was traditionally a gentleman's game that should be played in a quiet manner."

Like others—Larry Nelson, for example—he had something, in my opinion, more important than charisma. He was an honorable man who served in the U.S. Navy before turning pro and was devoted to his family above everything else. And, let's face it, that wasn't true about everyone on Tour.

Littler rarely played more than two weeks in a row and never more than three.

"When I thought I'd earned enough," he said, "I'd just go home and stay there for awhile. Who knows how much more successful I might have been if I'd had a different attitude, if I had been more like Palmer?"

Even his nickname, "Gene the Machine"—Jim Murray described his swing "as uncomplicated as a chorus girl, and twice as pretty"—was an indication that if excitement was what you were after, you were in the wrong place.

"I guess I don't meet people well," Littler said. "It's hard for me to give with what I really feel."

Little wonder that early in the final round at Oakland Hills, the gallery, if you can call it that, following him and Gardner Dickinson didn't reach double figures.

So if we are going to praise Gene Littler, who grew up in San Diego, and we most certainly should, it will have to be for his grit and determination.

And I don't mean just on the golf course.

In March 1972, Littler, after going in for a routine physical exam, was diagnosed with a malignant tumor of the lymph gland, which can spread very quickly.

"The first thing you think of is, am I going to die?" Littler recalled. "Then you say, Why me? I never drank or smoked. I know people who didn't take care of themselves at all, who did everything wrong and they were healthy."

Thank goodness he had the exam when he did.

The doctors, who took out muscles on his left side, including a large part of the pectoral, didn't mince words.

"We told Gene he'd never be able to play tournament golf again," said Dr. David Freeman, a San Diego neurosurgeon.

Early in his recovery, he met with a physical therapist twice a week, worked with light weights, and did some swimming.

Then, one day, while giving a lesson to his brother, Jack, he grabbed a wedge.

"I swung a club before I could raise my arm," he said. "It was amazing. I didn't hit it too bad."

He soon began to practice at La Jolla Country Club.

"I could see the progress each month," he said. "All along the medical people kept saying I wasn't supposed to be doing these things. Nobody could tell me whether I'd be able to play again. But I was determined to try."

Play again, he did. First, in October at a tournament in Japan, where he finished fifth, and then in Napa, where he tied for thirty-fifth.

The following summer, Littler won the 1973 St. Louis Children's Hospital Classic by a stroke over Bruce Crampton.

"This is the year of Secretariat, Tom Weiskopf, Henry Aaron, and lord knows what else," Jack Murphy, a San Diego columnist wrote, "but nothing compares with the grandeur of Littler's achievement."

Littler wasn't done.

He picked up four more victories, three in 1975 alone, including the Westchester Classic in a playoff over Julius Boros, before making his final Tour appearance in 1986.

Too bad it wasn't five victories, with one of them being at Pebble Beach in 1977.

That's the PGA where he blew a five-shot lead on the back nine and lost in a sudden death playoff to Lanny Wadkins.

I have nothing against Wadkins, but it would have been quite a story for Littler to win a second professional major sixteen years after his first—and five years after the surgery.

The loss "was incredibly devastating," his son, Curt, told me.

So when I think of Gene Littler, I don't think of promise unfulfilled. I think of a man with tremendous courage.

"He was my hero and my model for what a person should be," Mickey Wright said.

38

Willie Anderson

Three of the four players who have won the U.S. Open a record four times—Bobby Jones, Ben Hogan, Jack Nicklaus—are legends.

The fourth, not so much.

He was born too early, that was Willie Anderson's fault, playing in an era when golf meant little in America. He died too early, as well, which is a whole other story, a mystery worthy of Scotland Yard.

Speaking of Scotland, that's where Anderson grew up. His father was a greenskeeper at West Links in North Berwick, a course that has been around since the 1830s. He became a caddie when he was eleven and in his early teens apprenticed as a clubmaker in the town of Gullane.

Only, his destiny wasn't in Scotland.

His destiny was in the United States, which relied on Scots with his expertise to teach this difficult new sport.

Anderson, who got off the boat at Ellis Island in the spring of 1896, was fortunate to survive the long voyage. Of the ninety-seven passengers, twenty-one did not. From New York, he made his way to Watch Hill, Rhode Island, serving as the pro at the Misquamicut Club. Over his fourteen years in the United States, Anderson worked at ten different courses.

It didn't take long for people to realize: *This kid can play.*

In September 1897, competing in his first U.S. Open at Chicago Golf Club—the third Open, period—which was thirty-six holes back then, Anderson, only seventeen, almost won the damn thing. England's Joe Lloyd nipped him by one, nailing his approach on the final hole to within eight feet and converting the putt for a birdie. Anderson finished third in 1898, fifth in 1899, and tied for eleventh in 1900.

In 1901, he broke through at Myopia Hunt Club near Boston, defeating Alex Smith by a shot in the first eighteen-hole playoff in Open history. The playoff was held on a Monday because the members had taken over the course the day before. Boy, how times have changed.

Anderson made another statement at Myopia.

When informed by an officer of the club, an Englishman, that the pros would have to eat lunch in the kitchen and not the clubhouse—the upper-class gentlemen who ran country clubs didn't think very highly of anyone who played the game for money—he blew his stack.

"Na, na, we're no goin' t' eat in the kitchen!" said Anderson, who, "standing on the velvety lawn before the clubhouse swinging an iron . . . whether intentionally or not, made a vicious swipe, cutting an enormous divot that flew high, before the astonished gaze of the transplanted Briton."

The pros were allowed to dine in a tent. Not the same as the clubhouse, but it sure beat the kitchen.

When he won his first Open, Anderson played with a gutta-percha ball made from the rubber-like sap of the gutta tree. Two years later at Baltusrol, he used the wound Haskell Ball with a rubber core. No one else has won the Open with two different types of golf balls.

Anderson prevailed in 1904 and 1905, as well, to give him four titles in five years and three in a row. He also claimed four Western Opens. A superb iron player and straight hitter, he possessed what was known as the *St. Andrews swing,* a flat and full-sweeping motion, and needed just eight clubs to get around.

*

For all his success, Anderson wasn't pleased with the impression he made with the public.

"They don't know me—they don't know me," he complained.

It may have been his own doing.

"Willie was somewhat dour at times," according to Tom Mercer, a club pro. "There was this about Willie; if he didn't like a person, he couldn't pretend that he did. He was not what you would call a gladhander."

In addition to his club jobs, Anderson earned money in exhibitions.

Over five days in October 1910, he took part in three thirty-six-hole matches with top pros and amateurs. That's a lot of golf. No wonder Anderson said he didn't "intend to play another game this year."

He didn't. He died two days later at the age of thirty-one.

Only how?

What killed him, according to the *Philadelphia Record,* was "a hardening of the arteries," though many would come to believe, due to an article in *The American Golfer* about twenty years later, that he drank himself to death. Or perhaps it was caused by an "abscess on the brain," as *The Philadelphia Public Ledger* suggested, or epilepsy, as another writer discovered in the city archives.

However Willie Anderson met his maker, he certainly made his mark.

"In my struggles to land the Open," Alex Smith said, "Willie Anderson seemed to be my Nemesis. . . . His untimely death was a blow to his friends, who looked upon him as a player most likely to set a record for Open Championships that would never be beaten."

37

Kathy Whitworth

In 1959, Kathy Whitworth was thinking about giving up the game she loved. It wasn't loving her back.

In three months on the LPGA tour, Whitworth, nineteen, had yet to earn a dime. "I was too confident at the start," she said. "I didn't think winning would be any problem. But it was terrible."

Thank goodness her parents who ran a hardware store in Jal, a small town in the southeast corner of New Mexico near the Texas border, didn't agree. Stick with it, they told her, and if your game doesn't come around in three years—that's how long her father and a couple of businessman in town were subsidizing her for—we will figure out something else.

"When they said that, it kind of took the pressure off me," Whitworth said.

Around the same time, she read a quote in a magazine from Betsy Rawls.

"I work harder for an 80 than I do for a 70," Rawls said.

She couldn't believe it. "I didn't know she ever had a bad day," Whitworth said. "Whenever I missed a shot, I sort of gave up. I made a commitment to myself that from then on, I was never going to give up."

Sure enough, she tied for sixteenth in Asheville, North Carolina, earning $33. "I thought I had won the tournament," she said. "I was so excited. I'll never forget that day as long as I live." She picked up her first victory in the 1962 Kelly Girls Open in Maryland thanks to a three-putt on the final green by Sandra Haynie. Still, a win is a win, and Whitworth got her second one the same season in Phoenix, beating the legendary Mickey Wright by four.

More victories started to come, one after another, and when she notched her last in 1985, the total was up to eighty-eight (including six majors), more than anyone ever, male or female, as well as ninety-five second-place finishes. In seven different seasons, Whitworth won at least seven tournaments. Not too shabby for someone who didn't pick up a club until she was fifteen, and that was only because her friends wouldn't take no for an answer.

Using clubs that had belonged to her late grandfather, she didn't do very well that first time out but was smitten, and before long started taking lessons from Hardy Loudermilk, the pro at Jal Country Club, a nine-hole course. "We played preferred lies, you might say," she said. "It was never in that good a shape to not tee it up somewhere, put it even on a weed in the fairway. You got a club length, as I recall, to move the ball."

Loudermilk called an instructor he knew in Austin, which was about four hundred miles away.

Will you work with her? he asked Harvey Penick.

Send her over, Penick said.

During her audition, "I was petrified," said Whitworth, who had been playing golf for about eighteen months.

After watching her for a while, Penick said he could help, but she would have to do whatever he told her. If not, he said, "I'm afraid it will be a waste of your time and my time." No problem. For three days, with her mother taking notes, she hit balls, day and night, working mainly on her grip. In 1957, Whitworth won the New Mexico Women's Amateur. A year later, having dropped out of Odessa Junior College in Texas, she turned pro.

The tour back then was a far cry from what the LPGA is today. In addition to the small fields and the meager prize money (less than $10,000 per tournament), the women, at times, teed off between groups of club members.

They didn't complain.

"We were glad to be playing," she said. "We did whatever we could and whatever they required."

No one required more from Kathy Whitworth than Kathy Whitworth. She played practically every week, feeling she owed it to the tour. "Everything had been so good for me that I wanted to do my part," she explained.

After the 1973 season was over, Whitworth headed home. All she needed was a few months off and she would be ready to tee it up again.

Not this time.

"When the next year rolled around, I wasn't looking forward to going back," Whitworth said.

One day, she looked like the player she had been for the last decade. The next, she looked like she hadn't touched a club in her whole life. Whitworth didn't have a clue of what was wrong. A friend of hers did.

"Every time you get in contention," the friend told her, "you find a way to get out of it and so you shoot a bad score."

In other words, Whitworth was sabotaging herself to take the pressure off of needing to win. The pressure she had been feeling for a long time.

From then on, if she didn't feel like playing for a week or two, so be it. The tour would survive. There were plenty of young stars to take her place.

"It extended my career," she said.

In the spring of 1982, Whitworth picked up victory number eighty-three, passing Mickey Wright for the most all time.

"Thrilled to death for you," Wright wrote in a telegram. "Know you're relieved. Keep winning."

Whitworth played until 1991 when she was in her early fifties. She had no choice, having lost virtually all of her retirement savings, about $400,000, which she had invested in Technical Equities Corp., a California-based financial management company that went into bankruptcy in 1986, its founder going to prison for fraud.

"It was described as a sure-win thing, but a couple of years later," she said, "there were rumors it was having problems.... Athletes, doctors, professional people, a lot of lives were ruined and there were a number of suicides.... That was a very difficult time in my life, because I had never played golf feeling like I had to do it to survive. The fun was gone, and I didn't play worth a darn."

Yet she made it through, which didn't surprise anyone who knew her. Kathy Whitworth, who died on Christmas Eve in 2022, made it through every challenge she ever faced.

Thank goodness her friends insisted they play that day in Jal.

"I have no idea what I would have been doing if that hadn't happened," she said.

36

Greg Norman

I will not write another letter, I promise. No way. The Shark didn't respond to my last letter about Craig Wood, and I know how to take a hint.

So, where do I start?

I got it: on August 11, 1986, the final round of the PGA at Inverness.

I was in the gallery. Not as a golf writer. As a fan.

After Norman birdied the 9th hole to seize a four-stroke lead, I figured, like everyone else, it was over.

It wasn't.

A double bogey at 11 and the lead was down to two. A bogey on 14 and the lead was gone.

Norman's playing partner, Bob Tway, won it by holing out from the bunker on the 72nd hole.

I was ecstatic.

Not because I liked Tway or disliked Norman, but because of how fortunate I was to witness such an historic moment in person.

Nonetheless, I felt bad for Norman as I drove back to my place in Michigan. He didn't lose the tournament. Someone else won it.

How wrong I was.

Greg Norman shot a 40 on the back nine for a five-over 76. I'm sorry, but if you shoot a 40 on the last nine holes of a major championship, you deserve to lose.

That isn't bad luck. That's bad play.

I'm not suggesting he didn't suffer his share of bad luck over the years. Exhibit A: the Larry Mize chip-in on the second playoff hole of the 1987 Masters. Only that the narrative of Greg Norman as a victim of fate is misleading: he, and no one else, is responsible for him winning only two majors (the British Open in 1986 and 1993).

Think I'm being too harsh?

Well, consider this: from 1986 through 1996, Norman held at least a share of the lead during the final round of thirteen majors.

Do the math. That means he failed to come through in eleven of those thirteen—and failed, I'm afraid, is the only way to describe it no matter how many others might rave about him.

"To me, the incredible quality of his golf over a very long time," said fellow Aussie Geoff Ogilvy, "should give him the equivalent status of a ten-time major winner. But it doesn't work that way."

No, mate, it does not.

Nothing, of course, matches his meltdown at Augusta in 1996 when Norman, leading by six after three rounds, closed with a 78 to lose by five to Nick Faldo. Everything that could go wrong did go wrong. On the back nine, especially, beginning with a bogey at 10. Give him credit, I suppose, for not leaving the Tour and entering the witness protection program.

"I've let this one slip away and I've let others slip away," he acknowledged, "but it's not the end of my life.... I'm not going to fall off the face of the earth because of what happened here."

Slip away is one way of putting it.

I prefer *throw* away.

Take the four-iron he hit into the gallery on the last hole of the 1986 Masters that cost him a playoff, at the very least, with Jack Nicklaus.

Or the three bogeys on the back nine of the 1987 Masters.

Or the tee shot into the fairway bunker on the last playoff hole of the 1989 British Open at Royal Troon that pretty much ended his hopes of the Claret Jug.

I could go on, but I think you get the point.

So, why did Norman self-destruct in the biggest moments?

"Greg can only play one way, and that's aggressively," Johnny Miller explained after the '96 debacle. "When he tries to play conservatively his brain short-circuits. His wires get crossed and the sparks start flying." Or as the late Jack Newton, the runner-up in the 1975 British Open, put it: "The biggest flaw in his game is his course management. The bottom line, it sucks." One might get away with trying low-percentage shots over the first three days "but in the last round of a major," Newton said, "that ain't gonna work."

Many back home recognized the potential in Norman early on.

"I think we may have a helluva player," Peter Thomson said in 1976 when Norman was in his early twenties. "He may not win five Opens because the competition is greater, but this kid is going to be world class."

In 1981, when most of us first took notice—he finished fourth in the Masters, three shots behind Tom Watson—he wasn't Greg Norman from Australia.

He was the *Great White Shark.*

Norman mentioned in a press conference that he hated sharks, though he had never actually shot one.

He checked that box soon enough.

"When I got back to Australia later that year," he said, "I decided to put my conscience at ease." He found one in Queensland and, using a .303 rifle, "buried several bullets into the thick skin of an ugly hammerhead and hoped those America golf writers understood."

In the 1984 U.S. Open at Winged Foot, he lost to Fuzzy Zoeller in an eighteen-hole playoff.

That's the Open where Zoeller waved a white towel of mock surrender from the fairway after Norman canned a forty-foot putt on the 72nd hole—Zoeller, tied for the lead, assumed it was for a birdie, not par—the last of three straight clutch saves that kept his hopes alive.

When Norman, arguably the best driver of his generation—he combined length and accuracy—was on his game he was unbelievable.

Which makes his failures in the majors feel like an even bigger loss.

Of what could have been.

Norman, who finished with twenty victories, teased us with rounds that took our breath away. Like the 63 he shot on Day Two of the 1986 British Open at Turnberry. Tom Watson called it "the greatest round ever played in a tournament in which I was a competitor." (It would have been historic—no one had ever shot a 62 in a major—if not for a three-putt on the 18th hole from twenty-eight feet away.)

Or the 64 he turned in on the final day of the 1993 Open at Royal St. George's, when he hit every fairway and sixteen greens in regulation to hold off Faldo by two.

"Anybody who doesn't believe Greg wasn't one of the best players the game has ever seen only needs to look at that tournament," said his former instructor, Butch Harmon. "There was a twenty-five-mile-per-hour wind that day. Greg never missed a shot, had complete control with every club. That was the perfectionist being perfect."

I often think of the day I followed Norman in Toledo.

What if Norman hadn't fired a 40 on the back nine? What if Bob Tway hadn't holed the bunker shot?

In some strange, mystical way, beyond the powers of us mere mortals to comprehend, is it possible—forgive me, I'm a huge *Star Trek* fan— that the entire course of golf history from that moment on would have been forever altered?

"I honestly, genuinely feel bad for him," Faldo said after beating Norman at Augusta. "What he has been through is horrible."

And a lot of it his own doing.

35

Louise Suggs

She wasn't as popular as Babe Didrikson Zaharias. Or some of the greats that came after her.

Nope, all Mae Louise Suggs did was win. A lot.

Sixty-one tournaments, to be exact, including eleven majors, third most behind Patty Berg (fifteen) and Mickey Wright (thirteen). In the 1949 U.S. Women's Open, she defeated Babe by fourteen strokes, and from 1950 to 1962, Suggs, the first woman to attain the career Grand Slam, won at least one LPGA tournament per season.

In the foreword to her book *Par Golf for Women,* Ben Hogan wrote:

"If I were to single out one woman in the world today as a model for any other woman aspiring to ideal golf form it would be Louise Suggs. Her swing combines all the desirable elements of efficiency, timing, and coordination."

In 1946, she picked up her first two majors, the Titleholders Championship and the Women's Western Open.

As an amateur.

A year later, she claimed another Western Open and in 1948, she captured the British Ladies Amateur at Royal Lytham & St. Annes, becoming only the second American—Babe was the first—to win the event. In the 1949 U.S. Open, Suggs, now a professional, closed with a five-under 70 at Prince George's Golf & Country Club in Maryland, while Babe faded away with an 80.

She and Babe, in case you're wondering, didn't exactly see eye to eye.

They met for the first time in 1945 in the locker room at the Western Open in Indianapolis.

Suggs, who had been hearing about Babe her "whole adult life," introduced herself.

"She stood there," she recalled, "and looked me up and down and said, 'So what?'"

Suggs thought Babe was a bully and a cheater.

"Everybody knew what was going on, but nobody could do anything about it," she explained. "So it just got to the point where it was a laughing stock situation, and you just kept your mouth shut and went on about your business as best you could."

Once, during a tournament in Illinois, Suggs claimed she saw Babe, the eventual winner, pick up her ball near a few trees and take an illegal drop at least fifty feet away. Protecting the field, she refused to sign Babe's scorecard. "Suggs lost all respect for Babe after that," Betsy Rawls said.

Suggs, all five feet six inches of her, never backed down to anyone. That included Hogan. In 1945, they were partners in the Chicago Victory Pro-Lady. Suggs, twenty-one, was still an amateur. "On the last nine the first day, from the same tees, I beat Hogan 35 to 36," she recalled. "I think the guys in the locker room really gave him fits. I know he wasn't too cordial the next day."

She let him have it:

"Mr. Hogan," she said, "I don't think you're a gentleman."

"What?" he responded.

"I came here to help you win. You're playing for money. I'm playing for a money clip, and you can't even be civil."

The two got along just fine after that.

As feisty as she could be—her license plate read TEED OFF—there was another side to Louise Suggs.

"On the course the wispy Miss Suggs gives the impression of being a nerveless, icy campaigner," wrote Beverly Hanson, a seventeen-time tour winner, "but beneath her controlled exterior, she's as jittery as a schoolgirl on her first date. One reason for her slim figure is the fact that, during tournaments at least, a constant case of 'butterflies' allows her to only go through the motions of eating."

Suggs had her father to thank for her life in golf.

Johnny Suggs, a left-handed pitcher for the Atlanta Crackers (his father-in-law was the owner) in the New York Yankees farm system hoped to get called up to the big leagues in 1923 but was passed over in favor of Herb Pennock, whom the team had acquired from the Boston Red Sox during the offseason. (Pennock won nineteen games his first year for the Yankees and is a member of the Baseball Hall of Fame.)

"Dad said, 'If I take off this uniform,'" Suggs said, "'I'll never put it back on again, because I've got a baby on the way.'"

The baby was Louise.

Leaving baseball behind, Johnny Suggs built a nine-hole golf course in nearby Lithia Springs, where the family would one day reside. The greens fees were seventy-five cents on weekdays, one dollar on weekends.

He taught Louise as much as he could, but like countless young golfers back then, she aimed to emulate the swing of another Georgian, Bobby Jones, whom she often saw at East Lake in Atlanta. "I never will forget," she said. "We were on the 11th hole, and I said, 'Mr. Jones, if you had one thing to tell me, to help me with my game, what would it be?' He said, 'Knock the hell out of it; it will come down somewhere.'"

When she was seventeen, Suggs, subbing for Babe, took part in a charity event with Bob Hope and Bing Crosby. The first to hit on number 1, she walloped her tee shot about 250 yards. As Hope was walking away from the tee, Crosby asked where he was going.

"I'm going to get a skirt," he said. "Where do you think?"

In 1946, Suggs was ready to add another title, "newlywed," the lucky man being Howard McCracken, an Army pilot she met on a golf course in Georgia.

The wedding, scheduled for September, never took place. His plane crashed in the Himalayas.

"My life would have been a whole lot different, I'm sure," said Suggs, who remained single until her death in 2015.

In 1950, she joined with a dozen others, including Babe and Patty Berg, to establish the Ladies Professional Golf Association.

"We figured if we could maybe get some tournaments together, we could at least pick up a little pocket change," she recalled. "We were so dumb that we didn't know we couldn't succeed. We survived and succeeded despite ourselves."

In 2024, the total purse for the LPGA tour rose to more than $120 million.

"It never dawned on any of us that it'd wind up like it is now," Suggs said decades later. "When I look at [the LPGA's] headquarters in Daytona Beach, when we worked out of the trunks of cars, it boggles the mind."

One might say the same about what she pulled off at the 1961 Royal Poinciana Invitational in Florida.

Suggs, in her late thirties, won the event, beating, among others, Sam Snead and Cary Middlecoff. Granted, it was on a par-3 course measuring only 2,688 yards, but everyone played from the same tees.

Snead, who finished third, wasn't too thrilled about losing to a woman.

"I finally had had enough," she said. "I said, 'Sam, I don't know what the hell you're bitching about. You weren't even second.'"

34
Jim Barnes

In July 1921, Jim Barnes had quite a week.

On July 22, Barnes, who stood six feet four and hit the ball a mile, won the U.S. Open at Columbia Country Club in Chevy Chase, Maryland, by nine strokes. There hadn't been a landslide like that since Abraham Lincoln defeated his former Civil War general George McClellan (212 electoral votes to 21) in the election of 1864.

Speaking of the White House, that's where Barnes headed for lunch a day or two after the tournament.

About a month before the inauguration, he and the president-elect, Warren Harding, had teamed up at a course in St. Augustine, Florida, to take on Fred McLeod, the 1908 U.S. Open champion, and a friend of Harding's.

Barnes was surprised to run into McLeod, his closest friend in golf.

"What are you doing here?" he asked.

"I'm here with the Big Boss," McLeod said.

"Your club president?"

"No, no, no. The Big Boss."

"What other boss you got?"

"The Big Boss... Harding."

Barnes didn't believe him... until he went to an area near the locker room.

"Jim Barnes," the president-elect said, "you're just the man I'm looking for. Now I've got a partner."

The two got along quite nicely, Harding telling Barnes he would show up for the Open at Columbia. "He was [there], too, every day," Barnes recalled. "When I putted out on the last hole, I walked over to him and the first thing he said to me was, 'Congratulations, partner.'"

For Barnes, who had led by seven with one round to go, the home stretch turned out to be a victory march.

Literally.

"You could hear them [the Marine Band] playing all over the course," he said, "and when I came up to the last couple holes I marched right along with the songs. I didn't know where the president was at the time, and I thought they might be playing for me."

Barnes, who was born in the village of Lelant in Cornwall, England, and moved to the United States in 1906, also won the PGA in 1916, the first ever, and 1919.

Rallying from four down in 1916, he knocked in a four-footer on the final hole at Siwanoy Country Club, just north of New York City, to prevail over Jock Hutchison one up. "Evidently Jim Barnes has no nerves," *The New York Times* reported. Because of his height, "when he leans forward to putt he is looking straight down into the bottom of the cup, the ultimate destination of his ball making a miss improbable if not impossible."

Defending his title in 1919 at the Engineers Country Club—due to World War I, the PGA wasn't held in 1917 and 1918—there was no suspense this time as Barnes had his way with Bob MacDonald in the semis (5 and 4) and McLeod in the final (6 and 5). In match play, according to *The Times,* "there is probably no other adopted foreigner or homebred who can compare to this tall Cornishman."

Two down to McLeod after ten holes, Barnes won seven of the next eight to go 5 up after eighteen.

"In baseball they would call this a rally," *The Times* put it. "In golf it is a Barnesism.... Golfers who give up easily, golfers who quit without half trying, should study Jim Barnes' game."

Which he learned as a caddie at the Lelant Golf Links, now the West Cornwall Golf Club, before advancing to clubmaker apprentice and assistant pro. After setting sail for a new life in America, Barnes went from one club job to another while winning his share of tournaments along the way.

In the final round of the historic 1913 U.S. Open in Brookline, Barnes shot a 41 on his first nine to stay within range of the leaders.

"He needed 34 on the back, two under par, not an easy assignment under the best of conditions," Mark Frost wrote, "but he'd done it already during the first round the day before ... [this time] Jim Barnes wasn't up to the task. Consecutive bogeys at ten and eleven left him three strokes down. His star faded fast; Barnes was done."

In 1914, he claimed the Western Open, the first of twenty-two Tour victories. In 1916, 1917, and 1921 no one won more tournaments than Jim Barnes.

His final major came in the 1925 British Open at Prestwick.

Barnes, who opened with a course-record 70, got help from Macdonald Smith who closed, you may recall, with a horrific 82; he prevailed by a stroke over Ted Ray and Archie Compston.

At age fifty-one, he won the 1937 Long Island Open, the first Tour victory for a player fifty or older. He is one of three Europeans—the others are Rory McIlroy and Tommy Armour—to claim three different majors. (Barnes never played in the Masters.) And the only golfer to be awarded the U.S. Open trophy by the president of the United States.

"The new champion has proved himself to be a player possessing courage, skill and poise," Harding said at the presentation ceremony. "He has proved himself to be a sportsman in the finest sense of the word."

33

Lloyd Mangrum

When he rejoined the Tour in 1946, Lloyd Mangrum didn't let a bad shot or bad break get him down, as it might have in the past.

Not after what he had been through.

Normandy and the Battle of the Bulge, for starters.

Mangrum, who had won five times before joining the U.S. Army in 1943, was one of only two men from his original unit to survive. Shortly before D-Day, he and his friend, Richard Green, tore up a $1 bill, vowing to put the bill back together after the war.

Green didn't make it.

Mangrum carried his half with him the rest of his life, the torn bill now in the World Golf Hall of Fame.

He wasn't part of the invasion on June 6, 1944, but broke his arm in two places a short time afterward when the jeep he was riding in flipped over in France.

"You'll be OK if you can raise your arm when the cast is taken off," the doctor said.

For months, while recuperating, Mangrum could do nothing but wait.

"Not even the thrill I got from winning the Open [in 1946] equaled the one I got that day I found I could lift my arm," Mangrum said. "Imagine a golfer who couldn't do anything but swing like a hockey player."

His days in combat, however, were far from over.

A member of Patton's vaunted Third Army during the Battle of the Bulge, which started around Christmastime in 1944, he was shot in the knee and left shoulder. Earlier, he had, reportedly, "averted death when he happened to turn his head just enough to miss a fatal bullet that harmlessly dinged his helmet instead."

As Mangrum put it: "An inch here and a half inch there is the difference between a dead sergeant and a live champion."

He came home with two Purple Hearts, which he thought was no big deal.

"Don't ever say I won a Purple Heart," he said. "You don't win it, you just get it. You're in the wrong place at the wrong time ... and you get it. Winning is something that's happy and I never saw any happiness over getting your tail shot off."

He should be admired, nonetheless.

For being on the battlefield at all. He had turned down an offer to be the head pro at the Army's course in Fort Meade, Maryland. "I'm in the Army to fight for my country," Mangrum said, "not to play golf."

In early 1945, the war coming to a close, he wrote a letter to Fred Corcoran, the top administrator in professional golf:

Hi Fred,

...I got to play four times when I was in a hospital in England ... but other than that you might say I haven't played for a year. I would need two a side from you these days.... Good luck to everyone back there. Maybe it won't be long before all of us can make the tour again.

So long for now,
Lloyd the Hacker.

Some hacker. In 1946, he finished in the top five in four of his first eight starts.

This wasn't his first comeback.

In the late 1930s, when Mangrum, living in the Los Angeles area, first tried to make it on Tour, he ran out of money. "What does a guy do when he's flat broke and 2,000 miles from home?" he asked Scotty Chisholm, a golf writer and tournament announcer.

"You go back and get together another few bucks, laddie," Chisholm told him. "Then you hit the circuit again."

Mission accomplished, and this time there would be no turning back.

In March 1940, Mangrum notched his first victory at the Thomasville Open in Georgia thanks to an eagle on the final hole to beat Bryon Nelson by two. A month later, in his Masters debut, he opened with a course-record 64 that stood until Nick Price shot a 63 in 1986.

Mangrum, who came in second in 1940 to Jimmy Demaret, finished in the top ten at Augusta National every year from 1947 through 1956.

His record in the U.S. Open was also outstanding, with six finishes in the top five.

In 1946, in a thirty-six-hole playoff at Canterbury with Nelson and Vic Ghezzi, Mangrum trailed by three with six to go. He promptly birdied 13, 15, and 16 and lined up a seven-footer on 18 in the middle of a downpour for the victory.

"He didn't even hesitate," Bud Ward, a two-time U.S. Amateur champion recalled. "Just stepped up like nothing was at stake and banged it in."

Another time, at a tournament in Phoenix, he was in the hunt down the stretch when his ball got stuck in a tree, forcing him to take a penalty.

"Lloyd never said boo," said Frank Stranahan, who was paired with him. "He just went about his business. I said, 'Jeez, Lloyd, I never saw a tough break like that, under pressure, handled so well.' He said, 'Frank, after surviving a jeep rollover and getting out of World War II alive, I promised myself I'd never get upset about anything in golf ever again.'"

Mangrum was afraid of no one.

In his rookie year, he was playing ahead of Gene Sarazen, who twice drove into his group.

"Mr. Sarazen," he said on the tee at number 10, "you'll probably win this tournament. I'm trying to make $100 to get out of town on. But if you play into me again, I'm going to take your bleep-bleep ball and hit it back over your bleep-bleep head."

Years later, prior to the final round of the St. Paul Open, Mangrum, who was in the lead, got a call from someone warning that if he didn't lose the tournament, he'd lose his life.

The police told him he should withdraw.

The police didn't know Lloyd Mangrum.

"Withdraw?" Mangrum said. "What do you think I'm playing for, tin cups? Just give me some bodyguards who will keep their heads up. In my racket, you need to keep your head down."

He shot a 70 and won going away.

Mangrum finished with thirty-six victories, including seven in 1948, although no majors after Canterbury.

One missed opportunity was the 1950 Open at Merion.

With three holes remaining in an eighteen-hole playoff with Ben Hogan and George Fazio, he trailed Hogan by one. At number 16, he faced a critical fifteen-footer for par. He converted the putt but was assessed a two-stroke penalty for marking his ball a second time; he had been getting rid of a bug. Mangrum was now three behind Hogan, the eventual winner.

As usual, he took it in stride:

"Fair enough, we'll eat tomorrow no matter what happens."

In 1962, Mangrum, who was rarely seen without a cigarette in his mouth and sported jet-black hair and a pencil-thin mustache that made him look like a movie star—"our answer to Errol Flynn," some of his peers said—suffered a heart attack, the first of twelve.

The last one killed him in 1973. He was fifty-nine.

He spent his final years as the head pro at Apple Valley Country Club on the edge of the Mojave Desert about a hundred miles from Los Angeles. Bob Tinsley, who played with him on several occasions in the early 1970s, told me what Mangrum did one day on the 18th hole, a par-5 measuring over 500 yards.

A one-iron down the middle of the fairway.

Another one-iron . . . into the cup for a double eagle.

"I couldn't believe my eyes," he recalled.

Mangrum, according to Tinsley, didn't get too excited. My guess is he had enough excitement to last a lifetime.

32

Bobby Locke

Gary Player, eighty-six years young, offered his opinion—he's never been short of those—about fellow South African star Bobby Locke: "There are people who get robbed in life," Player told me, "and the highest robbery ever is the ranking of Bobby Locke. Every time I see a ranking of the top twenty golfers, I don't see his name there. It's quite hilarious." (I didn't dare tell him that he wasn't in my top twenty, either.)

Player brought up Byron Nelson who, he said, is always ranked in the top ten.

"Bobby Locke," Player said, "would have eaten Bryon Nelson for breakfast." (I didn't dare tell him I, too, have Nelson in the top ten. I'm a coward, I admit it.)

"Locke was an amazing putter, wasn't he?" I asked him.

Player pounced on that softball.

"Not an amazing putter," he replied. "The best putter who ever lived. And he played on Bermuda greens with bad mowers and spike marks. The wear and tear on them by the end of the day was terrible. I played a hundred rounds with him. You had to see how he putted to believe it. What would have happened if he played with the conditioned greens of today?"

What about his swing? I asked, knowing it didn't get the praise his play on the greens did. And that's putting it mildly.

His right foot a few feet behind his left, his shoulders, according to one account, "rolled and spun like a wallowing whale. Every shot would start way right, then curl slowly back to centerfield."

Player said Ben Hogan once spoke up in defense of Locke at the Masters Champions Dinner. "Everybody thought he had a crazy swing," Hogan said, according to Player. "I loved his swing."

In any case, I don't get the feeling Locke was too concerned with how he looked from tee to green. He is the one, after all, who came up with the famous line: *You drive for show and putt for dough.*

The numbers do not lie.

Locke won six Tour events between May 11 and July 27, 1947, finishing second on the money list, just $3,600 behind Jimmy Demaret, who played in twice as many tournaments (twenty-eight to fourteen). Locke ended his career with thirteen victories, including four British Opens.

As outstanding as his record was, it should have been better, and it was no fault of his.

In 1949, shortly after capturing his first Open at Royal St. George's, Locke was barred from the U.S. tour.

The official reason was that he had reneged on a commitment to compete in the Inverness Four-ball tournament and the Western Open.

The PGA of America required players in those days to give a thirty-day notice for withdrawing from any event.

Claude Harmon, the 1948 Masters champion, and he wasn't alone, recognized a more sinister motive.

"Locke was simply too good," he said. "They had to ban him."

He was reinstated in March 1950—Hogan, Nelson, and Sam Snead pressured the PGA on his behalf—but would never again feel welcome in the United States, opting to play the majority of his tournament golf overseas. Locke won only once more in the States: the 1950 All American Open in Illinois.

I can't help wondering: What kind of numbers would he have put up if he had spent more time in America? (In seven U.S. Opens, from 1947 through 1954, he finished in the top five on five occasions.)

A bomber pilot for the South African Air Force in World War II, Locke made his first big impression in 1947 when, back home, he defeated Snead in twelve (two were halved) of sixteen exhibition matches.

Snead, unless I'm mistaken, hadn't received a whippin' like that since losing to Paul Runyan in the 1938 PGA.

"I could beat him from tee to green 15 times out of 18 and still lose," Snead said. "He'd hit a 20-footer, and before the ball got halfway, he'd be tipping his hat to the crowd. He wore out his hats tipping them."

Shortly afterward, Locke made his first trip to the States.

"Before I left, Locke asked me, 'D'you think I could come to America and make a bean or two?'" Snead wrote. "'With that putter, I told him you could get rich.'"

Others weren't convinced and paid the price.

That includes Lloyd Mangrum, who lost $500 betting against Locke in the 1947 Houston Open, which was his first victory, by five over Johnny Palmer and Ellsworth Vines.

Locke was all business on the course, but off the course, he knew how to have a good time.

"He would be the last to leave the bar," Player said. "He called everyone 'Captain.' He would say, 'I got to sing a few more songs for you.'" Locke loved to play the ukulele. "I've never been very good," he admitted, "but after six or seven Pabst Blue Ribbons, I begin to sound reasonable."

The Locke story, I'm sorry to tell you, took some unfortunate twists in his later years.

The first was not of his own doing.

In February 1960, three days after his wife, Mary, gave birth to their daughter, Carolyn, he was a passenger in a car that was struck by a train at a level crossing in South Africa. Thrown through the back window, Locke was unconscious for two days in the same hospital where Mary was recuperating from the delivery. He was fortunate to survive but "suffered blinding, violent headaches," according to Janette Makin, a friend. "After the train hit Bobby, everything changed."

The next two incidents were definitely of his own doing.

In 1969, he was arrested for drunk driving. Refusing to allow the police to move the vehicle, he got in and tried to drive it but the back wheels were stuck. The police moved it anyway with Locke still inside.

In 1978, Locke, who owned a block of apartment flats, shot a man he had hired for a paint job. Not satisfied with the work, he refused to pay him.

"I thought there was going to be a drama," Locke told the court. "I returned to my cottage and fetched my gun. He was about to turn when I fired a shot. He was obviously coming back to make a contest."

Locke was found guilty of attempted murder but got off easy with a $140 fine and suspended three-month sentence.

His reputation, on the other hand ...

"The incident banished Locke to a dark corner of the public memory," one writer suggested.

Maybe so, but remember him we should.

You drive for show and putt for dough.

31
Vijay Singh

One low point, and there are a number to choose from, in the long journey of Vijay Singh to the top of his sport was when he was leaving his native Fiji in 1982 to play golf in Australia. Being "dead broke," as he put it, he visited a businessman who had told him he would help out when Singh was ready.

"After trying to avoid me," Singh recalled, "he took me in his office, told me his business wasn't going well, and handed me $20."

Another low point was when he was banned from the tour in Australia.

"He owed me money, and a lot of others, too," according to Ray Graham, administrator of the South Pacific PGA. "He was told he couldn't play here again until those debts were settled."

Then there were the two years he spent as the pro at the Keningau Club in Borneo, an island in the Pacific. Talk about being off the beaten path. One writer described Borneo as "the tournament player's equivalent of Devil's Island." Singh and his wife, Ardena, went weeks without running into another human being.

He made $160. Per month. Not counting lessons.

"I was out there in the jungle hitting balls and practicing in 100-degree heat and trying to think about what I'm going to do next," Singh recalled. "I had to earn some money so I could go out on the tour again...I never thought about coming to America, let alone winning a golf tournament here."

Finally, and this is a low point that followed him for years, Singh was suspended by the Asian Tour for allegedly altering his scorecard by a stroke in the 1985 Indonesian Open.

Ever since, he has pleaded innocent.

"It was a misunderstanding between the marker and myself," Singh insisted. "It so happened that my card showed me one more than I actually shot, but instead of just disqualifying me, they banned me from the whole tour. My marker was the son of a VIP in the Indonesian PGA, so to save some embarrassment, they chose to get me."

Another player who was in the field that week begged to differ:

"It was not a misunderstanding. All of us who were around are very upset that Vijay denies this."

Anyway, if Vijay Singh is so special, why am I going on and on about his low points?

To show how much he has overcome. Very few in the top one hundred overcame more.

In Fiji, Singh learned the game from his father, a nine-time club champion at Nadi Airport Golf Club.

"My brothers would go to the hotels and bars," he said. "I would never do that, even when I was fifteen or sixteen. Golf was what I did."

Singh did whatever it took to get in his reps. That included jumping over the airport fence and sprinting on the runway between takeoffs and landings... with his clubs on his shoulder. (I might be wrong but I don't think Jordan Spieth ever did that.)

In 1984, Singh won the Malaysian PGA Championship.

Then came the incident in Indonesia, which was how he ended up in Borneo.

Singh took part in his share of money games. One time, there was $700 on the line, maybe more.

Only, he didn't have $700. He had $10.

On the final hole, a par 5, he hit his tee shot out of bounds.

"The feeling I had when I stood over the next drive," he said, "was the worst feeling I've ever had in the game. How would I pay if I lost? Would I lose my job? What would I tell my wife?"

After reaching the fairway with his second ball, he made a par while his opponent found the water on his way to a double bogey. "So I won the hole and a lot of money," Singh said years later. "Now, whenever I'm in contention in a tournament, I think about that. I never told my wife, either."

Singh left Borneo in 1987 for the Safari Tour in Africa. A year later, he captured the Nigerian Open.

"Guess what?" he told his wife. "I've just won nine thousand pounds."

"Vijay, my God!!!" she said.

The next stop was the European Tour, Singh having tied for second at the qualifying school. In 1989, he won the Volvo Open Championship in Italy for his first tour title and tied for twenty-third in the British Open at Royal Troon. He picked up another victory overseas in 1990 and two more in 1992.

America, here we come.

Singh won seven times in his first six years on the PGA Tour, capped by his triumph in the 1998 PGA Championship at Sahalee Country Club in Washington state. Tied with Steve Stricker after three rounds, Singh closed with a two-under 68 to prevail by two.

"It's something I never thought was going to happen," he said. "It's unbelievable."

He claimed his second major at Augusta National in 2000.

Singh shot an even-par 72 on Day One, hitting sixteen of eighteen greens, but with winds gusting to twenty-five miles per hour, that was a more than respectable score; only two players broke 70. On Day Two, he made one putt after another, including a thirty-five-footer for a birdie at number 9, to turn in a 67. Over the weekend, he recorded rounds of 70 and 69 to win by three over Ernie Els.

"Wearing this green jacket tops it all," Singh said. "I can't describe the feeling."

Nonetheless, despite his accomplishments, he didn't receive the best press in the world—and a lot of it was his own fault.

"Maybe if I joked around more around the press tent, your image of me would be different," he told one writer. "But that's not me. And the golf course is my office. If I come up to you when you're writing a story, are you going to drop everything to talk? Or are you going to say you're too busy doing your job?"

On the other hand, he got along well with the people who mattered the most to him. His peers.

"He was very aloof with the media and the public," Gary Koch said, "but there are a lot of players that will tell you that he was as willing to share his knowledge of the game and the golf swing as any player on Tour."

In 2004, he won the PGA at Whistling Straits in a three-hole play-off over Justin Leonard and Chris DiMarco. A few weeks later, Singh, who would collect nine victories that year—he finished his career with thirty-four—rose to number one in the world rankings, replacing Tiger Woods, who had occupied the spot since 1978 when, at the age of two, he appeared on *The Mike Douglas Show*. (It sure seemed that long, didn't it?)

Singh, unlike other players, wasn't intimidated by Woods. Not after everything he had been through.

"It's incredible the success he had after the age of forty," Koch said.

Singh, who won twenty-two times in his forties, did it the only way he knew how. Practice, practice, practice.

"I wonder how much earth he [Singh] has moved over the years,"

Nick Price said. "I don't know if Mr. Hogan practiced as hard as Vijay did. Certainly no one in my era even comes close to him."

30

Harold Hilton

His first came at age twenty-three in the 1892 British Open at Muirfield, his last at forty-four in the 1913 British Amateur at St. Andrews. In all, Harold Horsfall Hilton, a lifelong amateur from West Kirby, a seaside town near Liverpool, won seven major championships. Only two amateurs—Bobby Jones (thirteen) and John Ball (nine)—have won more.

Hilton wasn't a particularly long hitter, but it didn't matter. "The stroke is repeated, time after time, with unvarying accuracy by Mr. Hilton," Horace Hutchinson wrote. "With accuracy perhaps more unvarying than anyone else has ever attained."

He could also get the ball in the hole.

"Fewer strokes are thrown away by him on the putting green, probably, than by any other living player," Hutchinson wrote.

Hilton, who smoked as many as fifty cigarettes on the days he played golf, endured his share of losing before he became a champion.

In the 1887 British Amateur at Royal Liverpool, his first, he was eliminated in the second round.

Two years later, in the Amateur at St. Andrews, he lost his opening match to John Laidlay, learning an important lesson.

"I am afraid that I began that round with the idea that if I gave mine enemy a good run I should have done well, and when the match had finished I felt I had done well," Hilton wrote. "But that is not the spirit in which to approach a Championship. You must go out to win whatever your chance may be on paper."

In the 1891 British Amateur on the Old Course, after storming back from three down with five to go to even the match, Hilton came up short against Laidlay once more. He missed a makeable putt on the first extra hole for the win and another on the second that would have kept him in the game.

"It was evident that Mr. Hilton had not got his nerves under perfect control," *The Scotsman* reported.

In 1892, he lost in the final to John Ball, 3 and 1.

"I always consider that this was the only final I ever played in which fortune was a little unkind to me," Hilton wrote.

Fortune, however, was kind to him a few months later at Muirfield.

He wasn't planning to go to Muirfield at first, he said, "chiefly for the reason that I did not think it was worth the financial outlay." Only when a friend offered him a place to crash did Hilton decide to make the trip.

A wasted trip, it first appeared: after rounds of 78 and 81, he stood seven behind the leader, Horace Hutchison.

Poor Horace. If only the tournament had been thirty-six holes, instead of seventy-two, as it was every year before 1892. He hit his tee shot on the first hole into the woods and wound up with an 86. Meanwhile, Hilton, the hottest player on the course, fired a 72 that left him only two behind Ball with one round to go. Ball was the next to fall back with a 79, paving the way for Hilton to win his first major by three. He chipped in twice and made everything in sight.

As Hilton walked up 18, he was "chatting volubly with his friends," Hutchison wrote, "very pleased with himself, as well he might be, brimful of confidence and with the smoke trailing up from his cigarette even while he was playing the ball so that it seemed impossible that he could see through it to hit the ball correctly. But he did hit it mighty correctly, for all that, and won the Championship."

He won his second British Open five years later, and it couldn't have come at a more appropriate place, Royal Liverpool, which was hosting the tournament for the first time.

Trailing James Braid by three entering the final round, Hilton, who made a forty-five-footer on number 1, needed just eighteen strokes to get through the first five holes and finished with a 75. Braid, who turned in a 40 on the front, barely missed a twenty-footer on 18 that would have forced a playoff. "An endorsement of the previous win [in 1892] was particularly gratifying to me," Hilton wrote, "even though in this second success I had the advantage of playing over a course with which I was well acquainted."

Hilton won the British Amateur in 1900, 1901, and 1911, when he also competed for the first time in the U.S. Amateur at the Apawamis Club in Rye, New York.

The press referred to it as "Childe Harold's Pilgrimage," the title of an early nineteenth-century poem by Lord Byron about a young man—Hilton, forty-two, wasn't exactly young, but still—searching for distractions in a foreign land.

Hilton was 6 up on the long-hitting Fred Herreshoff of the United States with thirteen holes to go.

Game, set, and...

No, not match. Definitely not match.

Herreshoff won three of the next four holes. The fans came alive.

"When he [Herreshoff] began to outplay the Englishman and picked up hole after hole," *The Washington Post* reported, "the crowd was swept off its feet by his masterful work and driven to applauding and shouting at every American stroke."

Through thirty-four holes, the match was all square. Hilton then got bailed out when his opponent missed a five-foot putt at 17 and a seven-footer on 18.

His biggest break was yet to come.

On the first playoff hole, an uphill 377-yard par-4, Hilton, using a spoon (a seven-wood today), pushed his approach to the right, the ball heading toward the woods. Even Seve—hell, Harry Houdini—wouldn't have been able to escape from there.

Harold Hilton never had to try.

The ball bounced off something—some said the turf, others swear it was a rock—and rolled onto the putting surface.

Herreshoff, perhaps shaken by the turn of events, half-topped his approach and hit a poor third, allowing Hilton to become the first foreign-born player to leave the United States with the championship cup in his possession.

"Hilton's spoon to the 37th green," Herbert Warren Wind wrote, "became the most-discussed single shot ever played in an American tournament."

The fans, Wind went on, "were not at all pleased over the idea that a foreigner had carried one of our championship cups out of the country, and men who had never cared a straw about golf before now wanted to know the real inside story."

29

Raymond Floyd

Forget about all the wonderful shots he hit. The two chats, that's what we should focus on when it comes to the life and career of Raymond Floyd. Both were with his wife, Maria.

The first took place in March 1974 at the Greater Jacksonville Open.

Floyd, playing poorly for the second day in a row and almost certain to miss the cut, spoke to Bob Rosburg at the turn.

"Withdraw and let's go back to Miami," Rosburg said. "We can make the racetrack."

Floyd agreed with Rosburg and didn't bother to finish the round. When he got back to his hotel room, he told Maria, whom he had married a few months before, about the change in plans: "Get packing. We got a plane to catch."

She didn't pack a damn thing.

"You've got a long life ahead of you," she would tell her husband, who was thirty-one. "If golf isn't what you want to do for a living, now is the time to get out and think about doing something else. You're not giving it your best."

Floyd was taken aback.

"That was like hitting me in the head with a baseball bat," he said. "I had never dreamed of doing anything other than being a golf professional.... When she said that, the whole realization came home. Had I let it get out of hand that badly?"

In a word, yes.

For the longest time, Floyd applied himself to his craft only when "the bank account got low," hanging out with the likes of New York Jets quarterback Broadway Joe Namath, former Heisman Trophy winner Paul Hornung, Dean Martin, and Clint Eastwood.

Raised in Fayetteville, North Carolina, he couldn't resist the limelight. "It's a life not many get to see or live," he recalled. "I had never been to these big cities or met these other celebrities. It was an incredible life."

So was his next life. Thanks to Maria.

Floyd practiced more, and as the years rolled by, won more.

Prior to claiming the Kemper Open in 1975, his last victory had been six years earlier at the PGA Championship outside Dayton, Ohio. From '75 through '82, he won thirteen tournaments, including a second PGA at Southern Hills. He finished with twenty-two wins overall.

"He went from a guy who was having a great amount of fun," Gary McCord told me, "to a guy who became really comfortable in his own skin, in how he played the game and how he could best defeat everybody. It was something to watch. You didn't want to be in the way of it."

Floyd would have an intense look in his eyes when he got on a roll. There was even a name for it.

The stare.

"He wanted to absolutely bury you," Lee Trevino said.

Floyd claims he didn't give his fellow players the look on purpose.

"That's just when you're in the zone," he pointed out. "I mean, if I could have induced it, I would have won a heck of a lot more tournaments."

The second chat with Maria took place on Sunday, June 8, 1986. She and Floyd were driving from Rye, New York, where he had played in the Westchester Classic to Shinnecock Hills in Southampton, Long Island, site of the U.S. Open. Their three kids, ages six to eleven, and nanny were in the back seat.

Floyd was not in a good mood. The co-leader entering the final round at Westchester, he had closed with a six-over 77 to finish in a tie for twelfth.

"What happened?" Maria asked.

"Just one of those days," he told her. "I blew an engine."

"What made you blow the engine?"

"I don't know."

Floyd wanted to let it go. It had been a long day, and his wife was making it longer.

Maria wouldn't.

"What if it happens this week?" she said. "What if you're leading this week in the last round? You have to understand why you did that."

To this day, Floyd told me, he doesn't "know how you have those rounds. We've all done it at some point in our career."

The two kept going at each other. Floyd became so fed up that he pulled over to the emergency lane on the Long Island Expressway and stopped the car. The kids were crying.

"You're getting out or I'm getting out," he told Maria.

No one got out, although I'm sure the Floyds couldn't have arrived at their final destination soon enough.

One week later, Floyd, forty-three, who in twenty-one starts had never finished higher than a tie for sixth in the Open, became, at the time, the oldest champion in history.

The chat with Maria played a huge role.

"When I got in that position again [leading in the final round at Shinnecock]," Floyd said, "it wasn't going to get away from me this time."

On Sunday's back nine, on a leaderboard crowded with big names, Floyd kept hitting fairways and greens and made one key putt after another to prevail by two over Chip Beck and Lanny Wadkins. He had told Maria—I assume they weren't arguing anymore—after a Monday morning practice round that Shinnecock was so well routed that even the USGA, which set up the Open layouts and not very well in his opinion, "couldn't mess it up."

Four years later, Floyd, poised to win his second green jacket—in '76, he had played the par-5s in fourteen under par to lap the field by eight—was up by three with five holes to go. On 14, his chip from behind the green was tracking until the ball bumped into a penny left by John Huston, his playing partner.

Huston had asked Floyd if the marker was in his way. He told him it was not.

"It sure was on line when that kicked it off," Floyd said.

Yet it was still his tournament to win. Or lose.

As he prepared to hit his approach on 17, Floyd was still ahead by a shot over the defending champion, Nick Faldo, who was playing the final hole. If he could avoid any mistakes, he'd soon be in Butler Cabin.

He couldn't.

"I played it a little too safe [on 17] and the ball went a hair long," Floyd said, "and I had a near-impossible putt. I was thinking par-par and I win the tournament. Bad thinking...I should have tried to birdie 17."

On number 10, the first hole of the sudden death playoff, Floyd had a chance to put Faldo away, but his birdie attempt from fifteen feet came up about a foot short.

"I thought I made it," he said. "But it was uphill and there was dew starting."

He lost the Masters on the next hole, number 11, when his second shot found the pond on the left.

"Hey, I've put things behind me in my life," Floyd said a few years later, "but there's one thing that will disappoint me the rest of my life, and that is giving that golf tournament away.... I had it won and didn't close. I've never said that about another golf tournament."

In September 2012, he lost Maria to bladder cancer.

"We have our arguments and little fights, just like every other good marriage," he once said, "but Maria's my best friend. She's unbelievable, really the most amazing person I've ever met in my life."

28

Jimmy Demaret

Before there was Doug Sanders and Payne Stewart, the flashiest dressers on Tour in their day, there was Jimmy Demaret.

"I learned early," said Demaret, a three-time Masters champion, whose father was a painter, "that color puts life into things."

Purple, pink, peach, royal crimson, hunter green, tangerine, canary yellow, you name it. There wasn't a color or combination of colors he wouldn't try. By the mid-'50s, he owned seventy-one pairs of slacks, fifty-five shirts, thirty-nine sport coats, and twenty sweaters. As for the number of shoes, Imelda Marcos would have been impressed.

"Everybody looked like pallbearers," Demaret said about his fellow competitors. "I went to a New York tailor, Harold Dryer, who made clothes for Adolphe Menjou and Cary Grant, and picked out some material for slacks. Harold told me I had chosen ladies' material. But that's what I wanted."

Demaret, in fact, might have been a nightclub singer—he sang with a dance band as a youth and later performed at clubs and bars with Bob Hope and Bing Crosby—if not for that other calling.

When he was eight, he walked by Camp Logan, a nine-hole army hospital course near his home in Houston, and saw wounded World War I veterans hitting balls. One day, a doctor handed him a pitching iron in pretty bad shape. "Proudly I walked over to a corner of the course," Demaret wrote, "took a few swings—and I was a slave for life. The golf bug had taken its toll. I swung that rusty iron, and any other club I could get my hands on, until the course closed, day in and day out."

One of nine children, he grew up not knowing where his next meal would come from.

"He had quit school and was caddying and shining shoes by the time I came along," said Mahlon, his younger sister by thirteen years.

Luckily, he found his way to Jackie Burke Sr., leading to a life he could have never imagined.

Burke was the head professional at River Oaks Country Club where Demaret was a caddie before becoming an assistant pro. The job wasn't easy. "All the clubs were carbon and steel," said Mike Burke, Jackie's grandson. "He [Demaret] would stand in front of a buffing wheel and buff all the rust off the clubs. He'd hold the iron under a buff and developed really strong forearms as a result."

Demaret was practically adopted by the Burke family, babysitting three-year-old Jackie Jr., who called him Uncle Jim. The two would be friends for life.

In 1934, he won the Texas PGA in Dallas with a record score of 286. However, after earning $25, Demaret skipped town without paying the hotel bill.

"We [he and his caddie] agreed that the $25 was our get-home money," Demaret wrote, "so he waited outside with the clubs, under the window of our fourth-floor room, and I went upstairs and packed our meager belongings. I leaned out the window and dropped them [to him]. As a postscript to this story, I might add that two years later, I sent [the hotel] a check and a note of explanation. Ever since, I've considered them old friends who helped me out when I most needed it."

In 1935, he tied for third in the Sacramento Open, pocketing $250. "It seemed like a million dollars to me then," Demaret wrote.

He went winless in 1936 and 1937, but in 1938, he finally broke through, knocking off Sam Snead in the 36-hole final of the match play tournament in San Francisco, 4 and 3, despite being outdriven by thirty to forty yards.

In 1940, Demaret won six times, including his first Masters title. He opened with a 67, including a 30 on the back. "If there ever was one round a golfer could point to and say, 'that made me for life,' I can point to that back nine at Augusta," he wrote many years later. "Whenever things get tough nowadays in my middle age, I pick up my scrapbook and read about that round."

He followed with a 72 to share the lead with Lloyd Mangrum at the halfway mark.

His next stop: the emergency room?

His stomach hurt so badly on Saturday morning that he couldn't eat a thing.

"There was grave doubt," O. B. Keeler wrote, "if the amiable Texan would be able to start at all."

He started, all right, with help from a little bromide, shooting a two-under 70 to go up by one over Mangrum and three over Snead and Craig Wood. On Sunday, Demaret recorded seventeen pars to prevail by four. "He clicked off the final round in machinelike precision," one writer suggested, "despite tremendous pressure, never once appearing concerned about how it all might end."

In 1941, Demaret won the Inverness Invitational Four-Ball with his partner, the stoic Hogan—could any two people on the planet have been more different?—six months before the Japanese attacked Pearl Harbor. Stationed in Corpus Christi, Texas, he served in the Navy, the kind of cushy posting Mangrum turned down.

"Every war has a slogan," Demaret quipped. "'Remember the Alamo,' or 'Remember Pearl Harbor.' Mine was 'That'll play, admiral.'"

Demaret finished his career with thirty-one victories, but there's no telling the numbers he might have put up if he hadn't lost three years due to the war. He was thirty-five when the fighting came to an end.

"He was the most underrated golfer in history," Hogan said. "This man played shots I hadn't even dreamed of. I learned them. But it was Jimmy who showed them to me first."

In 1947, Demaret won for the second time in Augusta. The first golfer to shoot under par each day, he beat Nelson and Frank Stranahan by two.

"I wanted to win this one ['47] more than anything I know," Demaret said. "I kept thinking about what Walter Hagen used to say. He said if you win once you are lucky, but if you win twice you're just plain good."

And if you win three times...

In the 1950 Masters, he needed help, and as you may recall, Jim Ferrier, the Aussie, gave it to him. Demaret, dressed for the occasion—bright green slacks, a white and green shirt, green shoes, and a green cap—birdied 15 and 16 to win by two as Ferrier made one mistake after another.

Once his playing days were over, Demaret stayed busy, co-hosting Shell's *Wonderful World of Golf* series on TV, building the Champions course in Houston with Jackie Burke Jr., and launching the Legends of Golf tournament in the late 1970s, which led to the establishment of the Senior tour.

The way he left us, of a heart attack in 1983, says everything you need to know about the man.

The night before, writer Charles Price was told, "he had a drink with some friends, a drink his doctors told him he shouldn't have because of his heart."

"Get out and live," Demaret once said. "You're dead for an awful long time."

27

Ernie Els

In 1991, in eight starts on the Ben Hogan Tour, the developmental tour in men's golf, the six-foot-three Ernie Els, aka *The Big Easy* for his rhythmic, effortless swing, earned only $6,143.

"Those guys are survivors out there," Els said. "They play for a living, and they kicked my butt."

They didn't kick his butt for long.

He continued to work with instructor David Leadbetter, who corrected his hook by rotating his grip and adjusting his weight shift. In 1992, Els became the first since Gary Player to win the South African Open, PGA, and Masters in the same year.

In 1994, he defeated Greg Norman by six to capture the Dubai Desert Classic.

"He's got a lot calmer temperament than I had fourteen years ago," Norman said. "It's taken me fourteen years to get to where he is now."

Els was just getting started.

In June '94, he captured the first of his four majors, the U.S. Open at Oakmont in a playoff over Colin Montgomerie and Loren Roberts.

It was far from easy.

Els bogeyed the 1st hole of the playoff and tripled the 2nd after hitting his approach into a bush. He rebounded with a birdie on 3 and shot even par the rest of the way for a three-over 74, tying Roberts. Monty, meanwhile, was eliminated with a 78.

"I shot 74, but it could have been 80," said Els, who hit only six fairways the entire day. "I made all kinds of putts on the back nine."

Els, twenty-four, put Roberts away with a par on the second extra hole, becoming the third youngest to win the Open since World War II.

"He showed me what I used to see in Jack Nicklaus," Player said. "Jack could play badly and still get the ball in the hole and win. That to me is more impressive than long drives and all the other things that matter."

Yet Els didn't get ahead of himself.

"This has come pretty early for me," he said. "If people want to say I'm the next whatever, good for them.... People have to be patient with me. They're going to expect me to win every week, but that's not going to happen."

No, it wasn't, but I can't help feeling that despite the four majors—a second Open in 1997 at Congressional (he parred the final five holes to edge Monty by one) and two British Opens (2002, 2012)—and nineteen victories overall, Els is another who, as great as he was, didn't reach his potential.

"He should have won more majors," Nick Price told me, "certainly in the seven to eight range." Which Price wanted to make very clear is intended as a compliment.

Why didn't Els win more?

I'll give you two words: The first is Tiger. The second is Woods.

"Maybe six or seven," responded Els, who had three at the time, when asked how many majors he would have captured by then if there hadn't been a Tiger Woods.

Woods said "Hello, world" in Milwaukee two years after Els won at Oakmont. In 2000, Els came in second to Woods in the U.S. Open at Pebble Beach by fifteen and in the British Open at St. Andrews by eight.

"Ernie had all the tools," Frank Nobilo, a former Tour player, said. "You knew he was going to inherit the number one spot. It was just a matter of time. And in three years, everything was shaken up."

Phil Mickelson got in the way, as well.

In the final round of the 2004 Masters, Els eagled 13 to go up by three and birdied 15—"he's got the green jacket by the collar," CBS's David Feherty said—but was caught by Lefty, who birdied 12, 13, 14, and 16. Even so, as Mickelson lined up an eighteen-footer on the 72nd hole, the odds were good that Els, practicing on the putting green, would be headed to a playoff.

Then came the roars.

Els went six under the last twelve holes for a 67, and it still wasn't low enough.

"The frustrating thing for me is I felt I had more to give [on the last three holes] but I played it too safe," he said. "I didn't want to make a mistake coming in, knowing Phil's record in the majors to that point [he was winless] and that 17 and 18 are tough driving holes. I thought I'd be okay."

Even so, the loss to Mickelson, coupled with the losses to Woods, doesn't let Els off the hook.

He was in a great position on three occasions when one, or both, weren't in contention but couldn't close the deal.

The 1995 PGA at Riviera

Leading by three after fifty-four holes, Els, who had turned in rounds of 66, 65, and 66, closed with a 72 to miss the playoff between Montgomerie and Steve Elkington, the eventual champion, by two.

"What was supposed to be a walk in the park for Ernie Els," Jim Murray wrote, "became a walk through Dracula's castle."

The 2004 British Open at Royal Troon

He lost by a stroke in a four-hole playoff to Todd Hamilton, who would never win on Tour again.

Els missed a twelve-footer on the final hole in regulation that would have given him the title.

"I'm going to think about that putt for quite a while," he said.

The 2010 U.S. Open at Pebble Beach

In the final round, Els, poised to pick up his first major in eight years, was tied with Graeme McDowell.

Then came a bogey at 9, a double at 10 and another bogey at 11. He wound up finishing third, two back.

He didn't talk to the press afterward. That wasn't like him.

"There's been quite a few close ones over the last couple of years," Els explained a few weeks later, "and I didn't quite have my thoughts together. I wasn't trying to have a swipe at anybody or deliberately being rude. To be honest, I just wanted to go and throw myself in the ocean. Sorry."

I know I sound like a broken record, but I shouldn't be too hard on Els. Over the last thirty years, only Woods, Mickelson, Vijay Singh, Dustin Johnson, and Rory McIlroy have won more tournaments.

Furthermore, he has been a class act his whole career and that should count for something.

In the late 1990s, I was supposed to meet Els in the locker room at a tournament in the Midwest. I waited for a half hour, perhaps longer. He never showed up.

I ran into him the next day in the media center. He couldn't have been more gracious.

"Hey, I'm sorry I wasn't there," he said, wondering if we might be able to reschedule.

I've been a fan of his ever since.

26

Annika Sorenstam

The twentieth century came to an end with Annika Sorenstam in a slump.

A slump by her standards, that is.

After winning six tournaments in 1997 and four in 1998, Sorenstam, no longer the best female golfer in the world—that was now Karrie Webb—won just two in 1999. At Old Waverly in Mississippi, going for her third U.S. Women's Open title in five years, she missed the cut by two strokes.

Something had to change and fast.

In September 1999, she hired Terry McNamara, who had caddied for Rosie Jones, a ten-time tour winner up to then.

"I realized I hadn't reached my full potential," Sorenstam said. "I felt like it was in me, but how do I get it out of me?"

Practice, practice, practice.

"When Annika practiced," McNamara recalled, "there wasn't time for anything else except for what we were trying to get out of that practice. We weren't talking about the movie that was on TV last night or what we had for dinner. I've had players say, 'Yup, I was practicing for eight hours,' but in the eight hours, they might have practiced two and a half. Annika went to the course for three and a half hours and practiced for three and a half hours."

She worked with Dave Stockton, one of the top putters of all time, and trainer Kai Fusser. "To hit it further, I had to train like another athlete," she told me. By bulking up, Sorenstam went from ninety three to one hundred and three miles per hour in clubhead speed with her driver.

The bar all along was Karrie Webb.

"I knew that if I didn't play my best," Sorenstam said, "she would beat me by far. She inspired me."

Goodbye, slump.

In 2000, she won five times, posting fifteen top tens in twenty two starts.

Still, that wasn't good enough.

That fall, Sorenstam handed her caddie a check with a nice bonus. Enclosed was a note that said it all:

"Five wins is great but our goal is to win major championships and get back to world No. 1. And let's not take our mind off of that."

They didn't. Not for a second.

In March 2001, she became the first—and remains the only—female golfer to shoot a 59, with birdies on the first eight holes and on twelve of the first thirteen. It happened during the second round of the Standard Register Ping tournament at Moon Valley Country Club in Phoenix, which she won by two over Se Ri Pak.

"It was the first time," McNamara said, "that I thought, 'We can do this. We can get to the top of this mountain.'"

The week after the 59, Sorenstam captured the Dinah Shore, her first major title since the 1996 U.S. Open, and not a moment too soon. Her inability to secure one of the big ones had prompted a multiple major champion (anonymously, of course) to label Sorenstam as the "Queen of the ShopRite Classic." Ouch.

From 2001 through 2006, she won 46 of the 124 events (37.1 percent) she played in, including eight majors; in 30 of the 124, she came in second or third.

And missed only two cuts.

"If you're kicking yourself because you didn't see Wayne Gretzky, Michael Jordan, Sandy Koufax, or Nolan Ryan in his prime, you should come see Annika Sorenstam," LPGA commissioner Ty Votaw said. "You're seeing a once-in-a-lifetime excellence in a sport."

For Sorenstam, who compiled nineteen victories in 2001 and 2002 compared to Webb's five, there would soon be another mountain to climb.

In January 2003, asked at a press conference in Orlando if she would consider competing in a PGA Tour event, the answer was yes.

"Do you have any idea what you said up there?" her agent, Mark Steinberg, said afterward.

"I do," she responded. And she wasn't about to walk it back.

Before long, invitations from tournaments arrived, Sorenstam choosing Colonial Country Club, one of the shorter courses on Tour, where accuracy is paramount. Some thought her taking on the men was a terrific idea. Others thought it was a terrible idea. What if she were to play poorly? Would it set back the cause of women's golf?

"She's looking at it from her perspective," suggested Kelli Kuehne, the U.S. Women's Amateur champion in 1995 and 1996. "She's not looking at it overall, to help grow the women's game. She has a lot to lose and nothing to gain."

Sorenstam couldn't have disagreed more.

"This wasn't about proving women can play against the men," she said. She saw it as "an internal motivation so I could take my game to the next level. Which, in my opinion, would only help the LPGA tour."

Of all the support she received, a letter from Arnold Palmer stood out:

It's certainly your privilege to do what you think is best for you and the game. Just ignore all the comments you are hearing. Do your thing, have fun, and get it done.

Sorenstam got it done, all right, hitting every fairway except one in her opening round to post a one-over 71.

On the second or third hole, McNamara said, she told him: "I am so nervous I can't feel my hands."

"Well," he replied, "they're the only ones we got."

So what if she followed with a 74 to miss the cut by four? She beat about a dozen Tour players and, if she had putted better, would have been around for the weekend.

The lasting image wasn't any particular shot she hit. It was her reaction to her first shot.

After ripping a four-wood about 250 yards down the center of the fairway, a club she usually hit about 225, she pretended to collapse while walking away from the tee box, showing the world the pressure she had been under.

"Everybody took a collective breath," said Meg Mallon, a two-time U.S. Women's Open champion. "She became relatable."

She still had plenty of game when she retired in 2008, but has never regretted the decision.

"Winning another tournament wasn't going to change my life," said Sorenstam, who finished with seventy-two victories, third behind Kathy Whitworth (eighty-eight) and Mickey Wright (eighty-two). She also won seventeen times in Europe. "I had reached my full potential."

Sorenstam, a great ambassador for the game, has come a long way from the shy teenager in Sweden who, on occasion, three-putted the final hole of tournaments on purpose to avoid the spotlight. "It was the speech problem," she explained. "I hated standing up and having to say something.... In school, I very seldom raised my hand and answered the questions. I just sort of stayed by myself."

By herself she remains.

The top female golfer of the last half century.

25

Rory McIlroy

Let me make one thing perfectly clear, as Richard Nixon used to say— what, I couldn't quote Churchill?—Rory McIlroy is my favorite golfer of this century, and I felt that way long before he spoke out so force- fully against LIV, although I wasn't thrilled to see him soften his stance in 2024.

He almost always strikes the proper note whether he is up or down. I even forgive him for blowing off the media after blowing the 2024 U.S. Open in Pinehurst.

Give credit to his parents, Gerry and Rosie, from Northern Ireland. They brought up a mensch.

"I told him at a young age," Gerry said, "it's nice to be nice, and it doesn't cost you a penny."

Unfortunately, no twenty-first-century golfer, however much it kills me to admit it, has been a bigger disappointment than McIlroy.

He appeared destined for double digits in majors—he had four at the age of twenty-five, matching only Jack Nicklaus and Tiger Woods—but with none since 2014, in thirty-eight appearances, which is hard to believe, double digits now seems out of reach. Each time he was in position to break the drought, someone played better, as Cam- eron Smith did in the 2022 British Open at St. Andrews or Wyndham Clark in the '23 U.S. Open in Los Angeles. Or Bryson DeChambeau in Pinehurst.

On the Old Course, he reached every green in the final round but made only two birdies.

"Far too often, I've seen him hit it 320 down the middle," Nick Faldo said, "then flare or pull wedge to fifty feet and three-putt it. That is a killer. It does more damage than just on the scorecard. It eats away at your self belief and trust."

And if the pressure on him wasn't enough already, McIlroy now has Pinehurst—he missed two putts of less than four feet the last three holes to lose by one—to overcome.

There is no guarantee he will. Arnold Palmer never overcame Olympic.

*

McIlroy had a cut-down wedge placed in his hands before his second birthday. When he was seven years old, he played off a 36 handicap.

A 19 by age eight, a 12 by ten, a five by twelve. A one by thirteen.

"I can remember the exact moment, sitting at home, working out all the numbers," he said, "when I realized that I was a scratch player."

Faldo was an early influence.

"Nick emphasized course management, correct side of the fairway, correct size of the pins," McIlroy said. "...Just the things you need to know to get around a golf course. As much as possible I worked on flexibility and core strength and waited around for the length to come. By the time it did, I wasn't afraid of anybody."

Everyone who came in contact with McIlroy sensed something special.

Darren Clarke, a future British Open champion, met him when he was thirteen and they were playing the 7th hole, a 160-yard par-3, at Portmarnock Golf Club outside Dublin. "It was windy as hell and cold enough to be winter," said Dermot Gilleece, an Irish journalist, "and this diminutive kid with a cherubic face and a mop of unruly hair pulls a seven-iron. 'Okay, Rory,' Darren says, 'Show us what you got.' When his ball dropped out of the sky and stopped eight feet from the pin, Darren smiled at me and said, 'Look out for this kid, Dermot.'"

Look out, indeed.

As an eighteen-year-old amateur, McIlroy tied for forty-second in the 2007 British Open at Carnoustie, and in 2009, he won the Dubai Desert Classic by a stroke over Justin Rose. "I was super impressed," recalled Mark O'Meara, who played with McIlroy the first two days. "He had everything."

In 2010, he was victorious for the first time in the United States, at Quail Hollow by four strokes over Phil Mickelson. Making the cut on the number, he shot a 66 on Saturday and a course-record 62 on Sunday. That's what I call sealing the deal.

In 2011, McIlroy, twenty one, led by four heading into the final round of the Masters.

The tournament was his to win or lose.

He lost. And it was ugly.

On number 10, McIlroy hit his drive so far left that . . . CBS didn't have any cameras near enough to show us how far left. His ball came to a rest between two white cabins about 125 yards from the tee.

"Now have you ever seen anyone anywhere close to this on 10?" anchor Jim Nantz asked Faldo, the network's lead analyst.

"Never," Faldo said.

"He's lucky that's even found," Nantz said.

McIlroy, who walked away with a triple, proceeded to bogey 11, double 12, and bogey 15, and that, ladies and gentlemen, is how you shoot an 80 in the final round of the Masters and finish in a tie for fifteenth.

Two months later, he won the U.S. Open at Congressional. By eight strokes.

McIlroy, with a score of sixteen-under 268, set an Open record in relation to par and became the youngest champion since Bobby Jones in 1923. After the third round, his fellow Irishman Padraig Harrington declared McIlroy, who was up by eight, the favorite to surpass Jack Nicklaus in major victories. "Oh, Paddy, Paddy, Paddy," McIlroy told reporters. "You know, I'm looking for my first one. I've put myself in a great position to do that tomorrow, and we'll see what happens from there."

In 2012, McIlroy won the PGA on the Ocean Course at Kiawah Island, again by eight strokes, to be, at twenty-three, the youngest player since Seve Ballesteros to win two majors.

Maybe Paddy was onto something.

McIlroy picked up two more in 2014: the British Open at Royal Liverpool by two over Rickie Fowler and Sergio Garcia—he went wire to wire, playing the sixteen par-5s in twelve under par—and the PGA at Valhalla Golf Club in Louisville, Kentucky, by one over Mickelson. McIlroy bogeyed two of the first six holes to fall three behind but birdied number 7 and eagled the par-5 10th after hitting a three-wood to within seven feet.

"I didn't think in my wildest dreams," he said, "I would have a summer like this. I played the best golf of my life. I really gutted it out today."

Nicklaus himself was looking into the crystal ball.

"I think Rory has an opportunity to win fifteen or twenty majors or whatever he wants to do if he wants to keep playing. I love his swing," he said prior to the PGA.

As Tony Jacklin told me in 2024: "When he is on his game, there's nobody better."

When.

"Sometimes I look at him," Jacklin continued, "he doesn't look as comfortable as others. I'm sure in many cases he is probably trying too hard. It makes you realize how fickle sport can be."

Perhaps I am being too hard on McIlroy. Just as I might have been too hard on Ernie Els and Davis Love III and (fill in the blank).

Imagine if the four majors he won had been spread out over a decade or so instead of coming in a four-year span early in his career. No one would believe he's underachieved, and that includes yours truly.

"He's easily good enough," Harrington said in the summer of 2023. "We all know that…but it's a little bit more complicated than just being good enough. The standard is very deep….Rory has to bring his A game."

McIlroy will turn thirty-six in May 2025. There is still time to pick up at least a couple more. Hogan won eight of his nine majors after turning thirty-five; Nicklaus, six, and Sam Snead, five.

"We're going to get one of these [bleep] things sooner or later," he said in the locker room after losing to Wyndham Clark in Los Angeles.

I sure hope so.

24

Cary Middlecoff

The plan for Cary Middlecoff was to become a dentist, like his old man, Herman, and his uncle, Charnell.

For a few years, the plan worked beautifully.

Middlecoff attended the Tennessee College of Dentistry, and after graduating in 1944, he served in the U.S. Army Dental Corps, filling 12,093 teeth in eighteen months.

When he got out of the army, however, the plan hit a snag.

"I didn't want to see any more teeth," he said.

He wanted to play golf.

His son could surely do both, as he did, figured Herman Middlecoff, who was a club champion in Memphis and ran a successful practice. So to get his point across, he enlisted the help of another lifelong amateur who played at a high level while having a day job. His name was Bobby Jones.

It did no good.

Cary Middlecoff picked up the game at seven and was a city champion at seventeen. In 1945, as an amateur, he won the North and South Open at Pinehurst No. 2 by five shots, playing the final thirty-six holes with Ben Hogan and Gene Sarazen.

"It made me believe I could make a living playing golf," Middlecoff said.

He was long and straight with the driver and made his share of putts.

Middlecoff turned professional in 1947. He was going to give it two years to see if he could be successful.

He didn't need two years.

Middlecoff tied for twelfth in his first tournament in Jacksonville and won his second, the Charlotte Open, in a playoff over George Schoux. He picked up two more victories in 1948, and six in 1949—he would finish with thirty-nine—including the U.S. Open at Medinah.

He trailed by six strokes after Day One. Fortunately, the players leading the way at Medinah weren't the familiar suspects. They were likely to falter.

Falter they did.

On Day Two, Middlecoff shot a 67 to climb within one. A 69 in his morning round on Saturday put him ahead by one.

As usual, he had cope with more than his opponents and the golf course.

"I was high-strung," he admitted. "It was a constant fight within to control myself."

Middlecoff took so much time that Doug Ford Jr., remember, carried a stool for his father in the 1955 PGA.

"I can remember a couple of times I really got into it with him," Bob Rosburg said. "Doc was a nice guy but sort of a pain in the ass to play with or behind."

Middlecoff, for his part, didn't offer any apologies.

"I have always maintained that a man who is not nervous is either an idiot or has never been close enough to winning to get nervous," he said. Besides, he pointed out, he was hardly the only one to take his time. "Nicklaus," he said, "is one of the slowest players that ever played. But it was all right because he kept winning.... Everybody said, 'This is Jack, and he is trying hard.' Well, s---, I tried hard, too."

He let things get to him. Case in point: round three of the 1953 U.S. Open at Oakmont.

On number 10, after finding the bunker with his first and third shot, he let it rip.

Toward the Pennsylvania Turnpike.

Fore!

Well, that's one way to drop out of a golf tournament. A major championship, no less.

"A collection of things had happened," he explained. "Not very good luck, and I had bad starting times. They started me last or next to last two or three times in a row, which is always a disadvantage. I just got pissed off."

Really? We didn't notice.

"I wasn't very proud of that," Middlecoff confessed.

Anyway, back to 1949 and Medinah, a U.S. Open with fonder memories.

Closing with a 75, Middlecoff opened the door to Samuel Jackson Snead. The golfing gods owed Snead, who had thrown away a couple of Opens. With two holes to go, it seemed as if they might finally pay up.

Then it happened again, Snead bogeying the 17th hole—he took three from the fringe—to miss a playoff with Middlecoff by one shot.

In 1955, Middlecoff arrived at Augusta National in good form, having won the Crosby and St. Petersburg Open earlier that season. In good spirits, as well, no doubt, being a fan of the course he got to know quite well while stationed in Georgia during the war. He turned in a 65 on Day Two to put him up by four over Hogan and six over Snead and Jackie Burke Jr. and wound up winning by seven.

Bobby Jones was impressed. Good thing he didn't convince Middlecoff to do more fillings.

"The way he filled those seventy-two cavities during the last four days," Jones quipped, "makes me think I may have been wrong."

In 1956, Middlecoff, the co-favorite with Hogan at 3–1, captured his second U.S. Open at Oak Hill. He passed Peter Thomson, the thirty-six-hole leader, with a 70 in his morning round on Saturday and got up and down from forty yards for a huge par on the 72nd hole. Hogan came up one short, missing a thirty-inch putt on 17.

Middlecoff, who notched twenty-eight victories in the 1950s, just one fewer than Snead, might have won more if it hadn't been for his health. He had a bad back, a right leg a half-inch shorter than his left, and problems with his vision that started when a piece of the drill he had used to put in a filling in 1945 got into his right eye.

And he was allergic, of all things, to grass.

"One of the main reasons I took a lot of time over the ball was that I couldn't see very well," he explained. "The hay fever was part of it, and the problem with the eye was also a factor."

Nonetheless, he nearly made it two Opens in a row at Inverness in 1957.

Down by eight at the halfway mark, he fired a 68 in the third round to cut the deficit to three, and birdied 16 in the fourth to trail Dick Mayer by just one.

On 18, he lined up a ten-footer for the tie, but an eternity went by and he still hadn't brought the putter back.

Finally, a fan shouted what everyone else was thinking:

"Hit the damn thing!"

Middlecoff did, once he responded to the fan and the gallery stopped laughing. And it went in.

"As the putt fell," according to one writer, "a great roar burst from the crowd. Fans leaped about, yelled, clapped each other on the back, and said they'd never seen such a finish."

Too bad Middlecoff had nothing left for the playoff, turning in a 79 in near-hundred-degree temperatures to lose by seven. He won just three more times before leaving the Tour in the early 1960s.

"It is true that Cary Middlecoff played golf slowly, fidgeted, fiddled around over club selection to the point that it's the first thing that pops up when the name comes up," wrote Furman Bisher, the longtime Atlanta writer. "How unjust, how cruelly unjust."

23

John Ball

The Royal and Ancient Golf Club of St. Andrews proclaimed John Ball Jr. as "the first great amateur golfer."

Without question, and in my opinion, he's the third-greatest of all time, behind Bobby Jones and Francis Ouimet.

Ball, who was born near Liverpool in 1861, won nine majors, the same as Ben Hogan and Gary Player and one more than Arnold Palmer and Tom Watson. Yes, the competition wasn't anywhere near as fierce as it would be in the decades ahead, and yes, the fields were smaller.

So what?

Jones, let me remind you, put it best:

"I think we must agree that all a man can do is beat the people who are around at the same time he is. He cannot win from those who came before any more than he can from those who may come afterward."

Ball won the British Amateur eight times, the first in 1888 at Prestwick, the last in 1912 at Royal North Devon when he was fifty years old, the only golfer besides Phil Mickelson to win a major in his fifties. His other major came in the 1890 British Open, also at Prestwick, when he became the first of only two players—Jones would be the second in 1930—to capture the British Amateur and Open in the same year.

By doing so, author Stephen Proctor wrote, it set off such "a frenzy of passion for golf in England that within a decade Scotland's hegemony over its own national pastime would be in jeopardy."

In his first British Open in 1878, Ball, sixteen, tied for fourth at Prestwick, eight behind the winner, Jamie Anderson. He earned one pound sterling for his efforts.

Fortunately, it didn't cost him.

That's because, when the first British Amateur was held at Royal Liverpool in 1885, the committee in charge ruled that any player who hadn't received a prize during the last five years would be allowed to keep his amateur status.

In addition to his eight victories in the Amateur—three more than anyone else—he made it to the quarterfinals on eight other occasions, including at Liverpool when, in the third round, he defeated John Ball Sr.

Yup, his dad.

The elder Ball, who owned the Royal Hotel, the headquarters for the Royal Liverpool Golf Club, reached the semifinals himself in 1887, taking down Harold Hilton, before dropping the final two holes to lose to Horace Hutchison one up.

Too bad. A victory would have set up an all-Ball final.

Let's skip to the 1899 Amateur at Prestwick, where John Ball Jr. squared off against a two-time champion, Scotland's Freddie Tait.

Prestwick was packed. This was the match everyone was hoping for.

"The variegated costumes of the ladies, who formed a considerable part of the crowd," *The Scotsman* wrote, "and the bright scarlet and tartan of a contingent of the 4th Battalion Princess Louise's Regiment, from their encampment in the neighbourhood, gave a lively aspect to the scene."

Tait was 4 up through nine and 3 up through eighteen, Ball missing one short putt after another. During the lunch hour, he took a putting lesson from Hilton. It paid off. By the 6th hole of the afternoon eighteen, the match was all square and stayed tight the rest of the way.

On the 37th hole, Ball lined up a seven-footer for the win.

"A man standing beside me remarked, 'These are just the ones he misses,'" Hilton said. "I thought to myself, no, these are just the kind he holes."

He holed it, all right, and was carried by his fans to the clubhouse.

"I shall always maintain," Bernard Darwin wrote, "that this was the greatest golf match I ever saw, not by any means the most perfect in play, but the most nearly divine in terms of god-like thrusts by either side."

Tait and Ball shared something in common—and it had nothing to do with golf.

They both were in the Second Boer War around the turn of the century. Tait, thirty, was killed in action while Ball served in a cavalry unit, the Cheshire Yeomanry.

With distinction, I should add.

Once, while he was fleeing a Boer farm on fire, "one man's horse came down, and John Ball immediately pulled up and went to his assistance," another soldier recalled, "getting the horse up from the poor beggar's legs—all this of course under very heavy crossfire."

In 1921, Ball, now fifty-nine, made it to the round of sixteen in the Amateur. He won a record ninety-nine matches in all, losing his bid for number one hundred in the second round at Royal Liverpool when he was sixty-five. Five down with five to go, he took the next two holes before his opponent, J. R. Abercrombie, knocked in a long putt to put him away.

Ball, who never took a lesson—I'm not counting the putting tip from Hilton—stood with his feet wide apart and gripped the club tightly with the palm of his right hand.

"He was superbly accurate," Darwin wrote, "and he seemed to have an almost unique power of stopping his backswing at any point he desired."

Darwin said he derived more "aesthetic ecstasy from watching [Ball] than from Bobby Jones and Harry Vardon put together, and it is hardly possible to say more than that."

He was in control of his emotions, as well.

"To my mind, if there was ever a man in golf," possessing a "lack of nerves, it was John Ball," wrote Jerry Travers, the four-time U.S. Amateur champ. "It has been recorded how on one occasion, just before a final round for the British championship...he was found working in his garden, with no thought of golf in his head."

The limelight didn't interest Ball. When his portrait was hung on the stairway in the Royal Liverpool clubhouse, he did "everything he could to avoid walking up the stairs," Stephen Proctor wrote, and in 1912, when the folks at Hoylake prepared an elaborate welcome for him after he won his eighth British Amateur, the guest of honor didn't show up, leaving the train one stop early to walk home along the beach.

"John's soft, whispering voice, his stoicism, his pawky jibs at easy rules and innovations, his relentless criticism of moderns with their fuss, and his total outlook on the game were the very essence of golf," Scottish amateur golfer Robert Harris wrote. "He just played."

22

Nick Faldo

Nick Faldo, who won three Masters and three British Opens from 1987 through 1996 and was number one in the world for nearly one hundred weeks, was the best player to come from the United Kingdom since Harry Vardon.

And yet there was a time in his career when he was known as *Nick Fold-o*, a nickname given to him by the English press for his tendency to fade away in the biggest moments.

So, naturally, one of the things I asked Faldo, who left his job as the lead analyst with CBS in 2022 and now lives on a farm in Montana, was how he felt about the folks on Fleet Street.

He didn't hold back. I didn't expect he would.

One time, he said, he didn't hand in his score in a pro-am and the headline the next day read: *"Faldo Tears Up His Card."*

"I called [the reporter] up," Faldo explained, "and said, 'here's the card in my hand; it's still in one piece. So why the headline?' 'I'm not in charge of the headline,' he said."

Another time, after finishing his round, he told a writer that the greens were slow and bumpy, which led to another damning headline he said he didn't deserve: *"Faldo Slams the Golf Course."*

Faldo grew so irate over how he was portrayed by one particular journalist that he decided to fight back. He told him, "if you are ever in the group [that huddled for an interview after a round], either you stay or I stay. Not the both of us." The writer held his ground the next time, and so did Faldo, who walked away.

He couldn't win no matter what he did.

"Everyone thought I was an ass," Faldo said. "It was sad to have to be defending yourself all the time."

Even so, and he would be the first to admit it, he could have done a better job dealing with the media.

After winning the British Open at Muirfield in 1992, Faldo said at the presentation ceremony: "I want to thank the press from the heart of my bottom."

He claims the comment was totally spontaneous and in jest, and after watching the ceremony on YouTube—he had started to say "bottom" first—I am inclined to believe him. Yet given his history with members of the fourth estate, he had no room for error.

We also spent some time talking about his golf swing. The one he changed even after he had been the leading money winner on the European Tour in 1983 and had won at Harbour Town in 1984.

A lot of guys would never have taken that kind of risk.

And not just a few small changes. A total overhaul.

"The little person sitting on my shoulder said to me, 'You haven't got it, mate. This is not good enough,'" said Faldo, who made the decision in the spring of 1985.

Faldo, working with David Leadbetter, searched for answers in the same place Ben Hogan did.

In the dirt.

"I'd go until I couldn't close my hands," said Faldo, who hit roughly 1,500 balls a day.

Nonetheless, as the months dragged on, there was little or no progress. If anything, his game was headed in the opposite direction.

As were his sponsors.

"My manager used to arrive [at the house]," Faldo recalled, "and I used to say, 'Here he comes to bring the gloom and doom.' That somebody is pulling out, or this [business deal] is not happening."

The only major sponsor to stick with him was Pringle, the sweater manufacturer. Faldo said he earned about twenty thousand pounds a year from the relationship.

In the 1985 British Open at Royal St. George's, he tied for fifty-

248 of The Golf 100

fourth, while Sandy Lyle, also from the UK, walked off with the Claret Jug. A few months later, in the Ryder Cup at the Belfry, Faldo, after losing a foursome match on Friday morning, told captain Tony Jacklin:

"Don't pick me again. I'm no good."

Jacklin, who had been harboring doubts of his own, obliged.

When Team Europe beat the Americans (16½–11½) for the first time since 1957, Faldo, who fell to Hubert Green in the singles, 3 and 1—he couldn't sit that one out—didn't celebrate as enthusiastically as his teammates.

"I didn't feel like I had done my part," he explained.

He finished fifth in the 1986 British Open at Turnberry, but his game really rounded into shape during the week of the 1987 Masters.

Not at Augusta National, mind you. He hadn't played well enough to earn an invitation.

Instead, Faldo entered the Deposit Guaranty Golf Classic in Hattiesburg, Mississippi. The scene at the airport in Atlanta, where he bumped into players and members of the media, summed up how far he had fallen. "Everyone was turning right and going to Augusta," he recalled. "I was turning left and going to Hattiesburg. It didn't feel good."

He told himself: "I'm not going through this again. I'm turning right next year."

In Hattiesburg, where Faldo quipped "there were probably more people inside the ropes than outside," he posted four straight rounds of 67 to come in second, a stroke behind David Ogrin.

A month later, he captured the Spanish Open, his first victory in three years, and shortly afterward, the British Open at Muirfield. That's the Open where he parred every hole on Sunday to edge Paul Azinger by a stroke.

Nick Fold-o, no more.

"Nick struggled at times and was criticized for the changes," Leadbetter said, "but the proof is in the pudding. He hit only one shot off line into the heavy rough all week."

Over the next five years, Faldo won four majors: the Masters in 1989 and 1990, the British Open in 1990 and 1992.

No one else won more than two.

Leading by four through fifty-four holes of the '92 Open, he bogeyed 11, 13, and 14, but was bailed out by John Cook, who missed a short birdie putt on 17 and bogeyed 18 to lose by one. "I would have been scarred from that Open if I had lost it," Faldo admitted. "I've lost majors but I don't walk around carrying any scars from them."

Thanks, Sir Nick—he was knighted by Queen Elizabeth II at Windsor Castle in 2009—for giving me a perfect transition to your battle with Greg Norman in the 1996 Masters.

I won't give Norman a pass—shocking, isn't it?—but it's often overlooked how well Faldo played in the final round (like Billy Casper in the final round at Olympic), his five-under 67 the best score of the day. If he hadn't applied the pressure with birdies on 2, 6, and 8, maybe the Shark wouldn't have imploded.

Maybe.

"I travel the world and we're nearly thirty years on," Faldo told me, "and I get stopped in every airport, every golf course, and [people] say, 'tell us about '96.' Of course, I'm happy to rattle on about it. So many people watched that. I'm blessed with that one. I really am. It's huge for me."

As for what he said to Norman during their famous hug on the 18th green, Faldo guarded it like it was a state secret until he finally spilled the beans about a decade later when he came out with a new book.

"Don't let the bastards [the media] get you down over this," Faldo told him.

He was speaking from experience.

21

Young Tom Morris

He was the Tiger Woods of his time. If only his time had lasted longer.

A lot longer.

The signs that Young Tom Morris would be something special were there from the start. "Most golfers saw only one way to play a hole," author Kevin Cook noted, "but Tommy could picture a dozen, and as he grew, he gained the strength to hit the shots he imagined."

In April 1864, Young Tom, who was about to turn thirteen, went with his dad to play in a tournament in the Scottish city of Perth. When they got there, they were told Young Tom was too young. So as Old Tom and other pros battled against each other, his son took part in a another match on the same course.

The opponent was William Greig, considered by many in those parts to be a star in the making. The real star in the making was Young Tom, who crushed young Greig.

Young Tom was fortunate. With his family secure, he didn't have to be a caddie or clubmaker like his father and others.

Still, he was young and young people make mistakes.

In 1865, playing in his first British Open, he walked off the course with twelve holes to go. Bobby Jones would do the same thing at St. Andrews more than a half century later and regret it for the rest of his life.

In 1867, Old Tom and Young Tom ran into Willie Park Sr. at a tournament in Carnoustie.

"Tom," Park asked Old Tom, "what have you brought this laddie here for?"

Park knew perfectly well why Young Tom was there.

"You'll see what for," Old Tom responded. "You'll see."

Park saw, all right, losing to *this laddie* in a playoff.

Young Tom finished ninth in the Open in 1866 and fourth in 1867.

His turn to take home the championship belt came a year later.

When someone he'd known for as long as he could remember put up one hell of a fight.

Old Tom, of course.

In the first twelve holes of the 1868 Open at Prestwick, Young Tom turned in a 51, the lowest round in tournament history. Old Tom answered with a 50 on the second twelve to assume a one-stroke lead over Young Tom. Park was four back.

Over the final twelve—keep in mind this was all happening on the same day—Young Tom broke the record once more with a 49 to beat his father by three and become, at seventeen, the youngest British Open champion to date.

He still is.

"Spectators, bettors and golfers gathered round to see the Earl of Stair present the Belt to the new champion," Kevin Cook wrote.

"Tommy held the Belt up for all to see, spurring the loudest cheers of the day."

A year later, he brought the championship belt back to Prestwick and picked up his security deposit.

He needn't have bothered.

Young Tom won by eleven strokes. His opening twelve holes included an ace on number 8, the 166-yard Station Hole, the first recorded hole-in-one in professional golf. Young Tom was making history every time he stepped on the course.

In 1870, he won his third straight Open, allowing him to keep the belt for the rest of his life.

He started off in spectacular fashion.

On the first hole, which measured 578 yards, he got it out there far enough in two shots to leave himself roughly 200 yards to the green.

Making a 4 on what was, essentially, playing as a par-6—the term *par* wouldn't be invented until 1911—would be a strong opening statement.

Only he didn't make a 4. He made a 3.

No, it's nowhere near as famous as Gene Sarazen's double eagle in the 1935 Masters, but Young Tom's shot was every bit as incredible. He wound up winning by twelve.

"A new star rose in the golfing firmament, one before which all others had to pale their ineffectual fires," according to one account.

Young Tom didn't make it four straight in 1871.

There was no British Open in 1871.

Because he took the championship belt home for good, the organizers needed to come up with a new prize, as well as determine where the tournament would be held.

For the longest time, they couldn't make up their mind—until, finally, the Prestwick Golf Club, the Honourable Company of Edinburgh, and the Royal and Ancient Golf Club of St. Andrews decided the Open would rotate between St. Andrews, Musselburgh Links, and Prestwick, the clubs splitting the costs of a silver claret jug to replace the belt.

In 1872, Young Tom got that fourth straight title, beating Davie Strath by three. He tied for third in 1873 when the tournament was played for the first time on the Old Course and came in second the following year at Musselburgh.

The 1874 Open was Young Tom's last.

It all started when he fell in love.

Her name was Margaret Drinnen, and on November 25, 1874, they were married.

Margaret, who was ten years older, came with a lot of baggage—she'd had a child out of wedlock—but that didn't deter Young Tom. She was the woman he wanted to spend the rest of his life with, and he didn't give a damn what anyone else might have thought. Before long, a child was on the way.

In September 1875, he teamed up with his dad to take on Willie and Mungo Park at North Berwick.

Young Tom was hesitant to play, with Margaret in her last month of pregnancy, but figured he could hurry back, if necessary, to their home in St. Andrews.

With two holes to go, the match was all square.

A telegram then arrived from St. Andrews with a message for Thomas Morris. Old Tom opened it:

"Come home posthaste."

The message was meant for Young Tom.

Old Tom should have shown it to his son immediately. He didn't.

There was a match to finish, with twenty-five pounds on the line, as well as some side bets. Besides, the next train out to Edinburgh wouldn't take off for hours.

"We must go," Old Tom finally told Young Tom after they prevailed one up. "Your wife is ill."

By the time he got home, she was dead and so was the baby.

Young Tom was shattered. His friends hoped to get him back onto the course to take his mind off his grief, if only temporarily, but, Cook wrote, he "was more inclined to take long, late-evening walks or to sit and drink, a habit he indulged more often as the days grew shorter."

He played more golf that fall and showed signs of his old self, though after one match, Young Tom, according to one writer, "continued to be seen on the links and in his old haunts, looking ill and depressed."

On Christmas Day, he died in his sleep. He was twenty-four.

Word is he died of a broken heart, but not everyone is convinced.

"It makes a nice story, but it is shite," according to David Malcolm, a St. Andrews golf historian and scientist. "He died of a pulmonary embolism due to an inherited weakness. He could have gone at any time."

However Young Tom left this planet, and some will always choose the romantic version, the game has never seen anyone like him.

"I am often asked who was the greatest golfer I have known," wrote Andra Kirkaldy, the Scottish pro who saw Vardon, Taylor, and Braid, "and my answer is always the same—Young Tommy Morris.... I could go on for hours, telling of Tommy's triumphs and singing his praise, for we were all his worshippers."

20

Francis Ouimet

Mark Frost, who wrote *The Greatest Game Ever Played,* a wonderful book about Francis Ouimet's triumph in the 1913 U.S. Open at Brookline, spent months poring through old newspapers.

If he hadn't read the stories, he later wrote, "I'd swear myself it was fiction."

After all, how could Francis, a twenty-year-old amateur, aided by a ten-year-old caddie, Eddie Lowery, take down the legendary Harry Vardon and Ted Ray, the 1912 British Open champion, both from the UK, the game's birthplace, to win America's national championship?

On a course, adding to the absurdity of it all, where Francis had been a caddie and still lived across the street?

Who knows? The golfing gods have never clued us in.

One thing's for certain: from Jones to Hogan to Nicklaus to Woods, nothing has topped 1913, and nothing ever will.

Francis wasn't intending to play in the Open, despite a strong showing in the U.S. Amateur at Garden City two weeks before, losing 3 and 2 in the second round to Jerry Travers, the champion in 1907, 1908, and 1912. After taking a vacation from his job in sales at the Wright & Ditson sporting goods store, asking for more time off was out of the question.

"Why don't you let me worry about Wright & Ditson," USGA president Robert Watson told him.

Francis was in the office not long afterward when he saw his name in the paper among the players entered for the Open's two qualifying rounds.

"This is some kind of terrible mistake," he informed his boss, George Wright.

There was no mistake.

Watson had submitted his name without telling him, and Wright, who received a heads-up from the USGA president, was totally on board.

"It seems to me," Wright told Francis "that as long as you're entered in the Open tournament, you had better plan to play."

*

Francis Ouimet collected golf balls before ever hitting one.

He found them on the way to and from school. One day, he took a few swings with a club that a member had given his older brother, Wilfred, a caddie at The Country Club. Francis swung the club every chance he could and, at age ten, was a caddie himself.

Soon fate, and not for the last time, intervened on his behalf.

Theodore Hastings, a member he was caddying for, asked him if he played golf. When Hastings found out he did and that he lived across the street, he told Francis to get his sticks.

He didn't have to tell him twice.

After a 39 on the front nine, Francis came home with a 45 and it should have been a lot better. He got flustered when he noticed Dan McNamara, the caddie-master, watching him on number 15. Caddies were not supposed to play the course; he got a 10 on the hole.

From that day forward, however, he was permitted to play with the members, and as the years went by, his game continued to improve.

In 1912, he made it to the final of the Massachusetts State Amateur. A year later, he won it. Over the last six holes of his semifinal match versus John G. Anderson, Francis went six under par.

After his loss in the Amateur at Garden City, you may recall, was when he had that most instructive chat with Travers.

"He learned something from every match he lost," Herbert Warren

Wind wrote, "and from some matches he won. He did not copy the mannerisms of other players and allowed his admirable competitive temperament to develop unforced. He knew himself."

The Open was next.

No one was paying attention to Francis.

Why should they?

Not when the field included John McDermott, the two-time defending champion, Macdonald Smith, and, of course, Vardon and Ray. (The tournament had been moved from June to September to accommodate the two Brits who wouldn't arrive in the United States until August.)

Francis hit some tee shot on the 1st hole, and that's not a compliment.

The ball went no more than forty yards, ending up behind a tree. He half-topped his next one into the rough and found the bunker with his third, resulting in a bogey, followed by a double bogey on 2 and another bogey on 3.

His confidence could easily have been shattered. It wasn't.

He played the final fifteen holes in even par for a 77, just six behind the co-leaders, Smith and Alec Ross. In the afternoon—they played thirty-six holes a day—Francis made a double at 16 when he left one in the bunker, but still shot a splendid 74 to trail Vardon and another Englishman, Wilfrid Reid, by four.

The next morning, Francis, with encouragement from his mother, who would later join the ever-expanding gallery—his father, similar to James Braid's old man and Paul Runyan's, saw no future in the sport—turned in another 74 to tie Vardon and Ray atop the leaderboard. In the afternoon, both Brits shot a 79 to finish at twelve-over 304.

Francis, who teed off later, double bogeyed 10 to fall two behind.

Time was running out.

"Walking to the 11th tee," he wrote, "I heard a man say, 'It's too bad he's blown up.' I knew he meant me, and it made me angry. It put me in the proper frame of mind to carry on. There was still a chance, I thought."

He chipped in from about thirty-five feet for a birdie on 13 and saved par with a nine-footer on 16. On 17, with Vardon and Ray in the gallery, Francis hit his approach to within twenty feet.

And knocked it in.

The fans went berserk.

"They yelled, pummeled each other joyously, swatted their friends with umbrellas, and shouted delirious phrases they had not thought of since boyhood," Wind wrote.

Francis wasn't home free just yet.

On 18, he made a five-footer for par—"those five feet may as well have been half a mile," Frost wrote—to live another day.

And what a day it was.

There was no blood on the front nine, each player shooting a 38. Francis was fortunate. On number 5, a 420-yard par-4, he hit his second shot out of bounds but escaped with a bogey and after a par on 10, took the lead for the first time.

On 17, a 360-yard dogleg left, clinging to a one-stroke advantage over Vardon, he hit his drive down the fairway to almost the same spot he hit it the day before. His approach came to a rest about eighteen feet from the cup.

And only a few hundred yards from his front door.

I agree with Mark Frost. I'd swear it was fiction, too, if there wasn't proof.

With Ray too far behind and Vardon already in for a bogey, here was a chance for Francis to go up three and put the tournament away.

He didn't waste it.

"For a while," Frost wrote, "it seemed all the world had lost its mind, and justifiably. The roars wouldn't stop."

Francis finished with a 72 to defeat Vardon by five and Ray by six.

"In every direction," Frost continued, "people staggered, exhausted, wrung out, more than a few self-medicated from a personal flask, all astonished by what they'd had seen and been through, stunned by how they felt, more thrilled by such an experience than they'd ever known was possible."

Francis Ouimet, who would never turn pro, won the U.S. Amateur in 1914 and 1931 and lent his name to a fund that has awarded millions in college scholarships.

I'll leave it to Vardon, the opponent but never the villain, to have the final word:

"While I was naturally a little disappointed at failing to achieve my object, I did not begrudge the young Boston player his well-earned victory. I felt afterwards on thinking over the outcome of this meeting that the American's success would do more for the advancement of the game in the United States than anything which could have possibly happened."

19

Patty Berg

In 1933, playing in her first Minnesota City Women's Championship, fifteen-year-old Patty Berg shot a 122 in the medal round to put her in the last flight of match play, where she lost 10 and 8.

"In fact," Berg recalled, "I think they made an extra flight just for me and another girl who shot 120."

Walking toward the clubhouse, she came up with a plan:

From that moment on, until the next city championship in 1934, Berg would devote herself fully to the game, which included lessons from Lester Bolstad, a two-time Big Ten champion. He would be her instructor for forty years.

Her first day in the sand trap was one he would never forget.

"She hit a line drive that almost beheaded a golfer 30 yards away," Bolstad said. "I yelled 'fore' just in time, and he ducked."

Lo and behold, she won the title in 1934, launching one of the most distinguished careers in the history of women's golf. Of golf, period. Of her sixty professional victories, fifteen were majors, more than anyone, male or female, except for Jack Nicklaus and Tiger Woods.

"I didn't think I'd win [the Minnesota title]," Berg said. "When I did, I started to dream.... That's a long time to spend on one endeavor, isn't it—365 days? But I'll tell you, it was worth every freckle on my face."

Berg, who stood only five feet two, was quite an athlete. She ran like the devil, was a champion speedskater, and played quarterback for the 50th Street Tigers, a neighborhood football team. One boy on the team, a tackle, was Charles "Bud" Wilkinson, the future Hall of Fame coach for the Oklahoma Sooners.

The Bergs weren't crazy about their little girl playing football. She went there right after school, ruining one skirt after another.

Golf was another matter entirely. Her father, a grain merchant and

10-handicapper, was a member of Interlachen Country Club, where a few years earlier Bobby Jones secured the third leg of his Grand Slam.

Herman Berg Sr. gave his daughter a few of his old clubs and cut down a two-wood to fit her. She was smitten.

A year after winning the city title, Berg, seventeen, captured the Minnesota State Amateur Championship. That same summer, in the U.S. Women's Amateur at Interlachen, she sank a forty-five footer to defeat Peggy Chandler two up in the quarterfinals and a twenty-five footer on number 18 to stay alive versus Charlotte Glutting in the semifinals, winning the match on the third extra hole.

Next up: Glenna Collett Vare, the five-time U.S. Amateur champion.

Playing in front of seven thousand spectators, Berg was four down with six to go.

Yet there was no quit in her. There was never any quit in her.

After converting an eighteen-foot putt on the 33rd hole, she was only two down.

She lost the match on the next hole but gained the respect of the woman who beat her. Asked to rank the top young players she'd seen in the Amateur that year, Collett Vare placed Berg at the very top.

"In fact," she said, "quite a distance ahead of the rest, and they all were good."

The future couldn't be brighter. As long as she could manage her nerves.

One time, the morning after an exhibition match with Walter Hagen, Horton Smith, and Johnny Revolta, another highly regarded pro, Berg told her father: "I don't think I want to play competitive golf anymore. I was sick all the way over to this thing, all the way back, all last night and I don't feel too good today."

"They're little butterflies and they'll go away," her father assured her.

"If they don't, I won't live past seventeen."

In the 1936 Curtis Cup, the headline in a Scottish paper read: *Patty Berg Suffers from Stage Fright.*

The U.S. retained the Cup, although Berg lost in the singles to Helen Holm, 4 and 3.

Stage fright or not, she was something else in 1938: Ten victories in thirteen starts.

In the final of the U.S. Women's Amateur at Westmoreland Country Club in Wilmette, Illinois, she got revenge against Estelle Lawson Page, 6 and 5, who had beaten her 7 and 6 in the final the year before.

"As bonny Mrs. Page ran over to the new champion and plopped a kiss on her cheek," *Time* magazine reported, "the gallery of 3,000 yelled themselves hoarse for the temperamental little red-head, the darling of all golf galleries, who had just climaxed one of the best seasons any woman golfer has ever had."

In 1940, Berg turned pro, signing with the Wilson Sporting Goods company for $7,500 a year, a relationship that would last the rest of her life. One writer called it "quite a gob of dough for a girl twenty-two, years old and taking her first job."

The clinics Berg gave—more than fifteen thousand, it was estimated—brought many women to the sport. Judy Rankin, a twenty-six-time winner on the LPGA tour, was seven years old when she attended a clinic in St. Louis. "I had never seen a woman professional golfer," Rankin told me. "She had a bit of a star quality to her. I realized, even at a very young age, that she was somebody."

In 1941, on the day after Pearl Harbor, Berg broke her knee in three places in a car accident while headed from Texas to Tennessee with fellow pro Helen Dettweiler to take part in an exhibition for British War Relief.

"I was laid up for eighteen months," she recalled, "and when they took the cast off, I couldn't get the leg bent because of the adhesions. The knee started to turn blue, so they gave me gas and ether and hit it or manipulated it. They did that twice, and I fell once, so I ended up with about seventy-five percent use of the leg in terms of bending it."

Once she got out of the hospital, Berg worked hard. Just as she did after shooting the 122.

"I rode a bicycle and did two hours of gym work a day [in Mobile, Alabama] with Tommy Littleton [a middleweight boxer]," she said. "I got so I could hit golf balls, then so I could pick them up, and then finally so I could play." During an exhibition at the Tam O'Shanter Country Club outside Chicago, she shot a 78 from the men's tees. "The course was playing long because it had rained a lot," she said, "so I thought I was back."

In 1946, Berg, who had traveled around the country to raise money for the war effort, won the first U.S. Women's Open at Spokane Country Club in Washington. After recording a 145 (thirteen strokes lower than anyone else) in two qualifying rounds—that's the only time the Open featured a match-play format—she rolled past one opponent after another, defeating Betty Jameson in the thirty-six-hole final, 5 and 4.

"When that kid gets to the green," Helen Hicks, a two-time major winner, said about Berg, "she expects to hole every putt. When she misses one of ten feet, she is provoked. And, when she misses, she practices until the turf cries out for mercy. You can't go far wrong that way."

18

Babe Didrikson Zaharias

It was August 8, 1932, which is as good a day as any to begin the story of Mildred Ella "Babe" Didrikson Zaharias, the greatest athlete of the twentieth century, and that includes Babe Ruth, Muhammad Ali, Jim Brown, Jim Thorpe, Willie Mays, Michael Jordan . . . etc., etc., etc.

Babe, twenty-one, had just won two gold medals in the Summer Olympics at the Coliseum in Los Angeles with record-setting performances in the eighty-meter hurdles and javelin. (She should have won a third in the high jump but the judges robbed her, ruling she committed a foul on her third attempt because her shoulders went over the bar first. They hadn't said a word when the same thing happened in both of her first two attempts. She had to settle for a silver.)

On this August day, she played a round of golf at Brentwood Country Club on the west side of L.A. with Grantland Rice and three other newspapermen.

Babe, who did not possess a humble bone in her body, had been "bragging during the Olympics," according to biographer Don Van Natta Jr., "that she once shot an 82 and could drive the ball 250 yards."

At Brentwood, she recorded a 52 on the front nine but came home with a 43, which included one tee shot that went 260.

Rice couldn't contain himself.

"She is the longest hitter women's golf has ever seen," he wrote. "For she has a free, lashing style backed up with championship form and terrific power in strong hands, strong wrists, and forearms of steel.... If Miss Didrikson would take up golf seriously, there is no doubt in my mind...she would be a world beater in no time."

Rice was right. To a point.

Babe, who hit almost 1,500 balls a day, did become a world beater—she won forty-one tournaments, including ten majors—but it took a lot longer than it should have and it wasn't her fault.

Her crime: She was from the wrong side of the tracks.

In the 1935 Women's Texas Amateur, Van Natta Jr. pointed out, "nearly all the competitors were members of Texas high society, wealthy wives of prominent husbands who didn't think someone as crass as Babe belonged" at River Oaks, which was hosting the event.

Peggy Chandler, one of the top female amateurs in the state, didn't mince words:

"We really don't need any truck drivers' daughters in our tournament," she said. (Ole Didrikson was a furniture restorer from Norway who also did some construction, but you get the point.)

Babe was allowed to play anyway and made the most of it, rallying from three down to defeat Chandler in the final, 2 up.

In no time, those opposed to Babe appealed to the USGA. If she was a professional in other sports—baseball, basketball, and billiards—the argument went, she shouldn't be an amateur in golf.

The USGA agreed, barring her in "the best interest of the game."

The real interest, Van Natta Jr. put it, "was to protect the game as the province of the wealthy, and, at the same time, boost the chances of the high-society golfers to win future tournaments."

She found other ways to stay involved, such as going on an exhibition tour with Gene Sarazen. The two hit it off, Babe picking up tips whenever she could. "If I was going to be the best," she pointed out, "I wanted to learn from the best. And he was the best in championship golf at that time."

Babe got to where she thought she could hold her own against at least some of the men but she failed to make the cut in the 1938 Los Angeles Open at Griffith Park Golf Course.

The week wasn't a total loss.

In her group was George Zaharias, a pro wrestler who played the bad guy. And wrestling fans love to root against the bad guy. Zaharias cried and begged for mercy when, near the end of the match, his opponent had him on the canvas.

The two got married later that year.

George, with help from Babe's cooking, ballooned to over three hundred pounds. He also drank to excess. Later, when the two were having problems, she delivered one of her classic one-liners:

"When I married George, he was a Greek god. Now he's nothing but a goddamn Greek."

He had been exactly what she needed—friend, lover, manager, breadwinner, you name it.

The relationship served another purpose, as well.

"George also helped Babe win over some cynical members of the public and press," Van Natta Jr. concluded, "the ones who had doubted that she was a 'real' woman or wondered whether she really had eyes for men."

In 1952, however, if I might jump ahead for a minute, when Babe started to hang out a lot with Betty Dodd, an LPGA player about half her age, some women suggested they were lovers.

"What began as a youthful admiration for a charismatic idol on Dodd's part and desire for a 'running buddy' on Didrikson's grew," according to another biographer, "into a mutually enriching and satisfying intimate relationship. She and Babe became constant companions.... Although a sexual relationship was never publicly acknowledged, they became each other's primary partner."

Peggy Kirk Bell, a fellow pro, didn't believe the rumors about Babe and Dodd for one second.

"Gay? Babe wasn't gay!" she claimed. "We had a lot of trouble keeping her away from the men!"

Anyway, in 1940, five years after she was banned, Babe applied to the USGA to regain her amateur status. While waiting for an answer, she won the Women's Western Open and Texas Open, both professional events, but didn't accept any prize money.

The waiting finally came to an end in January 1943: she was an amateur once more.

In 1944, Babe won the Western Open and before too long, the war was over.

She captured the U.S. Women's Amateur at Southern Hills in 1946, and a year later, at the Gullane Golf Club in East Lothian, Scotland, became the first American woman to claim the British Amateur.

Babe, during one stretch in 1946 and '47, won fourteen tournaments in a row, three more than Byron Nelson in 1945.

"In Texas we call someone like Babe Zaharais a 'piece of work,'" Nelson said, "but brash as she could be at times, she sure could back it up."

When asked in Scotland for the key to her success, Babe, who would soon turn pro, delivered another beauty:

"I just loosen my girdle and let the ball have it."

Her importance in the early days of the LPGA tour can't be overstated.

"Our sport grew because of Babe," Patty Berg said. "She had so much flair, color, and showmanship, we needed her. Her power astonished galleries."

Babe, at the same time, seemed determined to win at all costs. "Her self-worth," Betsy Rawls said, "was based on winning, on beating people at something—if not golf, anything."

At one tournament in 1951, Babe, the overnight leader, had been passed by Berg in the final round when it began to pour.

"They were near the clubhouse at the time," Rawls claimed, "and Babe marched in there and told the sponsors it was raining, and she wanted the round canceled. And they did it. They rescheduled for the next day. It wasn't even close to being rained out, or the course being unplayable." ("Patty beat Babe the next day anyway," Rawls said. "Played rings around her.")

Babe hated to lose even in the land of make-believe.

In *Pat and Mike,* a 1952 romantic comedy, the character played by Babe was supposed to lose in the final match to Pat, played by Katharine Hepburn. Change the script, Babe said, or I'm outta here.

They changed the script.

Babe didn't need any rewrites on the LPGA tour. In 1950, she won eight of the fifteen tournaments, including all three majors, and was the leading money winner. She followed with seven victories in 1951.

In 1952, however, Babe, who underwent hernia surgery in the spring, won only four times and finished fifth on the money list.

She wasn't her usual self again in early '53, her tee shots, as Van

Natta Jr. put it, lacking "their usual pop." Babe, who was constantly tired, worried something was seriously wrong, and those fears were soon confirmed.

"Babe," a doctor in Fort Worth told her, "you've got cancer."

The cancer was in the rectum, which was taken out, as well as part of her colon. She also underwent a colostomy, but the doctors discovered more cancer in her lymph nodes.

Babe lived only three and a half more years, and in those three and a half years, we witnessed a whole other level of greatness.

Exhibit A: the 1954 U.S. Women's Open at Salem Country Club in Peabody, Massachusetts, which took place fifteen months after her surgery.

She won by twelve strokes.

Wearing a colostomy bag.

"I don't like to keep bringing up this hospital deal," Babe said, "but when there were reports going out that I'd never play championship or tournament golf again, I said, 'Please, God, let me play again.' He answered my prayers, and I want to thank God for letting me win again."

When the cancer returned, she fought as hard as she could, but it was never a fair fight. Babe passed away on September 27, 1956. She was forty-five.

A 1935 poem from Grantland Rice said it all:

> From the high jump of Olympic fame
> The hurdles and the rest
> The javelin that flashed its flame
> On by the record test—
> The Texas Babe now shifts the scene
> Where slashing drives are far
> Where spoon shots find the distant green
> To break the back of par.

17
Seve Ballesteros

Many who played with the late Seve Ballesteros or saw him up close remember a shot he pulled off they still can't believe.

A shot no one else could have hit.

A shot no one else could have imagined.

Like the shot on the final hole of his singles match against Fuzzy Zoeller in the 1983 Ryder Cup at PGA National in Palm Beach Gardens, Florida.

The match all square, Seve hit what he later said was "one of the worst drives of my life," the ball ending up in a patch of Bermuda rough on a bank above the face of a bunker. The best he could do was advance it about twenty yards...into another bunker. The ball sat on an upslope just beneath the lip, still 245 yards from the putting surface.

His only option was to knock it onto the fairway and hope to get up and down for a par.

Seve grabbed his three wood.

"I was licking my chops," Zoeller said, "thinking, 'What the hell is he doing?'"

The impossible. As usual.

Aiming fifty yards left of the pin, Seve got the ball over the lip and it came to a halt on the fringe of the green. He got up and down for a par to halve the match.

Jack Nicklaus, the U.S. captain, called it "one of the greatest shots I have ever seen."

*

The son of a dairy farmer from a fishing village on the north coast of Spain, Severiano Ballesteros was seven years old when golf came into his life, and it wasn't long before the game took over his life. "Without a golf club in his hand, he was like a man with no legs," his older brother Manuel said. "It was part of him. You never saw him without a golf club."

Including on the beach, where he hit one ball after another with his precious three-iron. "I could do magical things with that three-iron," he'd later say.

In 1974, prior to his seventeenth birthday, Seve turned pro, finishing twentieth out of 110 players in his first event, the Spanish National Professional Championship in Barcelona, a debut anyone would be proud of.

Anyone but Seve.

He bawled his eyes out in the locker room.

"I think what surprised some of us was how angry he was with himself for not doing better," said fellow Spaniard Manuel Piñero. "I remember thinking at the time, 'This boy could be a very, very good player.'"

In 1976, playing in only his second major, Seve tied for second with Nicklaus in the British Open at Royal Birkdale, six behind Johnny Miller.

On the 72nd hole, after his approach ended up near a path leading to two bunkers by the green, he risked a bogey, or worse, by aiming for the path instead of going over the bunkers with a sand wedge. He pulled it off, the ball coming to a rest four feet from the cup, and made the putt. Seve captured the first of a record fifty European Tour titles a month later at the Dutch Open and won nine more times over the ensuing three years.

He was triumphant in the United States, as well, at the 1978 Greater Greensboro Open the week before turning twenty-one, in his first PGA Tour event. Trailing by five after fifty-four holes, he fired a 66 to become the youngest winner since Raymond Floyd in 1963.

In 1979, he won the British Open, the first of his five majors, and he did it, like the shot at Birkdale, the only way he ever did anything.

By being daring. By being Seve.

It happened on the 16th hole of the final round at Royal Lytham & St. Annes. Leading by two, Seve intentionally hit his tee shot to the right of the fairway, the ball ending up in a car park.

Was he out of his mind?

Nope. Quite the contrary.

"I knew the rough out there was not bad because the spectators had trampled it down," he said, "and that if I hit a big drive I could get close to the green and make a birdie. I also realized that if my ball finished among the cars I would get a free drop."

He hit a sand wedge to within twenty feet of the flag, converted the putt, and prevailed by three over Nicklaus and Ben Crenshaw.

So what if he sprayed the ball all over the place?

"The only thing that counts," Crenshaw said, "is your name on that big board and the score." As Hale Irwin, who was paired with Seve on the final day, described the victory: "It wasn't because he was lucky—it was because he created some shots that were unbelievable."

Even so, Tony Jacklin figured it was time to give Seve some friendly advice.

"This game is a lot easier out of the fairway than it is out of the rough," Jacklin told him as they shared a ride to London about a week after the Open.

Jacklin was wasting his breath. Seve continued to play the game his way, and for that we should be grateful. If he had become more methodical, like Nick Faldo, he might have won more tournaments but lost what made him special.

In the 1980 Masters, he was up by ten at one stage—the final margin was four—in a performance that inspired other Europeans. "He broke that barrier for us to think it was doable," Faldo suggested. "The Masters is a completely different golf course. We don't get anything like that in Europe."

In 1983, Seve won for the second time in Augusta, by four over Crenshaw and Tom Kite.

"It's like he is driving a Ferrari and the rest of us are in Chevrolets," Kite said.

A year later, he walked away with a second Claret Jug. At the Old Course this time, and as memorable as the victory itself—he outdueled Tom Watson, a five-time champion, to prevail by two—were the fist pumps he gave after after sinking the final putt on 18. He had more charisma than anyone since Arnold Palmer.

"The most excited I have ever been on a golf course," he said.

Seve, like Palmer, also made his share of blunders. And at the worst possible time.

In the final round of the 1986 Masters, he stood in the fairway at number 15, poised to take home the green jacket for the third time in seven years. Until he hit a fat, four-iron approach that found the pond in front of the putting surface, leading to a bogey—and a victory no one saw coming for the forty-six year-old Nicklaus.

A year later, also at the Masters, Seve missed about a four-footer for par on number 10, the first hole of a sudden-death playoff with Greg Norman and Larry Mize. It was a long walk back to the clubhouse as Norman and Mize moved on to the next hole.

"I lost faith in my putting when I missed that short one," he confessed. "I started missing a lot of short putts after that, especially the crucial ones."

Still, in 1988, he won a third British Open, a second at Royal Lytham, thanks to a final-round 65 that featured an eagle and six birdies. "I had begun to think I was finished," Seve said. "I was worried.... It is the greatest round of my life."

He tied for fifth in the 1989 Masters, tied for seventh there a year later, and tied for ninth in the 1991 British Open. Other than that, there were no more top tens in major championships.

Changes in his swing? A loss of desire? A bad back?

All of the above.

"To change the swing is not that hard if you have talent," he said, "but you have to be very good physically. I wasn't. I couldn't do it."

He worked with Butch Harmon and David Leadbetter but listened to anyone who offered advice, and that was another problem.

"I felt for him," Bernhard Langer told me. "I said, 'You need to work with one coach for a full year or two and do whatever he says because there are many ways to play this game, and having ten different swing thoughts is not going to help you. You'll get more and more confused.' He wouldn't listen, I guess."

In 2011, three years after doctors discovered a malignant tumor above his right temple, Seve Ballesteros died at the age of fifty-four.

"You can talk all you want about Arnie—and Arnie was great—but Seve was golf outside America," Ernie Els said. "He was the European Tour.... He was Tiger before Tiger was Tiger."

16
Billy Casper

Ask anyone about Billy Casper, and the first word that comes out of their mouth is almost always the same:

Underrated.

If that is, indeed, the case, one could blame Casper himself, who didn't seem concerned with how he came across. "If I was a little hypnotic on the golf course and in the pressroom," he said, "it was because I had to be to play my best golf.... I never played for history, either. I played for money, for my family."

One could also blame Mark McCormack, the founder of IMG, who billed his clients, Jack Nicklaus, Arnold Palmer, and Gary Player, in the 1960s as *The Big Three*. Which wasn't fair to Casper, who, from 1964 through 1970, won twenty-seven tournaments, more than Nicklaus (twenty-five). And six more than Player and Palmer.

Combined.

The Big Three, in the foreword to Casper's 2012 memoir, *The Big Three and Me*, made the case it could have been The Big Four.

"Inside the ropes," they wrote, "we were well aware of something the public at large didn't seem to know or appreciate. There was another player... we kept an eye on and worried about just as much, if not more, than each other. His name was Billy Casper."

Well, whoever is to blame, and you can throw in the press, as well, the narrative of the underrated Casper has been repeated so often that, being the skeptic I am, I began to wonder if maybe it had gone too far.

Yes, Casper won fifty-one Tour events—only six players have won more—but only three of the fifty-one were majors, which is why he doesn't belong on the same level as the other three—each won at least eight majors—and a dozen other all-time legends.

That is nothing to be ashamed of.

Casper, who won the Vardon Trophy five times, was known for his putting.

In the 1959 U.S. Open at Winged Foot, the first of his three major victories, he needed just 114 putts (only one three-putt) in seventy-two holes. Casper laid up each day on the 3rd hole, a 216-yard par-3, and made a 3 each time.

"Billy was a killer on the golf course," said Dave Marr, the 1965 PGA champion. "He just gave you this terrible feeling he was never going to make a mistake, and then of course he'd drive that stake through your heart with that putter. It was a very efficient operation."

What took place on Sunday, June 19, 1966, tells you everything you need to know about Billy Casper.

The player and the man.

Let's start on the 10th tee of the Olympic Club, Casper trailing Palmer by seven in the final round of the U.S. Open.

The only question was whether Palmer, who turned in a three-under 32 on the front nine, would beat the 276 that Ben Hogan shot at Riviera in the 1948 Open. All he needed was to come home in a one-over 36.

"It's Palmer against the record right now," ABC's Jim McKay told viewers as the King got ready to hit his second shot on 14.

Even Casper figured it was over.

"Arnie, looks like I'm going to have to work some to finish second," he told him as they headed to the tee at 10.

"Don't worry, Bill," Palmer assured him. "If you need some help, I'll help you."

He helped him, all right. More than Casper could have ever dreamed of.

I refuse to rehash the details of every Palmer blunder on the back nine, although there were some real doozies. Let the man rest in peace.

Better to rehash what Casper did.

A birdie at 12, pars at 13 and 14, and then the birdie at 15 that (along with a Palmer bogey) cut the lead to three and made it clear the tournament was far from over.

The birdie at 15 was vintage Casper, a left-to-right breaker from about twenty feet, the kind of putt he first learned how to make as a nine-year-old at San Diego Country Club. In the dark, if need be.

"I would memorize in my mind where the hole was and putt from various spots on the green completely blind," Casper wrote. "... It helped me develop at an early age a kind of sixth sense for the unseen parts of putting.... I got so I could make as many putts when I couldn't see the hole as when I could see it."

On 16, Casper made another birdie from fifteen feet while Palmer made another bogey, and after Casper gained one additional stroke at 17, the two were tied heading to 18.

Palmer, who putted first, left his birdie attempt about four feet short. Due to a new rule to speed up the game, he would have normally putted out without a second thought, but because the ball was in Casper's line, he wasn't sure what he should do.

"Go ahead, Arnold, you're hot," Casper said.

Some thought he was being a smart aleck. It was obvious that Palmer was anything but hot.

One writer called the response by Casper, whom he described as a "champion trash talker ... perhaps his most cold-blooded needle."

Not true, Casper claimed.

"I wasn't being a smart aleck," he said decades later. "It was just my answer."

However, Lee Benson, a co-writer on *The Big Three and Me*, said Casper told him that he wished he had never made the comment.

"He wouldn't hold that kind of guilt," Benson said, "if there hadn't been a little gamesmanship."

After leaving the Olympic Club, Casper, instead of grabbing a bite and getting to bed at a decent hour, drove to a church in Petaluma about forty miles north of San Francisco, where he delivered a fireside talk to his fellow Mormons. Casper had made the commitment before he knew he would play an additional eighteen holes.

"A deal's a deal," he wrote.

Casper, who had served in the Navy during the Korean War—he was stationed in the U.S.—spoke about the trip he had made a few months earlier to Vietnam. He put on exhibitions and clinics for the troops. "It's a sort of debt," he once explained. "I've been blessed by my talent as a golfer. This is my way to put something back into the game."

Shortly after eleven, he wrapped up the fireside talk and enjoyed a dinner of pork chops, green beans, and salad, not getting to bed until well after midnight.

The long night didn't set him back one bit.

Casper beat Palmer, who enjoyed a two-stroke lead at the turn but again faltered on the back nine, by four. One moment from the playoff stands out, and it has nothing to do with any shots struck by either player. It was when Casper put his arm around Palmer as they walked off the 18th green.

"He felt things deeply," his widow, Shirley, told me.

The Mormon faith meant everything to the Caspers. "It was like we joined a great big family," Shirley said.

The change in her husband was profound.

"Everything became easier," Casper said. "I began to live much more for others, and my life fell into balance."

The two went on to create a great big family of their own, adopting six children in addition to the five they had before joining the Church.

The other big change had to do with his diet.

Suffering from allergies for years, he began to eat a steady diet of buffalo meat, among other exotic foods, and organically grown vegetables. Casper lost fifty or so pounds to drop to around 170 and stopped having mood swings.

"The lethargy left and my depression lifted," he wrote. "My head was clear. I could focus again. I stopped being a grump."

Casper's most satsifying victory wasn't defeating Palmer in the Open. It was defeating Gene Littler, his boyhood rival, in an eighteen-hole playoff at the 1970 Masters.

He was, as usual, almost automatic on the greens, needing only twelve putts on the front nine.

"As I walked off the [final] green there was [tournament chairman] Cliff Roberts," recalled Casper, who won by five. "He stuck out his hand and I expected him to say, 'Congratulations, Billy.' Instead he said, 'thank you' twice. He'd been rooting for me to win Augusta for a number of years." Casper, who passed away in 2015, was buried in his green jacket, his wife receiving special permission from Augusta National.

I'm glad the Big Three wrote that wonderful foreword for his book and that other peers have recognized him for the great player he was.

Wherever he may fit in history.

"Casper had the thing figured out," Lee Trevino said. "When I got on tour (in 1967) everybody was talking about Nicklaus and Palmer, but I kept looking on the board and seeing Casper's name. I figured he was twice as good as me, so I watched how he practiced and decided I would practice three times as much as him. I focused on Casper."

15

Lee Trevino

The day for Lee Trevino in late 2022 started like every other day. Hitting one golf ball after another.

Just him and his thoughts.

"When I practice, it's like being in the classroom," Trevino told me over the phone a few hours later. "I'm trying to learn something. I'm looking to see what the ball is doing."

Good chance the ball was doing what it has been doing for decades.

Going wherever he wanted it to go.

Trevino, who grew up in a four-room shack with no electricity or indoor plumbing, came out of nowhere in the late 1960s to be one of the best the game has ever seen. His swing was unique—positioning his body to the left, he started the club well outside the target line and dropped it to the inside at the top of the swing—and his ability to amuse the gallery was second to none.

"They always talk about Hogan and Trevino, and it's a coin toss as to which one was the better ball striker," David Graham, a two-time major winner, said. "But Trevino could maneuver the golf ball better than anybody. What was even more incredible was he could hit all those shots on the driving range but then hit them on the golf course in competition, which we would never do."

Trevino, who won twenty-nine tournaments, including six majors, was never better than during a three-week stretch in the summer of 1971.

Some of the credit goes, of all people, to Jack Nicklaus. In March of '71, Trevino told him he was skipping the Masters for the second year in a row. "I told him I didn't like all the dogleg lefts," he explained.

Nicklaus thought he was making a mistake.

"You have no clue how good you are," he told Trevino. "You can play there as well as anybody."

What Nicklaus said had a huge impact.

"Coming from the GOAT," Trevino said, "are you kidding me?"

Soon afterward, he won the Tallahassee Open and the Danny

Thomas Memphis Classic and in early June tied for third in Atlanta and second in Charlotte. Leading to Merion where, going for a second U.S. Open—his first was at Oak Hill in 1968—Trevino was in top form.

As an entertainer and ball striker.

While he and Nicklaus waited on the first tee of their eighteen-hole playoff—both had finished at even-par 280—Trevino reached into his bag for a new glove to replace one full of sweat. Inside was a rubber snake he'd gotten for his daughter a few weeks earlier at the Fort Worth Zoo. When he pulled the snake out, everyone cracked up, including Nicklaus, who asked to see it for himself.

Trevino shot a two-under 68 in the playoff, defeating Nicklaus by three. The victory meant the world to the Merry Mex.

"It wasn't about the Open," he said. "It was about beating the GOAT. That's when I realized I belonged."

Did he ever.

Two weeks later, he defeated Art Wall Jr. in a playoff to win the Canadian Open.

He wasn't done yet.

The following week, he edged Taiwan's Lu Liang-Huan by a stroke to capture the British Open at Royal Birkdale. "I caught a streak of putting that summer that I'd never had before," Trevino said in 2013. "I spent the rest of my career trying to recapture the feeling I had over the putter during that spell."

Royal Birkdale was similar to Tenison Park, the municipal course in Dallas where he learned to master the bump and run.

Where he became Lee Trevino.

Born in Garland, Texas, he was raised by his mother and grandfather, a gravedigger, both immigrating from Mexico. Trevino, who didn't know his father, helped out in the onion and cotton fields at the age of five.

"I was twenty-one years old," kidded Trevino, "before I knew Manual Labor wasn't a Mexican."

One day, when he was sixteen, he and a friend stole the hub caps from another car. Trevino thought they would look real nice on his 1949 Powder Blue Ford.

A few hours later, the two were stopped by a police officer who let them go free after they returned the hub caps to their rightful owner.

"I was the luckiest man in the world," wrote Trevino, who was working at River Hills Country Club, about fifteen miles away. "I not only wasn't arrested but also wasn't fired. I don't know why. I should have been fired and barred from the club."

Either way, Trevino needed discipline in his life.

He found it with the Marines.

"The greatest experience I've ever had," he said.

Trevino, who learned how to operate a light .30-caliber machine gun while serving in Japan, was fortunate his tour ended when it did. Before Vietnam.

Only now what?

"I didn't have anything lined up," he said. "Nothing."

Good thing Hardy Greenwood came back into his life. Trevino was eight when he started going to a driving range Greenwood owned.

"I'd never seen an eight-year-old hit the ball like you did," he had told Trevino when he was fifteen. "I think you've got a future in golf if you really work at it."

Greenwood, who also owned a par-3 course, said Trevino could work nights and have his days free to play golf.

It couldn't have turned out any better.

Trevino played every day at Tenison Park, where a lot of gamblers hung out, including the one-and-only Titanic Thompson. Trevino took part in his share of money games at Tenison and at Horizon Hills Country Club in El Paso, where, beginning in 1966, he worked as an assistant pro and handyman.

The story has been told a million times. It is worth telling a million more.

The match pitted Trevino against Raymond Floyd, a Tour winner by then. When Floyd arrived at Horizon Hills, Trevino brought his bag into the locker room and polished his shoes.

"Well, who am I supposed to play?" Floyd asked.

"Me," Trevino replied.

"You? What do you do?"

"I'm a combination of everything. I'm the cart man, shoe man, clubhouse man, and pro."

Floyd played great the next two days.

Trevino played better.

He shot in the mid-60s to prevail by a stroke or two both times. On Day Three, Floyd—I wonder if he gave Trevino *The Stare*—got him back, thanks to an eagle on the final hole. Floyd couldn't get out of Dodge fast enough.

"Adios, amigo," he said.

In 1967, Trevino tied for fifth in the U.S. Open at Baltusrol.

And, to think, he almost didn't make the trip.

I can't play in that rough, figured Trevino who had tied for fifty-fourth the year before at the Olympic Club.

Thankfully, his wife helped change his mind and they mailed in the $20 entrance fee.

"She said you might as well try it again," Trevino said.

His performance wasn't a complete surprise. At least not to the caddie he had met only a few days before.

"They had to draw out of a hat, and he drew [me, a qualifier]," Trevino recalled. "He was not happy about it. Not at all. And so after I played about four practice rounds, he looked at [the other caddies] and I swear to God he said, 'Boys, you all can have whoever the hell you want. I got my man. I wouldn't trade this guy for anybody.'"

Trevino picked up $6,000 for his efforts. "I'm the richest guy in the world," he told himself.

He couldn't wait to celebrate with his buddies in El Paso. So, the following week, at the tournament in Cleveland, he told me he hit two balls in a row out of bounds on the 16th hole to make certain he would miss the cut.

There would soon be plenty more to celebrate.

Posting four top tens in twelve starts, he was the Tour's Rookie of the Year in 1967, and at Oak Hill a year later he became the first player in an Open to shoot four rounds in the 60s.

"I may buy the Alamo," he joked, "and give it back to Mexico."

Not that things always went smoothly in his life or career. Heavens no. He trusted the wrong people with his finances and got burned. Twice.

"If I had gotten the right people around me," he said, "I don't know what the heck I'd be worth today."

He also got divorced. Twice.

Trevino wasn't there like he should have been for the four children from those marriages.

"I spent a lot of time drinking with my buddies," he confessed. "I didn't have to do that. I put more value on my friends than I did my kids. It was selfishness."

Trevino didn't make the same mistake a third time.

He's been there every step of the way for Olivia and Daniel, his children with Claudia Bove, whom he married in 1983.

Claudia, who is eighteen years younger, got his financial house in order. "She sat me down," he said, telling him, "'I want to take care of you the rest of your life, but the buck stops here.' We finally got back on our feet. Thank God there was a Champions Tour," where he won twenty-nine tournaments.

In 1984, Trevino captured the PGA Championship at Shoal Creek in Alabama at the age of forty-four, his first major in ten years.

And first since he was struck by lightning.

It happened in 1975 during a rain delay in the Western Open at Butler National Golf Club outside Chicago.

"That changed everything," said Trevino, who was knocked unconscious and spent a few days in intensive care. "I don't know how good I would have been if that hadn't happened. It led to an operation on my back in 1976, and once they cut on you, you're never the same."

Perhaps not, but Trevino, eighty-five, couldn't be more grateful.

"I pinch myself every day," he said. "I could still be picking up range balls on some country club. I wouldn't have what I have right now. I owe my entire life not only to my family. I owe my entire life to the game of golf."

14

Gene Sarazen

If I could go back in time, other than trying to stop John Wilkes Booth or Lee Harvey Oswald, or warn the captain of the *Titanic*, or cancel the blind date with ... sorry, I digress ... I know where I'd go:

Augusta, Georgia. April 7, 1935. A little past 5:30 p.m.

Put me on the 15th fairway during the final round of the Augusta National Invitation Tournament as Gene Sarazen, trailing Craig Wood by three, prepares to go for the green in two. He was 235 yards from the hole.

Consider those who were nearby: Walter Hagen, paired with Sarazen; Bobby Jones, watching from a mound fifty yards away, and Byron Nelson, waiting to hit from the 17th fairway. Have there ever been so many golfing immortals in one place at one time?

I would take notes of everything: how the ball tracked toward the hole. How Sarazen reacted. How Hagen reacted. And how the fans—not patrons!—reacted.

No shot over the last ninety years can top it.

*

It's not just the shot itself, or that it happened at Augusta National that makes it so historic.

It's the man.

He wasn't a Larry Mize or a Bob Tway (a combined twelve victories), and I mean no disrespect. He was Gene Sarazen, the Squire—he owned a farm in New York state—the winner of seven major championships (thirty-eight victories overall) and the first player to attain the career Grand Slam.

He started out as Eugenio Saraceni, the son of Sicilian immigrants, Federico and Adela. To help his family—his dad was a carpenter—Eugenio, eight, was a caddie at Larchmont Country Club, about twenty-five miles from the Big Apple, before switching to the Apawamis Club in nearby Rye, where he became friends with another caddie, the future television star Ed Sullivan.

As a teenager, Sarazen, who was inspired by Francis Ouimet's Open triumph in 1913—"I copied everything (he) did, even the way he gripped the club"—made a hole in one at Beardsley Park, a nine-hole public course in Bridgeport, Connecticut, where his family now lived.

It got his name in the paper but when he saw *Eugenio Saraceni* in the headline, he thought it "sounded like a violin player. So I changed it.... That [Sarazen] wasn't in the phone book. I like the way it sounded, and I liked the way it looked. It sounded like a golfer."

Around the same time, he came down with a case of pneumonia, which developed into something called pleural empyema.

The prognosis wasn't good.

"I remember lying in the Bridgeport Hospital and these priests would come in and pull the curtain around," Sarazen said. "They figured I was going to go."

He was saved by an operation in which they drilled holes through his back between the ribs.

The doctors advised Sarazen to spend time outdoors to help his lungs.

He knew just the thing.

A friend hooked him up with George Sparling, the pro at Brooklawn, a country club a few miles away. He worked in the shop and later landed other club jobs.

In the spring of 1922, he played Oakmont with William C. Fownes Jr., the owner and former U.S. Amateur champion. Afterward, Fownes told Emil Loeffler, the course pro: "'I want you to take this boy [Sarazen was twenty] out to Skokie [Country Club, the site of the upcoming U.S. Open] and let him practice.'"

Skokie, Sarazen discovered, was "built right around my game."

He couldn't have been more confident when the tournament got under way in mid-July.

"I had a very strong hunch I might surprise the big boys," he said.

On Day One, he shot rounds of 72 and 73 to put him in a tie for third, only three back.

He then made a rookie mistake.

"I went down into Chicago and had dinner with a guy by the name of [George] Pietzcker," Sarazen recalled. "He was a photographer. He kept me out until twelve o'clock at night.... Finally I got back and [Leo Diegel, whom he was rooming with] says, 'You idiot, here you are almost in striking distance of the Open and you're staying out this late.'"

Sarazen turned in a 75 in his morning round on Day Two. It could have been worse. He birdied three of the last five holes to remain within four of the co-leaders, Bobby Jones and Bill Mehlhorn.

In the afternoon, he knocked in a forty-footer on 3 and a twenty-five-footer on 4, and on the 72nd hole, with the tournament still up for grabs, the fearless, five-foot-five Sarazen—"I had been so close to death as a boy. What could scare me on a golf course?"—with water left and out of bounds right, went for broke on the approach.

"My caddie wanted me to play safe," he said, "but I heard somebody say Jones and Mehlhorn were right back of me and I said, 'Oh hell, give me that brassie (a two-wood today).' I shot right for the green and put it about twelve feet from the hole."

In the end, he prevailed by a shot over Jones, who bogeyed 17, and Scotland's John Black, who made a double there.

"All men are created equal," Sarazen joked. "I'm just one stroke better than the rest."

It was no fluke. A month later, he captured the PGA at Oakmont, the first time the course hosted a professional major championship, out-dueling Bobby Cruickshank in the semis, 3 and 2, and Emmet French in the final, 4 and 3.

Then came the 1923 PGA at Pelham Country Club in New York state.

A PGA for the ages.

His opponent in the thirty-six-hole final was Walter Hagen, considered by many the premier match-play golfer of all time.

The two were tied after the morning eighteen, neither ever more than one up. Better yet, they weren't getting along.

Don't you love it when that happens?

On number 6, after Sarazen moved some leaves near his ball, which was in a patch by two poorly defined bunkers, and grounded his club, Hagen blurted out: "Say, what's going on here? You know that's illegal.... How about playing by the rules?" An official explained to Hagen that since Sarazen's ball wasn't in a hazard, he'd done nothing wrong.

Sarazen, who flubbed the chip and missed the putt, was furious.

"I'm glad you won that hole, Walter," he said. "I don't want to hear any squawking from you tonight." Neither said another word to each other the rest of the morning.

In the afternoon, Sarazen went 3 up, but Hagen rallied, evening the match with a twenty-footer on 17. After both parred 18, they went to sudden death. On the second extra hole, Sarazen hit his drive way left toward a few dwellings. A marshal indicated it was not out of bounds, the ball ricocheting onto the course, although, years later, Hagen attributed the ball's return, according to *Sports Illustrated,* to "some fans of Italian descent living near the corner of the dogleg."

Lo and behold, Sarazen, saved by good fortune—or a fellow Italian?—hit a superb approach, leading to his third major title in fourteen months.

Surprisingly, it took him nine years to pick up his fourth. Herbert Warren Wind suggested he tinkered too much with his swing.

In 1931, Sarazen designed—an earlier version had existed—the sand wedge as we know it today.

The game would never be the same.

"I guess the sand iron," he said, "would have to be one of the most important contributions I've made to golf.... I think the club saves everybody six shots a round."

He got the idea when his friend, the one and only Howard Hughes, showed him how to fly a plane.

"When I took off... I pulled the stick back and the tail went down and the nose of the plane went up," Sarazen said. "Something flashed in my mind, that my niblick should be lowered in the back... what I did was put a flange on the back of the club and angled it so that the flange hit the sand first, not the front edge, which was now raised. It was just like the airplane when it took off."

Sarazen took off as well, ending his drought in majors with a victory in the 1932 British Open at Prince's Golf Club in Sandwich.

He wasn't intending to play at first.

"No matter how much I made during the '20s," Sarazen pointed out, "I was absolutely flat in 1930, '31. All my securities were worthless. That's why I had to work so hard on my game."

His wife, Mary, told him to go regardless.

"Gene," she said, "I don't believe I've ever seen you playing better than you are right now.... I've got your tickets and your hotel reservations all taken care of. The only thing you have to do is get your passport fixed up. You're sailing a week from tomorrow."

The Open represented unfinished business. Sarazen came in second in 1928, tied for eighth in 1929, and tied for third in 1931.

In 1928, his caddie at Royal St. George's was Skip Daniels, who had been loaned to him by Hagen.

"I've won the British Open a couple of times, so winning it doesn't mean as much to me as it obviously means to you," Hagen told him when the two had a drink together on the *Berengaria,* the ship taking them to Europe.

Sarazen played well in '28, but in the second round he made a double on 14 after hitting a wood from the rough instead of the iron that Daniels had advised, and lost to Hagen by two. "We'll try it again, sir, won't we?" Daniels told Sarazen after the presentation ceremony. "Before I die, I'm going to win an Open Championship for you."

For the Open in '32, Sarazen planned to use him again but changed his mind after he shot a 67 in a practice round on another course with a caddie in his late twenties. "Dan," he told Daniels, who was in his sixties, "this bag is too heavy for you. I know you've been in bad health, and I wouldn't want you to try and go seventy-two-holes with it.... I'm sorry, Dan."

The young caddie turned out to be a disaster.

"He would never talk a shot over with me, just pull a club out of the bag as if he were above making a mistake," Sarazen recalled. "When I'd find myself 10 yards short of the green after playing the club he had selected, he [would say] 'I don't think you hit that shot well.' I began getting panicky as the tournament drew closer and my slump grew deeper."

Sarazen went back to Daniels, who had refused to caddie for anyone else, and "it was miraculous how my game responded to his handling."

The sand wedge was another weapon.

A secret weapon.

"I practiced and played with the club," said Sarazen, who won by five over Macdonald Smith, "and then put it under my coat and took it back to my room at night, because if the British had seen it before the tournament they would have barred it.... In the tournament, I went down in two from most of the bunkers."

He said goodbye to Daniels after the presentation ceremony.

"There was a good-sized lump in my throat," Sarazen recalled, "as I thought of how the old fellow had never flagged for a moment during the arduous grind of the tournament and how, pushing himself all the way, he had made good his vow to win a championship for me before he died."

Skip Daniels died shortly afterward.

*

The ball on that magical day in 1935 was on the right side of the fairway, nestled down in the grass, the pin on the right side of the green about fifteen feet from the back edge.

His caddie, known as Stovepipe—don't ask me—suggested a three-wood.

Sarazen chose a more lofted four-wood and let it rip.

"His swing into the ball was so perfect and so free," Jones wrote, "one knew immediately that it was a gorgeous shot. I saw the ball strike the tongue of the green, bound slightly to the left, directly towards the hole, and then the whole gallery began dancing and shouting."

I wish I had been there.

13

Phil Mickelson

Six major championships, the most of anyone in the twenty-first century, except for Tiger Woods.

Forty-five wins overall, tied for the eighth most with Walter Hagen.

The only player, male or female, to win a *professional* major—don't forget John Ball—after turning fifty.

I could go on and on to list the accomplishments of Philip Alfred Mickelson. And yet, and you must be sick of this theme by now—Lord knows, I am (I set out to commend the top one hundred players of all time, not criticize them, but facts, as John Adams said, are stubborn things)—Mickelson is another all-time great who underachieved.

Like Greg Norman, his accomplice in the LIV rebellion, he didn't know when to play it safe. "The difference between [Mickelson and Woods] is that Phil wants to hit an amazing shot, but all Tiger wants to do is hit the right shot," said Golf Channel analyst Brandel Chamblee.

You want examples? I have two words for you:

The first is Winged. The second is Foot.

I had no problem with the tee shot on the 72nd hole in the 2006 U.S. Open at Winged Foot that ended up in the left rough. Mickelson, leading by one, went with a driver.

I had a huge problem, and I'm far from alone, with his second shot.

Instead of playing for a five, at worst, and an eighteen-hole playoff with Geoff Ogilvy, by punching out to the fairway to set up a wedge, his biggest strength, for his third, he attempted to slice a three-iron around a tree. As with Palmer at Olympic in 1966, I won't rehash every detail of his implosion at 18. Bottom line: the gamble didn't pay off and another U.S. Open was lost. (Mickelson has come in second a record six times in the Open, two more than Sam Snead.)

"I just can't believe I did that," Mickelson said afterward. "I am such an idiot. I can't believe I couldn't par the last hole."

I know you think I'm being too harsh. Yet again.

Especially when one considers that Lefty, like Ernie Els, had the misfortune of playing in the Woods era. After all, only thirteen players—and, yes, I'm counting John Ball and Harold Hilton—have won more majors than Phil Mickelson.

Normally, you'd have a point.

Not in this case.

Not when Mickelson, who won everything there was to win as an amateur, was supposed to be the Next Big Thing.

He wasn't a natural lefty, but when he swung the club so smoothly left-handed, his father saw no reason to make a change.

In those early years, Lefty worked at Navajo Canyon (now Mission Trails), a course in San Diego. His job was to pick up trash and, later, range balls.

"Rainy days were my favorite time because nobody else would be there," Mickelson said. "So I'd put on my rain gear, grab a bucket of balls, and go out under a palm tree. I'd have the entire place as my private driving range...one time, it really started to pour and one of my friends who worked in the pro shop came out and asked me what I was doing. 'This extra practice right here is going to help me win a couple of Masters someday.'"

He won the Junior World Golf Championship in San Diego when he was ten, and at fifteen the first of a dozen American Junior Golf

Association tournaments. Then three individual NCAA championships while attending Arizona State, along with the 1990 U.S. Amateur at Cherry Hills.

In early 1991, he captured the Northern Telecom Open in Tucson, the first amateur to win a PGA Tour event in six years. (No amateur would accomplish that feat again until Nick Dunlap in 2024.)

Mickelson prevailed at Tucson in a fashion we would become accustomed to, a roller-coaster ride to the finish.

On number 14 he made a triple that included two unplayables to go from a one-shot advantage to a two-shot deficit. Yet he pulled himself together to birdie two of the last three holes, canning an eight-footer on 18 for the win.

"I never thought I'd see anyone come back from something like that," said Corey Pavin, who was paired with him.

Mickelson, who joined the Tour in 1992, collected his first victory as a pro at Torrey Pines a year later and by the summer of 1996 had a total of eight. In August of '96, he captured the World Series of Golf at Firestone.

I covered the event for *Golf World*. I couldn't have been more excited, working on the story until two or three in the morning.

Only Mickelson wasn't on the cover that week. Tiger Woods was.

Woods, turning pro, agreed to a $60 million deal with Nike and Titleist and had just won a record third straight U.S. Amateur.

It wouldn't be the last time Woods upstaged Mickelson.

To blame Woods, however, for Mickelson being an underachiever, wouldn't be fair.

In ten majors, starting with the 1997 U.S. Open at Congressional, while Woods retooled his swing and went winless, Mickelson posted just three top tens.

His best chance came in the 1999 Open at Pinehurst. Although Payne Stewart earned the victory with his clutch play down the stretch, the tournament was there for the taking—if only Mickelson didn't miss putts at 16 (eight feet) and 17 (six feet).

Not until the 2004 Masters, when he was thirty-three, did he break through, rallying, you may recall, from a three-stroke deficit on the back nine to steal the green jacket from Els.

A new Lefty?

Not really.

Two months later, in the Open at Shinnecock, Mickelson, tied for the lead, three-putted the par-3 71st hole for a double bogey . . . from four feet! He received a bad break when a small rock behind his ball in the bunker kept him from putting any spin on it, but as he later told Fred Funk, his playing partner: "I never should have been in the bunker in the first place."

On the other hand, when the gambles paid off—and even (especially) when they didn't—there was no one more exciting to watch than Mickelson and no one has been that exciting since.

He was a trapeze artist. Without a net.

Take the shot from the pine straw on number 13 in the final round of the 2010 Masters. His ball roughly two hundred yards from the green, Mickelson, leading by one, could have punched out into the fairway to set up a wedge for his third.

He didn't punch out. Of course he didn't.

Out came the six-iron, the Rae's Creek tributary be damned. It paid off, leading to his third green jacket.

Maybe we can't have it both ways.

Maybe taking the gambler out of the man would have taken out the soul.

Good thing he picked up two majors late in his career that would forever alter how he should be judged.

The first was the 2013 British Open at Muirfield.

Trailing the leader, Lee Westwood, by five through fifty-four holes, Mickelson birdied 13, 14, 17, and 18 for a five-under 66 to prevail by three.

The second was the 2021 PGA Championship on the Ocean Course at Kiawah Island.

No one saw it coming.

"This is just an incredible feeling because I just believed it was possible, yet everyone was saying it wasn't," said Mickelson, fifty, who hadn't recorded a top ten in a major since the British Open in 2016. "I hope that others find that inspiration. It might take a little extra work, a little harder effort, but gosh, is it worth it in the end."

While the two victories don't make up for the ones that got away, there is a big difference between winning four majors and winning six.

If only Phil hadn't been . . . Phil.

"He would have won a lot more," Jack Nicklaus said in 2021. "Right after he won the PGA this year I dropped him a note. I can paraphrase what I said: *Hey, you reined yourself in, you didn't try to do dumb stuff, and look what happened? You won.* . . . Golly, he's cost himself so many tournaments over the years with the double and triple and quadruple bogeys."

I can't close this chapter without addressing his fall from grace, which started when he joined LIV in 2022. It wasn't just that he abandoned the tour that made him rich and famous. A lot of guys did that. It was how strongly he defended the move, even after referring to the Saudis as "scary mother f . . . ers."

Is it a temporary fall, or has he tarnished his legacy forever? Too early to tell. Forever is a long time.

Mickelson, a huge gambler off the course as well, built up a lot of good will with the public—no one in his era signed more autographs— and that might still rescue him in the end.

The victory at Kiawah would have been one hell of a way to go out. Instead . . .

"I don't know if there has ever been a more disappointing figure in the game of golf than Phil Mickelson," Lanny Wadkins said.

I prefer to think of the Mickelson before LIV, my favorite moment occurring on the final hole at Torrey Pines in January 2011. His ball seventy-two yards from the pin, he needed to hole out to tie Bubba Watson. He walked up to the green, paced off the exact yardage, and had his longtime caddie, Jim "Bones" Mackay, tend the flagstick.

He didn't make it—the ball ended up a couple of feet away—but that didn't matter.

He thought he could make it, and so did we.

12

Tom Watson

When Tom Watson was a student at Stanford in the late 1960s and early '70s, every so often he would call Ray Parga, the starter at Pebble Beach, about an hour and a half away, to see if he could squeeze him in.

"Come on down, Tommy," Parga told him. "We'll put you off first."

Teeing off around seven, he played eighteen holes in roughly three hours.

Just him and his dreams.

"I always played a game," Watson said, "where I'm on the 15th tee and [he needs] to par in to win the U.S. Open against Jack Nicklaus. He was the guy."

Watson believes he rarely shot even par on those four holes to beat Nicklaus in those imaginary duels before driving back to campus. No matter. He beat Nicklaus—and it wasn't the first time—when the duel at Pebble was for real during the final round of the 1982 U.S. Open.

The chip he holed from off the green on number 17, when he and Nicklaus were tied, ranks as one of the greatest shots of all time.

"Get it close," his caddie, Bruce Edwards, said.

"Get it close, hell," Watson responded. "I'm going to hole it."

When he did, he did a little jog on the green and pointed to Edwards: *I told you I was going to hole it.*

*

Growing up, he was, like many kids, into baseball.

When he was eight years old, Watson, raised in Kansas City, Missouri, played for the Hen House Chicks. He hoped to join his friends on another team but was cut after a tryout. "I was out of baseball," he said. "So, what did I do? Well, I loved to play golf. I joke about it, but baseball is the reason I became a golfer."

Watson was blessed to be surrounded by older men he deeply respected who taught him about golf and about life.

The first was his dad, Ray, a World War II vet—he was a navigator on a B-24 bomber—who was the club champion at Kansas City Country Club and had reached the quarterfinals of the 1950 U.S. Amateur. The two were fiercely competitive. Exhibit A: the final of the club championship in the summer of 1964 at Walloon Lake Country Club in Michigan, where the Watsons had rented a cottage.

After Ray Watson knocked in a twenty-five-footer for par on the first playoff hole, his son, fourteen, missed a birdie attempt from fifteen feet. On the next hole, Tom lined up a three-footer to extend the match.

He hoped it would be conceded.

"I heard nothing but crickets," he said.

He missed.

"That," his father once said, "was the last time I beat him."

Fast-forward a decade later to when Byron Nelson approached him in the locker room at Winged Foot. Watson wasn't in a good mood.

He had just blown a chance to win the 1974 U.S. Open, closing with a nine-over 79 after starting the day with a one-stroke lead over Hale Irwin. Nelson told Watson how much he liked his golf swing and how he handled himself, but "if you ever need any help with your game, give me a call."

Watson didn't call.

Not until the fall of 1976. Meeting with Nelson at his ranch in Roanoke, Texas, the two hit it off.

"It was a friendship that grew," Watson said. "To listen to the history of the game from the man who made the history—who wouldn't love that? I ate it up. I loved being around Byron. It was very special."

Nelson shortened his swing, slowed down his tempo, and worked on his leg action. Watson also made a key discovery during an event later that year in Japan. In 1977, he won the Masters, the second of his eight majors—the first was the 1975 Open at Carnoustie—by two over Nicklaus.

From 1977 through 1984, he collected thirty-three of his thirty-nine victories. No one else in that span came close to that level of success.

Nowhere was the changing of the guard more evident than in the 1977 British Open at Turnberry, Watson and Nicklaus staging a duel unlike any the game had ever seen.

The Duel in the Sun.

Watson shot 65-65 over the last two days to defeat Nicklaus, who shot 65-66, by one. Hubert Green, who came in third, eleven back, put it best:

"I won this golf tournament. I don't know what game those other two guys were playing."

Beating Nicklaus, as it did for Lee Trevino at Merion, meant the world to Watson, who believed he needed to "confirm" his victory over the Golden Bear in the Masters a few months before.

"I felt right then and there I could play with the big boys," he said.

Watson, who ended up with five Claret Jugs, wasn't a fan of links golf at first.

"I preferred target golf to the luck of the bounce," he explained. "I didn't like having to aim drives at church steeples off in the distance."

So, what changed his mind?

"I got tired of fighting it," he told me. "I said to myself, 'You're taking the wrong attitude toward this. You've got to accept what it gives you. Links golf is not perfect.'"

As I listened to the seventy-three-year-old Watson, I couldn't stop thinking of what happened to the fifty-nine-year-old Watson in the 2009 British Open at Turnberry. I felt sad for him—and for us—all over again.

All Watson needed was one more lousy par and he'd own the greatest victory of all time, and not just in golf.

His drive on 18 found the fairway. So far, so good.

And then, from 189 yards away, with an eight-iron, Watson hit another solid approach, like so many other approaches his whole career.

As the ball was in the air, he was reminded of his second shot on the same hole in 1977, which ended up two feet from the cup, clinching his victory over Nicklaus. This time, however, the ball landed on the front edge of the green instead of a few yards short, where it needed to land, and with too much speed came to a halt below the putting surface.

If only he had gone with a nine-iron instead of an eight. If, if, if.

He rolled it up to about eight feet from the pin, but the putt for a par, and the Claret Jug, didn't come close to going in, sending Watson into a four-hole playoff against Stewart Cink.

In the playoff, Watson suddenly looked like the old man he was. It reminds me of the Broadway musical and film *Damn Yankees,* when the devil turns Joe Hardy, the star young ballplayer, back to the elderly Joe Boyd.

Cink beat Watson by six. It felt like six hundred.

Watson couldn't have handled the loss any better. "This ain't a funeral, you know," he told the press.

No, it wasn't, though it sure seemed like one.

Make no mistake about it: Watson was hurting. He was hurting bad.

A few hours later, he received a call from Nicklaus, who said he watched the final round from start to finish, which he'd never done before.

He told Watson he hit the putt on 18 "like the rest of us would have hit it."

Watson laughed.

"Just to have him call at that time of real sorrow, where I let it get away, made the bitterness of the situation a lot easier," he said.

Soon mail poured in from all over the world.

"The gist of many of the letters," Watson said, "was, 'I gave up doing things because I thought I was too old. But seeing you at the Open, I'm going to reinvigorate myself and get back with it.'"

There's a lot to admire in the man and that includes a willingness to speak his mind, regardless of the consequences.

In 1983, he accused Gary Player of cheating at the Skins Game by removing a rooted leaf resting against his ball. Player has always pleaded he did nothing wrong. A decade later, Watson wrote a letter to CBS, seeking the dismissal of analyst Gary McCord for irreverent comments about Augusta National. (McCord was later removed from the Masters telecasts.)

I asked Watson if he regretted his role in either matter.

"I felt I was doing the right thing," he said.

He has been honest, as well, in how he assesses his career.

"I had a short span where I really lit it up," he said. "Then things happen, and the play just doesn't stay that way."

The putter was the culprit, the short ones giving him the most trouble. It became painful to watch.

Watson won his final major, the 1983 British Open at Royal Birkdale, when he was thirty-three. (Phil Mickelson and Ben Hogan won their first majors at ages thirty-three and thirty-four, respectively.)

Earlier that year, Watson had dinner at Pebble Beach with a few friends, including Sandy Tatum, the former president of the USGA, the two frequent partners in the Pebble Beach Pro-Am. (I miss Sandy, who passed away in 2017 at age ninety six. He was the conscience of the game. No one would have been more eloquent in his criticism of LIV.)

The laughs kept coming, as did the alcohol. Late in the evening, Watson came up with an idea.

"Come on, let's go play the shot," he suggested, now holding a sand wedge and several golf balls.

There could be only one shot he had in mind.

Why not?

They headed to the 17th green but soon realized how foolish the idea was.

"It was pitch-black," Watson explained.

No one came close to knocking it in.

"It was absolutely hilarious," Tatum said. "I've got tell you, Tom would not have won the Open that night."

11 Gary Player

The first time I saw Gary Player up close was in March 1996 at a Senior tour event in the city of Ojai, California, about forty-five minutes from Santa Barbara.

Or, as us locals call it, Shangri-la.

Player, who almost always wore black, was in the practice area, hitting one bunker shot after another. He was sixty years old then and long established as one of the premier bunker players of all time.

I couldn't keep my eyes off him. So that's what dedication is, I told myself.

The dedication that Player, the son of a South African gold miner, displayed for decade after decade.

"There was nothing really exceptional about Gary's game except one thing: his desire to win," Jack Nicklaus explained. "I've seen him win tournaments you thought there was no way he could win, just do it on pure guts.... Gary, as much as anyone I ever saw, has that thing inside him that champions have."

Player recognizes it, as well.

"Some never reached their heights because they haven't done what was necessary," he told me in the spring of 2023. "It's a little thing called *it*, and that is a gift from God that very few people have."

Very few, indeed.

Player—not Billy Casper—might be the most underappreciated golfer ever, with more majors (nine) than Arnold Palmer, Sam Snead, and Tom Watson, and the only non-American to achieve the career Grand Slam, which he did before turning thirty.

If he has one regret, it's not moving to the United States and becoming an American citizen after winning the 1961 Masters.

"How many majors would I have won?" he asked. "That's the big question. I think it would have been thirteen."

Traveling was quite an ordeal when Player started out. To go from South Africa to the United States took forty-five hours. Half the time in the States, said Player, who estimates he's logged more than sixteen million miles in his eighty-nine years, "I was competing with one hand tied behind my back."

He overcame a great deal to become a pro golfer in the first place.

Much of his youth was spent alone, with a father twelve thousand feet underground and a mother taken away by cancer at forty-four when her son was only eight.

"Up till the age of thirty-two," he said, "I used to wake up at night crying, longing for my mother. I miss her and have a tear because she never lived to see me become world champion." Her death, he wrote, bred "an independence, a toughness of spirit, and an awareness of adversity, and discipline that have never left me."

Player was aware of the sacrifices his father was making—he earned only one hundred pounds a month, roughly $400—so his son might have a better life.

One that was aboveground.

"The best friends my father ever had were rats," Player said. "He gave a rat a piece of his sandwich every day because the rat knew when [the mine] was going to cave in, and when the rats ran out, the miners all ran like hell."

He once told his father: "I'd rather you were a beggar on the street than to go down there."

"It's all very well for you to say that," Harry Player replied, "but I've got to send you to school, put food on the table."

In his first round ever, at Virginia Park Golf Course outside Johannesburg, Player, fourteen, made three straight pars and by sixteen was telling everyone he would someday be the best golfer in the world.

One day, he and a few buddies jumped into a big compost pit near school.

"When it was my turn," he wrote, "I took a good long run and dived head first right into the pit just as I would off a diving board. Crashing through the layers of leaves and grass, I hit the bottom with terrific force—crunch. The impact broke my neck and knocked me out cold."

He wasn't allowed to play golf or swim or lift weights for over a year, but it didn't end his dreams.

Quite the contrary.

"The days seemed endless," he wrote, "but I continued...to visualize Gary Player striding confidently along fairways...holing long and difficult putts...winning tournaments around the world to the applause of appreciative galleries."

After turning pro at seventeen, Player captured the 1955 East Rand Open on the South African tour, and thanks to a collection from members of the Killarney Golf Club in Johannesburg, where he was an assistant pro, and an overdraft at the bank that his father arranged, he embarked on a journey that would result in 159 victories worldwide, including twenty-four on the PGA Tour.

In 1958, he won for the first time in America, the Kentucky Derby Open.

A year later, Player rallied from an eight-shot deficit at the halfway mark to capture the British Open at Muirfield, becoming, at twenty-three, the youngest champion in the twentieth century.

More majors soon came, one after another: the Masters in 1961, the PGA at Aronimink in Pennsylvania in 1962, the U.S. Open at Bellerive outside St. Louis (which gave him the career Grand Slam, Player donating his winnings to junior golf and cancer research) in 1963 and the British Open at Carnoustie in 1968.

One could argue, however, his most impressive performance was in defeat, at the 1969 PGA Championship outside Dayton.

Confronted with anti-apartheid protesters who threw a cup of ice and a program in his face, Player finished second, a stroke behind Raymond Floyd.

"If I ever won a tournament in life," Player said, "I won that tournament."

Before long, there were new names at the top of the sport, like

Miller and Wadkins and Crenshaw and Kite and Irwin and Watson, all as dedicated to their craft as Player was, but the Black Knight, as he was called, didn't step aside.

He was always younger than his years, a fanatic about fitness when no one else on Tour knew what a barbell was.

Player credits his late older brother, Ian, a leading conservationist, and a chat the two had before Ian headed off to fight for the Allies in World War II.

"The odds are I'm not going to come back," Ian told him. "What do you want to do [in the future]?"

"I want to be a professional sportsman," his five-foot-seven brother responded.

"You're too small and you're too weak. Now here are some second-hand weights. You promise me you'll exercise for the rest of your life?"

I promise, he told him, and he has kept that promise ever since.

"I wasn't the strongest guy on the Tour," Player said, "but I was the fittest by a mile and I was ridiculed left, right, and center for doing weight training. Even my brothers, Arnold Palmer and Jack Nicklaus, said, 'You can't do these heavy weights and play golf.'" (One time, before an interview, I watched Player, in his late sixties or early seventies, jog on a treadmill, and at a pretty fast clip. I never in my whole life felt like such a slacker.)

In 1972, he won the PGA at Oakland Hills, highlighted by a nine-iron approach over the trees and a lake at number 16—he stood on a gallery member's chair to get a better view of what he faced (Leo Diegel would have loved it)—to four feet, and two years later the Masters and British Open at Royal Lytham & St. Annes to bring his total of major titles to eight.

Leaving room for one more: the 1978 Masters. The most magnificent of them all.

Player, forty-two, who hadn't won on Tour in nearly four years, was tied for tenth, seven strokes behind Hubert Green, heading into the final round.

He birdied 10, 12, 13, 15, 16, and 18 for a six-under 30—right up there with the 30 that Nicklaus would shoot on the back nine in 1986, although it doesn't receive the same attention, which is unfortunate. (You got to watch the final moments of the '78 Masters on YouTube, an elated Player, wearing the green jacket from his two prior victories, shaking hands with Palmer after Green missed a short birdie putt on 18 to force a playoff.)

"That Masters is my crowning achievement," he acknowledged. "I was out of the tournament—out of it—but I simply never gave up. My focus was so intense, it was as if I poured every lesson I ever learned into that final nine holes. Do you know, I had two lip-outs on fifteen-footers and missed another birdie from six feet on the back nine? I could have shot 27. I was absolutely possessed!"

My wife and I moved to the Ojai area in 2000. Every so often, when I visit the Ojai Valley Inn, whose course hosted the Senior tour event, I think back to that day a lifetime ago.

To the man in black.

10

Harry Vardon

In 1878, eight-year-old Harry Vardon became a caddie.

Not because he was in love with the game, although that would come soon enough.

Because with the family not doing well financially, everyone was required to do their part, and Harry, who would quit school at twelve, was no exception. He headed over to the Royal Jersey Golf Club, a new course near the family's home in Grouville, offered his services, and changed his life. Forever.

"As far as I can remember," he wrote, "we did not think very much of this new game, but after carrying a few times we began to see distinct possibilities in it."

So what if they didn't have a place to play—Royal Jersey was out of the question—or any clubs or balls? They built their own four-hole course, each hole about fifty yards, using a big white marble called a taw (roughly half the size of a regular ball) for balls and tree branches for clubs.

"We played our elementary kind of golf whenever possible," he wrote, "and soon became very enthusiastic. I recall that most of our best games took place in the moonlight, which was exceedingly bright in Jersey, and enabled us to see quite well.... This was my introduction to the game of golf."

The rest is... you know the cliché.

From 1896 through 1914, Vardon won the British Open a record six times when the British Open was the biggest tournament in the world—some say it still is—taking home two of those Claret Jugs after a bout of tuberculosis had put him into a sanatorium and a bout with the yips turned every short putt into an adventure.

He hit "every ball perfectly cleanly," as Horace Hutchison put it, "with his club head always travelling in the right direction." It is the Vardon grip—the right pinkie overlapping the left index finger—that golfers of all levels have adopted ever since. (John Laidlay, a Scot, was the first top player to use the grip, but Vardon the most well-known.)

"It seems to create just the right fusion between the hands," Vardon explained, and "voluntarily induces each to do its proper work."

He received plenty of support from the start.

When Major Spofforth, the Captain of the Golf at Royal Jersey, saw Vardon take a swing (with no ball) he was so impressed that he took him onto the fairway and had him do it again, with a ball.

Vardon crushed it. Over and over.

The major had seen enough. He arranged for them to be paired together the next day in a match, which they won. Within a couple of years, Vardon, now around twenty, was the best player in the area.

"Henry, my boy," the major had told him, "never give up your golf. It may be useful to you one day."

It was useful to Vardon's younger brother, Tom, who left home to become a pro, winning twelve pounds and ten shillings by finishing second at a tournament in Musselburgh. The effect on Harry can't be stressed enough. "Although I had played very little," he wrote, "I knew in my own heart I was quite as good as my brother, and that if he could win such sums of money as this, there could be no reason why I should not be able to do the same."

He became a pro, as well, at Studley Royal Golf Club in Yorkshire and then at Bury Golf Club in Lancashire.

Vardon made his British Open debut at Prestwick in 1893—he tied for twenty-third—and three years later won his first Claret Jug, outdueling, you may recall, John Henry Taylor by four in a thirty-six-hole playoff. "I have frequently been asked my feelings when the last putt had been holed on the home green," Vardon wrote. "I can only say it was an occasion that I am never likely to forget as long as I live."

He claimed his second Open in 1898 when Willie Park Jr. (*A man who can putt is a match for anyone*) missed a three-footer to tie him on the final hole, and over the next twelve months Vardon won twelve of the fifteen tournaments he entered and came in second the other three times.

"I know that in those times," he wrote, "whenever I was within reach of the green with any club—brassie, cleek or anything else—I saw only the flag and thought only of the flag.... I knew that I could put the ball within a yard or two of any place that I wished. And so the game was especially easy for me."

As Bernard Darwin put it: he was "trampling down his adversaries like some ruthless juggernaut. Nobody could touch him."

In 1900, Vardon made the first of three trips to the United States.

The trip was organized by Spalding to promote the Vardon Flyer, a new gutta-percha ball the company hailed as "the longest flying ball in the market." Vardon became the first professional golfer to endorse non-equipment products, such as golf coats, health tonics, and muscle balm.

Facing the likes of Walter Travis and the reigning U.S. Open champion, Willie Smith, Vardon lost only thirteen of about ninety exhibition matches. He often took on the best ball of two or three local players.

The crowds who watched Vardon perform were blown away by drives that traveled as far as 275 yards.

One day, he made an appearance in the sporting goods section of Jordan, Marsh & Co., a major department store in Boston. Among those in attendance was a seven-year-old boy with the first name Francis.

Looking back years later, Vardon wrote, "it is with a feeling of the utmost satisfaction that I realize I was actually the means, through the medium of my visit there, of starting that which was to become in later years the great golf craze of America."

In October 1900, Vardon took a break from the tour to play in the U.S. Open at Chicago Golf Club.

John Henry Taylor, his fellow Englishman, rallied from a six-stroke deficit to make it a contest but Vardon, in front of the largest gallery that had ever attended a golf championship in the United States, put Taylor away with a sensational two-wood from 225 yards away on the final hole.

However, for all its success, the trip to America took a heavy toll on Vardon, "and it is doubtful," Darwin wrote, "if he was ever so brilliant again."

In 1903, Vardon claimed his fourth British Open, again at Prestwick, setting a scoring record by five strokes, but his body had begun to break down: dizzy spells, a hacking cough, blood in his handkerchief—which would turn out to be tuberculosis, a fatal disease in those days. Soon afterward, having suffered a nasal hemorrhage, he was confined to a sanatorium at Mundesley, close to the North Sea coast.

Fortunately, as the months went by, his condition steadily improved.

"I began to feel something like my old self," he wrote, "and slowly started to put on weight."

In February 1904, for the first time in eight months, he played a round of golf on a course that was owned by the hospital—and believe it or not, made a hole in one on number 4, the lone ace of his entire life. By June he was healthy enough to compete in the British Open at Royal St. George's.

At the halfway mark, Vardon was ahead by two, but in the third round, he missed a half dozen putts inside four feet—the yips—on his way to a 79 and followed with a 74 to finish fifth.

"The start of my falling from grace on the putting green," he wrote, "was undoubtedly the result of my illness, which somehow or other affected the nerves in my right arm."

Yet he kept plugging away and from 1905 through 1908, he finished in the top ten of the Open each time, finally picking up his fifth Claret Jug in 1911 in a playoff over Arnaud Massy at Royal St. George's with his brother, Tom, on the bag.

In 1913, Vardon, you recall, went on another tour of America, accompanied this time by the long-hitting, crowd-pleasing Ted Ray. The trip was a huge success.

Except for Brookline.

In the 1914 British Open, the last one before Europe went to pieces,

Vardon rallied from two back in the fourth round at Prestwick to beat Taylor by three for title number six.

I wish his story had ended there, in triumph.

It didn't. It ended at Inverness. In heartbreak.

Vardon was fifty years old when he played in the 1920 U.S. Open, his first since 1913. Incredibly, with seven holes to go, he led by four.

"Any golfer who was fortunate enough to follow Harry Vardon in his first 11 holes' play in the final round at Inverness knows what perfect style is," John G. Anderson wrote in *The American Golfer*. "Not the slicing or pulling of forced strokes, but the straight line to the hole with the amount of strength controlled."

Everything was going his way.

Except Mother Nature. Heavy winds came in from Lake Erie, "wrenching the leaves from the trees," as one writer put it, "and churning sand from the bunkers."

Vardon was no match for this opponent:

A bogey on 12. A missed two-footer on 13. Three putts apiece on 14, 15, and 16.

"Under ordinary circumstances these conditions would not have made very much difference," he wrote. "At the time, however, there is no doubt I was tiring fast, and having to complete the remaining holes under this adversity required too big an effort."

On 17, a long par-4, when he had to be bold, his approach carried the front bank of the brook roughly two hundred yards away, but the ball hit the ditch and bounced back in to end any hope.

Over the final seven holes, Harry Vardon was seven over par.

If he would have won the Open, he concluded, "I would have had to consider it as the outstanding performance of my golfing life."

I'll go a step further. It would have been the most outstanding performance of *any* golfer's life.

The game's first global star, Vardon, as Herbert Warren Wind wrote in the 1980s, "deserves a place on the same level as Nicklaus, Hogan, and Jones. There has surely never been a better golfer than Harry Vardon."

9

Byron Nelson

Byron Nelson, who lived to the age of ninety-four, was twice given up for dead before his twelfth birthday.

The first time was in 1912 when his mom, Madge, eighteen, was in labor for so long that the doctor, assuming the baby had no chance of survival, focused on the life he believed he could save. "He finally had to use forceps to deliver me and broke my nose doing so," Nelson wrote decades later. "I still have a few dents in my skull from it. After I was delivered, he just placed me on a table near the bed, thinking I was dead."

Enter Grandma to the rescue.

"Doctor, this child is alive," she shouted.

"To everyone's surprise," Nelson explained, "I did make it, thanks to an abundance of my mother's milk."

The second time was when he was around eleven, the cause typhoid fever.

His mom could tell he was sick from the odor, the same her husband, who survived, gave off shortly after they'd gotten married. Within a few weeks, Byron dropped from 124 pounds to sixty-five, while his temperature climbed to over 106 degrees.

"They were packing me in ice, and said I'd never live," he wrote.

Coming to the rescue this time was Mrs. Keeter, a member of the church the Nelsons attended who was a chiropractor. "She was an expert in giving enemas," Nelson wrote, "so she treated me once or twice a day, very gently and carefully, and after about ten days, I began to improve.... The fact that I survived both experiences is one of the reasons why I feel I've always been a blessed man."

At twelve, he became a caddie at Glen Garden Country Club.

"As it turned out, it was a pretty important step for me," Nelson explained, "even though at the time all I was concerned about was ... extra change in my pocket."

Nelson shot a 118 the first time he played, which didn't count the times he whiffed, but he learned quickly by practicing and watching others. In late 1927, he won the club's caddie championship over a kid seven months younger. His name was Ben Hogan. Nelson canned a thirty-footer on the final hole of regulation to tie Hogan and put him away when he knocked in another long one on the final hole of a nine-hole playoff.

In 1931, Nelson qualified for the U.S. Amateur in Chicago, but due to thirteen three-putts in thirty-six holes, missed making it to match play by a stroke. A year later in Texarkana, playing for the first time as a pro, in a field that included Hogan and Jimmy Demaret, he finished third and picked up $75.

"I had never even seen that much money in my hand at one time in my entire life," Nelson wrote.

He soon heeded the famous advice of nineteenth-century newspaper publisher Horace Greeley: *Go West, young man.*

With the $500 he received from friends in Fort Worth, Nelson, twenty, gave the Tour a shot in Southern California but didn't make a dime, and before he knew it, was back in Texas, milking cows and performing other chores around the house.

In April 1933, he became the head professional at Texarkana Country Club.

The job didn't pay much—about $60 a month—but it paid huge dividends.

"Very seldom did anybody come to the club before noon on any day," Nelson recalled, "so I had an excellent practice field and I'd hit balls. I hit 'em down there and go down and hit 'em back. I didn't need anybody to shag for me, although there wasn't anybody to shag anyway. So I got better and better."

So back to California he went in early 1934 for another go at it.

Nelson, who didn't fare much better this time, came up with a plan when he arrived in San Antonio for the Texas Open.

"I knew how much it was costing me per day," he wrote, "and I figured, 'Well, I've got enough money to play here and in Galveston, and then I'll go back to Texarkana and go to work.'"

The plan couldn't have worked any better.

He came in second in San Antonio, earning $450, and second in Galveston, picking up another $300.

"I jumped in the car," Nelson wrote, "and headed for Texarkana. I don't think the wheels hardly hit the ground the whole way."

There was no turning back now.

In 1935, he registered his first Tour victory at the New Jersey State Open. Still, getting ready for the winter tour in 1936, Nelson was thinking about buying a new set of clubs.

His wife, Louise, had a different idea.

"Byron, honey," Louise told him, "why don't you quit kidding yourself? It just can't entirely be the clubs. Your trouble is *you*."

Bingo.

"My immature and false sense of pride," he explained, "had prevented me from putting the finger on myself. I resolved to let the club makers worry about my clubs and to concern myself with my own use of the implements."

He became the most accurate player in the game, claiming his first major in 1937 at Augusta National by two over Ralph Guldahl. Trailing by four after fifty-four holes, he made a twelve-footer for birdie at 10, a six-footer for birdie at 12, and chipped in for eagle at 13 to prevail by two. In 1939, he won four times, including the U.S. Open at the Philadelphia Country Club, defeating Denny Shute and Craig Wood in a thirty-six-hole playoff, Shute eliminated after the first eighteen.

Nelson hit the flagstick six times that week.

With six different clubs.

"I was kind of in a trance for a few days before I fully realized I was indeed the U.S. Open champion," he wrote.

Nelson picked up his third major with a one-up triumph over Sam Snead in the 1940 PGA at Hershey Country Club in Pennsylvania and his fourth in a playoff with Hogan at the 1942 Masters.

His stomach acting up, he didn't get much sleep the night before the playoff.

"There were easier people to have a playoff against than Ben Hogan, you know," Nelson said. "I woke up on the morning of the playoff just miserable. Ben found out about it and came down to my room and said, 'If you're sick we'll just postpone.' I answered, 'No, Ben, let's go ahead and play it.'"

Nelson doubled the first and was three down after four, "but somewhere around the fifth hole," he said, "my adrenaline glands started to [get] going and pretty soon I felt just as strong as I could be. I had that old spring in my arms and legs." He gained two strokes on Hogan on 6 and two more with an eagle on 8 to take the lead. The final margin was one, just like the caddie championship at Glen Garden fifteen years before.

The two never staged a battle like that again.

One reason had to do with the battles taking place in Europe and the Pacific.

From late 1942 through early 1944, Nelson, who didn't serve in World War II—he was classified 4F due to hemophilia—and his buddy, Harold "Jug" McSpaden, also 4F, took part in more than one hundred exhibitions across the country to raise money for the Red Cross and USO. They also toured with Bob Hope and Bing Crosby.

In 1944, the Tour resumed a more regular schedule with twenty-three tournaments. Nelson won eight times and was the Associated Press Athlete of the Year.

Yet he wasn't satisfied. Keeping meticulous records of every round, he discovered two disturbing trends: poor chipping and careless shots. "So I made up my mind, like a New Year's resolution," he wrote, "that for all of 1945 I would try very hard to avoid a careless shot."

His dream for the longest time had been to own a ranch. Louise was wary of the idea and with good reason—her husband knew little about ranching—but she agreed to go along if they didn't borrow any money.

"All I had to do," wrote Nelson, who had earned almost $38,000 in 1944, "was continue to play well enough to keep winning or at least finishing in the top ten."

Mission accomplished.

In his first nine starts, Nelson won three times and came in second on five other occasions. In March, he and McSpaden—they were known as the *Gold Dust Twins* for all the occasions they finished first or second—teamed up to capture the Miami International Four-Ball. By mid-April, Nelson had won five in a row, and after the Tour took a break for two months, he claimed the Montreal Open by ten, recording just one bogey the whole week.

The streak went on and on—to nine when he rallied from three down through twenty-one holes to outduel Sam Byrd in the PGA at Moraine Country Club outside Dayton and to ten two weeks later at the All-American Open in Chicago.

Finally, Fred Haas, an amateur, won the tournament in Memphis to end the streak at eleven. Nelson, who tied for fourth, bounced back the next week in Knoxville to win again.

So what should we make of this unprecedented stretch of dominance?

Not merely the eleven consecutive wins. The eighteen wins overall, five more than anyone has ever compiled in a single season.

Some make less of it than you'd think, citing the weaker fields due to the war.

I see their point, but it should be noted that Snead played in nine of the eighteen tournaments Nelson won, while Hogan, who made eighteen starts in '45, won five times and finished second or third on seven other occasions. Nelson's scoring average over 120 rounds was 68.33, the lowest until Tiger Woods averaged 68.17 in 2000.

In any case, Nelson, who ended up with fifty-two wins, didn't let the skeptics get to him. "Most of the time when people make that comment [about the weaker fields]," he pointed out, "I say I'm just I'm glad I played when I did, and I never backed off from anybody and never had any problem beating people I wanted to beat."

Nelson, who made 113 cuts in a row, second only to Woods's 142, played his last full season in 1946, winning six tournaments. That year, he purchased a 630-acre ranch in Roanoke, Texas, about twenty miles from Fort Worth. He paid $55,000—in cash, of course—and it was worth every penny, giving him more happiness than a man could ever dream of.

"I just love chickens," he told a reporter who came to visit decades later. "There's no creatures alive that's more appreciative of what you do for them. They're as nice as a dog."

8
Walter Hagen

I love the stories about the larger-than-life Walter Hagen. Check out this one, for starters:

In the 1919 U.S. Open at Brae Burn, Hagen, tied with Mike Brady, who was done for the day, lined up an eight-foot birdie putt on the 72nd hole for the win.

Any player in his position would have thought only about the line and speed.

Not Hagen.

He had someone fetch Brady from the clubhouse so he could be on hand for the moment of triumph, or as Herbert Warren Wind put it, "watch his own funeral."

(Wouldn't it have been cool if Phil Mickelson had asked someone to fetch Ernie Els from the putting green in the 2004 Masters?)

"Mike obliged," Wind wrote, "and shivered in his spikes as Walter tapped his sidehiller into the corner of the cup, only to have it twist out again and linger on the lip."

The two squared off in an eighteen-hole playoff the next day.

Which leads to another story.

Hagen partied late the night before with his friend, entertainer Al Jolson, who was appearing in the show *Sinbad* in Boston. When someone suggested he get a little rest, with his opponent, presumably, having been in bed for hours, Hagen responded:

"He may be in bed but he ain't asleep."

Word is Hagen got no shut-eye at all, or very little, and that he took a shower at the hotel and downed two double Scotches in the clubhouse bar before showing up at the 1st tee to take on Brady. He won the playoff regardless—it wouldn't be much of a story if he didn't—by one shot.

As long as we're telling stories, here's another:

At dinner the night before the 1914 U.S. Open at Midlothian Country Club outside Chicago, Hagen ate lobster for the first time and had oysters as an appetizer.

He became so sick with food poisoning he thought about dropping out.

Good thing he didn't. "The Haig," as he was known, opened with a four-under 68 and went wire to wire to capture his first major.

Sorry, one more and that will be it, I swear.

During the 1920 British Open at Royal Cinque Ports in England, Hagen and the other professionals were treated as second-class citizens.

So he decided, like Willie Anderson two decades before, to make a stand.

Not permitted to dress or dine in the clubhouse, Hagen, who lived the high life, turned his limo, which was parked near the front door, into a locker room and dining car, hiring a footman to serve his meals.

Before long, the professionals would be second-class citizens no more.

"Walter Hagen did more for professional golf than anyone else," said Donald Smith, an officer with the Royal and Ancient Golf Club of St. Andrews.

Hold on, I need to tell you one more. I really mean it this time.

In 1928, he didn't show up at first to defend his PGA title at the Baltimore Country Club in Maryland. Officials had to track him down at an exhibition match in Pennsylvania.

Hagen lost to Leo Diegel in the quarterfinals, but when he was asked to hand over the Wanamaker Trophy—the winner keeps it for a year, like the Claret Jug—he said he didn't know where it was.

He had left it in a taxi … three years earlier!

The issue hadn't come up before because he won the PGA in 1926 and 1927. Keep in mind things were a lot more informal back then.

(In the early 1930s, the trophy was discovered at a sporting goods warehouse in Detroit. Maybe that's where they buried Jimmy Hoffa.)

*

Hagen was a flashy dresser—silk shirts, florid cravats, alpaca sweaters, black-and-white shoes at $100 a pair—and believed to be the first athlete to earn over $1 million. "All the professionals who have a chance to go after the big money today," Gene Sarazen said decades later, "should say a silent thanks to Walter Hagen each time they stretch a check between their fingers."

However, make no mistake about it: the Haig was more than a showman.

Among his forty-five Tour victories were eleven major championships, the fourth most behind Jack Nicklaus, Tiger Woods, and Bobby Jones. He also won the Western Open five times.

Along with Jones, he owned the Roaring Twenties.

No wonder their seventy-two-hole match in Sarasota and Pasadena, Florida, in the winter of 1926 was dubbed "The Battle of the Century."

Some battle.

Hagen made mincemeat of Jones, 12 and 11, despite a shot or two you wouldn't expect from a player of his caliber. He had a reputation, which might be exaggerated, of hitting more than his share of wayward shots, often following with a splendid recovery.

"Walter starts out knowing that he can't possibly play perfect golf," one writer suggested. "He figures in advance that he is bound to play a few bad shots and he allows for them before they happen. When they do, he isn't disturbed."

Needing only fifty-three putts, Hagen was 8 up over Jones through thirty-six holes. On one hole, after Jones knocked in a forty-footer, Hagen yelled:

"Whaddya know, he gets a half!"

He yelled it *before* attempting a twenty-footer of his own to match him. That's how cocky Hagen could be.

He made the putt, naturally, and a half it was.

Hagen wasn't the kind of opponent Jones liked to face.

"I would far rather play a man who is straight down the fairway with his drive, on the green with his second, and down in two putts for his par," he said. "I can play a man like that at his own game, which is par golf.... But when a man misses his drive, and then misses his second shot, and then wins the hole with a birdie—it gets my goat!"

Before he was ten, Hagen became a caddie at the Country Club of Rochester in New York state. At twelve, he walked out of school one day and never went back.

In his first tournament, the 1912 Canadian Open in Toronto, he finished eleventh. A year later, in the Open at Brookline, Hagen told

John McDermott, the two-time defending champion: "I'm W. C. Hagen from Rochester and I've come to help you boys take care of Vardon and Ray."

When he broke through in the Open at Midlothian in 1914, a legend was born—a legend who had thought about trying baseball instead.

The Philadelphia Phillies, he claimed, were ready to sign him to a contract... as long as he promised he'd work on his batting swing, not his golf swing.

That was fine with Hagen, until he had a chat with Ernest Willard, a member of the club in Rochester, who urged him to enter the 1914 Open.

"If you'll go," Willard said, "I'll pay all your expenses."

In 1920, Hagen set sail for England—that's when he got dressed and ate his meals in the limo—to conquer links golf.

Links golf conquered him. He finished fifty-third.

"Hagen's arching woods and irons were scattered as ruthlessly as the Spanish Armada," Wind wrote.

Hagen didn't make any excuses.

"I couldn't get it going," he admitted. "I didn't have the touch. I am discouraged now, but I am coming back to England. I hope someday to play well over here."

And play well he did, with victories in 1922, 1924, 1928, and 1929.

At Royal St. George's in '22, he became the first player born in America to take home the Claret Jug.

As for the PGA, which he won five times (tied for the most with Jack Nicklaus) his first title came in 1921 at Inwood Country Club on Long Island when he outdueled Jim Barnes in the final, 3 and 2. After skipping the tournament in 1922, he lost, as you may recall, in the final to Sarazen a year later.

He didn't lose again until 1928... when they found him in Pennsylvania.

No surprise he was so tough to beat when it was mano a mano, his errant shots costing him only one hole instead of perhaps two or three strokes. He got inside the head of his opponent like no one else. "His personality was completely dominating," Wind wrote. "If you tried to kid along with him between shots you could never get down to business when the strokes had to be played, but Walter could. If you tried to shut him out of your mind, the harder you fought to ignore him the more strongly his presence enveloped you."

Take Mike Brady, the unfortunate soul who was summoned by Hagen to watch his putt in the 1919 U.S. Open. Early in the playoff the following day, when Hagen noticed how high up Brady had rolled his shirtsleeves, he saw his opening.

"Listen, Mike," he said, "hadn't you better roll down those sleeves?"

"What for?" Brady responded.

"The gallery can see your muscles twitching."

Brady hit his next shot way left and wound up losing two strokes on the hole.

In the final round of the 1926 British Open at Royal Lytham & St. Annes, Hagen gave his fans another moment to remember.

He needed an eagle at the last hole, a par-4, to tie Jones who had already finished. So after his drive found the fairway, Hagen, like Phil Mickelson would one day at Torrey Pines, walked to the putting surface about 150 yards away to check out the best route for his approach. He asked his caddie to be ready to pull the pin if the ball had a chance of going in. It did, indeed, before it rolled past the cup.

"He was never monotonous, as Vardon and even Jones sometimes could be," Sarazen said. "He was always exciting."

7

Sam Snead

There is no shortage of stories about Samuel Jackson Snead, as well.

Snead arrived on the scene at the perfect time, when the game needed a big personality to stir interest in a public still reeling from the Great Depression.

He came from Ashwood, Virginia, a tiny hamlet close to Hot Springs. His dad, Harry, took care of the boilers and did other maintenance work at the Homestead, a resort hotel about three miles away, while raising chickens and cows for much-needed extra dough.

Come each Christmas, the Sneads were reminded of where they stood.

"I wasn't able to give everybody presents, on account of we were so poor," Snead wrote. "We didn't get much either. I'd go down and play with the toys the other kids got. After that, I disliked Christmas, although I participate in it with my own wife and two kids."

Not that he had an unhappy childhood. Far from it.

"I realize how pretty fortunate I was overall," he said. "An awful lot of what I later applied to my golf career came from either home or those woods around Hot Springs."

When he was seven, he shagged balls for his older brother Homer in a meadow near their house. Since Homer would bring only one club, Sam used the knotty end of a swamp-maple limb to hack away at rocks, hickory nuts, dirt clods, even dried-up manure.

On one Sunday, he wrote, he hit a rock that "took off like a bullet, even went through the church window, and sprayed the congregation with glass. The preacher . . . was the first one out the door, but all he found was an empty road. I stayed in the woods until dark, then wouldn't admit a thing when they gave me the third degree. They never did prove it on me."

Not permitted to play on Homestead's two eighteen-hole courses, Cascades and the Old Course, which were for the tourists, Snead sneaked onto The Goat, a nine-hole course for hotel employees. He had earlier designed a five-hole course of his own, sinking tomato cans into the ground as cups and setting up hazards such as a chicken pen and outhouse.

In high school, he twice finished second in a long-drive contest with drives of over three hundred yards.

When drives of over three hundred yards meant something.

Nonetheless, given his background, he needed a break to make something of himself. He got it.

One evening, while flipping burgers at a local restaurant, Snead spoke to a customer who knew Freddie Gleim, Homestead's head pro. One thing led to another, and by the end of the summer, Snead was working in the shop, cleaning clubs, keeping the place stocked, and sweeping the floor. The job paid only $25 a month, but he was allowed to use the driving range and tee it up on occasion. The following summer, he went over to the Cascades a few miles away, giving occasional lessons and sharpening his game.

Fast-forward to the 1935 Cascades Open, hosted by the Homestead.

Snead finished third in a field that featured a couple of past U.S. Open champions, and before long he was on the Tour. With a sweet, powerful swing envied by his peers—many consider it the sweetest of all time—he picked up five wins in 1937, and another eight in 1938.

He was thought of as a hillbilly but a lot of the stuff written about him was simply not true.

Snead, for example, did not bury his cash in tomato cans in the backyard.

Nor did he ask, after his picture appeared in a New York newspaper, "How'd they do that? I ain't ever been to New York." His manager, Fred Corcoran, made it up, as one writer put it, "to further depict Sam as a lovable hayseed."

No matter. The stories were told over and over, and that seemed fine with him.

"I don't think I was ever totally the rube they [the press] made me out to be," Snead said, "but they loved to hear about how I'd spend my time between tours back up at Ashwood with my folks."

For all his success, he went through his share of losing.

At the U.S. Open, especially.

In 1937, he finished second by two strokes to Ralph Guldahl at Oakland Hills. Snead didn't lose it so much as Guldahl, who closed with a 69, won it.

That wasn't the case two years later at the Spring Mill course in Philadelphia.

Snead lost it. In more ways than one.

First, he missed a five-footer for par on 17, though that's not what killed him. What killed him was what happened on 18, a par-5. On the tee, he figured he needed a birdie to win. So after hooking his drive into the rough and faced with a sandy lie from about 275 yards away, he still went for broke. The ball skidded into a bunker about one hundred yards from the green and was partly buried.

He didn't get on with his third. Or fourth. That's when he found out a par, not a birdie, would be good enough and that a bogey would tie him for the lead.

Snead was furious.

"Why didn't someone tell me that back on the tee so that I could have played it safe?" said Snead, who made a triple, missing the playoff between Byron Nelson, Denny Shute, and Craig Wood by two.

On second thought, furious doesn't begin to describe the state he was in.

"That night, I was ready to go out with a gun and pay somebody to shoot me," Snead wrote. "It weighed on my mind so much that I dropped 10 pounds, lost more hair, and began to choke up even on practice rounds."

He blew the 1947 Open, as well. With three holes to go in an eighteen-hole playoff at St. Louis Country Club, he was leading by two over Lew Worsham...until Worsham birdied 16, Snead bogeyed 17, and presto, the two were tied. On 18, each faced a par putt of about two and a half feet.

Snead was about to go first when Worsham weighed in: "Wait a minute, Sam. Are you sure you're away?"

Which led to Ike Grainger, the chairman of the USGA's rules committee, making a final determination.

With, I kid you not, a measuring tape.

"You could see the steam coming out of Sam," author Jim Dodson said, referring to a photo taken at the time. "He is standing there, the putter by his side, with this impatient stare that says, 'This is absolutely a sin against nature.'"

Snead was, indeed, away. By an inch.

He missed the putt, of course, while Worsham made his for the win. "Sam looked like he'd been shot through the heart," former U.S. Amateur champion Bill Campbell recalled. "I didn't want to go over and speak to him because I knew he was in absolute agony."

Never winning the Open takes something away from the greatness of Snead, there is no way around it, just as it takes something away from Phil Mickelson.

And from Nancy Lopez and Kathy Whitworth.

"If I could have shot 69 in the last round every time," said Snead, who also finished second in 1949 and 1953, "I would have won nine U.S. Opens. *Nine.*"

Snead didn't allow the defeats to define him. "I don't feel my career has not been fulfilled because I didn't win the U.S. Open," he suggested.

As for those who didn't think he could win the big one, Snead begged to differ: "Well, Jesus, what do you call those others?"

No argument on this end.

Of his record-tying eighty-two Tour victories, seven were majors: the Masters in 1949, 1952, and 1954; the PGA Championship in 1942, 1949, and 1951; and the British Open at St. Andrews in 1946.

He didn't want to go to Scotland at first.

"I still had memories of the bad food and the sorry accommodations from the Ryder Cup in 1937 [in Southport, England]," he pointed out. "And when I learned they were putting up something like only six hundred dollars, why, I said no way to that. That wouldn't even cover my expenses."

Snead was urged to go by L. B. Icely, the president of Wilson Sporting Goods, who felt a victory, as Dodson put it, "would amount to a public relations windfall for both Sam and Wilson." Icely also, reportedly, agreed to pay for Snead's travel expenses.

The trip didn't get off to a good start.

First, he had to evacuate the plane that was to take him from New York when there was a fuel leak and an engine fire on the runway. Then, on the train from London to Scotland, Snead, who was sitting in a first-class compartment with Lawson Little Jr. and a British gentleman he had just met, blurted out:

"Say, that looks like an old, abandoned golf course. What did they call it?"

Ooops.

"My good sir!" the insulted Brit responded. "*That* is the Royal and Ancient Club of St. Andrews, founded in 1754! And it is not now, nor ever will be, abandoned!"

Snead's comment made its way into the papers, and from that point on, he claimed, "I was dodging reporters who had the knife out for me. The only place over there that's holier than St. Andrews is Westminster Abbey. I began to think the whole trip was a mistake."

It was no mistake.

Snead, who went through four different caddies in four days, which included practice rounds—"one of them whistled between his teeth when I putted"—prevailed by four over Bobby Locke and Johnny Bulla, becoming the first American to win the Open since Denny Shute in 1933. The two-under 290 Snead posted was lower than what Hagen shot in his four victories and two of the three winning totals from Bobby Jones.

Even so, Snead—God bless him for his bluntness—didn't fall in love with the place.

"The purse of $600 was such a joke," he wrote, "that I decided then and there not to defend the title. My traveling expenses alone were over $1,000, and nobody [not L. B. Icely, apparently] but me picked up that tab. On top of that, all my hitting muscles 'froze' in the icy wind at St. Andrews. For days I ached in every joint."

In 1950, he won eleven tournaments, as well as the Vardon Trophy with an average of 69.23.

Yet, believe it or not, Snead wasn't the Player of the Year.

Ben Hogan was. Even though he had just one win, the Open at Merion.

"In some ways," Snead said, "that was the toughest thing I ever had to swallow. I'd had the greatest year of my career—better than anyone had had since Byron Nelson's run—and Ben got all the honors. For a while, I seriously considered hanging it up. I couldn't do any better than I'd done. Once I got home to Virginia and thought about it some more, though, I decided to keep on going. But...the tour was never quite the same for me after that."

Perhaps not, but Snead, who defeated Hogan by one in a playoff at the 1954 Masters for his final major, played, and quite well on occasion, into his sixties. In 1974, at sixty-two, he tied for third in the PGA at Tanglewood Park.

Curtis Strange, also from Virginia, idolized Snead when he was growing up.

Hitting balls on the range one day while they were in high school, he and his twin brother, Allan, came to a sobering conclusion.

"We realized we can't swing like Sam and never will," Curtis said.

"Nobody ever will."

6

Mickey Wright

I was watching ESPN's *Pardon the Interruption* in the fall of 2023 when co-host Tony Kornheiser said Annika Sorenstam, who was turning fifty-three, was "at or near the top of the list for greatest female golfer of all time."

"Ever hear of Mickey Wright?" I wanted to tell him.

As awesome as Sorenstam was, she belongs near the top.

Not at the top.

Total tour victories: Wright, eighty-two; Sorenstam, seventy-two.

Total major titles: Wright, thirteen (including four U.S. Opens); Sorenstam, ten (three Opens).

Wright's thirteen majors came in fifty starts for a winning percentage of 26 percent; Sorenstam's ten in fifty-seven starts (17.5 percent).

And no, I don't want to hear how much better the competition was in the 1990s and 2000s than it was the 1960s when Wright was at her peak. I'm going to repeat what Bobby Jones said about comparing players in different eras, and I will keep repeating it, if need be, until my dying breath:

"I think we must agree that all a man can do is beat the people who are around at the same time he is. He cannot win from those who came before any more than he can from those who may come afterward."

Besides, Wright took time off from the tour in 1965, played in only about a dozen events in 1966, and scaled back even more after 1969 at age thirty-four. If she had kept a normal playing schedule all those years the gap between the two would be even wider.

She would have won ninety tournaments. At least.

"[Wright] by far, was head and shoulders above the rest of us," Kathy Whitworth told me. To win eighty-two times "in the span she did play, is remarkable."

One final point:

Her swing. The best of any female or male golfer. Ever. Even Hogan said so.

"It was just so gracefully athletic," said Carol Mann, a top player in the '60s. "Where the club was coming from, how fast it was going, and the unloading right at the moment of impact was extraordinary. She was a swinger, but she had one of the volatile impacts. It was almost like a whole new category."

I rest my case.

In 1993, more than one hundred LPGA members watched Wright, fifty-eight, play a few holes of a senior tournament in Florida. Some, including Australia's Jane Crafter, followed her for almost the entire thirty-six, asking for her autograph afterward. "We were like groupies," Crafter said.

Wright, playing with 1962 Wilson Staff irons and using the same putter from every one of her eighty-two victories, hadn't played competitive golf in eight years.

"I was extremely nervous," she admitted. "... I didn't want to fall off the first tee and embarrass myself. All I wanted to do was to break 80."

Embarrass herself? Mickey Wright? Not a chance.

She shot a five-over 78 on the first day despite having never played the course and a 74 the second day to share fifth place with Whitworth. Wright hit drives of up to 270 yards.

"It's just awesome," Crafter said. "Awesome! AWESOME!"

*

Wright's father, a 15-handicapper, introduced her to golf when she was ten.

"I took to it like a duck to water," Wright said, "and a little later there was a picture of me in the local paper with a caption, 'The Next Babe?' You can imagine what that does for an 11-year-old, and from that time on I was determined to become a professional golfer."

When Wright, who grew up in San Diego, was fourteen, her mother drove her about one hundred and twenty miles every Saturday morning to San Gabriel Country Club near Pasadena for a thirty-minute lesson with Harry Pressler, one of the top teachers in the state. "My swing really is Harry's swing," Wright recalled. "Harry was adamant there was one good swing. Club square going back. Right hand under the shaft in the 'tray' position at the top, the club at a 45-degree angle. Clubface square halfway down, at impact and into the follow-through."

In 1952, Wright, seventeen, captured the U.S. Girls' Junior Championship at Monterey Peninsula Club in Pebble Beach. In 1954, she lost in the final of the U.S. Women's Amateur to Barbara Romack, 4 and 2. The same year, she was paired with Babe for the last two rounds of the U.S. Women's Open in Massachusetts—the Open Babe won by twelve wearing a colostomy bag.

"I was 19 and scared out of my boots," said Wright, who tied for fourth. "Can you imagine suddenly competing against the greatest athlete of all time? Babe was larger than life, almost like something from another planet."

Wright went to Stanford but left after one year to turn pro.

"I can always get my college degree after I've had a fling at golf," she said. "I want to see just what I can do."

In 1956, her second season on tour, she picked up her first victory, in Jacksonville, and added three more titles in '57. Wright hit it a long way but her putting held her back.

"She figured that your score should be in direct proportion to the number of greens you hit in regulation," Betsy Rawls said, and that "it took skill to drive, but chipping and putting were just a matter of luck."

Wright wised up soon enough, realizing that it "took as much talent," Rawls said, "to hit good putts as good drives."

Her attitude also needed work. When asked about her two rounds in the 80s at a tournament in St. Petersburg, Florida, she blamed other players, the sponsors, her caddie, you name it.

Enter Rawls to the rescue. "No matter what you think or feel about it," she told Wright, "your golf game is your own responsibility. No one else can hit that ball for you."

Wright got the message loud and clear.

"Now every time I get over a chip shot—they used to give me trouble—I say to myself, 'This is your responsibility.' You can't imagine how much it helped," she said.

In 1958, Wright won five times, including her first two majors: the U.S. Women's Open by five over Louise Suggs and the LPGA Championship by six over Fay Crocker.

In 1961, working with Earl Stewart, a three-time winner on the PGA Tour, she went on a four-year run—forty-four victories, including thirteen in 1963—Tom Watson called "the best run anyone has ever had."

Give Stewart his due.

"[He] was a slave driver, much more of a perfectionist than I," Wright recalled. "And he didn't care how I hit it or swung the club. The object was to win."

Success, however, as it often does, came at a price.

"I took [winning] to an extreme," she said, "...but it is an easy trap into which to fall, especially when you have as much drive as I had to win.... Coming up to the last hole, you are scared to death, so afraid you will lose.... For me, it was as if you didn't exist if you lost, and then I couldn't wait until the next week to win again."

Worse yet, she didn't like the person she was becoming. "I found myself getting defensive and irritable," Wright said. The pressure grew so intense in the summer of 1964 that "I was always tired, my health was bad.... I knew something was going to happen."

It sure did.

In August, during the first round of a tournament in New Mexico, when a TV cameraman kept getting too close, she gave him an earful, the gallery catching every word. "I had completely lost control of myself," said Wright, who shot an 86 (including a six-putt). "And I figured it might happen again. Everything I had built up over the years, all my care about my public image, would be out the window. This finally made me decide to quit the tour. (Injuries were also a factor.)"

The pressure she faced wasn't just to win tournaments. It was to show up in the first place.

In the early '60s, Whitworth said, "Sponsors threatened to cancel their tournaments if she didn't play. And, knowing that if they canceled the rest of us wouldn't be able to play, Mickey would always play." As a result, Wright entered thirty-three events in 1962 and thirty in 1963, "more than I could physically and emotionally handle."

It was no mystery why tournaments needed her.

"Nobody ever made a difference at the gate like Mickey Wright," Carol Mann said. "She brought the game to the people...if you were running a golf tournament and didn't have Mickey Wright, you drew five thousand people. If you did have her, she drew ten thousand."

During her time off in 1965, she enrolled for a semester at Southern Methodist University in Texas, taking classes in math, philosophy, and psychology.

"I was hoping to find something equally as fascinating as golf," Wright said.

No such luck.

She went back on tour, winning seven tournaments in 1966.

The pressure returned, as well.

"I have a theory that the adrenaline supply runs out when your body has pumped so much adrenaline over the years," she said. "You have just so much of that to give."

From 1970 through 1979, Wright played in just sixty-six events, winning once, the Dinah Shore in 1973.

In 1979, she was in a sudden death playoff at the Coca-Cola Classic in New Jersey with Bonnie Byrant, Hollis Stacy, Jo Ann Washam, and . . .

Nancy Lopez.

"I was intimidated," said Lopez who defeated Wright on the second extra hole after the others had been eliminated. "She out-hit me, and I was pretty long then. I thought if I could beat her, what a great accomplishment it would be. I would be able to tell myself I had beaten Mickey Wright, the greatest of all time."

Wright, who played in her final LPGA event in 1980, granted few interviews in retirement. She passed away in 2020.

"My life now is not that exciting or interesting," she told a writer in 2000. "The interesting part was in the 1960s."

5

Arnold Palmer

Speaking of the 1960s, I won't start with the highs—the comeback at Cherry Hills in 1960, the Claret Jugs in 1961 and 1962, three of his four green jackets in Augusta, etc., etc., etc.

That's because, IMHO, the greatness of Arnold Palmer isn't only about what he won.

It's about what he lost.

Or, rather, how he lost.

How he reminded us how humbling the game of golf, and life, can be and how human and flawed we all are. He let us in and we loved him for it.

"Not a single time, in all the places we went," Peter Jacobsen recalled, "when people were falling all over themselves to get a picture or autograph or just shake his hand, did I ever hear him say, 'Geez, get me out of here. This is ridiculous. Get me away from this guy.' And whenever tournament organizers offered him security…he declined. He'd go with the people, no matter how long it took."

As far as losses go, nothing, of course, tops the Olympic Club in 1966. The *Hindenburg* doesn't top the Olympic Club.

"People who are close to him and close to me said he was never the same after that," Billy Casper said, "that he never totally recovered."

After the playoff, Palmer went back to the home where he and his wife, Winnie, were staying for the week.

"He came into the kitchen where I was making hors d'oeuves," recalled Rita Douglas, a club member. "He said, 'Oh, Rita, I could cry.' I just said, 'So could I, Arn.' He was very bitter about it; he really hated losing that one."

Another heartbreaking loss was the Masters in 1961.

Leading by a shot over Gary Player on the 72nd hole, Palmer found the fairway with his tee shot.

He then committed the biggest mental error of his career. Bigger, yes, than focusing on Hogan's record in 1966 instead of on Casper.

When his friend George Low, who was in the gallery, motioned him toward the ropes and said, "nice going, boy, you won it," Palmer should have done what Henry Cotton did in the 1934 British Open when others told him the tournament was over, and that was to shut his ears, "lest," as one writer put it, "the gods overheard and damned him for his presumption." Palmer accepted the congratulations from his friend and, in doing so, he wrote, "completely destroyed my concentration."

Lifting his head too soon, he found the bunker with his approach, sent his third across the green and down the slope toward the television tower, and failed to get up and down.

A double bogey on the final hole to lose the Masters by one. It doesn't get worse than that. (Well, except for the Olympic Club.)

"I'd lost because I'd failed to do what Pap [his father] had always told me to do—stay focused until the job is finished."

*

His father was Deacon Palmer, the superintendent and pro at Latrobe Country Club in western Pennsylvania.

"He put my hands on the club," Palmer said, "and told me in no uncertain terms, 'Don't you ever change this,' and I never really did. To most people, a proper golf grip is awkward as hell at first. But I was lucky. My hands were placed on the club so early that it always felt second nature to me."

Hit the ball hard, Deacon Palmer told his son, find it and hit it hard again.

That's how Arnold Palmer played the game growing up. And for the rest of his life.

When a club member suggested his boy was swinging too hard, Deacon Palmer didn't hold back: "You let me worry about the kid and you take care of your own game, all right?" As the distinguished English writer Peter Dobereiner put it: "Arnold never caught the golf bug. He was born with it like a hereditary disease."

His father taught him how to behave. On and off the course.

If he didn't hold his knife and fork properly, Palmer recalled, his dad would "go through the roof. And God forbid you dared to enter a dwelling or be in the presence of a woman and forget to remove your cap."

Palmer, aiming to please him, usually did the right thing.

Usually.

On the final day of the West Penn Junior tournament, he threw his putter over the gallery and a few small trees after missing a short one.

It made no difference that he won.

"If you ever throw a club like that in my presence or while you're living in my house," his father told him, "you'll never play another game of golf."

When Palmer was about thirteen, Babe Didrikson Zaharias played in an exhibition with him and his father at Latrobe.

"Up until then," he wrote, "I had my head down, competing. I just wanted to win. But while watching her showing off—both her skills and her personality—it occurred to me that I was a showoff, too. I wanted to entertain the people and earn their cheers."

In 1948, Palmer enrolled at Wake Forest. He had the time of his life, winning tournaments and making friends.

And learning how fragile life is.

His best friend, Bud Worsham, and Gene Scheer, another Wake student, were killed in a car accident after attending a dance in Durham. Worsham had wanted Palmer to join them. He went to a movie instead.

Palmer couldn't stay at Wake. Not with Worsham gone.

"I was haunted by a feeling I couldn't escape," he wrote, "that if only I'd gone that night to Durham with Bud and Gene things might have turned out very differently. I'd probably have been driving the Buick, and we would have all . . . gotten up that Sunday morning and maybe gone out and played golf and the world would have been exactly as it had always been for us, spinning happily on its axis."

Palmer left Wake to "outrun a grief," he explained nearly a half century later, "I still feel like a cool evening shadow."

He enlisted in the United States Coast Guard, starting basic training at Cape May in New Jersey in January 1951.

Although he didn't play much his first two years in the Coast Guard, the game remained the "one place," he wrote, "where I felt in control of what was happening to me."

In 1953, Palmer made it to the fourth round of the U.S. Amateur in Oklahoma City, losing one up to Don Albert. He won it the next year, rallying from two down after the first 18 to defeat Bob Sweeny, an investment banker, one up at the Country Club of Detroit.

Forget about the other major championships he won later on.

The 1954 Amateur, he always said, meant the most.

"I'd finally shown my father that I was the best amateur golfer in America," he wrote. "It was the turning point of my life, and I don't know if I've ever felt as much happiness on a golf course."

Palmer turned pro a few months later, signing a deal with the Wilson Sporting Goods Company for $5,000 a year, as well as a signing bonus of $2,000. In 1955, he collected the first of his sixty-two Tour victories, the Canadian Open, by four over Jackie Burke Jr.

He was on his way to becoming the most popular—and influential golfer—of his time.

Of any time perhaps.

It has often been said that Palmer brought the game from the country clubs to the masses and nothing could be more true.

When he won his first Masters in 1958, which led to the formation of Arnie's Army, one of those he had to thank (not personally) was Ben Hogan.

Early in the week, paired with Dow Finsterwald, Palmer played "abysmally," as he put it, in a money game against Hogan and Burke.

In the locker room afterward, Hogan asked Burke:

"How the hell did Palmer get an invitation to the Masters?"

Palmer heard every word.

"The question burned me up and set my mind on showing him why the hell I'd been invited to the Masters," he wrote.

He fired a 68 on Saturday to seize a share of the fifty-four-hole lead with Sam Snead.

Which brings us to the final round and the controversy on number 12.

Forgive me, but I don't have the bandwidth to go through it again—I spent a lifetime rehashing every detail about that hole with Ken Venturi, may he rest in peace, except to add that Palmer wisely avoided comment when the book was released in the spring of 2004. In his memoir, he wrote, "I knew the rule, and I believed I was well within my rights to do what I had done."

I prefer to focus instead on another final round, at Cherry Hills in the 1960 U.S. Open. There was nothing controversial about this one, I'm happy to report.

Simply a man on top of his game.

And on top of his sport.

I have read numerous accounts, but I will rely on what Dan Jenkins wrote in the August 1975 issue of *Golf Digest*:

Palmer, who was seven behind after fifty-four holes, was about to leave the locker room to play the final eighteen.

"You coming?" he said to Bob Drum, the golf writer for *The Pittsburgh Press*.

"I'm tired of watching duck hooks," Drum responded. "There's a guy named [Mike] Souchak leading the tournament. He's from Pittsburgh, too."

Palmer: "If I drive the first hole [a 346-yard par-4] I might shoot 65."

Drum: "Good, you'll finish fourteenth."

Palmer: "That would be 280. Doesn't 280 always win the Open?"

Drum: "Yeah, when Hogan shoots it."

Not only did Palmer drive the first hole, which led to a birdie, he birdied 2, 3, 4, 6, and 7 for a five-under 30 on the front nine.

On the 5th tee, he spotted Drum and Jenkins, who had hurried to join his group.

"Fancy seeing you here," said Palmer, who wound up finishing with a 65 to defeat Nicklaus, who was still an amateur, by two.

Palmer could have won more two or three more Opens, losing in playoffs to Nicklaus at Oakmont in 1962, Julius Boros at Brookline in 1963, and, of course, Billy Casper at Olympic in 1966. And he was in the hunt on the final day in 1967, 1972, 1973, and 1974.

Oakmont, about an hour from Latrobe, was a home game for Palmer.

And hostile territory for the twenty-two-year-old Nicklaus. The nerve of him, daring to dethrone a king.

"Someone standing in the deep rough," Gary Player recalled, "held up a sign that said, 'Hit it here, Ohio Guts!' It was shameful."

Nicklaus wasn't fazed.

"[He] had the ability to just close himself off from everything," Palmer said. "It's a great attribute. He could just shut himself off and go play."

Palmer couldn't.

For that, we should be grateful. He wouldn't be Arnold Palmer if he could.

He reached thirty-two of thirty-six greens on Saturday, but his putter let him down—on 17 and 18, especially, when he missed very makeable birdie putts.

Including the playoff, he three-putted ten times. Nicklaus three-putted once.

"I've always believed," he said, "if I could have just held him off [in the playoff], I might have been able to hold him off for a while. But not forever."

In the 1963 playoff, Palmer still had a slim chance of catching Boros, until he made a mess of things on number 11. After his tee shot ended up in the woods, he could have taken a penalty and perhaps saved himself a stroke.

Arnold Palmer, take the safe route? Are you kidding me?

I know what you're thinking:

Why am I nowhere near as critical of Palmer going for broke as I was of Greg Norman and Phil Mickelson? Because with Palmer, unlike those other two, I never felt he was trying to prove how great he was. He went for it because he loved the game and wanted to win badly. Probably too badly.

And, besides, we wouldn't have wanted it any other way.

"What's fun about a guy who hits fairways and greens and two-putts every hole?" Curtis Strange asked.

In reflecting on Arnold Palmer, the golfer and the man, I am reminded of George Bailey, the character played by Jimmy Stewart in the holiday classic *It's a Wonderful Life*.

Of where the game would be today if he had never been born.

Who would have carried the torch, as JFK might have put it, for a new generation of golfers now that Ben Hogan and Sam Snead were no longer in their prime?

Gene Littler? Billy Casper? Doug Ford?

I think not.

And who's to say that Nicklaus, coming along in the early 1960s, would have had the impact he did? Or Gary Player? Or Lee Trevino?

Or Tiger Woods?

"When Arnold died," Strange told me, "I felt like a piece of me died. I never thought he would die. He was our Superman."

4

Ben Hogan

In January 1938, Ben Hogan was getting ready to play in the Oakland Open, the next stop on the west coast swing.

For more than a paycheck. For a future in the game, period.

Of the $1,400 he started out with, he had only $86 left.

"If we don't make any money there," he told his wife, Valerie, "I'll sell the car, and we'll go home, and I'll never mention golf to you again."

Lo and behold, before the first round, someone stole the tires from his red Buick. Now he was really done for. Fortunately, Byron Nelson, who was staying nearby, gave him a lift to the course, and Hogan was able to make his tee time.

He picked up $285 by finishing in a tie for sixth and would live to see another day.

"I played harder [in the final round] than I ever played before," he said.

*

Ben Hogan faced one obstacle after another during his career. A nasty hook, the yips, and, of course, the accident.

First, however, it is essential to know what he faced before golf came into his life.

More than any human being should ever have to face.

When he was nine, his father, Chester Hogan, killed himself with a .38 revolver, and according to some accounts, his son saw him do it.

I'm going to resist the temptation to play shrink, and I hope future authors tread carefully, as well.

This isn't our area of expertise.

At the same time, it doesn't take a PhD in psychology to know that what happened that day in 1922, as much as Hogan avoided the subject—Valerie did not find out about the suicide until long after they had gotten married—had an enormous impact.

"I always got the feeling that Ben had been his father's favorite," she said, "and that he had felt very close to his father. I'm sure the way he died had a lot to do with the way Ben's personality was. I don't think he ever got over it."

Like Byron Nelson, Hogan started out as a caddie at the Glen Garden Country Club in Fort Worth.

His older brother, Royal, told Ben, then eleven, that other kids were earning sixty-five cents per bag, an opportunity he couldn't pass up. He later worked in the shop, polishing clubs until three in the morning on weekends. "Boy, I would look at those clubs and they were the most beautiful things, Nickels and Stewarts, all made in Scotland," he said. Working on the clubs gave him a "much better understanding of the game."

Hogan, who would drop out of high school during his senior year, had some success as an amateur, finishing second in the state public links championship in Waco and losing in the final of the Southwestern Amateur in Shreveport, Louisiana.

In the 1930 Texas Open at Brackenridge Park in San Antonio, his first event as a pro, Hogan withdrew after rounds of 78 and 75 even though he had made the cut. "Right then and there, I decided," he said, "if I couldn't learn to handle the pressure and play any better than that, why, I had no right to be out there at all."

A week later, in Houston, after turning in a 76 and 77 and making another cut, he quit again.

Hogan struggled so mightily in those early years that to pick up a few extra bucks he mopped floors at a restaurant and worked as a bellhop at the Blackstone Hotel.

And believe it or not, was the stickman at a gambling house called Top of the Hill Terrace.

While he received help from his peers, and from Marvin Leonard, a local department store owner and father figure who loaned him money on several occasions, it was Hogan's work ethic which led to his winning nine majors (sixty-four tournaments overall), and being the best golfer (not Snead or Nelson) of his generation.

And, in the opinion of many, the best ball striker the game has ever known.

"Very few times in my life I laid off maybe two to three days," Hogan explained in a rare 1983 television interview with Ken Venturi. "It seemed like it took me a month to three months to get back those three days to where I was when I took a rest. . . . I had to practice and play all the time."

His peers paid close attention. "Practicing as much as Ben did," Tommy Bolt, the 1958 U.S. Open champion, suggested, "which I swear was twice as much as anybody I ever saw, he basically reduced the margin for human error to damn near nothing."

No one was more focused on his own game.

One time, his playing partner, Claude Harmon, made an ace on number 12 at Augusta National. You would have never known it by Hogan's response.

"I think that's the first time I ever birdied that hole," he told Harmon as they headed to the 13th tee.

Find fault with his self-absorption, if you must, but it worked for him.

In September 1938, Hogan teamed up with Vic Ghezzi at the Hershey Four-Ball in Pennsylvania to win for the first time on Tour. Two years later, he collected his first individual title, the North and South Open in Pinehurst, by three over Sam Snead, and took the next two events, as well, to finish the season as the tour's leading money winner.

As for that hook of his, thank God for Henry Picard who, you may recall, urged Hogan to move his left hand to the left and weaken his grip.

Harry Cooper claimed he also gave him a lesson.

"Ben never made mention of that tip in public," Cooper said, "but I think he was grateful. Every time I see him, he comes over and gives me a big hug."

If only a war hadn't gotten in the way, Hogan serving as a second lieutenant in the U.S. Army Air Corps and joining the Civilian Pilot Training Program.

In 1946, Hogan replaced the retiring Byron Nelson as the best golfer in the world. He captured the PGA, his first major, at Portland Golf Club, outdueling Ed Oliver 6 and 4 in the final, one of thirteen victories that season.

"He almost couldn't be beaten," Jackie Burke Jr. said.

Hogan won seven tournaments in 1947 and ten in 1948, including the U.S. Open at Riviera and a second PGA at Norwood Hills Country Club outside St. Louis.

In 1949, he took two of the first three tournaments. He was so much better than the competition that players began to believe he had found the secret to the golf swing.

The only secret, as Hogan memorably put it, "is in the dirt." Translation: The practice area.

Secret, or no secret, there seemed no limit to what he could accomplish.

Yet there are always limits in golf, as in life, some self-imposed or, in his case, brought on by bad luck, fate ... who the hell knows?

How else to describe the Greyhound bus that veered into the wrong lane on Highway 80 and collided with him and his wife on the morning of February 2, 1949, as they were driving their Cadillac from Phoenix to Fort Worth? Hogan, trying to save Valerie by hurling himself across the seat, wound up saving himself as his side of the vehicle was crushed.

His injuries included a double fracture of the pelvis, a chipped rib, broken collarbone, and broken left ankle.

"Ben's legs got all mashed," Snead recalled. "For a while we all thought he was done for. Nobody expected him to play golf again, let alone win tournaments."

Hogan made it through those early days, but when a series of blood clots threatened to block a key artery to his lungs, the Associated Press sent an advisory to radio stations and newspapers: "The following is a biographical sketch of Ben Hogan, professional golfer, now ill at El Paso. It is intended primarily for use in the event of his death." Surgery, thank goodness, got him out of danger.

In January 1950, eleven months after the accident, Hogan made his much-anticipated return in the L.A. Open at Riviera.

He lost to Snead by four in an eighteen-hole playoff but was a winner just by showing up.

From then on, his body wouldn't allow him to play very often—the most starts in any season were six—but Hogan was more successful (not necessarily better) than he was before.

Beginning with the 1950 U.S. Open at Merion, immortalized by the classic Hy Peskin photo of Hogan's one-iron approach on the 72nd hole, he won six of his nine majors after the accident, and they all came in his first nine starts. Counting the 1948 U.S. Open and PGA, that made it eight out of his last eleven.

"If anything," Bolt suggested, "that wreck made Ben an even more dangerous critter. He saved everything inside for the titles he wanted most and the rest of the time he just practiced, practiced, practiced."

Hogan won the 1951 Masters and his third Open a few months later at Oakland Hills, setting the stage for 1953, the best year a golfer, pro or amateur, has ever had, and that includes Jones's Grand Slam in 1930, Nelson's streak in 1945, and Woods's three majors in 2000.

None of them did it with the body Hogan was stuck with.

He won five of the six tournaments he played in, including three majors, and tied for third the other time.

The Masters by five over Ed Oliver.

The U.S. Open at Oakmont by six over Snead.

The British Open at Carnoustie by four over Peter Thomson and three others.

(He didn't compete in the PGA, which was to conclude on the day before the first round of the British and, even if it wasn't, the thirty-six hole matches would have been too hard on his legs. Hogan didn't play in another PGA until 1960, when it was a stroke play format.)

Like Snead in 1946, Hogan wasn't inclined to make the trip to Scotland—"it was a big deal for him to go so far after the accident," Valerie said—but he followed the advice of some top players who said his career wouldn't be complete unless he played in the Open. Hogan, dubbed by the Scots as the *Wee Ice Mon,* bested the tournament record at Carnoustie by eight strokes in what would be his only Open appearance.

The week had exacted a heavy toll on him.

"He looked utterly and completely drained, a man on the verge of collapse," said future CBS commentator Ben Wright. "Still, the way the crowd quietly and respectfully parted as he approached—well, it reminded me of passing royalty."

The British Open turned out to be his last major title, though he came close on a number of occasions, most notably in the 1955 U.S. Open at the Olympic Club.

What is it about that course, anyway, that it felt compelled to break the hearts of the game's most iconic figures?

After Hogan putted out on 18 for a final-round 70 and a total of seven-over 287, everyone figured it was over, including Gene Sarazen, who congratulated him on the NBC telecast. Sarazen, more than anyone, should have known better.

"I'm through with competitive golf," Hogan said after he lost by three in a playoff with Jack Fleck, a relatively unknown pro from Iowa who had rallied down the stretch in the final round to force a tie.

He wasn't through, far from it, and in 1960, at age forty-seven, made a heck of a run in the Open at Cherry Hills.

Tied for the lead with Arnold Palmer on the 71st hole, a par-5, Hogan, who had reached thirty-four greens in a row that Saturday, hit a wedge that looked perfect until it spun back into the water, leading to a bogey he couldn't afford. He followed with a triple on 18, finishing in a tie for ninth.

What happened on 17 wound haunt him for a long time.

"I find myself waking up at night thinking of that shot, right today," he told Venturi in 1983. "There isn't a month that goes by that that doesn't cut my guts out. I didn't miss it. I just didn't hit it far enough."

Hogan is tied with Jack Nicklaus, Bobby Jones, and Willie Anderson for the most Open victories at four, though in the opinion of some (Hogan, himself, felt that way) he has five. In 1942, he won the Hale America Open at Ridgemoor Country Club in Illinois, which was co-sponsored by the USGA, and received a medal almost identical to the one Open champions were awarded.

In 1967, Hogan, fifty-four, turned in a 30 on the back nine—a 66 overall—in the third round of the Masters to climb within two of the lead.

The fans couldn't stop cheering.

"You talk about something running up and down your spine," said Hogan, who would finish in a tie for ninth. "I'd felt those things before. I'd had standing ovations before. But not nine holes in a row. It's hard to control your emotions. I think I played the best golf of my life on those last nine holes. I don't think I came close to missing a shot."

3

Bobby Jones

Of the twenty-one majors that Bobby Jones played in from 1923 until his retirement in 1930, he won thirteen and finished second in four others. While that doesn't put him above Jack Nicklaus or Tiger Woods, neither had a run like that.

The most victories Nicklaus or Woods compiled over a span of twenty one majors were seven.

Jones, I should add, won his thirteen while having a day job.

And, again, I don't care what the competition was like in the 1920s compared to later generations.

I think we must agree that all a man can do is beat the people . . .

*

Bobby, who grew up in Atlanta, weighed a little over five pounds at birth, and due to a digestive ailment, less than forty pounds when he was five. Thank God his father took the family out of the city during the summer. The fresh air did his boy a world of good.

Thank God, too, for Stewart Maiden, the pro at East Lake which opened in 1908.

Bobby, now six, loved to watch Maiden, who had just come over from Scotland, play a couple of holes. He'd promptly head to the 13th green in hopes of replicating Maiden's swing with three clubs in his possession: a cut-down two-wood, cleek, and short iron.

Around this time, he took part in his first golf competition:

Six holes of stroke play at East Lake against three others including eleven-year-old Alexa Stirling, the future three-time U.S. Women's Amateur champion who would inspire Glenna Collett Vare and, no doubt, many others. Stirling was the winner but suggested the trophy, a three-inch-tall cup, be awarded to Bobby.

"He slept with his little silver prize that night," Mark Frost wrote, "and hung on to it for as long as he lived, always polished, in place of pride alongside some of the greatest trophies in the world."

When he was nine, he knocked off Howard Thorne, 5 and 4, in the final of the junior championship of the Atlantic Athletic Club.

Howard Thorne was sixteen years old.

In 1913, Jones kept close track of what was going on in Brookline.

If Francis Ouimet could do it, so could he.

Soon afterward, Harry Vardon and Ted Ray came to East Lake to play an exhibition match against Stewart Maiden and Willie Mann, another local pro.

Ray knocked in an eight-footer on 18 for a one-up victory.

"Young Bobby could hardly sleep that night," Frost wrote, "lying in bed replaying every shot over and over. . . . He wanted to be in that place, try to hit those shots under pressure, feel what those men felt."

Let's skip a few years to the 1916 U.S. Amateur at Merion, his first national event, where Jones, fourteen, was supposed to get the putting lesson from Walter Travis but arrived late on the train from Philly. He defeated Eben Byers 3 and 1 and Frank Dyer 4 and 2 before falling in the quarterfinals to Robert Gardner, a two-time champion, 5 and 3.

"At his age," Grantland Rice wrote, referring to Jones, "the game in this country has never developed anyone with such a combination of physical strength, bulldog determination, mechanical skill and coolness against the test. He is the most remarkable kid prodigy we have ever seen."

He also had a temper.

"At a missed shot," Rice wrote in 1940, "his sunny smile could turn more suddenly into a black storm cloud than the Nazis can grab a country. Even at the age of 14, Bobby could not understand how anyone could ever miss any kind of golf shot."

In 1921, he quit in the British Open at St. Andrews.

As Young Tom Morris did in the 1865 Open at Prestwick.

During the third round, after a 46 on the front nine and a double bogey on the tenth, Jones according to an eyewitness, grabbed his ball from the bunker on 11—he had failed three times to get out—and ripped up his card.

"I have some sterling regrets in golf," he wrote. "This is the principal regret—that I quit in competition. I've often wished I could offer a general apology for picking up my ball."

More than a century later, it is still hard to picture Bobby Jones, of all people, quitting. At St. Andrews, of all places.

I'm glad he did.

From then on, his respect for the game and displays of sportsmanship were second to none. (In the 1925 U.S. Open he called a penalty on himself when his ball moved at address—no one else saw it—costing him a victory in regulation; he was defeated by Willie MacFarlane in a thirty-six hole playoff. Jones dismissed the credit he received for being honest: "You'd as well praise me for not breaking into banks.")

Jones, who had lost in the final of the U.S. Amateur in 1919, and by one stroke to Gene Sarazen in the 1922 U.S. Open, won the 1923 Open at Inwood Country Club for his first major title. It had taken longer than he and others expected.

He certainly didn't make it easy on himself.

Starting the final round with a three-shot advantage, he bogeyed 16 and 17 and doubled 18.

"Well, I didn't finish like a champion," he told O. B. Keeler. "I finished like a yellow dog." He was lucky that Bobby Cruickshank, his closest pursuer, bogeyed 13 and 15 and doubled 16, giving Jones an opportunity to redeem himself in a playoff the following day.

On number 18, with the players tied, Jones, whose ball was in a patch of dry, hard ground about 200 yards from the green, knocked a driving iron over the water to six feet and two-putted to prevail by two.

"Taking into consideration the lie of the ball, the club selected and the distance," Francis Ouimet said, "it was the finest shot I've ever seen."

I don't have enough space here to go over the other eight majors he won from 1923 through 1929—my editor is having a fit as it is (135,000 words, Michael? Really?), and besides, I need to save room for the Grand Slam—with one exception: the 1929 U.S. Open at Winged Foot.

Jones, who led Al Espinosa by six with six holes to go, bogeyed 13 and made a triple on 15, his second of the day. He needed to par the final two holes just to get into a thirty-six-hole playoff.

He got the first one on 17, but was left with a sidehill, downhill twelve-footer on 18 for the second.

If Jones would have missed it, Keeler said, "it would have remained a spreading and fatal blot, never to be wiped from his record."

He almost did, the ball falling in on its final rotation.

To a playoff the two went, if you can call it that.

I prefer to call it the first Massacre at Winged Foot (the second, of course, being the U.S. Open in 1974), Jones defeating Espinosa by twenty-three strokes, even after going three over the first three holes.

"There are many," Herbert Warren Wind wrote, "who think that the career of Bobby Jones would have tapered off then and there, that there certainly would have been no Grand Slam had he missed that curving 12-footer."

Something to think about, isn't it?

*

The possibility of winning the Grand Slam—the name was coined by Keeler after a term in bridge—first occurred to Jones in 1926.

He captured the British Open and U.S. Open that year and lost to George Von Elm in the final of the U.S. Amateur, 2 and 1, and to Andrew Jamieson in the quarterfinals of the British Amateur, 4 and 3.

Jones probably shouldn't have played the match against Jamieson. When he woke up that day, he felt "the muscle up the left side of [his] neck give a loud, rasping creak like a rusty hinge." He played because he didn't want to give up after coming so far in the championship and believed that if he were to beat Jamieson, his neck might be better by the next match.

"It was certainly no discredit and no accident to be beaten by a player of his ability," Jones wrote. "On the other hand I was left with some reason for believing that things might have been different had I remained fit."

The next time he competed in all four majors was in 1930, the British Amateur coming first, in late May at St. Andrews.

He wasn't a fan of the Old Course in the beginning, but by 1930, Jones, who won the Open there in 1927, had "come to love it."

In the fourth round, he faced Cyril Tolley, the defending champion. The match was tight from start to finish, Jones prevailing on the first extra hole thanks to a stymie. "The release from the tension," he wrote, "was almost unbearable." (The tension often got to Jones. It was not uncommon for him to lose between twelve and eighteen pounds during a tournament week, with occasional vomiting.)

In the semifinals, he was two down with five to go, but rallied to knock off George Voigt one up, and in the final, beat Roger Wethered, 7 and 6. "Honestly," Jones said, "I don't care what happens now. I'd rather have won this tournament than anything else in golf. I'm satisfied."

The British Open at Royal Liverpool was the second leg.

He held off Macdonald Smith and Leo Diegel, prevailing by two. While waiting for both players to finish, Jones "relieved his exhaustion with a good stiff drink," Wind wrote, "using two hands to steady his glass."

Upon returning to the United States, he was treated to his second ticker-tape parade down Broadway—the first was after he won the

British Open in 1926—though not every New Yorker was excited about the celebration.

"What's the parade for?" one person asked.

"Oh, for some goddamn golf player," a police officer told him.

Jones went on to defeat Smith by two at Interlachen for his fourth U.S. Open title, tying him with Willie Anderson.

Ahead by one, with Smith still on the course, Jones left his approach on 18 about forty feet from the hole. "As I stepped up to the putt," he wrote, "I was quivering in every muscle.... It is impossible to describe the sensation I felt when I saw my ball take a small break five or six feet from the cup, so that I knew it was in."

One major remained: the U.S. Amateur at Merion, and how appropriate, where he made his national debut in 1916.

He'd grown a lot since then.

As a player and a man.

With the tournament still two months away, Jones, an attorney, hoped to get his life back to normal but normal was impossible. Interview requests poured in from all over the world along with stacks of fan mail.

September was here before he knew it.

First, as usual, he had to make it through the two qualifying rounds, which was no guarantee. Not even for Bobby Jones.

"Each evening," Wind wrote, "Americans squirmed in their chairs by the radio waiting for the word from Merion."

The wait was worth every second: Jones, who shot a 69 and 73, was one of the thirty-two golfers headed to match play.

The moment was getting to him.

"There's something on my mind I can't shake off," he told Keeler. "I go to sleep all right from fatigue, but then around midnight, I wake up and have to get up. I've always been able to sleep. Something's bearing down on me in this tournament that was never there before."

He didn't appear anxious on the course, however, easily getting past his first two opponents, Charles Ross Somerville and Fred Hoblitzel. On Day Two, Jones eliminated Fay Coleman of California, 6 and 5, and Jess Sweetser, the 1922 champion, 9 and 8. Sweetser had beaten him 8 and 7 in the semis of the 1922 U.S. Amateur at Brookline, his worst match-play loss in a major championship.

Now all that was standing between Jones and history was one man: Eugene Homans.

Eugene who?

It was a mismatch from the start, Jones 7 up through the first eighteen. On the 29th hole, Homans lined up his putt from twenty-five feet to stay alive.

The ball was barely on its way when he walked over to congratulate Jones.

"And then shouts and cries and tumult filled the air," Mark Frost wrote. "They all came at him in a wild rush, hundreds and thousands... the cheering would not dissipate for five full minutes."

Jones was relieved as much as anything else.

"I had completed a period of most strenuous effort," he wrote. "Nothing more remained to be done."

Nothing, indeed.

"So tell me," Keeler had asked him after the U.S. Open, "are you going to quit this damned game now?"

"I'm going to play in the Amateur in September at Merion, anyway," Jones replied. "Don't print it yet, but that's going to be the end."

The end it would be.

In 1932, the Augusta National Golf Club, designed by Jones and Alister MacKenzie, opened for play. Two years later, the best golfers on the planet assembled there for the first time and, except during World War II, have been assembling every year since. You can't walk the grounds without feeling his presence.

In 1948, Jones played in the Masters for the final time, finishing fiftieth.

His body gave out on him in the worst way. The diagnosis would eventually be syringomyelia, an extremely rare disease that leads to paralysis.

Most people back then lived five to seven years after they contracted the disease.

Jones lived for twenty-three.

What he achieved as a player "after those years when nothing would quite come right was an epic victory in itself," Roger Wethered said at a service for Jones in St. Andrews five months after he passed away in 1971, "but the second victory—the one in which he was reduced to walking with difficulty with a cane and finally to a wheelchair—was a victory of the spirit that will also live as long as his name is remembered."

2

Tiger Woods

I will never forget Sunday, September 15, 1996.

The day I saw Tiger Woods in person for the first time.

I was blown away.

Not by how he played. Heavens, no. He played poorly. On the greens, that is.

From what happened afterward.

In the final round of the Quad City Classic at Oakwood Country Club in Coal Valley, Illinois, Woods, who was leading by three, hooked his drive on number 4, a 460-yard par-4, into the swamp. After taking a drop, he tried to squeeze the ball through a small opening, but it hit a tree trunk and bounced back into the water.

Woods ended up with a quad. In the Quad Cities.

On number 7, he four-putted for a double bogey ... *from eight feet.* And missed short par putts on 11 and 12.

To lose by four to Ed Fiori, a forty-three-year-old journeyman who would never win again.

In the media center afterward, I asked Woods, twenty, competing in just his third event since turning pro a few weeks earlier, what he might learn from the experience. He stared at me—who did he think he was, Raymond Floyd?—for what felt like an eternity before responding.

"It's kind of hard for me to tell you exactly what I'm going to learn from it," he said. "I will tell you one thing. I am going to learn a lot."

I believed him. To this day, I haven't seen anyone look more determined. On or off the course.

It was as if the future had already been written and all Tiger Woods had to do now was to make it official.

One month later, he picked up his first two Tour victories, in Las

Vegas and Florida. In 1997, he won the Masters by twelve strokes. In 2000 and 2001, he collected four straight majors: the Tiger Slam.

He became the greatest golfer of all time.

Correction: He *should* have been the greatest golfer of all time. He isn't and has only himself to blame.

This is going to sound ludicrous, but I'm going to put it out there anyway:

Tiger Woods underachieved.

Before you try to have me committed—if you haven't tried already—consider this:

On June 16, 2008, Woods, thirty-two, outdueled Rocco Mediate in a playoff at Torrey Pines to capture the U.S. Open, his fourteenth victory in forty-six majors as a professional, a winning percentage of 30.4 percent.

The question was not *if* Woods would win nineteen majors and surpass Jack Nicklaus.

The question was *when*.

How wrong we were.

Woods, who will turn fifty in December 2025, has won only one major since Torrey Pines, the 2019 Masters.

No doubt injuries (too many to mention, except for the car accident in February 2021) have played a huge role—he's missed twenty-two of the sixty-five majors staged since Torrey Pines—and perhaps he tinkered too much with his swing, but I kept thinking, there had to be more to it.

So in the summer of 2024, I reached out to a friend, Jaime Diaz, who first wrote about Woods when he was in his early teens.

To Diaz, who believes that Tiger, in addition to his supreme talent, benefited from seeing himself as an overachiever, everything changed after the scandal of his serial womanizing broke in late 2009.

"That was a crusher," Diaz told me. "His aura was damaged as far as how others perceived him, and maybe how he perceived himself. It took away that ability to be almost impervious to pressure. He lost the sense of invincibility. Tiger imploded, and Jack never did. If Tiger doesn't implode, he's better than Jack because he would have gotten to 18 and beyond, probably."

Is he an underachiever then?

"I would never call him an underachiever," Diaz replied, "but once he reached that point [winning his fourteenth major] I think it's reasonable to say he underachieved from that point."

*

"Honey, get out here!" Earl Woods said to his wife, Kultida. "We have a genius on our hands." The genius, less than a year old, had just grabbed a cut-down club and taken a swing, the ball going into the net.

In 1978, when Tiger was two, his father reached out to Jim Hill, the sports anchor for the CBS affiliate in Los Angeles. Hill, who met him on the driving range of the Navy Golf Course in Cypress, California, was overwhelmed.

"He was only a couple of feet tall," Hill recalled. "Yet he was hitting it fifty yards, and he was hitting the ball flush every time."

Soon afterward, Tiger—his father gave him the nickname of Lieutenant Colonel Nguyen T. Phong, who saved his life in Vietnam—appeared on *The Mike Douglas Show,* knocking in his first big putt on national television.

So it was from a few inches away. Got to start somewhere.

I could be mistaken but I swear I heard NBC's Dan Hicks in the background: "Expect anything different?" (His memorable call on the 72nd hole of the Open at Torrey.)

Skipping way ahead to the spring of 1986, a ten-year-old Woods watched Nicklaus collect his sixth green jacket. "I wanted to be where he was, and doing what he was doing," recalled Woods, who put the list of the Golden Bear's achievements on his bedroom wall.

In 1992, Woods, sixteen, played in the L.A. Open at Riviera, his first PGA Tour event, thanks to a sponsor's exemption.

With rounds of 72 and 75, he missed the cut by six and was disappointed. Of course he was.

Others were anything but.

"So, in a very important way, you won the L.A. Open," Jim Murray wrote. "I hope you like it in the limelight because it looks as if that is where you will spend your career. The game is starved for a hero and it looks like you are elected."

In 1994, Woods won the first of three straight U.S. Amateurs to go along with the three straight U.S. Junior Amateurs that he captured in 1991, 1992, and 1993.

Which brings us to the 1997 Masters. There's never been another Masters like it, and there never will be.

Woods, twenty-one, finished with a record total of eighteen-under 270. As Jim Nantz put it when the final putt dropped on the 72nd hole, it was "a win for the ages."

Not for just what Woods shot.

For what it meant.

Prior to the 1998 Masters, I asked about two dozen well-known figures for their reflections on what Woods accomplished.

The late activist Dick Gregory said it all:

"It was great to be black. Watching him do that had the same aura as watching Nelson Mandela come out of jail. Whenever he came up for a shot, you didn't make a phone call. It was moving to me because I knew what it was doing to people across the country. All black folks were on their knees praying for their son."

In May of '97, Woods, in his first post-Masters appearance, won the Byron Nelson tournament in Texas.

Then came the first of his well-chronicled swing changes.

"I was in it to find the answer to one question: How good can I be?" he explained years later. "I suppose I was searching for perfection, although that's not attainable in golf, except for short stretches."

As far as short stretches go, the summer of 2000, which began with his fifteen-shot triumph in the U.S. Open at Pebble Beach, has to be near the top.

"It's not a fair fight," NBC's Roger Maltbie said after Woods found the putting surface on Pebble's par-5 6th from four-inch rough 205 yards away.

With a seven-iron.

In the 2000 Open, "I felt he was really at his best," Ernie Els said. "...The ball flight and the velocity of the ball coming off the club, I've never seen anything like that."

A month later, Woods won the British Open at St. Andrews by eight. There are 112 bunkers on the Old Course. His ball didn't end up in any of them. "He has raised the bar to a level," Tom Watson said, "that only he can jump."

Next up was the PGA Championship at Valhalla in Louisville, Kentucky.

On the 72nd hole, Woods needed to knock in a seven-footer to stay alive against the unheralded Bob May, who had matched him shot for shot down the stretch. Which he did, of course. I don't recall Woods, with a major on the line, ever missing a putt that he absolutely had to make. When he defeated May in a three-hole playoff, he became the first since Ben Hogan to win three majors in the same year.

Woods made it four in a row in the 2001 Masters while paired in the final group on Sunday with his chief rival, Phil Mickelson.

"To have it go right four straight times, some of the golf gods are looking on me the right way," Woods said.

If the 1997 Masters was the greatest victory of his career, the 2008 U.S. Open at Torrey Pines was the gutsiest.

He played with a fractured tibia and a ruptured ACL.

His doctor said the normal treatment for stress fractures was six weeks on crutches and a month of rehab.

"I'm playing in the U.S. Open," Woods told him. "And I'm going to win it."

Grimacing and limping from one shot to the next, Woods struggled at times—he double bogeyed the first hole every day but Friday—but was also as magnificent as ever. On Saturday, he knocked in a sixty-six-footer for an eagle on 13 and a forty-footer for an eagle on 18 to post a one-under par 70.

Leading to Sunday. And the biggest birdie of his life.

Give credit to his caddie, Steve Williams. Woods, who needed to get up and down from about one hundred yards on 18 to force an eighteen-hole playoff with Mediate, was intending to hit a fifty-six-degree sand wedge until Williams persuaded him to go with a full sixty-degree wedge so the ball might produce more spin and stop quicker.

It came to a rest twelve feet from the pin.

Dan Hicks was right. Just like the putt at Valhalla, and so many others, I didn't expect anything different.

I also assumed, like everybody else, that he would get to nineteen majors, despite him missing the last two in '08 and the surprising loss to Y. E. Yang (the first time Woods blew a fifty-four hole lead in a major) in the 2009 PGA at Hazeltine.

Then came the scandal, and although he issued a public apology, I stopped caring about how many more majors he might win. To me, Woods had failed a much bigger test.

A test of character.

Besides feeling sad for his wife and family, I felt sad for what we lost. For what the game lost.

Someone who was great in every sense of the word—worthy of our admiration, respect, and dare I say ... love.

Woods has tried hard over the past fifteen years to regain our trust, and to some extent he has succeeded. I was moved, like many, by his triumph in the 2019 Masters and the hugs he gave his mother; son, Charlie; and daughter, Sam, behind the 18th green, evoking memories of Tiger and his father embracing at the same spot twenty-two years before.

"The return to glory," Nantz said after the final putt dropped.

I disagree. Those days are gone for good.

So if it's okay with you, I'm going to take a mulligan on what I wrote in the chapter on Gene Sarazen. If I could go back in time, I'd go to the Quad City Classic on September 15, 1996, after the loss to Ed Fiori.

After Woods finished speaking to the press, I would have shown him a crystal ball of the future, the trials, as well as the triumphs, on and off the course, hoping to give him something to think about:

Tiger, you will be the greatest player ever.

If you don't screw it up.

Jack Nicklaus

The topic in our conversation a few years ago had switched to major championships, something Jack Nicklaus knows a thing or two about.

"Do you have eighteen or twenty?" I asked.

"I had twenty and then all of a sudden, I had eighteen," he told me. "Where did that come from? I don't know who in the world was the guru at the time that took them away."

Who, indeed?

Don't get the idea Nicklaus feels robbed. Not in the slightest. He said he's fine with either number.

I'm giving him twenty, which is consistent with how I've counted majors all along.

In addition to the eighteen he claimed as a professional, I'm including, as *Golf Digest* and other publications did for the longest time, the U.S. Amateurs he won at Broadmoor in Colorado in 1959 and at Pebble Beach in 1961, both considered majors at the time.

"When I won the Open at St. Andrews in 1970," Nicklaus explained, "I walked in the pressroom and Bob Green [the longtime golf writer for the Associated Press] said, 'Well, that's ten, only three more to tie Bobby Jones.' When I turned pro, we considered the Amateur a major championship. Jones's record of thirteen was based on that."

With that matter resolved, I asked what he wants his legacy to be.

"My greatest legacy," he said, "is being a father and a grandfather. Golf's a game. The family is life and that by far is the most important thing to me. People can think of me whatever they want to think of me as a golfer. My golf record was pretty good. It could have been a lot better if I hadn't done the other things. But my record as a father would not be as good."

The golf record was more than pretty good.

And it's not just the twenty majors he won; it's the nineteen times he finished second and nine times he finished third. (Woods, in comparison, has seven seconds and four thirds.)

Which is why Jack Nicklaus is the greatest golfer ever.

As Wayne Gretzky told me, greatness "comes from the bigger the moment, the more pressure there is, the more they respond."

Many argue, and I don't disagree, that when Woods was at his best, he was better than Nicklaus at his best and was more dominant.

Like Roger Maltbie said during the 2000 U.S. Open, it wasn't a fair fight.

Even so, in the end, it still comes down to which player, Nicklaus or

Woods, whatever the reasons (injuries, scandal, etc.), responded more often in the big moments—and again, the numbers do not lie.

*

I'm not going to go through each of the majors Nicklaus won. We'd be here all day.

The following five will suffice:

1: The 1962 U.S. Open

To dethrone the king in his backyard at Oakmont, with Arnie's Army rooting fiercely for its hero, was something to behold. Trailing by two after fifty-four holes, Nicklaus closed with a 69 to tie Palmer. "I wasn't at all nervous getting ready that morning [for the playoff] and the reason is simple," he wrote. "I was hitting the ball from tee to green very well and I was putting very well." Indeed. Nicklaus, ahead by four after six holes, prevailed by three for his first major title. His first title, period.

2: The 1965 Masters

Winning by nine over Palmer and Gary Player, Nicklaus finished at seventeen-under 271, three strokes fewer than Hogan's previous low in 1953. The record (tied by Raymond Floyd in 1976) would stand for more than thirty years. "I was at last beginning to emerge from the shadow of Arnold," Nicklaus wrote, "and was becoming a golfer people could enjoyably follow and yell and holler and whoop for."

As Bobby Jones famously put it at the time: "He plays a game with which I am not familiar."

3: The 1975 Masters

This Masters might not be the most compelling—it would be difficult to put it above 1986—but it's right up there.

Knocking in a forty-footer for a most unlikely birdie at 16 on Sunday, Nicklaus won by a shot over Tom Weiskopf and Johnny Miller, who both missed makeable putts on the 72nd hole. He became the first player with five green jackets. "Holing a putt of that length over that difficult a line at that moment was a humongous break," he wrote. "The excitement was almost unbearable."

4: The 1980 U.S. Open

The words on the scoreboard near the 18th hole said it all:

JACK IS BACK.

Nicklaus, who hadn't won on Tour in nearly two years, was back, all right, prevailing at Baltusrol by two over Japan's Isao Aoki. "The look on his face as [a critical birdie putt on number 17] dropped," his wife, Barbara, said, "eyes squeezed tight shut, so relieved, so ecstatic, showed the world just how much golf mattered to him, and how wonderful it was to know that winning wasn't over."

5: The 1986 Masters

At forty-six, many assumed he was washed up, including Tom McCollister, a columnist for *The Atlanta Journal.*

Nicklaus couldn't avoid McCollister's column, a friend taping it to the refrigerator door at the house where he was staying.

"To tell you the truth, I kind of agreed with Tom," he said years later, "but it helped get me going."

His six-under 30 on the back nine, which included an eagle on number 15, and birdies on 16 and 17, propelled him to a one-stroke victory over Greg Norman and Tom Kite.

"We stopped counting the pieces of mail when they reached five thousand," Nicklaus wrote.

*

During my interview with Nicklaus in late 2022, I didn't ask about his wins and losses as a professional. He had been asked about them long enough.

I focused on who he was before he became Jack Nicklaus.

An early break...

In 1946, his father, Charlie Nicklaus, broke his ankle playing volleyball, and when it didn't heal properly, the doctor told him: "You better take up something where you start to exercise or you're going to end up in a wheelchair very shortly."

So in the spring of 1950, he returned to golf, which he had played growing up, and took his son along.

Charlie, however, couldn't walk for long. After each hole, he sat down for fifteen or twenty minutes before playing the next one. "I started [carrying his] clubs," recalled Nicklaus, who was ten at the time, "fiddling around, chipping around the green, waiting for him to go to the next hole."

"If not for the ankle injury, would your father have ever gone back to golf?" I asked him.

"He had no reason to," Nicklaus said. "He played volleyball."

Another Jack enters the picture....

"Jackie," Charlie Nicklaus said in the summer of 1950, "we have a new pro who has just come to Scioto [Scioto Country Club in Columbus, Ohio]. His name is Jack Grout. Would you like to get enrolled?"

Absolutely.

In a class with about fifty others, Jackie Nicklaus stood out.

"After about three weeks," he recalled, "J. Grout turned to me and said, 'Jackie boy, come out here and show these kids how to hit a hook, how to hit a proper fade, how to hit the ball in the air.' He used me as an example all the time. I was flattered."

One of Grout's jobs before coming to Scioto, you may recall, was to serve as an assistant to Henry Picard at Hershey Country Club in Pennsylvania, where he picked up the same theories about the golf swing that Picard had picked up from the highly respected Alex Morrison.

So here's another one of those what ifs in life: What if Grout hadn't worked at Scioto? Who's to say another instructor would have had the same impact on Charlie Nicklaus's boy?

"I thought he was the greatest teacher in the world," Nicklaus said. "He took an interest in me and wanted to see me grow. We developed a relationship. I wanted to please him."

The Ohio Open and the Slammer...

In 1956, Nicklaus, sixteen, received an offer to play in an exhibition with Sam Snead which would take place on the second day of the Ohio Open, which he had already entered.

He couldn't do both.

Or could he?

After he finished his round in the Open at Marietta Country Club he hopped onto a Beechcraft D-18, his first private plane, to Urbana about two hundred miles away to join Snead.

Imitating the Slammer's smooth tempo, Nicklaus shot a 71 while Snead, forty-four, turned in a 68. That was when Nicklaus learned how to "cock my head to the right," he said. "If that was good enough for Sam Snead, it would be good enough for me."

The next morning, he fired a 64 and followed with a 72 to capture the Ohio Open.

"I wouldn't have won the tournament," said Nicklaus "without [watching Snead]."

The only thing he didn't seem thrilled with was that Snead kept referring to him as junior. "He called me junior until I was probably about twenty," Nicklaus said.

The King and I...

In September 1958 at a course in Athens, Ohio, Nicklaus played for the first time with Palmer, the occasion to honor Dow Finsterwald, the 1957 PGA champion, who was from the area. Palmer and Nicklaus were paired in a better-ball match against Finsterwald and Howard Baker Saunders, an amateur.

Prior to teeing off, they held a driving contest on the 1st hole, a 320-yard par-4.

"Arnold drove the ball on the green and I drove it over the green," he recalled.

Nicklaus would kid Palmer that, "when we played that first time, I just outdrove you something awful.'

Palmer was always ready with a needle of his own:

"But I shot 62 and you shot 68."

*

Got to start somewhere...

The same year, Nicklaus, eighteen, playing in his first Tour event, the Rubber City Open at Firestone, was in contention at the halfway mark with rounds of 67 and 66.

In round three, he was paired with Art Wall Jr., the leader, and Tommy Bolt, the reigning U.S. Open champion.

"He [Bolt] put his arm on my shoulder as we walked off the first tee," Nicklaus said. "'Okay, Jackie boy,' he said, 'don't worry about a thing. Old Tommy's got you covered. You don't have to worry about Tommy. You just relax and play golf.'"

Easier said than done.

Nicklaus made six bogeys in his first nine holes.

"I was basically out of the tournament," said Nicklaus, who tied for fifteenth. "Tommy didn't have to worry about me anymore, so he didn't talk to me anymore."

The love of his life...

Nicklaus met Barbara Bash during freshman orientation week at Ohio State.

"Barbara stopped by to say hello to a gal named Mary, who I was dating," Nicklaus said. "I walked up to say hello to Mary, and Mary introduced me to Barbara. Mary and I had already decided we were going to date around. So, I called Barbara that night and asked her out." She said yes but "couldn't work me in for about two weeks."

Finally, he and Barbara went on their first date.

To a fraternity party.

"She's been a teetotaler her whole life," he said, "so I had no issues with that."

They saw each other until around Christmas, when they split up for a couple of months.

I didn't ask him why. I was prying too much as it was.

"She dated a fraternity brother of mine," he said, "and I went back and dated Mary a little more."

In February, he sent Barbara a birthday card.

"We started going out again," Nicklaus said, and "neither one of us dated anyone else after that."

The two got engaged in Christmas of 1959 and were married in July 1960.

"She picked the week of the PGA Championship," he said, "because she knew I couldn't play in it."

There would be no Jack Nicklaus without Barbara Nicklaus. He knows that better than anyone.

A blessing in disguise...

Prior to the 1960 U.S. Open at Cherry Hills, Charlie Nicklaus told his son:

"Jack, the odds for the tournament just came out. You are 35-1. You want some of that?"

Why not?

Putting $20 on himself, he stood to pick up $700 if he were to prevail. It was the first, and last, time Jack Nicklaus placed a bet on himself in a golf tournament.

"I was getting married [the next month]," he told me, "and I could sure use it."

The investment didn't pay off, Nicklaus finishing second, two strokes behind Palmer.

"I played 36 holes today," Ben Hogan said afterward, "with a kid who could have won this Open by 10 shots if he'd known what he was doing."

Good thing he didn't know what he was doing.

"Had I won that golf tournament," Nicklaus told me, "I would have had to stretch my arms out as far as I could to scratch my ears, my head would have been so big. I don't know if I would ever have gone back to work and learned from it. You learn far more from losing than you do from winning."

The rest is history...

"As a golfer," Nicklaus wrote, "it definitely turned me on to be compared with my longtime hero, Bob Jones, and particularly to think that I might someday approach his record. Obviously, the only way to do that was to remain amateur.... The prospect of the endless travel and superficiality of lifestyle inherent in such a nomadic [professional] career was a turnoff."

In the fall of 1961, however, he decided to turn pro.

The money, from endorsements especially, was too tempting to resist, but it wasn't the only factor.

"I really want to be the best that I can be at what I'm doing," Nicklaus told Barbara. "The only way I can do that is by playing against the best on a consistent basis."

"Great, go do it." she said.

Afterword

I never felt I had a mission in life until I started working on *The Golf 100*. Until I found out what made these men and women so heroic.

And so human.

I also saw the book as an opportunity to check in on players I got to know when I worked at *Golf World* in the late 1990s.

Did they view their successes—and setbacks—any differently in their seventies and eighties than they did back then? Any regrets, on or off the course? Any deeper awareness of their fellow competitors and the times they lived in?

I'm on the back nine, as well, and am eager to know what it has all been about before it's too late.

I was probably asking for too much.

They are the greatest golfers, not the greatest thinkers.

Still, from time to time, I detected, and I hope it wasn't my imagination, a slight pause, a softer tone—something, anything, that suggested the losses that were painful in the past weren't as painful anymore.

Not with the toughest loss of all to come.

Speaking of loss, I was deeply affected by the passing of Tom Weiskopf in August 2022 and Kathy Whitworth four months later.

On one level, it made no sense. I interviewed Weiskopf and Whitworth only a couple of times over the phone.

On another, it made all the sense the world.

They were members of a special group I was putting together. They couldn't die.

I was also eager to bring back to life the tournaments that meant so much for so long: The U.S. Amateur and British Amateur.

When the best golfers in the world played for something more important than money.

They played for pride.

"The word *amateur*," Sandy Tatum, the late USGA president, wrote, "derives from Greek words meaning, as a verb, to love, and, as a noun, lover. That word, therefore, puts amateur golfers in the right frame of reference, because they are the lovers of it whose love provides the heart, and indeed the soul, of the game of golf."

*

The list took two and a half years to compile—two and a half years of second-guessing and third-guessing and fourth-guessing ... wait, is it too late to call the printer?

Maybe, if I had used different metrics there would have been room for other deserving players who were left out:

Like Willie MacFarlane, who won twenty-one tournaments.

Or Doug Sanders, who won twenty. Or Bill Mehlhorn, nineteen. Or Tommy Bolt, fifteen.

And what about those with two majors such as Dave Stockton, Fuzzy Zoeller, John Daly, Lee Janzen, David Graham, Bubba Watson, Zach Johnson, José María Olazábal, etc. etc.?

Or women with five or more majors, including Inbee Park, Amy Alcott, Patty Sheehan, Yani Tseng, Betsy King, and Pat Bradley?

I could go on and on. I sometimes wish I had written *The Golf 200*.

So did I make any mistakes?

A bunch, no doubt, and I'm sure you won't hesitate to point them out.

All I ask is you be as nice to me as I was to Phil Mickelson and Greg Norman and Tiger Woods and several others.

On second thought, please be nicer. Like I indicated before, this wasn't a "tough task," as Jim Furyk told me. This was an impossible task.

Starting at the top.

I had finally settled on Jack Nicklaus over Woods as number one— the numbers were in the Golden Bear's favor—until late 2023 when it dawned on me that Bobby Jones, not Nicklaus or Woods, might be the GOAT.

Not only because of the golfer he was but because of the man he was and the impact he made.

Greatness, permit me to explain once again, is about more than what takes place between the ropes.

Is the individual someone we admire? Someone who inspires us to be our best selves... in our families, our jobs, our communities?

Unable to keep the revelation about Jones to myself, I called my friend, Ron Cherney, whom I consulted with throughout the whole process. Ron, who played in the 2007 U.S. Senior Amateur, thought I was out of my mind.

He thought that a lot of times.

"Bobby Jones was an amazing player," Ron said, "but come on, he wasn't as good as Nicklaus or Woods. They played such a different game. It's no contest."

In the end, the numbers for Jones, even with the bonus points, weren't enough, though he was able to pass Hogan for third. Nothing against Hogan, but he didn't impact the sport the way Jones did. Not even close.

As for Arnold Palmer, on his record alone he would have come in seventh, but similar to Jones, there was much more to his greatness, and once I factored in the bonus points, he moved up to fifth.

Lee Trevino, meanwhile, was penciled in at number sixteen, a spot behind Billy Casper, until I inserted his bonus points for outdueling Nicklaus in the 1971 U.S. Open, the 1972 British Open, and the 1974 PGA.

Likewise, I originally had Gary Player at fifteen until his bonus points for winning the career Grand Slam and playing a huge role in growing the sport all over the world moved him up several notches, barely past Tom Watson. If you have Watson, the best golfer in the game in the late 1970s and early 1980s ahead of Player, I won't argue. Watson passed Phil Mickelson with the additional points he picked up for his major victories over Nicklaus.

Many will wonder, and I won't blame them one bit, how I could possibly keep Scottie Scheffler and Justin Thomas off the list with two majors and more than a dozen Tour victories apiece.

While including Padraig Harrington, who has only six victories.

The numbers for Scheffler and Thomas simply didn't add up—not after I had factored in the bonus points for John McDermott, Roberto De Vicenzo, Tony Lema, Macdonald Smith, Padraig Harrington, Bernhard Langer, Ken Venturi, Tony Jacklin, and Henry Cotton. Other current players who came up short, though they will likely earn enough points before they finish their careers, include: Bryson DeChambeau, Collin Morikawa, Jon Rahm, and Xander Schauffele. (The last tournament to count in the rankings was the 2024 British Open at Royal Troon.)

Besides, I decided from the outset that any male golfer with at least three majors—it is incredibly hard to win one—since 1900 would go in automatically.

In my opinion, three majors signifies greatness, no matter what else the individual may or may not have accomplished.

*

I constantly traveled back and forth between the past and present.

One moment, I was reading how the Old Man, Walter Travis, overcame one slight after another to claim the 1904 British Amateur at Royal St. George's.

The next, I was watching Rory McIlroy attempt to fend off DeChambeau in the 2024 U.S. Open at Pinehurst in hopes of picking up his first major in ten years.

I wanted to scream at the TV set:

Hey, Rory, forget about your damn drought. Do you realize that if you win the Open, you will move up in my rankings?

The game has changed in numerous ways since Willie Park Sr. won the first major championship ever, the 1860 British Open at Prestwick.

And yet, in some ways, it is exactly the same:

Human beings coping with their demons, as well as their opponents. God bless every one of them.

There has been one remarkable comeback after another:

Harry Vardon from tuberculosis, Ben Hogan from the car accident, Babe Didrikson Zaharias and Gene Littler from cancer surgery.

And let us not forget those who returned from the battlefield, wounded but not defeated, such as Tommy Armour (the First World

War) and Lloyd Mangrum (hopefully, the last). One of the biggest takeaways for me in assembling this list was to appreciate how many golfers served their country, from the Boer War through Vietnam.

The players in the top one hundred are frequently in my thoughts. And in my dreams.

I haven't felt the presence of the dead so viscerally since I visited Gettysburg in 2004, where I could almost hear the yells of Confederate General George E. Pickett and the other rebels as they stormed toward the Union lines.

If God could grant me one wish—yes, rather than getting rid of the FedExCup—it would be to watch Old Tom Morris, Young Tom Morris, Francis Ouimet, Joyce Wethered, Glenna Collett Vare, Harold Hilton, John Ball, Jerry Travers, Willie Anderson, Ralph Guldahl, Louise Suggs, and countless others play the game they loved.

Just once.

Acknowledgments

I must begin by thanking the late editor of *Golf World,* Terry Galvin.

Terry took a chance on me in the spring of 1996, although I had written just a dozen or so golf stories.

If not for him, it is possible I would have never become a golf writer. I can't begin to imagine how different my life would have turned out.

Golf World, a weekly, along with *Golf Digest,* a well-known monthly, whose headquarters was in the same building in Trumbull, Connecticut, was filled with talented editors and writers who had a tremendous impact on my career. I also learned a lot from the exceptional journalists I got to know at *Golf Week, Sports Illustrated, Golf,* and other publications.

I couldn't be more fortunate, as well, for the support I received from many friends while I worked on this project. I can't mention them all, but there are a few who must be singled out.

Starting with Ron Cherney.

Ron, who possesses the most extensive library of golf memorabilia you could imagine, loaned me roughly one hundred books, along with dozens of magazines.

I kept telling him I would give them back to him someday. I still plan on doing that.

Maybe.

I will be forever grateful for his wise counsel and friendship. Even if he has never been able to appreciate the greatness of John Ball.

Another invaluable ally from start to finish was Tom Cunneff, the editor of *The Met Golfer* magazine, whom I have known since the early 1990s. In our conversations, he always gave me something to think about.

I'm indebted, as well, to Jim Dodson, a wonderful writer and better friend, who was always there with an encouraging word. Same goes for longtime friends Lorenzo Benet, Bill Courtney, Judy Rakowsky, Ron Shelton, and my stepdaughter, Jade.

Many others who were helpful include Michele Babin, Frank Beard, Lee Benson, Mike Burke, Jay Burton, Donna Caponi-Byrnes, Shirley Casper, Jonathan Coe, Jim Colbert, John Cook, Kevin Cook, Jane Crafter, Beth Daniel, Jay Danzi, Crystal Davis, James Davis, Janet Davis, Bruce Devlin, Jaime Diaz, Bobby Farrell, David Fay, John Fischer, Doug Ford Jr., Kelly Fray, Mark Frost, David Graham, Rick Grayson, Rachel Harris, Larry Hasak, Astrid Jacklin, Peter Jacobsen, Mike Johnson, Rich Katz, Christina Kim, Esther Sehee Kim, Gary Koch, Gregg Krusoe, Joe LaCava, Maggie Lagle, Christina Lance, Connor T. Lewis, Curt Littler, Fiona MacDonald, Danela Mada, Meg Mallon, Julius Mason, Gary McCord, Mike McGee, Terry McNamara, Pattie Melnyk, Doug Milne, Adrian Mitchell, Jim Nantz, Andy O'Brien, Alejandro Ochoa, Jamie Palatini, Amanda-Leigh Player Hall, Judy Rankin, Lynn Roach, Holly Roberts, Jeff Runyan, Jack Ryan, Craig Smith, Ed Sneed, Connor Stange, Tracey Stewart, Dave Stockton, Scott Tolley, Laurie Weiskopf, David Winkle, Mike Woodcock, and Guy Yocom.

I want to give a special thanks to Laury Livsey, the PGA Tour historian; Amy Mills, the Senior Manager of Statistical Research for the LPGA; and Bob Denney, PGA Historian Emeritus. I kept asking questions, and they kept providing answers.

Safe to say the book would not have been possible without cooperation from players in the top one hundred.

They include JoAnne Carner, Fred Couples, Ben Crenshaw, Nick Faldo, Raymond Floyd, Jim Furyk, Padraig Harrington, Juli Inkster, Hale Irwin, Tony Jacklin, Dustin Johnson, Tom Kite, Bernhard Langer, Nancy Lopez, Larry Nelson, Jack Nicklaus, Lorena Ochoa, Mark O'Meara, Se Ri Pak, Gary Player, Nick Price, Betsy Rawls, Annika Sorenstam, Jordan Spieth, Curtis Strange, Lee Trevino, Lanny Wadkins, Tom Watson, Karrie Webb, Tom Weiskopf, and Kathy Whitworth.

Working on the book revived memories of how golf came into my life in the early 1970s. And at a crucial time.

My father had recently passed away when my uncle Abe and aunt Anna began inviting me to their country club outside Albany, New York. I will be forever grateful to them.

As usual, I was very fortunate to have Jay Mandel of William Morris Endeavor as my literary agent.

Jay has represented me since the late 1990s. I can't overstate how important he has been to my development as an author.

The group at Doubleday has been exceptional, as well, beginning with my editor, Jason Kaufman.

Jason was passionate about the book from the start. Whenever I struggled with some part of the manuscript, his sound advice got me back on track. I also want to thank editorial assistant Lily Dondoshanksy, who made one superb suggestion after another, and Nora Reichard, the production editor, for guiding me through the final stages.

Finally, I would have never made it through the journey—and every book is a journey, some rockier than others—without my wife and co-conspirator in life, Pauletta Walsh.

The patience Pauletta displayed in listening to me go on and on about Walter Travis and Leo Diegel and JoAnne Carner and Patty Berg and Lloyd Mangrum—and everyone else in the top one hundred—was something to behold.

Talk about bonus points.

Bibliography

A significant portion of the material in this book comes from interviews I conducted between December 2021 and October 2024. I also relied on these sources, among others, for my research:

Sports Illustrated

USA Today

ESPN.com

Golf Digest

Golf World

USGA.org

Wikipedia.org

Associated Press

The Washington Post

The New York Times

Los Angeles Times

The San Diego Union-Tribune

Golf Journal

Glasgow Herald

Augusta.com

Netflix documentary *Full Swing*

For the Good of the Game, a podcast

The Memorial Tournament publication that profiles players honored at the annual Jack Nicklaus tournament in Ohio.

Here, too, are the books that proved invaluable to my work:

Barkow, Al. *Gettin' to the Dance Floor: An Oral History of American Golf.* Atheneum, 1986.

Barrett, David. *Miracle at Merion: The Inspiring Story of Ben Hogan's Amazing Comeback and Victory at the 1950 U.S. Open.* Skyhorse Publishing, 2010.

Benedict, Jeff, and Armen Keteyian. *Tiger Woods.* Simon and Schuster, 2018.

Burke Jr., Jackie, with Guy Yocom. *It's Only a Game: Words of Wisdom from a Lifetime in Golf.* Gotham Books, 2006.

Callahan, Tom. *Arnie: The Life of Arnold Palmer.* HarperCollins, 2017.

Casper, Billy, with James Parkinson, and Lee Benson. *The Big Three and Me.* Genesis Press, 2012.

Cayleff, Susan E. *Babe: The Life and Legend of Babe Didrikson Zaharias.* University of Illinois Press, 1995.

Collett, Glenna. *Ladies in the Rough.* Alfred A. Knopf, 1928.

Cook, Kevin. *Tommy's Honor: The Story of Old Tom Morris and Young Tom Morris, Golf's Founding Father and Son.* Avery, 2007.

Crenshaw, Ben, with Melanie Hauser. *A Feel for the Game: To Brookline and Back.* Doubleday, 2001.

D'Antonio, Michael. *Tour '72: Nicklaus, Palmer, Player, Trevino The Story of One Great Season.* Hyperion, 2002.

Demaret, Jimmy. *My Partner, Ben Hogan.* McGraw-Hill Book Company, 1954.

Dodson, James. *American Triumvirate: Sam Snead, Byron Nelson, Ben Hogan, and the Modern Age of Golf.* Alfred A. Knopf, 2012.

———. *Ben Hogan: An American Life.* Doubleday, 2004.

Evans, Charles, Jr. *Chick Evans' Golf Book: The Story of the Sporting Battles of the Greatest of All Amateur Golfers.* Thos. E. Wilson & Co., 1921.

Fields, Bill. *Arnie, Seve, and a Fleck of Golf History: Heroes, Underdogs, Courses, and Championships.* University of Nebraska Press, 2014.

Flaherty, Tom. *The U.S. Open 1895/1965: The Complete Story of the United States Golf Championship.* E.P. Dutton & Co., 1966.

Frost, Mark. *The Grand Slam: Bobby Jones, America, and the Story of Golf.* Hyperion, 2004.

———. *The Greatest Game Ever Played: Harry Vardon, Francis Ouimet, and the Birth of Modern Golf.* Kingswell, 2002.

Goodwin, Stephen. *The Greatest Masters: The 1986 Masters & Golf's Elite.* Harper and Row, 1988.

Halberstam, David. *The Best American Sports Writing of the Century.* Houghton Mifflin, 1999.

Harig, Bob. *Tiger & Phil: Golf's Most Fascinating Rivalry.* St. Martin's Press, 2022.

Jones, Robert Tyre, Jr. *Golf Is My Game.* Doubleday, 1960.

Kahn, Liz. *The LPGA: The Unauthorized Version: The History of the Ladies Professional Golf Association.* Group Fore Productions, 1996.

Keeler, O. B., and Grantland Rice. *The Bobby Jones Story.* The Fireside Press, 1953.

Kirkaldy, Andra. *Fifty Years of Golf: My Memories.* E. P. Dutton and Company, 1921.

Lema, Tony, with Gwilym S. Brown. *Golfers' Gold: An Inside View of the Pro Tour.* Little, Brown and Company, 1964.

Love, Davis, III. *Every Shot I Take: Lessons Learned About Golf, Life and a Father's Love.* Simon & Schuster, 1997.

Lowe, Stephen R. *Sir Walter and Mr. Jones: Walter Hagen, Bobby Jones and the Rise of American Golf.* Sleeping Bear Press, 2000.

Miller, Richard. *Triumphant Journey: The Saga of Bobby Jones and the Grand Slam of Golf.* Holt, Rinehart and Winston, 1980.

Nelson, Byron. *How I Played the Game.* Taylor Publishing Company, 1993.

Nicklaus, Jack, with Ken Bowden. *My Story.* Simon and Schuster, 1997.

Palmer, Arnold, with James Dodson. *A Golfer's Life.* Ballantine Books, 1999.

Player, Gary, with Floyd Thatcher. *Gary Player, World Golfer.* Word Books, 1974.

Player, Gary, with Michael McDonnell. *To Be the Best.* Pan Books, 1991.

Price, Charles. *The American Golfer.* Random House, 1964.

Proctor, Stephen. *The Long Golden Afternoon: Golf's Age of Glory 1864–1914.* Arena Sport, 2022.

Sampson, Curt. *Hogan.* Rutledge Hill Press, 1996.

Scott, Tom, and Geoffrey Cousins. *The Golf Immortals.* Hart Publishing Company, 1969.

Shipnuck, Alan. *Phil: The Rip-Roaring (and Unauthorized) Biography of Golf's Most Colorful Superstar.* Avid Reader Press, 2022.

Snead, Sam, with Al Stump. *The Education of a Golfer.* Simon and Schuster, 1962.

Snead, Sam, with George Mendoza. *Slammin' Sam.* Donald I. Fine Inc., 1986.

Sommers, Robert. *The U.S. Open: Golf's Ultimate Challenge.* Atheneum, 1987.

St. John, Lauren. *Seve: Ryder Cup Hero.* Partridge Press, 1993.

———. *Shark: The Biography of Greg Norman.* Rutledge Hill Press, 1998.

Tatum, Frank, Jr. "Sandy." *A Love Affair with the Game.* The American Golfer. 2002.

Travers, Jerome D. *Travers' Golf Book.* The Macmillan Company, 1913.

Trevino, Lee, and Sam Blair. *They Call Me Super Mex.* Random House, 1982.

Van Natta, Don, Jr. *Wonder Girl: The Magnificent Sporting Life of Babe Didrikson Zaharias.* Little, Brown and Company, 2011.

Vardon, Harry. *My Golfing Life.* Hutchinson & Co., 1933.

Venturi, Ken, with Michael Arkush. *Getting Up & Down: My 60 Years in Golf.* Triumph Books, 2004.

Wethered, Joyce. *Golfing Memories and Methods.* Hutchinson & Co., 1933.

Wind, Herbert Warren. *Following Through*. Ticknor & Fields, 1985.

———. *Herbert Warren Wind's Golf Book*. Simon and Schuster, 1971.

———. *The Story of American Golf: Volume One 1888–1941*. Callaway Editions, 1948.

Wind, Herbert Warren, Sarah Ballard, Frank Deford, Rick Reilly, and Dan Jenkins. *Golf: Four Decades of Sport's Illustrated Finest Writing on the Game of Golf*. Oxmoor House, 1994.